Authors & Artists for Young Adults

ISSN 1040-5682

Authors & Artists for Young Adults

VOLUME 33

Thomas McMahon
Editor

GALE GROUP

Detroit
New York
San Francisco
London
Boston
Woodbridge, CT

Thomas McMahon, *Editor*

Alan Hedblad, *Managing Editor*

Victoria B. Cariappa, *Research Manager*
Tracie A. Richarson, *Project Coordinator*
Andrew Guy Malonis, Gary J. Oudersluys, Cheryl L. Warnock, *Research Specialists*
Tamara C. Nott, *Research Associates*
Tim Lehnerer, *Research Assistants*

Maria Franklin, *Permissions Manager*
Edna Hedblad, *Permissions Specialist*
Sarah Chesney, *Permissions Associate*

Mary Beth Trimper, *Production Director*
Stacy L. Melson, *Buyer*

Randy Bassett, *Image Database Supervisor*
Michael Logusz, *Graphic Artist*
Robert Duncan, *Imaging Specialist*
Pamela A. Reed, *Imaging Coordinator*

The paper used in this publication meets the minimum requirements of
American National Standard for Information Sciences—Permanence Paper
for Printed Library Materials, ANSI Z39.48-1984.

Library of Congress Catalog Card Number 89-641100
ISBN 0-7876-3233-3
ISSN 1040-5682

10 9 8 7 6 5 4 3 2 1

Printed in the United States of America

Contents

Introduction

Authors and Artists for Young Adults is a reference series designed to serve the needs of middle school, junior high, and high school students interested in creative artists. Originally inspired by the need to bridge the gap between Gale's *Something about the Author*, created for children, and *Contemporary Authors*, intended for older students and adults, *Authors and Artists for Young Adults* has been expanded to cover not only an international scope of authors, but also a wide variety of other artists.

Although the emphasis of the series remains on the writer for young adults, we recognize that these readers have diverse interests covering a wide range of reading levels. The series therefore contains not only those creative artists who are of high interest to young adults, including cartoonists, photographers, music composers, bestselling authors of adult novels, media directors, producers, and performers, but also literary and artistic figures studied in academic curricula, such as influential novelists, playwrights, poets, and painters. The goal of *Authors and Artists for Young Adults* is to present this great diversity of creative artists in a format that is entertaining, informative, and understandable to the young adult reader.

Entry Format

Each volume of *Authors and Artists for Young Adults* will furnish in-depth coverage of twenty to twenty-five authors and artists. The typical entry consists of:

—A detailed biographical section that includes date of birth, marriage, children, education, and addresses.

—A comprehensive bibliography or filmography including publishers, producers, and years.

—Adaptations into other media forms.

—Works in progress.

—A distinctive essay featuring comments on an artist's life, career, artistic intentions, world views, and controversies.

—References for further reading.

—Extensive illustrations, photographs, movie stills, cartoons, book covers, and other relevant visual material.

A cumulative index to featured authors and artists appears in each volume.

Compilation Methods

The editors of *Authors and Artists for Young Adults* make every effort to secure information directly from the authors and artists through personal correspondence and interviews. Sketches on living authors and artists are sent to the biographee for review prior to publication. Any sketches not personally reviewed by biographees or their representatives are marked with an asterisk (*).

Highlights of Forthcoming Volumes

Among the authors and artists planned for future volumes are:

Kevin J. Anderson	Thomas Harris	Kristen D. Randle
James Baldwin	Sonya Hartnett	Spider Robinson
Joan Bauer	Sheila Solomon Klass	J. K. Rowling
Francesca Lia Block	Tracy Kidder	Louis Sachar
Judith Clarke	George R. R. Martin	William Shakespeare
Douglas Coupland	Henri Matisse	William Sleator
Richard Donner	Anne McCaffrey	Todd Strasser
Lois Duncan	Hayao Miyazaki	John Updike
Charles Frazier	Mike Myers	Rich Wallace
Paul Fleischman	Gordon Parks	Andrew Lloyd Webber
Kaye Gibbons	Randy Powell	Tim Winton
Matt Groening	Anna Quindlen	John Woo

Contact the Editor

We encourage our readers to examine the entire *AAYA* series. Please write and tell us if we can make AAYA even more helpful to you. Give your comments and suggestions to the editor:

BY MAIL: The Editor, *Authors and Artists for Young Adults,* 27500 Drake Rd., Farmington Hills, MI 48331-3535.

BY TELEPHONE: (800) 347-GALE

Authors & Artists for Young Adults

Douglas Adams

ning 1978, script editor for television series "Doctor Who," 1978-80; writer, 1978—.

■ Awards, Honors

Best Books for Young Adults List, American Library Association (ALA), 1980, and Golden Pen Award, 1983, for *The Hitchhiker's Guide to the Galaxy.*

■ Writings

"THE HITCHHIKER'S GUIDE TO THE GALAXY" SERIES

The Hitchhiker's Guide to the Galaxy, Pan Books (London), 1979, Harmony (New York City), 1980.
The Restaurant at the End of the Universe, Pan Books, 1980, Harmony, 1982.
Life, the Universe and Everything, Harmony, 1982.
So Long, and Thanks for All the Fish, Pan Books, 1984, Harmony, 1985.
The Hitchhiker's Trilogy (omnibus volume), Harmony, 1984.
The Original Hitchhiker's Radio Scripts, edited with an introduction by Geoffrey Perkins, Harmony, 1985.
The Hitchhiker's Quartet (omnibus volume), Harmony, 1986.
More Than Complete Hitchhiker's Guide, Longmeadow Press (New York City), 1987, revised edition published as *More Than Complete Hitchhiker's Guide Fifty-One Point Eighty*, 1989, unabridged edition, 1994.

■ Personal

Born March 11, 1952, in Cambridge, England; son of Christopher Douglas (a management consultant) and Janet (a nurse; maiden name, Donovan, present surname, Thrift) Adams; married Jane Elizabeth Belson, 1991; children: Polly Jane Rocket. *Education:* St. John's College, Cambridge, B.A. (with honors), 1974, M.A. *Hobbies and other interests:* Purchasing equipment for recreations he would like to take up.

■ Addresses

Home—London, England. *Office*—The Digital Village Ltd., 101 Bayham St., London NW1 0AG. *Agent*—Ed Victor Ltd., 6 Bayley St., London WCIB 3HB, England.

■ Career

British Broadcasting Corporation (BBC), London, producer and scriptwriter for "Hitchhiker's Guide to the Galaxy" radio and television series, begin-

Mostly Harmless, Crown (New York City), 1992.
The Illustrated Hitchhiker's Guide to the Galaxy, Crown, 1994.
The Ultimate Hitchhiker's Guide, unabridged and complete version, Wings Books (New York City), 1996.

Also author of scripts for the "Hitchhiker's Guide to the Galaxy" radio and television programs, BBC-TV; author, with Steve Meretzky, of interactive computer program.

OTHER

(With others) *Not 1982: Not the Nine O'Clock News Rip-Off Annual*, Faber (London), 1981.
(With John Lloyd) *The Meaning of Liff*, Pan Books, 1983, Harmony, 1984.
(Editor with Peter Fincham) *The Utterly Utterly Merry Comic Relief Christmas Book*, Fontana (London), 1986.
Dirk Gently's Holistic Detective Agency (novel), Simon & Schuster (New York City), 1987.
The Long Dark Tea-Time of the Soul (novel), Heinemann, 1988, Simon & Schuster, 1989.
(With Mark Carwardine) *Last Chance to See* (non-fiction), Crown, 1990.
(With Lloyd) *The Deeper Meaning of Liff: A Dictionary of Things There Aren'tWords for Yet—But There Ought to Be*, Crown, 1990.
Two Complete Novels (*Dirk Gently's Holistic Detective Agency* [and] *The Long Dark Tea-Time of the Soul*), Wings Books, 1994.
Dirk Gently's Holistic Detective Agency: Two Complete Novels (contains *Dirk Gently's Holistic Detective Agency* and *The Long Dark Tea-Time of the Soul*), Random House (New York City), 1995.

Contributor to *The Great Ape Project: Equality Beyond Humanity*, edited by Peter Singer, St. Martin's, 1993. Also author of episodes of "Doctor Who" for BBC-TV; co-author of interactive computer program, "Bureaucracy" and designer of a CD-ROM adventure game, "Starship Titanic," 1997.

■ Adaptations

The Hitchhiker's Guide to the Galaxy has been produced as a stage play, as a television series for BBC-TV and PBS-TV, 1983, as a computer game, Infocom, 1984, as an abridged audio-cassette, Listen for Pleasure, 1986, and unabridged audio-cas-sette, Minds Eye, 1988; producer Ivan Reitman holds the movie rights to the *Hitchhiker* trilogy; *The Restaurant at the End of the Universe* was adopted for cassette by Listen for Pleasure; *Life, the Universe and Everything* was adapted for cassette by Listen for Pleasure, and for a comic book by John Carnell; *So Long, and Thanks for All the Fish* was adapted for cassette by Listen for Pleasure, 1985; *Dirk Gently's Holistic Detective Agency* was adapted for cassette by Simon and Schuster, 1987. Adams's "Starship Titanic" video game has spawned a spin-off novel, *Douglas Adams's Starship Titanic*, by Terry Jones, 1997, and *Douglas Adams's Starship Titanic: The Official Strategy Guide*, by Neil Richards, 1998.

■ Work in Progress

A novel, *The Chaos Engineer*; possible sixth installment in the "Hitchhiker" series.

■ Sidelights

"Every particle of the universe . . . affects every other particle, however faintly or obliquely. Everything interconnects with everything. The beating of a butterfly's wings in China can affect the course of an Atlantic hurricane. If I could interrogate this table leg in a way that made sense to me, or to the table leg, then it would provide me with the answer to any question about the universe." Or so Douglas Adams's offbeat private detective, Dirk Gently, supposes in *The Long Dark Tea Time of the Soul*. At another point in that same novel, Gently contends that the impossible has "integrity," while the improbable is quite commonplace. The themes of universal questions to be asked—if not answered—of the interconnectedness of all things, and the vitality of the improbable play throughout all the works of Douglas Adams with silly gusto.

Improbable is a word that quite well describes Adams's own meteoric rise to popularity and an odd sort of fame. It all started with Adams lying drunk on his back in a field. This took place in Innsbruck on a hitchhiking trip around Europe before he entered university. "I sort of laid down on the ground and stared up at the stars," Adams told Susan Adamo of *Starlog* in a 1981 interview, "and it occurred to me then that somebody ought to write a hitch hiker's guide to the galaxy. The thought didn't come back to me for years afterward." When it did, after Douglas had been writing scripts for England's BBC radio for several years, it returned with the resounding thud of the planet Earth being destroyed, and one Arthur Dent being propelled into space to become the first galactic hitchhiker.

Adams's quirky idea for a radio program spawned a multimedia blitz for the young writer: a series of five novels in the "Hitchhiker" group (the first one of which sold 100,000 copies in less than a month and ultimately sold morethan two million in England alone); a stage play; a television series; and a computer game. Adams became a loopy cultural hero for the young; his tongue-in-cheek antics in the formerly strictly non-humorous precincts of outer space and sci fi earned him a legion of eager fans around the globe. Adams has gone on to write of a "film-*blanc*" private eye, endangered species, and a galaxy of objects, actions, and feelings for which no words exist. The production of video games has taken up much of his working time in the 1990s, but fans hope for a sixth instalment in the "Hitchhiker" series twenty years after publication of the first. As Marc Conly summed up in *Bloomsbury Review*, "Douglas Adams is a dismayed idealist in jester's clothing. His portrayal of modern society, and his unrelenting dissection of the modern style of self-centeredness, make us think, make us laugh, and make us look forward to his next book."

A Proper British Upbringing

Adams was born in Cambridge, the son of a theology teacher and management consultant, Christopher Douglas Adams, and a nurse, Janet Donovan Adams. Adams stayed in his home town for his university training, attending prestigious Cambridge University, where he majored in English literature. But more importantly, Adams spent nearly every free moment at school writing sketches for Cambridge Footlights, a college theatrical club that has long proved a breeding ground for actors, comedians, and writers alike. "It's not so much that being a member of Footlights gives you a guaranteed entrée into show business, which a lot of people kind of assume simply because so many people have come out of it," Adams told D. C. Denison of the *Boston Globe* in a 1985 interview. "The reason why so many people of that type have come out of it is

because they've gone into it. Certainly in my experience, when I was deciding on what kind of university career I was going to have, I wanted to go to Cambridge because I wanted to do Footlights—mainly because I knew I had a reasonable opportunity to meet people of like mind. . . . It's just sort of a rallying flag." Some of those likeminded people included core members of what would later become the Monty Python group: John Cleese, Eric Idle, and Graham Chapman.

After graduation, while trying to start a writing career, Adams toiled at a series of menial jobs, including hospital reporter, barn builder, chicken shed cleaner, and bodyguard for the royal family of Qatar, work for which his 6'5", 210-pound frame—if not his disposition—suited him well. During this same period, he also worked with Chapman, later of Python fame, on numerous unsuccessful projects. Finally Adams began writing scripts for BBC radio and TV, among them for the long-running *Dr. Who* sci fi series. Then he recalled the inebriated night in Innsbruck and his idea for a guide of a very different stripe.

The Hitchhiker's Guide to the Galaxy

Adams presented his idea for a radio show to BBC Radio 4 and received pocket change as upfront money to develop a pilot script. Adams sketched out the basic premises of his story: clueless Englishman Arthur Dent and his alien friend Ford Prefect hitch rides across the galaxy after Earth is destroyed in order to make room for an intergalactic highway. What started out as an experiment—almost a write-off—on radio soon garnered loyal fans who loved the send-up humor and piercing glances at contemporary life. Adams and the producers of the show revolutionized the way BBC radio did things, by taking days to record each segment, using stereo sound effects, and occupying studio after studio. "We wanted the sound to be the verbal equivalent of a rock album," Adams told James Brown of the *Los Angeles Times* in a 1982 interview.

By 1978, the BBC radio series was so popular that Pan Books in England asked Adams to novelize the story. "I never set out to be a novelist," Adams once told *Contemporary Authors*, "because I thought I was just a scriptwriter." But with his novelization for Pan, Adams went beyond simply filling in "he said" in the proper places in radio

Bestselling author of *Mostly Harmless*

Douglas Adams

"Extremely funny...Inspired lunacy...[and] over much too soon."
—*The Washington Post Book World*

The first in the increasingly inaccurately named *Hitchhiker's* Trilogy

THE HITCHHIKER'S GUIDE TO THE GALAXY

Ballantine Books
0-345-39180-2

Adams's sci-fi farce began as a popular BBC radio show, which he then wrote down in this 1980 novel featuring clueless Englishman Arthur Dent and his many misadventures traveling the galaxy.

scripts. Instead, he rewrote the entire story. The published book was an instant success, reaching the top of British bestseller lists.

The first of what has become five books in the "Hitchhiker" series, begins with Earth destroyed to make way for an express route in hyperspace. Ford Prefect, a researcher for a guide to hitchhiking the galaxies, manages to rescue low-keyed Arthur Dent just as the planet disintegrates. They end up on a spaceship operated by Zaphod Beeblebrox, a two-headed adventurer and sort of cousin to Ford. Others aboard the spacecraft are

Zaphod's girlfriend, Trillian, and a robot, Marvin, who is forever depressed. Together they make their way to Magrathea where custom-made planets are manufactured. There Slartibartfast, who helped design Earth, informs the crew that the planet was part of a project to come up with the meaning of life, the universe and everything, and that the answer is forty-two. The rest of the novel and indeed the series are an extended and hilarious faux-sci fi adventure to discover the question for which forty-two is the answer. Plot, it becomes rapidly obvious, plays second place to witty dialogue and outlandish characterizations.

Michael Adams, writing in *Dictionary of Literary Biography Yearbook: 1983*, noted, "One of Adams's main virtues is his gift for characterization. The adventures of Arthur and his friends are entertaining not only for all the last-second escapes from disaster but for how the characters respond to the whims of fate." Adams told James Brown of the *Los Angeles Times* that Dent, the putative main character, was something of an autobiographical rendering, and that moving "from one astonishing event to another without fully comprehending what's going on," he is an Everyman. Using the literary devices of science fiction, Adams, in fact, managed to spoof most of the sacred cows of contemporary society: technology, health fads, literary critics, and rock 'n roll. Most of society's shibboleths provided grist for the Adams irony mill.

Critics on both sides of the Atlantic applauded Adams's antic wit. The *Listener*'s Peter Kemp called the first volume "a sardonically funny exercise in galactic globe-trotting," and noted that what makes the book "almost unputdownable is its surreal, comic creativity." Kemp concluded that "for most of the book, the characters zoom exuberantly through other worlds." In the United States, a critic for *Kirkus Reviews* called Adams's book an attempt at science fiction "Monty Python style," concluding that "fans of absurd deadpan-parody will happily flip through this likable send-up in order to extract a couple of dozen fine giggles." Reviewer Lisa Tuttle noted in the *Washington Post Book World*, "There's nothing dull about the *Guide*, which is inspired lunacy that leaves hardly a science fictional cliché alive." And Gerald Jonas commented in the *New York Times Book Review* that while humorous sci fi usually has "notoriously limited audiences," Adams's novel "is a delightful exception."

Critics have noted Adams's debt to earlier authors including Jonathan Swift, Lewis Carroll, Kurt Vonnegut, and the antics of Monty Python. Adams himself has also credited the British humorist, P. G. Wodehouse. Michael Adams noted in *Dictionary of Literary Biography Yearbook* that the "human characters [in *Hitchhiker's Guide*] are space-age variations on Wodehouse's Bertie Wooster and all his eccentric friends and relatives, and know-it-all Marvin is a neurotic version of Jeeves." The same critic went on to note that while the characters of Slartibartfast and Trillian are underdeveloped, "Marvin [the chronically depressed robot] delightfully complements Arthur, Ford, and Zaphod in Adams's satire of Me-generation manifestations." Indeed, many critics agree that satire is Adams's main goal in the novels.

Hitching a Ride on a Sequel

To date, Adams has written four more "Hitchhiker" novels. The immediate sequel to the first book appeared in 1980 with *The Restaurant at the End of the Universe*, in which Ford Perfect and his friends continue their ultimate road-adventures. The restaurant in question is the fabled Milliways, where the clients can witness the end of the cosmos. Adams himself in *Dictionary of Literary Biography Yearbook* pronounced the novel to be "the [series's] most entertaining satire." As Philip Howard noted in the *Times* of London, the story "has attracted a cult even among those normally impervious to the mechanical charms of science fiction." Howard went on to note that a "summary of the plot [of the sequel] would read like case notes of a nervous breakdown" involving "a sequence of episodic disasters and hilarities." *Kirkus Reviews* concluded that Adams's second venture into hyperspace was "[s]ometimes lame, limp, or just plain silly——but, at its best, very funny indeed." Claudia Morner noted in *School Library Journal* that Adams's sequel "is both an entertaining, silly story and a successful satire of the worst of S. F. novels." Morner concluded that it "maintains the disrespectful, crazy tone [of the first] and should be popular."

In the third instalment, *Life, the Universe and Everything*, Dent and Ford "find themselves caught up in the malevolent plan of the rulers of the planet Krikkit to destroy everything that isn't cricket and to seize the Golden Bail that will give them great power," according to Richard Brown writing in *Times Literary Supplement*. Featured here is the computer Deep Thought which came up with the answer to the mystery of the universe as being the number forty-two. Arthur Dent is also still bumbling along, attempting to discover the Ultimate Question to Life. As Richard Brown explained, "Much of the comedy arises from a variety of pseudo-high-tech mis-information." Tom Hutchinson pointed out in the *Times* of London: "There is a serious undertow to all this, of course, a Vonnegut-appreciation of the universe's futility which allows Mr Adams to slip in some moments of sly terror so that the smile freezes on our faces like ancient winter." Michael Brown noted in *Dictionary of Literary Biography Yearbook* that the "strongest satire comes with the attack on war, imperialism, and xenophobia."

Most reviewers and Adams himself felt the fourth volume of the "Hitchhiker" chronicles was a mistake. *So Long, and Thanks for All the Fish* is set back on earth and Arthur Dent is in love with the beautiful Frenchurch who is the only earthling to remember that the planet was once destroyed. As Robert Reilly commented in *Twentieth-Century Science Fiction Writers*, despite the changed venue, this fourth novel "proves to be too much of the same thing. The freshness which lent such force to *Hitchhiker* is gone; the joke has been carried too far."

For nearly a decade Adams steered away from further forays into the "Hitchhiker" realm, busying himself with other book projects as well as computer games, which continue to occupy much of his creativity. The "Hitchhiker's Guide" computer game was released in the mid-1980s, and as Adams told Denison of the *Boston Globe*, "I've just become totally engrossed [with computers], and now there seem to be more things to do than I can possibly encompass." His "Starship Titanic" came out on CD-ROM in 1997, the product of several years of work by his London-based production company, Digital Village.

In 1992 the fifth book in the "Hitchhiker" series appeared, *Mostly Harmless*, a book that again won praise for the concept as a whole. Ford Prefect discovers a Vogon plot to take over the *Hitchhiker's Guide to the Galaxy* imprint and notifies Arthur Dent, now a resident Sandwich Maker on the isolated world of Lamuella. There are Grebulons galore colonizing a new planet and a daughter for Arthur who comes from a time distant in space.

Writing in *Locus,* Carolyn Cushman observed that "This time, [Adams] sinks his teeth into a basic human problem [looking for a purpose in life] and uses it as a theme, giving *Mostly Harmless* a coherence lacking in the other novels in the series. And it's funny to boot." A reviewer for *Analog Science Fiction and Fact* noted that Adams's new novel was "a bit of bubbly seltzer in a dour, dour world," adding that "Adams's cock-eyed logic is bound to make you smile."

Life After Hitchhiking

Adams took a rest from Dent and Ford with a pair of nonsense dictionaries inspired by more

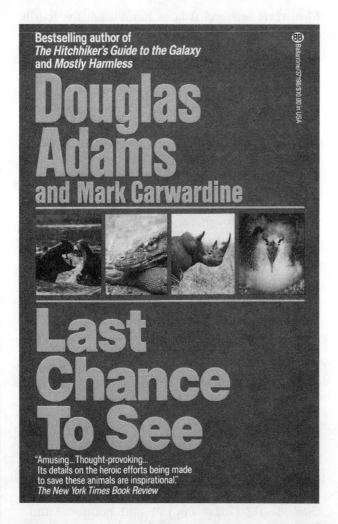

Bestselling author of
The Hitchhiker's Guide to the Galaxy
and *Mostly Harmless*

Douglas Adams
and **Mark Carwardine**

Last Chance To See

"Amusing...Thought-provoking...
Its details on the heroic efforts being made
to save these animals are inspirational."
The New York Times Book Review

Written with zoologist Mark Carwardine, Adams's 1990 book is a combination travelogue and chronicle of endangered species living in Indonesia, China, New Zealand, and Mauritius.

youthful inebriation—this time with a group of friends in Greece in 1978. The basis of that game was to come up with new words or phrases or existing words to be used in a new sense. These neologisms, which were scribbled on sheets of scrap paper, filled a drawer and later became the core of *The Meaning of Liff* and *The Deeper Meaning of Liff.* A reviewer for the London publication *Observer* called the latter book "One of that rarest of things, a good, original idea for a funny book."

Another fictional turn came in the companion volumes *Dirk Gently's Holistic Detective Agency* and *The Long Dark Tea-Time of the Soul,* both featuring the private detective Dirk Gently and his adventures with strange supernatural forces. Dirk is usually most competent with missing cat cases, but takes on the murder of a computer executive in the first of the novels. Adams assembles his usual zany cast of characters and incidents to propel the plot: a time machine, a spaceship, an Electric Monk, and the ghost of Samuel Taylor Coleridge. While reviewer Christopher Farley of the *Chicago Tribune* faulted the novel for "too much" plot, others found the book on a par with Adams's earlier work. H. J. Kirchoff stated in the Toronto *Globe and Mail* that it was Adams's "best novel." Kirchoff felt the author's characters were "more fully delineated . . . the settings more credible and the plot more . . . well, linear." John Nicholson concluded in the *Times* of London that "what signifies here is the quality of the writing, the asides and allusions, and—above all—the jokes. Mr Adams scores very high on all counts."

"In *The Long Dark Tea-Time of the Soul,* Adams has thrown a smattering of Norse Mythology, a pinch of detective fiction, and a good helping of fantasy into a stew of satire and sardonic observation that the fans of *Hitchhiker's Guide to the Galaxy* . . . will easily recognize," according to Marc Conly of *Bloomsbury Review.* This second Dirk Gently novel was not meant as a sequel, but as the ongoing adventures of an unlikely detective. Gently is trying to get to the bottom of the murder of his only client and the explosion at an airport check-in counter. These are apparently unrelated crimes, but holistic Dirk Gently sees a connection and teams up with Kate the American with an attitude to investigate Thor, the Norse god of Thunder, who is none too pleased with Odin. Along the way Adams shoots barbs at religion and modern mores. Conly noted that Adams's "social awareness and the accuracy of his barbs

If you enjoy the works of Douglas Adams, you may also want to check out the following books:

James Gurney, *Dinotopia,* 1992.
Harry Harrison, *Planet Story,* 1979.
Piers Anthony, *Castle Roogna,* 1979.
John DeChancie, *Paradox Alley,* 1987.

keep the narrative . . . from becoming too frothy." Kathleen Schine concluded in the *New York Times Book Review* that Adams's "humor, crisp and intelligent, and his prose—elegant, absurdly literal-minded understatements or elegant, absurdly literal-minded overstatements—are a pleasure to read."

More of a departure for Adams was his 1990 *Last Chance to See,* co-authored with zoologist Mark Carwardine. Traveling to Indonesia, China, New Zealand, and Mauritius, the two authors chronicle endangered species around the world, and provide a droll travelogue at the same time. Jack Beatty observed in the *Atlantic* that Douglas Adams was not your sanctimonious type of nature writer. "He smokes, he drinks, he has unflinching things to say about certain representative people of the Third World, a type often treated as a protected species, and he is an Englishman, which means that he would rather be clever than profound any day. Above all," Beatty continued, "he packs his irony with his shaving kit." The book is an episodic narrative of several of Adams's and Carwardine's travel-adventures, research journeys as originally planned for a series of radio programs on endangered species. "Don't expect any great insights here" commented Beth Levine in *New York Times Book Review,* "but *Last Chance to See* is enjoyable and accessible, and its details on the heroic efforts being made to save these animals are inspirational." Reviewer Melissa Greene of *Washington Post Book World* hailed *Last Chance to See* as a "rambunctious . . . and moving travel book, a kind of catalogue of the civilization that exists at the fringes of civilization." Greene went on to conclude that "despite the backdrop of ecological disaster and colossal human stupidity, the book is funny and a sort of rollicking good read, and the animals themselves are among the most wonderful characters in it."

Adams took a hiatus from book publishing through much of the 1990s, putting aside a Dirk Gently book that went haywire to concentrate instead on his Digital Village projects. Adams participates not only in writing the computer-game adventures, but also in the overall production phase as well. As Brad Stone noted in *Newsweek,* "Adams, who applies a sort of comical Murphy's Law toward technology in the 'Hitchhiker' books, has also become something of a new media guru. Companies like Dell and Canon pay to hear his humorous take on our digital future and the power of new technologies." Stone went on to note, "But [Adams] also has a serious message: 'If you approach the future pessimistically, then you can be pretty certain the things you most fear are going to happen." Stone goes on to quote Adams as saying, "I would never claim technology is going to make the world better, but it certainly makes it more and more interesting."

■ Works Cited

Adamo, Susan, "Douglas Adams," *Starlog,* June, 1981.

Adams, Douglas, *The Long Dark Tea-Time of the Soul,* Simon and Schuster, 1989.

Adams, Michael, "Douglas Adams," *Dictionary of Literary Biography Yearbook: 1983,* Gale, 1983, pp. 175-78.

Beatty, Jack, review of *Last Chance to See, Atlantic,* March, 1991, p. 267.

Brown, James, "Thumbs Up for the Hitchhiker," *Los Angeles Times,* April 4, 1982.

Brown, Richard, "Posh-School SF," *Times Literary Supplement,* September 24, 1982, p. 1032.

Conly, Mark, "Ruminations on the State of the Universe," *Bloomsbury Review,* May-June, 1989. p. 16.

Cushman, Carolyn, review of *Mostly Harmless, Locus,* October, 1992, p. 37.

Review of *The Deeper Meaning of Liff, Observer,* December 2, 1990, p. 64.

Denison, D. C., "Twenty One: Douglas Adams," *Boston Globe,* January 20, 1985.

Farley, Christopher, review of *Dirk Gently's Holistic Detective Agency, Chicago Tribune,* August 25, 1987.

Greene, Melissa, review of *Last Chance to See, Washington Post Book World,* March 24, 1991, p. 4.

Review of *The Hitchhiker's Guide to the Galaxy, Kirkus Reviews,* July 15, 1980, p. 941.

Howard, Philip, review of *The Restaurant at the End of the Universe, Times* (London), February 7, 1981, p. 9.

Hutchinson, Tom, "Hitching Another Hike to the Stars," *London Times*, September 9, 1982, p. 7.

Jonas, Gerald, review of *The Hitchhiker's Guide to the Galaxy, New York Times Book Review*, January 25, 1981, pp. 24-25.

Kemp, Peter, "Wise-Guy-Sci-Fi," *Listener*, December 18 & 25, 1980, p. 866.

Kirchoff, H. J., review of *Dirk Gently's Holistic Detective Agency, Globe and Mail* (Toronto), April 14, 1987.

Levine, Beth, review of *Last Chance to See, New York Times Book Review*, March 17, 1991, p. 22.

Morner, Claudia, review of *The Restaurant at the End of the Universe, School Library Journal*, April 15, 1982, p. 87.

Review of *Mostly Harmless, Analog: Science Fiction and Fact*, September, 1993, pp. 164-65.

Nicholson, John, review of *Dirk Gently's Holistic Detective Agency, Times* (London), June 18, 1987.

Reilly, Robert, "Adams, Douglas," *Twentieth-Century Science Fiction Writers*, St. James Press, 1986, pp. 1-2.

Review of *The Restaurant at the End of the Universe, Kirkus Reviews*, December 1, 1981, p. 1490.

Schine, Cathleen, review of *The Long Dark Tea-Time of the Soul, New York Times Book Review*, March 12, 1989, p. 11.

Stone, Brad, "The Unsinkable Starship," *Newsweek*, April 13, 1998, p. 78.

Tuttle, Lisa, "As Other Worlds Turn," *Washington Post Book World*, November 23, 1980, p. 6.

■ For More Information See

BOOKS

Bestsellers 89, Issue 3, Gale, 1989.

PERIODICALS

Bloomsbury Review, December, 1982.

Chicago Tribune, October 28, 1982; March 13, 1985; March 17, 1985; March 31, 1989.

Chicago Tribune Book World, October 12, 1980.

Globe and Mail (Toronto), June 27, 1987.

London Times, December 13, 1984; November 5, 1988.

Los Angeles Times, April 19, 1985; June 13, 1987; March 17, 1989.

Los Angeles Times Book Review, December 7, 1980; February 3, 1991, p. 4.

Magazine of Fantasy and Science Fiction, February, 1982.

Newsweek, November 15, 1982.

People, January 10, 1983.

Publishers Weekly, January 14, 1983.

Spectator, December 15, 1990, p. 35.

Voice of Youth Advocates, April, 1993, p. 33.

Washington Post, July 23, 1987; March 16, 1989.

Washington Post Book World, December 27, 1981.*

—Sketch by J. Sydney Jones

Allen Appel

Time after Time; nominations for ALA Best Book for *Twice upon a Time* and *Till the End of Time.*

■ Personal

Surname is pronounced "apple"; born January 6, 1945, in Bethlehem, PA; son of Allen R., Jr. and Irene (a homemaker; maiden name, Trippett) Appel; married Sharon Conway (a publicist), 1980; children: Allen R. IV, Leah Helen, Charles David. *Education:* West Virginia University, B.A., 1967.

■ Addresses

E-mail—appelworks@email.msn.com.

■ Career

Photographer, illustrator, and writer. *Member:* Mystery Writers of America, Authors Guild.

■ Awards, Honors

Recognition as one of year's best novels from American Library Association (ALA), 1986, for

■ Writings

FICTION

Time after Time, Carroll & Graf (New York City), 1985.
Twice upon a Time, Carroll & Graf, 1988.
Till the End of Time, Doubleday (New York City), 1990.
(With Craig Roberts) *Hellhound,* Avon, 1994.

NONFICTION

From Father to Son: Wisdom for the Next Generation, St. Martin's Press (New York City), 1993.
Thanks, Dad, St. Martin's Press, 1994.

OTHER

(Illustrator) *Proust's Last Beer,* Viking, 1979.

Also the author of the screenplay, "The Ebony Streak." Appel's works have been translated into Chinese and Korean.

■ Work in Progress

Two mystery novels; gift books for St. Martin's press on babies and dogs; screenplays.

■ Sidelights

Allen Appel takes his readers on fictional flights to Russia during the 1917 Revolution, to the Reconstruction Era America of Mark Twain, and to Japan during the 1945 bombing of Hiroshima. His time-traveling protagonist, Alex Balfour, at the center of his "Pastmaster" series, has won readers of all ages since publication of the first novel, *Time after Time.* Often classified as a science fiction writer, Appel is first of all a fiction writer. His professional historian-hero Balfour does not climb into an ornate time machine for his travels, nor does he take lessons in breaking the membrane of temporality. Instead, Alex Balfour steeps himself in a time period, falls asleep, and quite unwillingly wakes up in another world:

"The headache was gone. Alex Balfour was lying face down in a shallow trench. The ground was cold and hard and smelled of clay and mold. He had just enough time to lift his head up out of the dirt before the first shell slammed into the earth. A howling rush of air and then the explosion. . . . His ears rang with it. He flinched as a flare burst high in the air with a flat pop and drifted slowly down, hissing, emitting a cold magnesium light that drenched his limited landscape, coloring it a pale, monochromatic blue."

Such is the way that the reader and Balfour himself are introduced to his latent abilities in *Time after Time:* waking up *in medias res,* in the muddy hell of World War I trench warfare. "An editor friend of mine told me never to try and explain the unexplainable," Appel remarked to *Authors and Artists for Young Adults (AAYA)* in an interview. "So I don't bother with trying to tell how Balfour does his time-traveling. He just does it." And does it and does it. Balfour makes two encore appearances, in *Twice upon a Time* and *Till the End of Time,* shuttling back and forth between historical time zones like a frequent flyer. A writer for the *Washington Post Book World* summed up the appeal of the trilogy of books in reviewing the first of the series: "Part historical novel, part science fiction, part love story."

This "total adventure" is what Appel serves up in all the "Pastmaster" books, though it is also leavened with hard-hitting historical truths. As Gregory Benford noted in a *Washington Post Book World* review of *Till the End of Time,* the book is "a lively page-turner," but "not without moral purpose." Benford pointed out that "Appel is after larger game than the reader's attention span." It is this concern with historical accuracy and ethical questions that have helped to make Appel's books as popular in the classroom as at the beach. Appel explained to *AAYA* that he "tried to put things into the novels that history teachers wouldn't tell students."

A West Virginia Upbringing

Born in Bethlehem, Pennsylvania, on January 6, 1945, Appel moved with his family to West Virginia when he was six. "I grew up and lived in West Virginia through college," Appel told *AAYA.* One of three siblings, Appel formed an early love

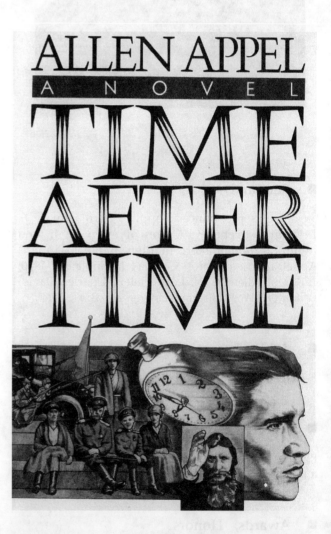

Time-traveling history teacher Alex Balfour finds himself transported back to the beginning of the Russian Revolution in this 1985 work.

of reading. "My mom was always reading," Appel recalled in his interview. "And I just naturally picked up the habit too, as did my brother and sister. We had a rule in the family: fewer than three people at dinner and it was okay to read at the table. We spent a lot of silent meals together." At age eleven, laid up with a high fever, Appel was introduced to the Tarzan books by his mother who had an entire set of works by Edgar Rice Burroughs in the attic. "I raced through them," Appel said. "And from there I went on to science fiction. And soon I was reading everything. My sister is two years older and I would read the books she brought home. I read everything two years too early."

Thoughts of actually becoming a writer himself were put on hold, however. After high school graduation, Appel attended West Virginia University, where he earned a B.A. in 1967. Thereafter he worked primarily as an illustrator and photographer. "I was self-taught in both," Appel told *AAYA*. "I can't draw to save my life, but I worked in collage illustration, often using my own photographs. I created something of a niche for myself, and worked as a freelancer for the *Washington Post* with their Sunday magazine sections." One day, however, sitting at his desk at the newspaper, Appel had a sudden epiphany: "I looked around and everybody I saw in the room was a writer. And I figured they weren't any smarter or imaginative than I was. Why couldn't I become a writer, too?"

A Matter of Time

It was a rhetorical question that led Appel on a several-year pursuit to learn how to write. By this time he had already earned a book credit with his 1979 work, *Proust's Last Beer*, which he illustrated and also conceived. A book describing how famous people died, this nonfiction debut gave him little in the way of education about how to construct fiction. Appel, who is self-taught, simply sat down and began a novel about the crossing of a chimp and a human. "When the dust settled I had a book told only with dialogue. Not even a 'he said' or 'she said.' So I went back in for a second draft and inserted that sort of stuff. The third draft I actually got around to adding descriptive passages." Though this first novel made the rounds of New York publishers, none were enthusiastic enough to buy it. Yet it served

Appel examines the issue of race in this second Alex Balfour novel, published in 1988.

as an apprenticeship, or at least the beginnings of one.

Over the next several years, Appel tried his hand at westerns and romances, penning five more unpublished novels, but gaining confidence in his craft as he went along. Then a fortuitous meeting with Kent Carroll, an editor just setting out on his own in publishing, led to the "Pastmaster" series. Working with the germ of an idea about spending one's summer vacation not at the beach but in the Russia of 1917, Appel set to the task of crafting a hybrid novel—part sci-fi and part historical fiction. Like his protagonist, Alex Balfour, Appel immersed himself in the time period. "I'd never been to Russia, at that time the Soviet Union, and clearly had never been anywhere in 1917, so it was my job as a researcher to get the feel of the time and place right." He read histories, memoirs, and correspondence from the time. "I found out that Lenin had a lisp, something we don't really think about when you mention the name of that revolutionary. So in my book he sometimes sounds like Elmer Fudd." Photograph books of the time were also an aid in recreating the scene. "But they were all in black and white," Appel recalled. "I got the objects right, the look of the street and the things you might find in a drawing room, but I lost sleep over the colors. So I made a house yellow. What if houses weren't painted yellow then? What if some expert found out?"

However, concerns over such details faded in the urgency of plot; no experts on house paint stepped forward. Appel's fictional world came across whole and clear. Balfour, a history teacher at the New School and a gourmet cook, awakens from an incredibly realistic dream of being in the trenches of World War I. He puts it down to nightmare, overwork, too much drink taken. Except that his jeans are smeared with the same red clay he saw in his dream. Balfour continues to dream, going back to Russia during the first World War and the beginning of the Russian Revolution. Molly, his lover in the present, tells him that in fact at times he seems to disappear. Slowly Balfour begins to accept the fact that he is actually time-traveling.

In the course of such journeys in time and quite by accident, Balfour becomes an unwilling participant in the murder of the mad monk, Rasputin, after which he reappears in the present to confront Molly in the monk's sables. During further time travels he encounters Maxim Gorky speaking to workers and puts a word in the ear of the British consul about a spy named Mata Hari. But Balfour himself is arrested by the Czar's police as a suspected spy, and spends weeks imprisoned. More meetings with famous men occur: Pavlov busy walking three dogs, and Lenin, spluttering his words.

His guide through all these adventures is the young American, Maxwell Surrey, whom Balfour knows from the present as the old man who cared for him after he was orphaned as a teenager. And most surprising of all, Balfour meets another time traveler—his own father, who is leading a band of ruthless Cossacks and is intent on changing history. He tells his son, Alex, that he must pre-

In this 1990 novel, Alex Balfour travels back in time to prevent the Japanese from developing an atomic bomb during World War II.

vent the assassination of the Czar and his family, but Alex Balfour has suddenly had too much of history, and goes back to the present. However, nagged by his own morality, he makes one final trip to the past, having learned "that we are responsible for things. For ourselves, other people, events. That inaction can be as destructive as out-and-out evil."

Upon publication of *Time after Time*, reviewers were generally positive if not enthusiastic about this first novel. Sybil Steinberg, writing in *Publishers Weekly*, felt that readers ready to withhold incredulity "will be rewarded by scenes of cliff-hanging and head-bashing, slaughter, torture and hairsbreadth escapes, . . . true romance and wholesome sex." Steinberg went on to conclude that *Time after Time* is an engrossing read. A reviewer for the *Washington Post Book World* dubbed the book a "compelling journey back in time" and an "absorbing first novel," while a contributor in *Booklist* called it "Riveting adventure, replete with romance and drama." Writing in the *New York Times Book Review*, Perry Glasser commented that Appel's novel was on one level "fine entertainment," but more than that in its entirety. Glasser praised *Time after Time*'s "vivid writing," and called the novel "something of a historical novel, something of a science fiction novel, partly the story of a son's bitter relationship with his father, partly a romance." These features are "pleasingly balanced," concluded Glasser, "with grace and skill."

Further Travels in Time

Sales of this initial title were encouraging enough for Appel to continue with the intended series. For his next title, *Twice upon a Time*, Appel chose an American setting. "And I wanted to talk about what I consider to be *the* issue of our time—race," Appel explained to *AAYA*. "I wanted to write about black people and Native Americans, both then and now. The moral issues were very important for me in the writing." In this second novel, Alex Balfour has come to feel truly alive and free only when he is in the past, yet still he receives no warning when such journeys are beginning nor does he have any overt control over his destination. Molly, his partner and a reporter for the *New York Times*, sets things in motion when she takes on an assignment to cover a story about one John Raven, a Native American who claims to be a direct descendant of Crazy Horse, the "Architect, or rather strategist, of the Battle of the Little Bighorn," as Balfour tells her for background. Raven has shot two white men doing a land study on a South Dakota reservation, and Molly soon heads out to that state to interview him.

Studying up on the history of Native Americans and their struggles vis-à-vis the whites sets off a series of time travels for Balfour, journeys which at first seem to be unrelated to any one main event. Then Balfour finds himself taken back to the Philadelphia Exhibition of 1876 where he checks out the latest in technological advances and meets Mark Twain. Living with a group of emancipated slaves, Balfour conspires with one of them to release two captured Indians who are at the

exhibit, and with Twain in tow, the five of them light out for the territories. Their trek westward includes a raft trip down the Mississippi. Meanwhile, back in the present, Molly is kidnapped by Raven just before the centenary of Custer's Last Stand, and Balfour, lost in time, arrives at the Little Big Horn in an attempt to stop the slaughter that he knows will soon happen.

Once again, critics praised Appel for his historical reconstruction. Andrea Caron Kempf noted in *Library Journal* that "Appel again demonstrates his unique blend of history and science fiction in a riveting novel that says much about freedom and slavery and the innate dignity of human beings." Kempf gave the book a "highly recommended" rating. Other reviewers applauded Appel's blend

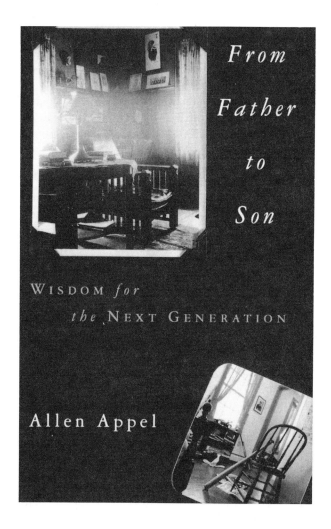

In this 1993 work, Appel provides advice for his son that is useful for any reader.

of entertainment and history. *Kirkus Reviews* dubbed the novel a "high-speed, deftly handled sequel" which blends "time-travel, authentic backgrounds, and speculative fancy." *Publishers Weekly* remarked that "Appel maintains a firm hold on the strands of his plot, keeping Alex's sensibility consistently modern without becoming patronizing or sentimental toward the times." "Suspense" and "period detail," this same reviewer concluded, "will keep readers turning these pages." High praise was given by Susan Jelcich in *Voice of Youth Advocates*, who commented that "Appel has created a perceptive, insightful, sometimes passionate blend of history, adventure, and moral responsibility." Jelcich concluded that "*Twice upon a Time* is entertaining, worthwhile reading that packs a punch as it amuses."

The third book in the series, *Till the End of Time,* finds Balfour transported back to World War II, attempting to stop the Japanese from developing their own atomic bomb. Appel again has Balfour making the acquaintance of the high and mighty from history: taking tea with Albert Einstein, meeting with Franklin Delano Roosevelt, having an affair with Betty Grable, and even lending a hand to a young lieutenant named John F. Kennedy as he saves the crew of his PT boat. The crux of the story deals with Balfour's attempt to stop the destructive use of the atomic bomb, a mission on which Einstein sends him to Roosevelt. But F.D.R. is too canny a politician to be limited in the use of this new weapon; he sends Balfour to the South Pacific on a fact-finding mission to get him out of the way. Meanwhile in the present, Molly is following a story about Japanese germ warfare that resonates with the historical tale which culminates at the bombing of Hiroshima, where Appel has set the Japanese atomic program (it actually was in Tokyo).

"This novel seems at first to be a simple action gambol," Benford noted in the *Washington Post Book World*, "but it raises issues seldom treated in our press." *Publishers Weekly* found this third title in the "Pastmaster" series to be a "thoroughly absorbing and enjoyable adventure," concluding that "insights into the effects of time on human nature and on one man's actions attest to Appel's continuing ability to keep readers glued to the page." According to *Kirkus Reviews*, "Appel's generous dollops of history are as painlessly informative, and the tale he spins as rousing, as ever." Marcia R. Hoffman, writing in *Library Journal*, re-

marked that Appel "has assembled some believable and very human characters" in the bomb scene "which is exciting and well researched."

The popular series came to an abrupt end, however, when Appel delivered his fourth Balfour manuscript, "Sea of Time," to Doubleday, only to have it rejected because the subject matter supposedly would not have wide enough appeal. "That limited subject matter just happened to be the sinking of the Titanic," Appel said in his interview. "I think maybe that editor was just a little bit wrong in light of the movie and the spin-offs that came a few years later. But at the time I was so angry that I just put the manuscript on the shelf and moved on to other projects. I still send it out to fans who write, asking about a sequel."

Since the last of the "Pastmaster" series, Appel has embarked on numerous projects. In 1994 he collaborated with Craig Roberts, a retired helicopter pilot, policeman, and Vietnam veteran, to write the thriller, *Hellhound,* about a conspiracy by Iraqi and Palestinian terrorists to kill former president Ronald Reagan and destroy Southern California. A Russian colonel discovers the plot and teams up with a disgraced Los Angeles cop to ground the mission by outmaneuvering the deadly Hellhound helicopter en route. *Publishers Weekly* noted that Appel and Roberts "make a good team and deliver an imaginative novel of clear, direct military suspense" with a "rousing climax." Appel has also created a line of gift books, partly in collaboration with his wife, Sherry Conway Appel, in appreciation of parents. Additionally, he has largely left novel writing behind—at least for the time being—to work on screenplays. His first endeavor, "The Ebony Streak," tells the story of Marshall "Major" Taylor, one of the greatest athletes of his day at the turn of the twentieth century and one of the first black world champions in any sport. A bicyclist in a time of worldwide passion for the sport, Marshall held the one-mile speed record. Though cheered in Europe, Marshall faced bigotry in his native America, dying penniless and unknown. As Appel put it, "Marshall is the most famous athlete that America ever forgot."

A full-time writer, Appel is brimming over with new plans and projects. But for many readers, it is still the "Pastmaster" series that makes his name known. "I receive fan letters all the time," Appel told *AAYA*. "Lots of them are from young readers, too, ones who find truth in these books

If you enjoy the works of Allen Appel, you may also want to check out the following books and films:

Richard Peck, *Voices after Midnight*, 1989.
Stanley Shapiro, *A Time to Remember*, 1986.
Karen Weinberg, *Window of Time*, 1991.
Star Trek 4: The Voyage Home, a film starring William Shatner and Leonard Nimoy, 1986.

and write to me that they never knew history could actually be interesting. I think part of the draw of the books is that I never fudge. I never cheat. I don't let Alex Balfour get himself out of trouble by suddenly going back to the present. He is in the past and in trouble and he has to deal with it. He has to save himself. There is a level of engagement that young readers especially respond to. I have young kids myself, and find that so often in books intended for younger readers that the writer cheats at the end. 'It was all a dream.' The hero or heroine is saved by that device. With Alex Balfour the dream becomes reality. And reality can be deadly serious."

■ **Works Cited**

Appel, Allen, *Time after Time*, Carroll and Graf, 1985.

Appel, Allen, *Twice upon a Time*, Carroll and Graf, 1988.

Appel, Allen, interview with *Authors and Artists for Young Adults*, conducted July 20, 1999.

Benford, Gregory, "What Is and What Might Have Been," *Washington Post Book World*, August 15, 1990, p. 4.

Glasser, Perry, "The Professor Vanishes," *New York Times Book Review*, January 26, 1986, p. 12.

Review of *Hellhound*, *Publishers Weekly*, May 30, 1994.

Hoffman, Marcia R., review of *Till the End of Time*, *Library Journal*, September 1, 1990, p. 253.

Jelcich, Susan, review of *Twice upon a Time*, *Voice of Youth Advocates*, October, 1988. p. 190.

Kempf, Andrea Caron, review of *Twice upon a Time*, *Library Journal*, April 1, 1988, p. 56.

Steinberg, Sybil, review of *Twice after Time*, *Publishers Weekly*, September 27, 1985, p. 83.

Review of *Till the End of Time*, *Publishers Weekly*, June 29, 1990, p. 85.

Review of *Till the End of Time*, *Kirkus Reviews*, July 1, 1990, p. 893.

Review of *Time after Time*, *Booklist*, October 1, 1985, pp. 189-90.

Review of *Time after Time*, *Washington Post Book World*, May 24, 1987, p. 12.

Review of *Twice upon a Time*, *Kirkus Reviews*, February 1, 1988, p. 139.

Review of *Twice upon a Time*, *Publishers Weekly*, February 19, 1988, pp. 72-73.

■ **For More Information See**

PERIODICALS

Booklist, September 1, 1990, p. 24; March 15, 1991, p. 1473.
Kliatt, spring, 1987, p. 19.
Locus, April, 1990, p. 35; September, 1990, p. 57.
New York Times Book Review, March 1, 1987, p. 34.
Washington Post, November 30, 1985; April 21, 1988.

ON-LINE

Allen Appel's Web site is located at http://www.appelworks.com.

—*Sketch by J. Sydney Jones*

Robert L. Asprin

■ Personal

Born June 28, 1946, in St. Johns, MI; son of Daniel D. (a machinist) and Lorraine (an elementary school teacher; maiden name, Coon) Asprin; married Anne Brett (a bookkeeper), December 28, 1968; children: Annette Maria, Daniel Mather. *Education:* Attended University of Michigan, 1964-65.

■ Career

University Microfilm, Ann Arbor, MI, accounts payable clerk, 1966-69, accounts receivable correspondent, 1969-70, payroll-labor analyst, 1970-74; junior cost accountant, 1974-76, cost accountant, 1976-78; freelance writer, 1978—. *Military service:* U.S. Army, 1965-66. *Member:* Science Fiction Writers of America.

■ Writings

SCIENCE FICTION NOVELS

The Cold Cash War, St. Martin's (New York City), 1977.

The Bug Wars, St. Martin's, 1979.

The Star Stalkers, Playboy Press, 1979.

(With George Takei) *Mirror Friend, Mirror Foe,* Playboy Press, 1979.

Tambu, Ace Books (New York City), 1979.

Tambu Anthology (short fiction), Ace Books, 1980.

(With Lynn Abbey) *Act of God,* Ace Books, 1980.

(With Bill Fawcett) *Cold Cash Warrior,* Ace Books, 1989.

Phule's Company, Ace Books, 1990.

Phule's Paradise, Ace Books, 1992.

(With Lynn Abbey) *Catwoman: Tiger Hunt,* Warner (New York City), 1992.

(With Linda Evans) *Time Scout,* Baen, 1995.

Wagers of Sin, Baen, 1996.

(With Peter J. Heck) *A Phule and His Money,* Ace, 1999.

FANTASY NOVELS

Another Fine Myth, Donning (Norfolk, VA), 1978, revised edition, illustrated by Phil Foglio, 1985.

Myth Conceptions, illustrated by Polly and Kelly Freas, Donning, 1980.

The Demon Blade, St. Martin's, 1980.

Myth Directions, illustrated by Foglio, Donning, 1982.

Hit or Myth, illustrated by Foglio, Donning, 1983.

Myth Adventures (includes *Another Fine Myth, Myth Directions,* and *Hit or Myth*), Doubleday (Garden City, NY), 1984.

Myth-ing Persons, illustrated by Foglio, Donning, 1984.

Little Myth Marker, illustrated by Foglio, Donning, 1985.

(With Kay Reynolds) *M.Y.T.H. Inc. Link,* illustrated by Foglio, Donning, 1986.

Myth Alliances (includes *Myth-ing Persons, Little Myth Marker,* and *M.Y.T.H. Inc. Link*), Doubleday, 1987.

Myth-Nomers and Im-Pervections, illustrated by Foglio, Donning, 1987.

M.Y.T.H. Inc. in Action, illustrated by Foglio, Donning, 1990.

Sweet Myth-tery of Life, illustrated by Foglio, Donning, 1994.

GRAPHIC NOVELS

(With Phil Foglio) *Myth Adventures One* (previously published in magazine form), art by Foglio, Starblaze Graphics (Norfolk, VA), 1985.

(With Foglio) *Myth Adventures Two* (previously published in magazine form), art by Foglio, Starblaze Graphics, 1985.

(With Mel White) *Duncan and Mallory,* Starblaze Graphics, 1986.

(With Lynn Abbey) *Thieves' World Graphics,* art by Tim Sales, 6 volumes, Starblaze Graphics, 1985-87.

(With Mel White) *Duncan and Mallory: The Bar-None Ranch,* Starblaze Graphics, 1987.

(With White) *Duncan and Mallory: The Raiders,* Starblaze Graphics, 1988.

EDITOR

Thieves' World, Ace Books, 1979.

Tales from the Vulgar Unicorn, Ace Books, 1980.

Shadows of Sanctuary, Ace Books, 1981.

Sanctuary (includes *Thieves' World, Tales from the Vulgar Unicorn,* and *Shadows of Sanctuary*), Doubleday, 1982.

Storm Season, Ace Books, 1982.

(With Lynn Abbey) *The Face of Chaos,* Ace Books, 1983.

(With Abbey) *Wings of Omen,* Ace Books, 1984.

(With Abbey) *Birds of Prey,* Ace Books, 1984.

(With Abbey) *Cross-Currents* (includes *Storm Season, The Face of Chaos,* and *Wings of Omen*), Doubleday, 1984.

(With Abbey) *The Dead of Winter,* Ace Books, 1985.

(With Abbey) *Soul of the City,* Ace Books, 1986.

(With Abbey) *Blood Ties,* Ace Books, 1986.

(With Abbey) *The Shattered Sphere* (includes *The Dead of Winter, Soul of the City,* and *Blood Ties*), Doubleday, 1986.

(With Abbey and Richard Pini) *The Blood of Ten Chiefs,* Tor (New York City), 1986.

(With Abbey) *Aftermath,* Ace Books, 1987.

(With Abbey and Pini) *Wolfsong: The Blood of Ten Chiefs,* Tor, 1988.

(With Abbey) *Uneasy Alliances,* Ace Books, 1988.

(With Abbey) *Stealers' Sky,* Ace Books, 1989.

(With Abbey) *The Price of Victory* (includes *Aftermath, Uneasy Alliances,* and *Stealers' Sky*), Doubleday, 1990.

OTHER

The Capture (script for comedy slide show), Boojums Press, 1975.

■ Adaptations

Several of Asprin's novels have been recorded on cassette tape.

■ Sidelights

With both science fiction and fantasy novels, as well as the script of several graphic novels to his credit, author Robert L. Asprin commands a loyal following of both teen and adult readers. Getting his start as an author of science fiction during the mid-1970s, Asprin quickly began a move toward the fantasy genre with such novels as *Another Fine Myth, Myth Conceptions,* and 1985's *Little Myth Marker.* As the titles alone should make clear to a reader unfamiliar with his work, Asprin liberally garnishes his writing with a full dose of farce, deliberately leaden puns, and blatant parody. Comparing his work to that of author L. Sprague de Camp, Richard A. Lupoff comments in the *St. James Guide to Science Fiction Writers* on the "typical Asprin characteristics of rapid pace, slapstick action, and broad humor."

The Cold Cash War was Asprin's first published novel. Drawing from his personal background working as a financial analyst in a large U.S. corporation, Asprin wove a futuristic tale about mega-corporations that behave like nations: they wage bloodless "warfare" on each other using war-game simulations. Ignoring the efforts of actual governments to stop them, these moneyed superpowers eventually lose control of the game when real weapons enter the picture and the hits become lethal. Calling it a "very good treatment of a SF concept popular in the 50s," a *Publishers Weekly* reviewer praised *The Cold Cash War*'s "satire, action, and character."

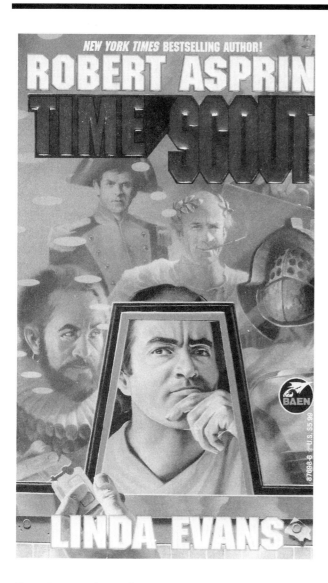

Co-written with Linda Evans, this 1995 sci-fi foray is about a near-future world where time travel is as common as summer family vacations.

criminals with assorted magical powers and the avaricious Queen Hemlock; dragons, demons, and an amazing assortment of fantastic ne'er-do-wells keep Asprin's fumbling heroes on their toes throughout other "Myth" books. While the series provides little in the way of the high-tech hijinks that appeal to some sci-fi followers, its light-hearted tone and steady barrage of puns, jokes, and bumbling antics have made it an entertaining read. "Asprin isn't trying to be profound," Tom Easton noted in a review in *Analog Science Fiction/Science Fact*. "He's having fun."

Writer and Editor

In his continuing effort to keep the job of writing fun, Asprin has strived to keep his subject matter from becoming stale. As he once noted, "my first three books are intentionally dissimilar. *The Cold Cash War* is speculative near-future fiction involving corporate takeover of world government. *Another Fine Myth* is a sword-and-sorcery farce full of dragons, stranded demons, and very bad puns. *The Bug Wars* does not have a human in the entire book. It was written 'first-person alien, reptile to be specific' and has been one of my greatest writing challenges to date." In addition to novel-writing, Asprin also branched out into editing, collaborating with fellow editor and writer Lynn Abbey to produce the popular series "Thieves' World." Called "the toughest, seamiest backwater in the realm of fantasy" by *Voice of Youth Advocates* reviewer Carolyn Caywood, the highly acclaimed "Thieves' World" anthology series brings together a collection of original short fiction written by a host of predominately women writers, including Abbey, Janet Morris, and C. J. Cherryh. Each book in the series centers around the ongoing struggle between the evil Queen Roxanne and her nemesis, a blood-sucking enchantress named Ischade. The continuing battle between these two powerful witches continues through such collections as *Soul of the City* and *Blood Ties*, each of which takes place in a mythic city called Sanctuary.

Asprin's second novel found him mapping terrain in a different genre: fantasy. *Another Fine Myth*, published in 1978, was inspired by such heroic characters as Kane and Conan the Barbarian, and Asprin leapt into the project with relish. Basing his two main characters—an apprentice wizard named Skeeve (who also serves as narrator) and his shifty-eyed cohort, Aahz—on the relationship between Bob Hope and Bing Crosby in their classic screwball "Road" films of the 1940s, Asprin developed a winning duo whose antics have fueled an entire series of humorous "Myth" books, in addition to spinoff graphic novels. In 1983's *Hit or Myth* the two come up against both a gang of

Asprin has characterized the overall message behind his writing as "the case for Everyman. Like all science fiction writers, I promote space travel and development. I feel, however, that we will never see it until the average guy on the street can see a place for himself in space. We will have to have the support of the common man, not just

If you enjoy the works of Robert L. Asprin, you may also want to check out the following books:

Lois McMaster Bujold, *Borders of Infinity*, 1989.

Kyle Crocco, Heroes Wanted, 1991.

Brian Daley, *Fall of the White Ship Avatar*, 1987.

L. Sprague de Camp, *Rivers of Time*, 1993.

George Alec Effinger, *Maureen Birnbaum, Barbarian Swordsperson: The Complete Stories*, 1990.

Neil Gaiman, *Good Omens: The Nice and Accurate Prophecies of Agnes Nutter*, 1990.

the scientists and test pilots." In 1979's *Tambu*, for example, Asprin assembles what he believes is a realistic crew for a spaceship. A renegade spaceworker who starts a kind of intra-stellar mafia, Tambu and this rough and ready crew use their collective street smarts to protect client planets from space pirates. Calling *Tambu* an "action-filled tale of how power corrupts," Claudia Morner notes in *School Library Journal* that Asprin's unusual sci-fi adventure yarn holds a great appeal for YA readers. "It is not only co-educational," the author explained of *Tambu;* "there are several racial types, ages ranging from teens to old-timers, and a wide cross-section of educational backgrounds. That is what life on Earth is all about, and that is what it is going to be like in space." Reflecting aspects of human reality within his fantasy has always been Asprin's goal; he maintains that the science fiction writer can be instrumental in changing the public's awareness of the amazing possibilities presented by travel to other worlds. "We are going to need grease monkeys as well as computer programmers," he once noted. "Few people see themselves as Superman, and as long as science fiction writers portray space travelers in that light, the taxpayers and voters could not care less about getting off the planet."

In 1990 Asprin added a new hero to his catalogue of space adventurers with *Phule's Company*. Willard Phule is a captain in the Space Legion, but his devil-may-care attitude soon finds him exiled to a remote command, where he is put in charge of a rag-tag band of fellow miscreants. Undaunted,

the savvy Phule eventually shapes his troops into a highly effective—and profitable—military outfit. "This lighthearted tale is part science fiction, part spoof, part heart-warmer," noted a *Publishers Weekly* critic of the novel, which would be followed in 1992 by the sequel, *Phule's Paradise.*

Another novel leaning more towards sci-fi than fantasy is Asprin's *Time Scout,* which he co-wrote with Linda Evans. Taking place in the near future, the 1995 novel features a world where time travel has become a common vacation pastime. Kit Carson, a retired "time scout"—one of the daring explorers who enter new passages through time in advance of the commonfolk—must train his headstrong granddaughter to survive as the first female time scout. Calling the novel "engaging, fast moving, historically literate," and reflective of Asprin's broad knowledge of the martial arts, *Booklist* reviewer Roland Green dubbed *Time Scout* "first-class action sf."

A Variety of Interests

"Philippine-Irish in ancestry, I look like a stereotyped revolutionary (which I'm not)," Asprin once commented. His offbeat "look" is reflective of several of his hobbies, which include a broad study of the martial arts. Fencing and coaching foil-, saber-, and epee-wielding, he has also served as divisional vice-chairman of the Amateur Fencing League of America. "Furthermore, I have studied the Japanese, Okinawan, and Chinese forms of armed and unarmed combat," Asprin added, "and am passable with firearms and archery. To round out the picture, I was active for several years in the Society for Creative Anachronism, which practices full-force combat with mock-ups of swords, spears, axes, and maces. As Yang the Nauseating, I organized and ran a 'household' patterned after a Mongol horde."

Fortunately, Asprin continues to take time away from his many hobbies to settle down and write. His creative side has also found other outlets: the raising and breeding of tropical fish, acting in several amateur stage productions, and playing folk guitar. But "I am first and foremost a storyteller," he will admit. Influenced by a youthful diet of action-adventure novels, Asprin has found the science fiction and fantasy genres to be another excellent outlet for both his interests and his imagination, ensuring that his novels are dependably lighthearted and entertaining. "I find long, drawn-out descriptions of explanations of mathematical theorems to be extremely boring," Asprin explains, "and therefore exclude them from my own stories. You do not have to know how to build a clock to tell time, or understand a jet engine to ride in a plane."

■ Works Cited

Caywood, Carolyn, review of *Soul of the City, Voice of Youth Advocates,* June, 1986, p. 84.

Review of *The Cold Cash War, Publishers Weekly,* July 11, 1977, p. 75.

Easton, Tom, review of *Hit or Myth, Analog Science Fiction/Science Fact,* October, 1984, p. 147.

Green, Roland, review of *Time Scout, Booklist,* January 15, 1995, p. 689.

Lupoff, Richard A., "Robert Lynn Asprin," in *St. James Guide to Science Fiction Writers,* St. James Press, 1995, pp. 35-37.

Morner, Claudia, review of *Tambu, School Library Journal,* March, 1980, p. 146.

Review of *Phule's Company, Publishers Weekly,* June 8, 1990, p. 50.

■ For More Information See

PERIODICALS

Analog Science Fiction-Science Fact, September, 1987, p. 163; February, 1991, p. 181.

Booklist, December 1, 1977, p. 598; January 15, 1984, p. 715; April 1, 1986, p. 1120; March 15, 1987, p. 1097; June 15, 1990, p. 1960; January 15, 1992, pp. 915, 921; December 15, 1995, p. 689.

Library Journal, November 1, 1977, p. 2279; January 15, 1980, p. 228.

Publishers Weekly, January 20, 1992, p. 60.

Voice of Youth Advocates, April 1981, p. 52; February 1987, p. 290; December 1987, p. 241.*

Nevada Barr

■ Personal

Born c. 1952, in Nevada; daughter of a pilot and a pilot, mechanic, and carpenter; married (divorced). *Education:* California Politechnical University, B.A.; University of California, Irvine, M.A.

■ Addresses

Home—Mesa Verde National Park, CO, and Clinton, MS. *Agent*—c/o Putnam Publishing Group, 200 Madison Avenue, New York, NY 10016.

■ Career

Novelist and park ranger. Classic Stage Company, New York City, acted in off-Broadway shows; performed in television commercials and corporate and industrial films, Minneapolis, MN; United States National Park Service, law enforcement ranger in National Parks, including Guadalupe Mountains, TX; Isle Royale, MI; Mesa Verde, CO; Natchez Trace Parkway, MS; and, Horsefly Fire Camp, ID, 1989—.

■ Awards, Honors

Agatha Award for Best First Novel of 1993, and Anthony Award for Best Novel of 1993, both for *Track of the Cat.*

■ Writings

"ANNA PIGEON" MYSTERIES

Track of the Cat, Putnam, 1993.
A Superior Death, Putnam, 1994.
Ill Wind, Putnam, 1995.
Firestorm, Putnam, 1996.
Endangered Species, Putnam, 1997.
Blind Descent, Putnam, 1998.
Liberty Falling, Putnam, 1999.

OTHER

Bittersweet, St. Martin's, 1984.

■ Sidelights

Former actress-turned-national parks ranger Nevada Barr has forged a literary career for herself as the creator of the entertaining and much praised Anna Pigeon mystery novels. "What lifts the [series] far above most of the other contemporary amateur sleuths mysteries is Barr's exquisite writing—it swoops, soars, sails, then catches you unawares beneath the heart and takes your breath away," wrote a *Cleveland Plain Dealer* reviewer. "Like the parks and monuments she writes of, Nevada Barr should be declared a national treasure," echoed a reviewer in the *Bloomsbury Review.*

"Stars were starting to appear low in the sky; pinpricks of light in the summer-green evening..."

Bittersweet

NEVADA BARR

"This is a knockout." —Rita Mae Brown

This unusual western novel features two lesbian women who try to become Nevada innkeepers in a land dominated by men who can't understand them.

Writing in a 1995 edition of the magazine *Armchair Detective,* Dorman T. Shindler observed that Barr "comes by her love of the outdoors and her penchant for an adventurous lifestyle quite naturally. Raised within sight of the Sierra Nevada mountain range, she is the child of a mother who . . . ferried airplanes during World War II, and a father whose background included employment as a forest ranger and a pilot. In their later years, both parents flew planes for the Forest Service, fighting fires."

Barr, who was given the name Nevada after a character in one of her father's favorite movies, grew up at a mountain airport in the town of Johnsonville, California. As a girl, she dreamed of being an actress. That is what she worked at af-

ter graduating from college with a master of arts degree in drama; Barr acted for six years off-Broadway in New York and for another eight in regional theater, television commercials, and industrial films in Minneapolis, Minnesota. Her initial interest in writing grew out of her acting: she was frustrated with the weak roles that playwrights—most of whom were male—were creating for women. Barr's passion for nature came about because her first husband was involved with the parks service. Her interests in writing and the outdoors coalesced when Barr found work as a professional story teller, going on wilderness camping trips to tell dramatic campfire stories.

When she started writing down some of the stories that she was creating, Barr also began submitting them to magazines. One got published in a small magazine, earning its author a $100 fee. Encouraged by this, Barr decided to take her writing seriously, even if others did not. In 1979, she wrote a western novel called *Helena on Down,* which went unpublished. It was five long years, 1984, until her first novel appeared.

Makes Debut with *Bittersweet*

Barr described the book to interviewer John Rowen of *Booklist* as a "a neo-Gothic lesbian western." *Bittersweet* is the story of schoolteacher Imogene Grelznik, who, falsely accused of having a love affair with one of her pupils, leaves her native Philadelphia for a small Pennsylvania town, where she really does have a relationship with a female pupil—a sixteen-year-old abused wife named Sarah. Imogene and Sarah flee to Nevada, and there they become innkeepers, and maintain their independence in the face of a rough, male-dominated world that does not understand them. The plot—which many people regarded as an unusual premise for old west fiction—attracted favorable critical notice, as did the quality of Barr's writing skills. Sister Avila, writing for *Library Journal,* called *Bittersweet* "a first novel of power and vitality that will grip the reader." A *Booklist* reviewer stated, "Despite the novel's flaws . . . Barr succeeds in conveying the meaning of these brave and desperate lives."

After *Bittersweet,* Barr wrote two novels that remained unpublished. She told Dorman Shindler that one was based on the experiences of her flying parents in the 1940s and 1950s; the other was an historical novel about a 1913 coal strike in a town called Trinidad, Colorado. "These were big projects, they took three and four years to finish," Barr recalled in her *Armchair Detective* interview. "Then I started in the Park Service [in 1989], and I was wandering around Texas, and I wasn't working on a book." But the time was not wasted; Barr's imagination had lots of time and opportunities to work, and she devised whimsical plots to bump off some of the irksome people she encountered in her work. Said Barr, "And I thought, 'Let's be a little more constructive here.' And I decided to write a murder mystery novel."

In this third installment of the Anna Pigeon mystery series, Anna investigates the murder of a disliked park ranger in Mesa Verde National Park.

While it was almost a decade before the appearance of that novel, the wait was worthwhile. The book was a well-received mystery called *Track of the Cat*, the first volume in Barr's signature "Anna Pigeon" series. At the same time she was writing this and subsequent books, Barr worked as a law enforcement ranger in national parks such as Guadalupe Mountains National Park in west Texas, Mesa Verde National Park in Colorado, and Natchez Trace Parkway in Mississippi. She relied on her professional experience and understanding of natural lore to provide plots and background for the mysteries; in fact, her amateur-sleuth heroine is a tough-talking, wine-drinking park ranger. The originality of setting and occupational details in Barr's mysteries proved intriguing for reviewers and readers alike, for it gave her the chance to exercise one of her most praised talents: a gift for vividly describing nature.

In an on-line interview with Naomi Gesinger of Amazon.com, Barr explained the origins of her heroine's unusual name. "I stole it from this woman named Anna Pigeon who worked with my ex-husband in a museum," she said. "I thought it was such a wonderful name." Responding to a follow-up question about what other literary characters Anna is based on, Barr confided that "she started out being based on myself, because I was working as a park ranger in Guadalupe. But of course she was taller, stronger, smarter—you know, better looking. And over the years [Anna Pigeon] has kind of just evolved into her own person."

A Successful Mystery Series

In that debut book in the series, *Track of the Cat*, the heroine is working in Mesa Verde National Park when the body of a dead ranger is found. It appears that he has been killed by a mountain lion. However, Anna has her doubts, and so she investigates the lives and circumstances of everyone involved. At times, she is aided by her sister Molly, a New York City psychiatrist whose telephone conversations with Anna have become a running feature of the series. *Track of the Cat* proved a hit with critics, earning Barr much praise as well as both the Anthony and Agatha mystery writers' awards for best first novel.

Reviewer Paul Skenazy of *Washington Post Book World* commented that while *Track of the Cat* starts slowly and "bears some of the scars of the genre: overripe description, an occasional sincerity that approaches the sappy, [and] uneven writing," on balance it is "a wonderful and absorbing tale." Charles Champlin, of the *Los Angeles Times Book Review,* regretted that Anna's physical isolation forced her to use her horse excessively as a Dr. Watson-type sounding-board, but that was a minor quibble; Champlin hailed *Track of the Cat* as "an eventful, characterful story with a slam-bang denouement" that takes place in the wilds, a setting Barr "describes with poetic passion." A scholarly review, in *Women's Review of Books* more than a year after the novel's publication, treated Barr's work as inspiringly "ecofeminist." The critic, Mimi Wesson, praised Barr for allowing her protagonist a realistic ambivalence on social and human issues: "Some of the most rewarding parts of the narrative depict Anna's struggles to understand and satisfy her own needs for human connection," Wesson declared.

The follow-up to *Track of the Cat, A Superior Death,* finds Anna in a very different setting: Isle Royale National Park in the middle of Lake Superior, halfway between the upper peninsula of Michigan and Canada. The location gave Barr a chance to fill her heroine with fear of the immeasurable, as well as the spunk to conquer her trepidations. Again an assorted group of possible suspects, including park employees and tourists, are found in the otherwise thinly populated area; this time the trigger for the mystery is the discovery of an experienced diver's dead body on a sunken wreck shortly after his wedding. Paul Skenazy, again writing in the *Washington Post Book World,* hailed *A Superior Death* as "a wonderfully satisfying read." He had special praise for Barr's "tangled, rich descriptive language," which he wrote has "an engrossing pull." Marilyn Stasio of the *New York Times Book Review* echoed those comments, lauding Barr's "sternly beautiful" prose that "is best displayed in natural settings—like her eerie underwater landscapes of sunken ships and floating corpses—where human life makes itself scarce." Chicago *Tribune Books* critic Dick Adler also enjoyed the descriptions of nature found in *A Superior Death.* And anticipating a continuation of the Anna Pigeon mystery series, he mused, "Think of all the national parks Barr has left in which to turn Anna loose."

Adler's words presaged Barr's third mystery novel; *Ill Wind,* published in 1995, is set in Mesa Verde National Park, one of her old stomping grounds. This time a disliked park ranger's body is found at a "pathologically neat" murder scene. Surrounding the crime are questions about the fate of the Anasazi Indians and about local construction practices. Anna assists FBI agent Frederick Stanton, her love interest, in solving the mystery, and their interactions provide a developing focus for human relationships in the story. Like the first two Anna Pigeon mysteries, this novel won strong reviews; a critic for *Publishers Weekly* commenting that it is "common sense and appreciation for nature that makes [Anna Pigeon] such good com-

Barr continues to use her experience as a park ranger in her fifth book about Anna Pigeon, who is now investigating the deaths of two men whose plane was sabotaged at Cumberland Island.

pany." Writing again in the *New York Times Book Review*, Marilyn Stasio applauded the intelligence with which Barr formulated the answers to questions the novel posed, and she added that Barr's "stirring style is best illustrated by vibrant descriptions of the order and disorder in the natural world. In vivid images of life . . . and death . . . she shows us the very face of nature." Gary Dretzka in the Chicago *Tribune Books* used his review of *Ill Wind* as a forum to praise the Anna Pigeon books as "a rich new series."

Intricate, Suspenseful Works

Barr's 1996 novel *Firestorm* is a mystery with some new wrinkles. The setting is a northern California forest ablaze with a forest fire; the plot is of the "locked room" mystery style, which Barr "ingeniously resurrects," according to reviewer Maureen Corrigan writing in *Washington Post Book World*. While helping fight the fire, Anna Pigeon and eight others firefighters in her squad, one of whom is injured, are trapped in a canyon when the fire unexpectedly turns on them. They survive this inferno only because they find shelter inside the individual fireproof tents they carry for such dire emergencies. The deadly firestorm passes, razing the surrounding landscape in minutes; when the firefighters emerge from their foil cocoons they are in relatively good shape—except for one man, who is found dead with a knife in his back. The question of who could have committed murder in the midst of an inferno, and why, is the locked-room puzzle. "*Firestorm* is a brilliantly executed mystery," Corrigan observed; she then went on to compare the descriptions of forest fire favorably with Dorothy Sayers' descriptions of flood in *The Nine Tailors,* one of the classics of the mystery genre. Some of the fire scenes even "approach the reverent terror of Norman Maclean's posthumous 1992 masterpiece, *Young Men and Fire,*" Corrigan continued. A Chicago *Tribune Books* contributor went a step further, calling Barr's forest fire scenes "the best I've read anywhere" and pronouncing the novel to be "good, dirty, escapist fun of the first rank." Dick Lochte of the *Los Angeles Times Book Review* told readers that *Firestorm* describes natural disaster "with such authenticity and in such chilling detail that you can smell the smoke and taste the ashes." Lochte added, "Barr is a splendid storyteller, but it's her knowledge of the territory that ignites this fast-paced and suspenseful whodunit." *New York Times*

Book Review critic Marilyn Stasio extolled the novel's "striking visceral quality" which she called "remarkable because [Barr] writes with . . . a cool, steady hand" about nature's fury and man's inhumanity.

Endangered Species, the fifth novel in the series, finds Anna Pigeon spending the summer on presuppression fire duty on drought-stricken Cumberland Island National Seashore, an isolated park off the coast of Georgia. Anna's lazy routine is shattered by the crash of an airplane that kills the pilot, an anti-drug enforcement officer, and his passenger who is a district ranger. When it becomes evident that the plane was sabotaged and there's murder afoot, Anna develops a list of suspects that includes several members of her own park crew. The book also features an affecting subplot involving the first face-to-face meeting between FBI agent Frederick Stanton, who is Anna's lover, and Anna's psychiatrist sister Molly. Marilyn Stasio of the *New York Times Book Review* described *Endangered Species* as an "intricate mystery." Emily Melton of *Booklist* observed that "Anna's no-nonsense view of her unorthodox career, strong opinions, secret vulnerability, and soft heart" places her in the ranks of contemporary female detectives. A *Publishers Weekly* reviewer expressed a similar view, praising the strength of Barr's lead character. "A refreshing change from the brash, wisecracking order of female PIs, Barr's thoughtful and sensitive heroine . . . rings true on every page," the anonymous critic wrote.

In the 1998 novel *Blind Descent*, Anna Pigeon is a member of a rescue party that's dispatched to save a female National Park dispatcher who has been injured while exploring the ancient Lechugilla caves in New Mexico's Carlsbad Caverns, 800 feet underground. The plot thickens, of course, when Anna learns that the dispatcher's mishap was no accident, and someone in the rescue party is a murderer. "Barr's superbly unerring eye for natural setting and human conflict has made Anna's five earlier adventures . . . as distinctly memorable as the National Parks themselves," commented a *Kirkus Reviews* writer. *Library Journal* reviewer Alice DiNizo also liked the novel. "This will be as popular as Barr's other works, for the author is a master at the craft of prose," she wrote.

Pigeon appeared again in *Liberty Falling*, published in the spring of 1999. As always, trouble seems

If you enjoy the works of Nevada Barr, you may also want to check out the following books:

Alison Drake, *Tango Key*, 1988.
B. J. Oliphant, *The Unexpected Corpse*, 1990.
Dana Stabenow's "Kate Shugak" series, including *A Cold Day for Murder*, 1992, *Dead in the Water*, 1993, and *Breakup*, 1997.
Jessica Speart, *Gator Aide*, 1996.

to find Anna Pigeon wherever she goes. This seventh book in the series is set in an unexpected and unlikely locale—New York City. Anna has gone to the Big Apple to be near her psychiatrist sister Molly, who is deathly ill in hospital. Complicating Anna's life is the fact that FBI agent Frederick Stanton, her ex-boyfriend, lives in New York and is now in love with Molly. Seeking solitude as she attempts to deal with all of this, Anna crashes with a female parks ranger friend who's stationed on Liberty Island, the speck of land in New York harbour where the Statue of Liberty is located. Here Anna is drawn into a mystery surrounding how and why a teenage girl has leaped to her death from atop the monument. What at first seems like suicide begins to look like murder when other suspicious deaths occur on the island.

"Anna's snooping puts her own life in jeopardy," wrote reviewer Dick Adler in an on-line critique for Amazon.com. "She survives several attacks and a near drowning. . . . Barr neatly ties up her plot—ending with a brilliant chase scene across the water from Manhattan to Liberty Island." A *Kirkus Reviews* reviewer was less impressed. "Though Barr works her customary magic with the eerily deserted nightscapes of Liberty Island, they're just not as arresting as the Lechugilla caves (*Blind Descent*, 1998) or the wild scenes of any of earlier six adventures."

Barr's Anna Pigeon novels have also found wide favor with reviewers whose reservations about the main character and the off-the-beaten-track settings have become fewer and fewer with each new book. However, Barr has occasionally come in for criticism from Parks Department defenders who

have accused her of making the parks service and the people who work for it "look bad." Barr has responded to such criticism by explaining that she writes to entertain readers, not criticize, educate, or push for change. "I want people to love the parks," she told Linda Rancourt of *National Parks* magazine in a 1995 interview. "I point out the problems with the Park Service because I write about what I know, and what is true. I want the public still to believe that we're heroes, because I think everybody needs heroes. Why not let them be us? But I do think [the Park Service] needs to be deglamorized to the point that people realize there are needs."

■ Works Cited

Adler, Dick, on-line review of *Liberty Falling*, located at http://www.Amazon.com, 1999.

Adler, Dick, review of *A Superior Death, Tribune Books* (Chicago), March 6, 1994, p. 6.

Review of *Bittersweet, Booklist*, July, 1984, p. 1520.

Review of *Blind Descent, Kirkus Reviews*, January 15, 1998, p. 81.

Champlin, Charles, review of *Track of the Cat, Los Angeles Time Book Review,* May 23, 1993, p. 8.

Corrigan, Maureen, review of *Firestorm, Washington Post Book World*, April 21, 1996, p. 6.

DiNizo, Alice, Review of *Blind Descent, Library Journal*, March 15, 1998, p. 91.

Dretzka, Gary, review of *Ill Wind, Tribune Books* (Chicago), April 2, 1995, p. 7.

Review of *Endangered Species, Publishers Weekly*, January 6, 1997, p. 67.

Review of *Firestorm, Tribune Books* (Chicago), March 3, 1996, p. 6.

Gesinger, Naomi, "The Pigeon Swoops Manhattan: An Interview with Nevada Barr," located at http://www.Amazon.com, 1999.

Review of *Ill Wind, Publishers Weekly*, January 30, 1995, p. 87.

Review of *Liberty Falling, Bloomsbury Review*, May/June 1999, p. 15.

Review of *Liberty Falling, Cleveland Plain Dealer*, April 25, 1999.

Review of *Liberty Falling, Kirkus Reviews*, February 1, 1999.

Lochte, Dick, review of *Firestorm, Los Angeles Times Book Review,* April 28, 1996, p. 11.

Melton, Emily, review of *Endangered Species, Booklist,* February 15, 1999, p. 1006.

Rancourt, Linda, "Murder She Writes," *National Parks*, September-October 1995, pp. 30-36.

Rowen, John, "The *Booklist* Interview: Nevada Barr," *Booklist*, March 15, 1999, p. 1462.

Shindler, Dorman T., "The Law of Nature: An Interview with Nevada Barr," *Armchair Detective*, summer 1995, pp. 308-311.

Sister Avila, review of *Bittersweet, Library Journal*, September 1, 1984, p. 1684.

Skenazy, Paul, review of *Track of the Cat, Washington Post Book World,* July 18, 1993, p. 6.

Skenazy, Paul, review of *A Superior Death, Washington Post Book World,* March 20, 1994, p. 6.

Stasio, Marilyn, review of *A Superior Death, New York Times Book Review,* April 17, 1994, p. 19.

Stasio, Marilyn, review of *Ill Wind, New York Times Book Review,* April 2, 1995, p. 25.

Stasio, Marilyn, review of *Firestorm, New York Times Book Review,* March 24, 1996, p. 24.

Stasio, Marilyn, review of *Endangered Species, New York Times Book Review,* April 13, 1997, p. 24.

Wesson, Mimi, review of *Track of the Cat, Women's Review of Books,* January, 1995, p. 22.

■ For More Information See

PERIODICALS

New York Times Book Review, April 18, 1993, p. 24; March 24, 1996, p. 24; May 31, 1998, p. 30.
School Library Journal, July 1998, p. 113.
Tribune Books (Chicago), March 3, 1996, p. 6.
Washington Post Book World, July 2, 1995, p. 12.

ON-LINE

The Mississippi Writers Page, located at http://www.olemis.edu/depts/english/ms-writers/, November 24, 1997.

Putnam Berkley Group, located at http://univstudios.com/putnam/authors/nevada_barr/author/html, October 21, 1997.

Putnam Berkley Online, located at http://www.mca.com/putnam/books/endangered_species/txt_book.html, October 21, 1997. *

Jane Campion

Personal

Born April 30, 1954, in Wellington, New Zealand; daughter of Richard (a performance director) and Edith (an actress) Campion; married Colin Englert (a television director); children: Alice. *Education:* Victoria University, B.A.; attended Chelsea School of Arts; Sydney College of the Arts, diploma of fine arts; Australian Film, Television, and Radio School, diploma in direction, 1984.

Addresses

Home—Sydney, New South Wales, Australia. *Agent*—c/o New Zealand Film Commission, P. O. Box 11546, Wellington, New Zealand.

Career

Filmmaker and screenwriter. Director of television productions (later released as motion pictures), including *Two Friends*. Director of motion pictures, including *An Angel at My Table, The Piano,* and *The Portrait of a Lady.*

Awards, Honors

Best experimental film, Australian Film Institute, 1984, for *Painless Moments;* Rouben Mamoulian Award for best overall short film, Sydney Film Festival and best direction, best screenplay, and best cinematography awards, Australian Film Institute, all 1984, all for *A Girl's Own Story;* best short fiction award, Melbourne International Film Festival, 1985, for *After Hours;* Golden Palm for best short film, Cannes Film Festival, 1986, for *Peel: An Exercise in Discipline;* Golden Plaque for Television, Chicago International Film Festival and best director, best telemovie, and best screenplay awards, Australian Film Institute, all 1987, all for *Two Friends;* Georges Sadoul Prize for best foreign film, 1988.

New Generation Award, Los Angeles Film Critics, 1990, and awards for best director and best film, Australian Film Critics' Circle, 1990, all for *Sweetie;* Critics Award from Toronto Film Festival, Otto Debelius Prize from international jury at Berlin Film Festival, Si presci Award for best film from international critics, Elvira Notari Award for best woman director, and eight prizes from Venice Film Festival, all 1991, all for *An Angel at My Table;* National Society of Film Critics Award, best screenplay, 1993, Golden Palm award, Cannes Film Festival, 1993, Academy Award, best original screenplay, 1994, both for *The Piano.*

■ Credits

FILM DIRECTOR

(And screenwriter with Gerard Lee) *Sweetie,* Arenafilm, 1988.
An Angel at My Table, Fine Line Features, 1990.
(And screenwriter) *The Piano,* Miramax, 1993.
The Portrait of a Lady, Gramercy, 1996.
(And screenwriter with sister, Anna Campion) *Holy Smoke,* Miramax, 1999.

Also writer and director of short films, including *Tissues, Peel: An Exercise in Discipline,* 1982, (with Lee) *Passionless Moments,* 1984, *A Girl's Own Story,* 1984, *After Hours,* 1984, and *Two Friends,* 1986.

BOOKS

(With Kate Pullinger) *The Piano: A Novel,* Hyperion, 1994.
(With Anna Campion) *Holy Smoke,* Miramax Books, 1999.

■ Sidelights

The films of Jane Campion have brought the New Zealander an array of prestigious critical awards in just a few short years. Perhaps more rewarding, however, is the acceptance her work has found inside the corporate-run world of contemporary commercial entertainment, for the subject matter in Campion's films tends to center upon women whose inarticulateness or sense of devalued self-worth is often painful to watch on the large screen. Campion, who has written the screenplays for her most acclaimed works, creates or otherwise develops heroines with an unusually non-Hollywood type of femininity. Campion's "women are haunted creatures at the mercy of their emotions," wrote Hal Hinson in the *Washington Post.* "Their blood runs with sadness, and it is out of this sexual despair that Campion forges her melancholy poetry."

Campion was born in Wellington, the capital of New Zealand, in 1954. Both parents were seriously involved in the performing arts: her mother was a stage actress of some renown, while her father was a director for theater and opera productions; together the couple founded a touring company, the New Zealand Travelling Players. Campion's father Richard, who later became an assistant to his daughter on the sets for her films, remembered her as a headstrong child even at a young age. "I was doing the parental thing about what she might want to do later on," Richard Campion recalled of a moment when his daughter was just five in an interview with the *Guardian*'s Howard Feinstein. "She looked up at me with those big blue eyes and her golden hair and said, 'Dad, I am my own self!' And that's been the basic thing in her work."

> *"If nothing else, Campion's imperious originality reminds you how craven Hollywood directors are when it comes to expressing anything that can't be articulated for a studio press release. Watching her movies is like meeting those rare people who actually have the courage of their convictions. Liking them isn't the point."*
>
> —film critic Ty Burr

Leaving New Zealand, Campion studied anthropology at Victoria University in Australia, but after earning a bachelor's degree decided to pursue a fine arts degree. She graduated from the Sydney College of the Arts and then earned a 1984 diploma in direction from the Australian Film, Television, and Radio School. Her first short film, *Peel,* was made while she was still a student. The work is the tale of a family vacation in which members are confined inside an automobile; the father's order to his son to get out of the car and pick up an orange peel launches a massive conflict. A fourteen-year-old Nicole Kidman was originally cast as one of the leads in Campion's next work, *A Girl's Own Story,* but had to bow out of the wry and rather frank look at a group of teenage girls and their sexual awakening. Another short from this era, *Passionless Moments,* was merely Campion's chronicle of a series of uninteresting happenings. All three were collected for the 1991 rental *Films by Jane Campion.* "It's rocky stuff," assessed Ty Burr in *Entertainment Weekly* about the video, "but Campion's aggressive uniqueness—and her interest in the mundane nightmares of family life—is in every frame."

Campion next wrote and directed a 1984 film titled *After Hours*, and then filmed *Two Friends* for Australian television in 1986. This portrays two teenagers, Louise and Kelly—drastically different in temperament and outlook—and the demise of their friendship. But it was Campion's first feature film, *Sweetie*, that earned her somewhat unexpected critical and commercial success. The 1988 work, which she both wrote (with Gerard Lee) and directed, portrayed with comic flair the havoc a mentally unstable young woman creates among family members, who are partly to blame for her condition because of their attempts to ignore it. The plot centers around Kay, the shy, withdrawn sister of the title character. Sweetie is an exuberant, overweight, sexually uninhibited young woman who believes she is destined for a career as an entertainer. "Kay has been harboring a latent resentment towards Sweetie since childhood for getting all the attention from Mum and Dad," explained Desson Howe in the *Washington Post*, "and the enmity soon returns."

Kay has a boyfriend, Louis, whom she has lured away from a co-worker. His act of planting a young tree in their backyard angers Kay, who has a morbid fear of them; she uproots it, and their relationship begins to disintegrate. Sweetie's unannounced arrival with her odd boyfriend creates more tension in Kay's household. Sweetie is brash and childlike, and Kay cannot even bear to be around her. Louis is appalled when Kay tries to eject her sister, and when Kay returns from a visit to her mother—the parents have separated—she finds that Sweetie is now demanding to be treated as if she is a puppy; she even barks. Eventually Sweetie retreats to a childhood treehouse, refuses to come down, and her stomping on its floor causes it to split. The fall is a fatal one.

Critics Recognize Campion's Talent

When *Sweetie* was screened at the Cannes Film Festival, some members of the audience walked out. Roger Ebert reviewed it for the *Chicago Sun-Times* and attempted to explain why: "I imagine most people will have a hard time with *Sweetie*," he noted, after admitting he initially found it unpleasant at Cannes. "But this movie is real, it's the genuine article, and it's there on the screen in all of its defiant strangeness," he wrote after a second viewing. "Most movies slide right through our minds without hitting anything. This one screams and shouts every step of the way." Other critical assessments were similarly uncertain. "The film unfolds in a discomfiting cinematic universe," opined Burr in *Entertainment Weekly*. Writing in the *Washington Post*, Howe found the latter half of the film paced a bit more slowly, but remarked that Campion's "unique talent for open-ended exposition remains, as does the movie's innocent sense of grandiosity, its unorthodox belief about itself," noted the critic in an odd echo of the five-year-old Campion's own words to her father.

Campion's next film, *An Angel at My Table*, was originally conceived as a television miniseries in Australia. It was the first of her films to be written by Laura Jones, and chronicled the difficult

Holly Hunter and Anna Paquin starred in *The Piano*, Jane Campion's 1993 movie that won an Academy Award and a Golden Palm award at the Cannes Film Festival.

early life of New Zealand novelist and poet Janet Frame. Born in 1924, Frame achieved literary fame with her 1957 novel *Owls Do Cry*, but before her career, Frame had been wrongfully diagnosed as schizophrenic and institutionalized for several years. She also underwent numerous electroshock

---

Campion's "women are haunted creatures at the mercy of their emotions. Their blood runs with sadness, and it is out of this sexual despair that Campion forges her melancholy poetry."

—film critic Hal Hinson

---

therapy treatments. Campion's film follows Frame's life from her childhood as part of a close-knit, working-class family. With a mass of curly red hair, Frame was a shy and dreamy child whose poetic gifts were evident at an early age; by the time she reached young adulthood, however, two of her siblings had died, traumas which only exacerbated her shyness and sense of alienation. As a young schoolteacher after college, Frame found it difficult to talk to others—perhaps as a result of severe tooth decay—and began suffering from panic attacks; a suicide attempt led to her first hospitalization.

An Angel at My Table depicts how Frame's determined father battled to win her freedom from doctors who wanted to perform a lobotomy on his daughter. During her years in treatment, Frame had begun writing poetry. "When a cure seems improbable, sheer happenstance saves her from being lobotomized when a volume of her poems wins a prize, drawing outside attention to her evil circumstances," wrote Hinson in the *Washington Post*. The remainder of Campion's film follows Frame after she wins a grant to study abroad, befriends other unique artistic personalities, and begins to blossom as both a writer and person. In his review of the film, Hinson felt that Campion's heroine was portrayed as too detached for audiences to respond to with much sympathy, and also found fault with Campion and Jones's failure to explore how exactly Frame's personal difficulties fueled her literary talent. Hinson

termed the film "insufferably verbose and, at the same time, touched with magnificence."

Campion's Masterpiece

Campion's next film, *The Piano*, was her much-anticipated Miramax release, a big-budget opus that won her a slew of critical awards. The 1993 work brought Campion, as writer and director, several major prizes, including the Palme d'Or (Golden Palm)—the top honor at the Cannes Film Festival—as well as an Academy Award for best original screenplay and nominations for two Golden Globe Awards, for best director and best motion picture screenplay. Moreover, she became only the second woman in history to be nominated for an Oscar for best director from the Academy of Motion Picture Arts and Sciences.

The Piano is set in New Zealand in the nineteenth century, and begins with the arrival of Ada McGrath, played by Holly Hunter, to a muddy, windswept beach. Ada is mute, as she says in the first of two voice-overs that frame the narrative, and has been, inexplicably, since the age of six. With Ada is her young daughter, Fiona (Anna Paquin), who was born out of wedlock back in Scotland. Ada has agreed to marry an English farmer living in New Zealand, Stewart (Sam Neill), and is resigned to this new life far from home. She has also carried with her on the long sea journey her beloved piano, which is her only form of communication apart from the rudimentary sign language she and her daughter use; she also writes notes. Thus a dour Ada arrives in New Zealand dressed in her European finery, and her bridegroom, upon meeting her, refuses to bring the piano to their new house, deeming it too heavy to transport. It is left on the beach. "In a breathtaking long shot the lone piano is limned starkly against the rolling surf," wrote Harvey Greenberg in *Film Quarterly*. "It's suddenly a vivid icon of cultural collision, of yet another stifling of Ada's voice, of her delivery into paltry domesticity in a startling alien environment."

The marriage between Ada and Stewart remains unconsummated. One day, she plays the piano on the beach, and is heard by a strange neighbor, Baines (Harvey Keitel). He offers to trade a parcel of land to Stewart in exchange for the piano, to which Ada vehemently objects. Baines, an illiterate former whaler covered in Maori tattoos, tells

Campion takes her place behind the camera during shooting of *Portrait of a Lady*, the film adaptation of the famous Henry James novel.

her that she can visit his home to play it and give him lessons. She begins to do so, and Baines seduces her by offering to trade the piano back; he will give her one key for each sexual favor she allows. Dismayed and ashamed of his ruse when she is finally naked, he offers to end their "arrangement," which angers Ada. She overtakes him passionately, and her husband soon learns of their affair. He locks Ada inside their home with her piano, and their marriage falters. One day, she writes a declaration of her love on a piece of the keyboard, and gives it to Fiona to take to Baines; instead the girl gives it to Stewart. Enraged, her husband takes an ax to the piano, and then to Ada's hand before banishing her from the house. She flees to Baines.

The rest of *The Piano* chronicles Ada and Baines's journey to another part of New Zealand, when a storm endangers them and Ada willingly agrees to let her piano be thrown overboard to save them. But she becomes entangled in the ropes, and nearly drowns. In her final voice-over, she relates that she, Fiona, and Baines have settled elsewhere, and she is giving piano lessons as well as haltingly learning to speak. Campion "understands better the eroticism of slowness and restraint, and the power that Ada gains by pretending to care nothing for Baines," wrote Ebert in the *Chicago Sun-Times*. The critic termed it "one of those rare movies that is not just about a story, or some characters, but about a whole universe of feeling— of how people can be shut off from each other, lonely and afraid, about how help can come from unexpected sources, and about how you'll never know if you don't ask."

Other critics were equally effusive in their praise for *The Piano* and its writer/director. Campion's "script holds all the elements of tragedy and pathos of the Victorian romance," wrote Richard A. Blake in *America*, "but she refuses to offer her audience one moment of easy sentimentality." Though Blake did confess to feeling "profoundly disturbed" by the ending of *The Piano*, "the memory of this film will last a long time, and that may be the true test of a work of art," he declared.

Tackles Henry James Novel

After the critical and commercial success of *The Piano*, Campion delved into another ambitious film project. Her 1996 film, *The Portrait of a Lady*, was screenwriter Laura Jones's adaptation of the 1880 Henry James novel of the same name. Filmed in Italy and showcasing the regal looks of Nicole Kidman as American heiress Isabel Archer, Campion's film once more explored the difficulties a woman encounters regarding control over both her own destiny and conflicting, though sometimes subconscious, desires. As the film opens, Isabel, who is considered a great beauty, is in England with a wealthy aunt after the death of her father. Her consumptive cousin Ralph professes his love for her, which she rejects, and she also rebuffs the proposal from a wealthy aristocrat, Lord Warburton. "Campion makes us see— with really stunning support from Nicole Kidman—Isabel Archer as both eligible virgin and the bright, double-faced spirit of idealism that humankind perennially projects," wrote Kathleen Murphy in *Film Comment*.

Nicole Kidman plays Isabel Archer in Campion's *Portrait of a Lady*, Henry James's story of an American heiress who travels to Italy and struggles with destiny and desire.

Isabel travels to Italy with her aunt, where she falls in love with an older American man living in Italy. Gilbert Osmond, played by John Malkovich, proves a disastrous choice of husband; he is a dilettante, a fortune hunter, and abusive to Isabel. Her situation worsens, however, when she refuses to marry off the daughter of his mistress—a role for which Barbara Hershey won an Oscar for best supporting actress—to Lord Warburton; in the end, Isabel reunites with her dying cousin. Campion's talents as a director were offered rich visual opportunities in the lush Italian countryside and opulent Roman interiors; critics gave lavish praise to the film's cinematography.

As a film, *The Portrait of a Lady* won mixed reviews from critics, who often cited the densely nuanced text of James's original novel as a daunting obstacle for any filmmaker to tackle. *Commonweal* critic Richard Alleva wrote that "Campion doesn't just adapt Henry James. She refutes him. But it's a generous refutation which, on the whole, plays fair with the material. The novel isn't jazzed up or sent up. In some ways Campion's dreamy, sub-aqueous style is a good equivalent of James's prose, though she lacks his deadpan sarcasm. Campion honorably works to realize the drama of the novel even as she shapes it to her own ends." David Ansen, writing in *Newsweek,* summed up the mixed reactions of his colleagues: "The result is darkly gorgeous, fascinating, sluggish, undeniably audacious—and wrongheaded," and in conclusion Ansen called it "the kind of failure only a very gifted filmmaker could make: like it or not, it haunts you."

But liking Campion's work was not the point, *Entertainment Weekly* writer Burr once noted. Discussing Campion's unique perspective, and the sometimes difficult emotional terrain her films trod, Burr remarked that, "if nothing else, Campion's imperious originality reminds you how craven Hollywood directors are when it comes to expressing anything that can't be articulated for a studio press release. Watching her movies is like meeting those rare people who actually have the courage of their convictions. Liking them isn't the point."

Campion, who is married to Australian television director Colin Englert, with whom she has a young daughter, next immersed herself in a writing project with her sister, Anna Campion, director of the 1994 film *Loaded. Holy Smoke* was pub-

Campion's 1999 book and feature film, *Holy Smoke,* which she co-wrote with sister Anna, explores spiritual and sexual struggles in a young Australian woman.

lished in the United States in early 1999, and was the basis for Campion's fifth feature film of the same title. The Miramax project was cast with Kate Winslet in the lead, and reunited Campion with Keitel from *The Piano;* it also returned the director to the present-day and her interest in dysfunctional family dramas with a darkly comic side. Winslet portrays twenty-year-old Ruth Barron, the rebel daughter of a spiritually bankrupt, though not unpleasant, middle-class family in Sydney, Australia. "The most important things for them are paying the mortgage, having a nice barbecue every weekend, and having a routine to life," Campion explained about the Barrons in the *Guardian* interview with Feinstein.

If you enjoy the works of Jane Campion, you may also want to check out the following films:

Children of a Lesser God, starring Marlee Matlin and William Hurt, 1986.
Daughters of the Dust, directed by Julie Dash, 1991.
A Room with a View, starring Helena Bonham Carter, 1986.
Strictly Ballroom, a romantic comedy from Australia, 1992.

As the work opens, Ruth has joined a bizarre cult led by a charismatic guru, and fled to India. Her mother arrives to plead with her to leave the ashram, convincing her that Ruth's father is gravely ill. When she arrives home, Ruth learns that she has been tricked, and that her parents have arranged for a cult "deprogrammer" to return the daughter they assumed they knew. Keitel's character, P. J. Waters, hails from New York and was once involved in a cult himself; he appears fearless and tough, but Winslet's character soon breaks through his armor and seduces him. In a review of the book version of *Holy Smoke,* a *Publishers Weekly* review opined that Campion and her sister "successfully demonstrate the seductive pull of cults and are at their best when transforming Ruth's need for spiritual guidance into her psychosexual delirium."

In the interview with the *Guardian,* Campion admitted to Feinstein her fascination with alternative religions and belief systems. "What is curious to me is how scary beliefs are to people, and how religious commitment is frightening, yet none of us seems to have any beliefs ourselves. It's safer *not* to believe." It was a theme that she had also explored in a discussion with *Vogue* writer Kennedy Fraser. "I think both men and women are afraid to speak their own truth," Campion told Fraser, but pointed out that women, in the end, are more adept at it. "That culture of private truth-speaking is the compensation for not having power. You shut up, you see what's going on. Growing up as a woman—without power—is very interesting. You learn to get around it. To work without power but still feel expressed. It makes you very observant."

■ Works Cited

Alleva, Richard, review of *The Portrait of a Lady, Commonweal,* February 28, 1997, p. 19.

Ansen, David, review of *The Portrait of a Lady, Newsweek,* December 26, 1996, pp. 67-68

Blake, Richard A., review of *The Piano, America,* January 15, 1994, p. 14.

Burr, Ty, review of *An Angel at My Table, Entertainment Weekly,* May 20, 1994, p. 68.

Ebert, Roger, review of *Sweetie, Chicago Sun-Times,* March 23, 1990.

Ebert, Roger, review of *The Piano, Chicago Sun-Times,* November 19, 1993.

Feinstein, Howard, "The Jane Mutiny," *Guardian,* April 2, 1999, pp. 4-5.

Fraser, Kennedy, "Portrait of the Director," *Vogue,* January, 1997, pp. 144-149.

Greenberg, Harvey, review of *The Piano, Film Quarterly,* spring, 1994, p. 46.

Hinson, Hal, review of *Sweetie, Washington Post,* March 2, 1990.

Hinson, Hal, review of *An Angel at My Table,* June 21, 1991.

Hinson, Hal, review of *The Piano, Washington Post,* November 19, 1993.

Review of *Holy Smoke, Publishers Weekly,* April 5, 1999, p. 220.

Howe, Desson, review of *Sweetie, Washington Post,* March 2, 1990.

Murphy, Kathleen, review of *The Portrait of a Lady, Film Comment,* November-December, 1996, p. 28.

■ For More Information See

BOOKS

Jane Campion: Interviews, University Press of Mississippi, 1999.
Newsmakers 91, Gale, 1991.

PERIODICALS

Chicago Sun-Times, June 21, 1991.
Entertainment Weekly, March, 1994, p. 98; p. 108.
Interview, May, 1999, p. 66.
Library Journal, April 1, 1998, p. 139.
Los Angeles Times, February 14, 1990, p. F2.
Nation, February 3, 1997, pp. 35-36.
New Republic, June 3, 1991, pp. 28-29.
New Statesman and Society, September 28, 1990.

New Yorker, June 3, 1991, pp. 86-88.

New York Times, October 6, 1989; January 14, 1990; January 19, 1990; February 4, 1990; May 19, 1991, p. H22.

Washington Post, March 2, 1990; June 21, 1991; November 19, 1993.*

Kate Chopin

■ Personal

Born Katherine Chopin, February 8, 1851 (one source says July 12, 1850), in St. Louis, MO, United States; died following a cerebral hemorrhage, August 22, 1904, in St. Louis, MO; daughter of Thomas (a merchant) and Eliza (Faris) O'Flaherty; married Oscar Chopin (a cotton factor), June 9, 1870 (died 1883); children: Jean, Oscar, George, Frederick, Felix, Lelia. *Education:* Educated in St. Louis, MO. *Religion:* Catholic.

■ Career

Writer and translator.

■ Writings

FICTION

At Fault (novel), Nixon-Jones Printing Co., 1890.
Bayou Folk (short stories), Houghton, 1894, reprinted, Gregg Press, 1967, reprinted with introduction by Warner Berthoff, Garrett Press, 1970.

A Night in Acadie (short stories), Way & Williams, 1897, reprinted, Garrett Press, 1968.
The Awakening (novel), Herbert S. Stone, 1899, reprinted with introduction by Kenneth Eble, Capricorn, 1964, reprinted with introduction by Warner Berthoff, Garrett Press, 1970, reprinted in critical edition edited by Margaret Culley, Norton, 1976.

Contributor of articles, short stories, and translations to periodicals, including *Atlantic Monthly, Criterion, Harper's Young People, St. Louis Dispatch,* and *Vogue.* Also author of unpublished novel *Young Dr. Gosse.* Work represented in numerous anthologies.

COLLECTIONS

The Complete Works of Kate Chopin (two volumes), edited by Per Seyersted, Louisiana State University Press, 1969.
Kate Chopin: The Awakening and Other Stories, edited by Lewis Leary, Holt, 1970.
The Storm and Other Stories, with The Awakening (includes "Wiser Than a God," "A Point at Issue," and "The Story of an Hour"), edited by Per Seyersted, Feminist Press, 1974.
The Awakening and Selected Short Stories of Kate Chopin, edited by Barbara Solomon, Signet, 1976.
A Kate Chopin Miscellany, edited by Per Seyersted, Northwestern State University Press, 1979.
A Vocation and A Voice: Stories, Viking, 1991.

Matter of Prejudice & Other Stories, Bantam, 1992.

Kate Chopin, "The Awakening": Complete, Authoritative Text with Biographical & Historical Contexts, Critical History, and Essays from Five Contemporary Critical Perspectives, edited by Nancy A. Walker, St. Martin's, 1993.

The Awakening and Selected Stories, edited and with introduction by Nina Baym, Modern Library (New York City), 1993.

A Pair of Silk Stockings and Other Stories, Dover Publications (Mineola, NY), 1996.

■ Adaptations

The Awakening was adapted for film as *The End of August* in 1982; *The Story of an Hour* was adapted for film as *Kate Chopin's "The Story of an Hour"* in 1982.

■ Sidelights

Kate Chopin is considered among the most important women in nineteenth-century American fiction. She is best known for her 1899 novel, *The Awakening,* a once-scandalous account of one woman's growing sexuality in the American South during the Victorian era. For this novel, Chopin faced critical abuse and public denunciation as an immoralist, and she consequently abandoned writing. In more recent years, however, *The Awakening* has grown in stature and is now recognized as a masterpiece of its time. Critics such as Van Wyck Brooks and Edmund Wilson have commended the novel, and numerous others, including Cynthia Griffin Wolff, Anne Goodwyn Jones, and Elaine Gardiner, have subsequently revealed its social and psychological themes. The efforts of these and other critics have helped establish Chopin as a significant figure in American, particularly feminist, literature.

Chopin was born in St. Louis, Missouri, in 1851. Her mother, Eliza Faris O'Flaherty, was a member of the prominent French-Creole community and was thus a familiar figure in exclusive social circles. Chopin's father, Thomas O'Flaherty, was an Irish immigrant who had successfully established himself as a merchant and subsequently participated in various business ventures. Chopin was only a child when her father died. He had been a founder of the Pacific Railroad, and he was aboard the train on its inaugural journey when it plunged into the Gasconade River after a bridge collapsed.

After the train disaster, Chopin established a more intimate relationship with her mother, who had grown increasingly religious. Chopin also developed a strong tie to her great-grandmother, who guided her studies at the piano and in French and offered moral counseling. The older woman also regaled young Chopin with tales of French settlers from St. Louis's past. Among these stories, however, were accounts of notorious infidels, and more than one scholar has suggested that these tales made a vivid impression on Chopin.

During her school years Chopin read voraciously, showing an appetite for fairy tales, religious allegory, poetry, and novelists ranging from Walter Scott to Charles Dickens. Around age eleven, Chopin endured further heartache when her great-grandmother died. Soon afterwards, Chopin's half-brother, who had been captured as a Confederate soldier in the Civil War, contracted typhoid fever and died. These losses compelled Chopin to delve more intensely into literature, and for the next two years she secluded herself in the family attic—even missing school—and studied more books. When she resumed her formal studies at a Catholic school, Chopin worked diligently, though without great scholastic distinction. She did, however, gain repute as a proficient and creative storyteller.

Chopin graduated from the Catholic school in 1868, and for the next two years she enjoyed life as a belle in St. Louis's high society, earning admiration for both her beauty and her wit. She continued to read extensively, but her interests were not limited to the classics, and she showed familiarity with the works of many contemporary writers. In addition, Chopin devoted herself to music—practicing the piano and patronizing the city's symphony and its opera companies.

An Independent Woman

But as she reveled in St. Louis society, Chopin became increasingly independent. She began questioning Catholicism's implicit authoritarianism, which dictated subservience for women to male domination, and she showed heightened awareness of the inanities involved in socializing. In the spring of 1869, Chopin traveled to New Orleans and befriended a charismatic, independent—

though married—German singer and actress. Chopin was impressed with the woman, who seemed to maintain her individuality despite marriage. After returning to St. Louis, Chopin made another acquaintance, Louisiana native Oscar Chopin, who had arrived in the city to work in a bank. A year later the two were married.

The Chopins honeymooned in Europe, where they visited renowned cities and attended plays and musical performances. Their travels, though, were abbreviated by commencement of the Franco-Prussian War, and they returned briefly to St. Louis before establishing themselves in New Orleans. Although Oscar Chopin was French-Creole, the couple settled in the city's American district, thereby incurring the wrath of Oscar's father, who owned plantations in northern Louisiana and expected his son to maintain his Creole ties and perhaps even join him in operating the properties. But Oscar's father was a tyrant who had been known to violently abuse both his slaves and his son. Oscar, therefore, opted for a less troubling career as a cotton factor and began handling sales, finances, and supplies for other plantation owners. While her husband worked, Kate Chopin continued her relatively iconoclastic life. She pursued her interest in the performing arts, developing a preference for the operas of Richard Wagner, and she persisted in her habit, then considered highly unusual for women, of smoking cigarettes. Chopin also became familiar with her surroundings by adopting another habit, also unusual for young women, of walking unaccompanied through the city.

While walking alone through New Orleans, Chopin witnessed organized terrorism against blacks. Moreover, Oscar Chopin was a member of the White League, which clashed violently with Republicans sympathetic to blacks—one conflict claimed forty lives. Racial confrontations, however, were not the only cause for concern in New Orleans. Yellow fever was also spreading rampantly, killing four thousand citizens in 1878 alone. Per Seyersted, author of the critical biography *Kate Chopin*, speculates that Chopin—who had six children, including five sons, by 1879—may have been motivated by health considerations in making several trips to St. Louis with her offspring.

Also by 1879 Oscar Chopin's factoring business had collapsed, whereupon the family moved north to the family plantations in Natchitoches Parish.

There the Chopins became active members of the revived Creole community, and Kate Chopin won admiration for her convivial nature and superior intellect. But Oscar Chopin, whose health seemed consistently weak, contracted swamp fever during the winter, and, in January, 1883, he died. Kate Chopin remained in Natchitoches Parish for nearly one year and continued operating the plantations, but with little success. In 1884, she finally acceded to her mother's frequent requests to move with the children to St. Louis. The next year, Chopin's mother also died. In her critical volume *Kate Chopin*, Peggy Skaggs observes that Chopin's self-perception must have been affected by the various family deaths, and that the consequent tension may have resulted in the "search for self-understanding"that motivates so many characters in Chopin's fiction.

Following her husband's death, Chopin was consoled by the family physician, Frederick Kolbenheyer. With Kolbenheyer's encouragement, Chopin began writing about the Louisiana of her past. Her efforts resulted in "If It Might Be," a poem that Seyersted suggests may express Chopin's desire to join her late husband in death. "If It Might Be" appeared in the Chicago periodical *America* in early 1889, thus affording Chopin the rare luxury of publishing her first submitted work. But she then encountered technical difficulties in writing a pair of short stories, and only after reading a small collection of French writer Guy de Maupassant's tales did Chopin believe herself capable of producing fiction. After this realization, Chopin published the short stories "Wiser Than a God," which concerns a pianist who forsakes marriage for a music career, and "A Point at Issue," which chronicles the decline of an emancipated marriage into a conventionally restrictive, male-dominated union.

A Determined Writer

Chopin next produced a novel, *At Fault*, about morally complex—and unintentionally preposterous—romantic considerations. In this novel, a young widow, Therese, discovers that a prospective second husband, the Creole David Hosmer, had divorced his first wife after learning that she was an alcoholic. Therese's moral absolutism prompts her, despite her love for David, to promote his re-marriage to his ex-wife. Incredibly, he heeds her counseling and rejoins his former spouse, who eventually succumbs once more to alcoholism. Therese and David seem fated for more suffering until the alcoholic accidentally, but conveniently, drowns, thus allowing the lovers to unite without moral compromise.

At Fault addressed many of the themes, including women's emancipation and marital discord, that Chopin rendered more subtly in subsequent works. Upon its publication in 1890, the novel earned mixed reviews for its daring portrayal of a female alcoholic and its ambivalent perspective on divorce. Chopin had assumed financial responsibility for the book's publication and had sent copies to leading magazines and newspapers, including the local *St. Louis Post-Dispatch,* whose critic complained of *At Fault*'s allegedly immoral tenor but praised Chopin's skill in avoiding a moralistic tone. Similarly, a *Nation* reviewer noted that the novel's plethora of characters—in subplots involving arson and violence—all shared a lack of admirable traits. But the *Nation* reviewer added that Chopin possessed an "aptitude for seizing dialects of whites and blacks alike" and commended her "skill in perceiving and defining character."

Chopin followed *At Fault* with another novel, *Young Dr. Gosse,* for which she was unable to procure a publisher. Undaunted, she returned to writing shorter works, and in the next few years she produced more than three dozen stories and sketches. Chopin first found steady publication in children's magazines such as *Youth's Companion* and *Harper's Young People.* In 1893, she appealed to adult readers with two tales in *Vogue.* These stories apparently proved popular, for in the next seven years the magazine published an additional sixteen pieces by Chopin.

Chopin collected twenty-three of these stories and brief sketches and published them in 1894 as *Bayou Folk.* In this collection, Chopin established herself—at least to her contemporaries—as primarily a masterful colorist of Louisiana life. An *Atlantic Monthly* reviewer, for instance, cited Chopin's reproductions of Southern speech and lauded the simplicity and concision of the tales, while a writer for the *Critic* praised Chopin for her sincere, simple portraits of bayou life. The *Critic*'s reader also called *Bayou Folk* an "unpretentious, unheralded little book" and commended Chopin's "shrewdness of observation and. . . fine eye for picturesque situations."

First published in 1899, Chopin's novel about a woman's growing awareness of her own sexuality and self-worth, and her unsuccessful attempt to find happiness outside of Victorian norms, was highly controversial.

But *Bayou Folk,* despite the contentions of its initial readers, transcends mere portraiture in addressing such controversial subjects as infidelity and racial purity. Among the most famous tales in this collection is "Desiree's Baby," in which a woman disappears into the Louisiana bayou with her baby after her husband, distressed by the infant's features, accuses the woman of possessing Negro blood. This story offers chilling commentary on human behavior and fate, for no sooner has his wife vanished than the husband discovers that he is the parent with black ancestry. In another famous tale, "A Lady of Bayou St. John," a naive young wife falls in love with a visiting Frenchman while her husband is fighting in the Civil War. Before fleeing to Paris with her new love, the woman learns of her husband's death, whereupon she rejects the Frenchman and pledges herself to the dead man's memory. In this and other tales, Chopin proved herself an artist of great insight into human behavior. Her work's complexity, however, eluded critics until long after her death.

Although reviews of *Bayou Folk* were superficial and relatively unperceptive, they were nonetheless favorable and afforded Chopin sufficient motivation to continue writing. She still circulated her novel *Young Dr. Gosse,* but the manuscript met with further rejection, and, in 1896, she finally destroyed it. She found greater acceptance for her shorter fiction, and, by 1897, she had completed enough to form another collection, *A Night in Acadie.* This volume marked Chopin's growing interest in sexuality, passion, and the stasis of conventional marriage. Among the many acclaimed stories in this collection is "A Sentimental Soul," in which a devout, unmarried woman, Mamzelle Fleurette, falls in love with a married man. She confesses her feelings to a priest, who unsympathetically counsels discipline. After the married man dies from fever, the woman continues to love, but the priest warns her not to attend the funeral. Finally, Fleurette consults another priest, to whom she confesses only insignificant sins and not her profane love. Walking home afterwards, Fleurette experiences an exhilaration as she realizes that she must henceforth hold herself in confidence. *A Night in Acadie* also includes the celebrated tale "Athenaise," where a young bride twice flees her husband due to her diminished sense of self, and "A Respectable Woman," in which a wife represses her passion for her husband's friend. The best of *A Night in Acadie* thus indicates Chopin's increased concern for the plight of women in Victorian-era America.

Chopin produced the stories in *A Night in Acadie* despite a seemingly disadvantageous regimen. She wrote only one or two days each week, and even then she only wrote in her living room amid her playing children. With so little time for writing, Chopin considered most tales to be complete after an initial draft, which Chopin would then submit for publication. Aside from her strictly literary pursuits, Chopin presided over a modest sa-

lon that hosted prominent St. Louis intellectuals and celebrities. They convened at her home on Thursdays and debated timely philosophical and literary subjects. In addition, Chopin had been a member of the Wednesday Club, a women's organization co-founded by poet T. S. Eliot's mother devoted to both social and cultural issues. Chopin resigned from this group after two years due to dissatisfaction with the club's ideals and pretensions, reports biographer Per Seyersted in *Kate Chopin.*

When *A Night in Acadie* appeared in 1894, it too received critical praise for its convincing portraits of Louisiana life. Although it was not reviewed as extensively as was *Bayou Folk,* it nonetheless confirmed Chopin's reputation as an adept colorist. A reviewer in *Nation,* for instance, declared that Chopin "reproduces the spirit of a landscape like a painter," and the writer noted Chopin's skill in "seizing the heart of her people and showing the traits that come from their surroundings." Likewise, a *Critic* reviewer cited Chopin's ability to write about "the simple, childlike southern people who are the subjects of her brief romances."

By the time *A Night in Acadie* appeared Chopin was already preparing a third collection, *A Vocation and a Voice.* But this volume, which included tales previously rejected by magazines, was declined by publishers uncomfortable with Chopin's increasingly radical perspective on love, sex, and marriage. In some tales, she equated sexual passion with religious devotion, and in others she explored the power of passion. Chopin also explicitly denounced conventional marriage and its restrictive role for women. In this collection's most popular work, the often-anthologized "Story of an Hour," a semi-invalid learns of her husband's death and begins anticipating her newfound independence. Like "Desiree's Baby," however, this story ends in sudden, pessimistic fashion when the wife discovers that her husband is actually alive. She then dies of heart disease.

Chopin's Masterpiece

Chopin was undeterred by the rejection of her third collection and continued writing at an impressive pace. Aside from her short stories, she produced dozens of poems, translated several tales by de Maupassant, and contributed critical essays to various St. Louis periodicals. Fiction, however, was Chopin's greatest strength, and even as she vainly submitted *A Vocation and a Voice* for publication she was writing a second novel, *The Awakening*. This work, which would eventually be recognized as her masterpiece and a seminal work in American feminist fiction, first proved her most notorious publication and her literary undoing.

Like much of Chopin's fiction, *The Awakening* is about a dissatisfied wife in Louisiana. The protagonist, Edna Pontellier, is a reserved, sensitive young woman who first appears in the novel while vacationing at a summer resort with her children. On weekends she is met by her husband, a New Orleans broker. Otherwise she has only a few adult companions, including a young Creole named Robert Lebrun. Edna first responds cordially to Robert's constant attention. Early in the novel, however, she gains a greater sense of boredom with her life and becomes increasingly aware of passionate feelings for her male friend. But at dinner one evening, Edna is stunned to discover that Robert has hastily arranged his departure for Mexico, an arrangement doubtless intended to abbreviate their romance. Edna is consequently unnerved, but she understands that her life has been irrevocably changed: she has been awakened to her thoughts, her feelings, her potential.

After she and her family have returned to New Orleans, Edna begins neglecting her duties as wife and mother. She abandons housekeeping, refuses guests, denies her husband his conjugal privilege, and eventually moves from their home to a nearby cottage. With his life drastically disrupted, Edna's husband strives to maintain his social stature. Edna understands that, in his own way, her husband actually loves her, but she also knows that his own way involves perceiving her more as property than as a separate human entity with thoughts and feelings.

Edna eventually adopts a fairly Bohemian existence—painting and circulating among musicians and others who accept her independence. She also enters into a sexual relationship with a notorious philanderer, but she longs for Robert. Edna does not find fulfillment in her new life, however. Her art work is only mediocre, and her love affair is only satisfactory sexually. When Robert returns from Mexico, she seduces him and declares her devotion. While revelling in her love and her freedom, however, she is rushed away to assist a friend giving birth. When Edna returns home, she discovers that Robert has once again fled from her affection. "Good-by—because I love you," is all he has written as a farewell note. Despondent at her lover's desertion and her friend's anguished birthing experience, Edna returns to the seaside resort where she had first fallen in love with Robert. There she disrobes and drowns herself.

Critics React Strongly

The Awakening was received with indignation when it appeared in 1899. Critics claimed that Chopin was a pornographer and that her novel was immoral and even perverse. Among her many detractors was a reviewer for *Public Opinion*, who was "well satisfied" by Edna's suicide, and a critic for *Nation*, who noted the "unpleasantness" of reading about the allegedly headstrong protagonist. Willa Cather was also among the legion of readers who denounced *The Awakening*, complaining that Chopin had wasted herself on a "trite and sordid" theme. Of course, Chopin's novel was not entirely without its supporters. A critic for the *New York Times Book Review*, for example, noted Chopin's skill in exploring her subject and confessed "pity for the most unfortunate of her sex." But reviews such as this were rare in the overwhelmingly negative dismissal of the novel.

Chopin was understandably despondent over the reception accorded *The Awakening*. This public condemnation, coupled with the continued rejection of *A Vocation and a Voice*, is believed to have precipitated the end of her literary career. Contrary to popular belief, however, Chopin did not immediately cease writing in the wake of continued abuse. In the next year, she wrote several stories, including "The Storm," which anticipated the work of English writer D. H. Lawrence with its frank depiction of two lovers' infidelity during a thunderstorm. Gradually, then, Chopin abandoned her career. By 1904 her health was also in decline. Fascinated, however, by the World's Fair in St. Louis, Chopin made daily excursions. After a particularly exhausting day, she collapsed with a cerebral hemorrhage. Two days later, on August 22, she died.

In the ensuing years Chopin's notoriety for *The Awakening* faded, and her literary reputation became dependent on critics who considered her essentially a colorist. For many years it was thus

If you enjoy the works of Kate Chopin, you may also want to check out the following books:

Charlotte Perkins Gilman, *I Feel Like the Morning Star*, 1989.
Sarah Orne Jewett, *The Country of the Pointed Firs*, 1896.
Edith Wharton, *The Age of Innocence*, 1899.

commonly held that Chopin was foremost a re-creator of Louisiana life, particularly that of the bayou. But by the 1930's critical opinion began to change. Daniel S. Rankin, in his important study *Kate Chopin and Her Creole Stories*, hailed her as a masterful realist, and Shields McIlwaine wrote in *The Southern Poor-White* that Chopin was gifted at expressing "the emotional values" of her characters. By 1952, literary historian Van Wyck Brooks had even acknowledged *The Awakening* as an undeservedly slighted work. He called the book "one novel of the nineties in the South that should have been remembered, one small perfect book that mattered more than the whole life of many a prolific writer," and he commended the novel for its "naturalness and grace." Critics such as Robert Cantwell and Kenneth Eble followed Brooks's comments in the mid-1950s by hailing *The Awakening* as profound as well as evocative. Cantwell, writing in the *Georgia Review*, praised Chopin's "heightened sensuous awareness" and deemed *The Awakening* "a great novel," while Eble wrote in *Western Humanities Review* that Chopin was superb at characterization and that she had created a "first-rate novel." And in his 1962 volume *Patriotic Gore*, noted literary authority Edmund Wilson commended *The Awakening* as "quite uninhibited and beautifully written."

In more recent years Chopin and her work have become favored subjects among women critics. Priscilla Allen, in an essay included in the volume *Authority of Experience*, charged that the preponderance of male criticism had even served to distort the characterization of *The Awakening*'s Edna Pontellier and ignored her role as a representative of the oppressed. Taking a more sociological approach was Anne Goodwyn Jones, who wrote in *Tomorrow Is Another Day* that the plight of women in Chopin's fiction is not unlike that of black slaves. In her book, Jones analyzed

Chopin's perception of sexual repression and its effect on both individuals and their society. Still other women, including Cynthia Griffin Wolff in "Thanatos and Eros," an article for *American Quarterly*, contested these sociological interpretations of Chopin's work and argued for a more psychological approach, while critics such as Carol P. Christ, who wrote of women writers in *Diving Deep and Surfacing*, viewed Chopin's writing in largely spiritual terms.

But Chopin's work is not exclusively a subject of study for American women. It has exerted appeal in countries ranging from France to Japan. Indeed, the world's foremost authority on Chopin and her work is probably Per Seyersted, a Norwegian male. Thus Chopin's work, like that of any great writer, transcends specifics of time and place and holds relevance for readers regardless of gender or nationality.

■ Works Cited

American Quarterly, October, 1973.

Atlantic Monthly, April, 1894.

Review of *The Awakening*, *Nation*, August 3, 1899.

Cather, Willa, *The World and the Parish*, Volume II: *Willa Cather's Articles and Reviews, 1893-1902*, edited by William M. Curtin, University of Nebraska Press, 1970.

Christ, Carol P., *Diving Deep and Surfacing: Women Writers on Spiritual Quest*, Beacon Press, 1980.

Diamond, Arlyn and Lee R. Edwards, *The Authority of Experience: Essays in Feminist Criticism*, University of Massachusetts Press, 1977.

Georgia Review, Winter, 1956.

Jones, Ann Goodwyn, *Tomorrow Is Another Day: The Woman Writer in the South, 1859-1936*, Louisiana State University Press, 1981.

"Literature: 'Bayou Folk,'" *Critic*, May 5, 1894, pp. 299-300.

"Literature: Mrs. Chopin's 'Night in Acadie',", *Critic*, April 16, 1898, p. 266.

McIlwaine, Shields, *The Southern Poor-White: From Lubberland to Tobacco Road*, University of Oklahoma Press, 1939.

New York Times Book Review, June 24, 1899.

Review of *A Night in Acadie*, *Nation*, June 9, 1898.

Public Opinion, June 22, 1899.

Rankin, Daniel S., *Kate Chopin and Her Creole Stories*, University of Pennsylvania Press, 1932.

"Recent Fiction: 'At Fault',", *Nation*, October 1, 1891.

Seyersted, Per, *Kate Chopin: A Critical Biography,* Louisiana State University Press, 1969.

Skaggs, Peggy, *Kate Chopin,* Twayne, 1995.

Van Wyck Brooks, "South of the James," *The Confident Years: 1885-1915,* Dutton, 1952, pp. 337-52.

Western Humanities Review, Summer, 1956.

Wilson, Edmund, *Patriotic Gore: Studies in the Literature of the American Civil War,* Farrar, Straus, 1962.

■ For More Information See

BOOKS

Beer, Janet, Kate *Chopin, Edith Wharton, and Charolotte Perkins Gilman: Studies in Short Fiction,* St. Martin's Press, 1997.

Chopin, Kate, *The Complete Works of Kate Chopin* (two volumes), edited by Per Seyersted, Louisiana State University Press, 1969.

Chopin, Kate, *The Storm and Other Stories, with "The Awakening,"* edited by Seyersted, Feminist Press, 1974.

Dictionary of Literary Biography, Gale, Volume 12: *American Realists and Naturalists,* 1982, Volume 78: *American Short-Story Writers, 1880-1910.*

Gohdes, Clarence, editor, *Essays in American Literature in Honor of Jay B. Hubbell,* Duke University Press, 1967.

Kaur, Iqbal, editor, *Kate Chopin's The Awakening: Critical Essays,* Deep and Deep Publications (New Delhi), 1995.

Koloski, Bernard, *Kate Chopin: A Study of the Short Fiction,* Twayne, 1996.

Pattee, Fred Lewis, *The Development of the American Short Story: An Historical Survey,* Harper, 1923.

Petry, Alice Hall, editor, *Critical Essays on Kate Chopin,* G. K. Hall, 1996.

Pollard, Percival, *Their Day in Court,* Neale Publishing, 1909.

Ridgely, J. V., *Nineteenth-Century Southern Literature,* University Press of Kentucky, 1980.

Springer, Marlene, editor, *Edith Wharton and Kate Chopin: A Reference Guide,* G. K. Hall, 1976.

Toth, Emily, *Kate Chopin,* University of Texas Press, 1993.

Twentieth-Century Literary Criticism, Gale, Volume 5, 1981; Volume 14, 1984.

Ziff, Larzer, *The American 1890s: Life and Times of a Lost Generation,* Viking, 1966.

PERIODICALS

Georgia Review, Summer, 1974.

Kenyon Review, Summer, 1983.

Library Journal, December, 1990, p. 126; May 1, 1992, p. 81.

Louisiana Review, Winter, 1972.

Louisiana Studies, Fall, 1970.

Mississippi Quarterly, Spring, 1972; Winter, 1979-80.

Modern Fiction Studies, Autumn, 1982.

Nation, June 28, 1894.

New Republic, December 3, 1966.

New York Review of Books, September 23, 1971.

Novel: A Forum on Fiction, Spring, 1970.

Publishers Weekly, December 21, 1990, p. 49.

Revue de Louisiane, Winter, 1972.

Southern Literary Journal, Winter, 1968; Autumn, 1970; Spring, 1978; Fall, 1981.

Southern Review, October, 1970.

Studies in Short Fiction, Summer, 1974; Summer, 1981.*

Arthur C. Clarke

■ Personal

Born December 16, 1917, in Minehead, Somerset-shire, England; son of Charles Wright (a farmer) and Nora (Willis) Clarke; married Marilyn May-field, June 15, 1953 (divorced, 1964). *Education:* King's College, University of London, B.Sc. (first class honors), 1948. *Hobbies and other interests:* "Observing the equatorial skies with a fourteen-inch telescope," table-tennis, scuba diving, and "playing with his Rhodesian Ridgeback and his six computers."

■ Addresses

Agents—Scott Meredith Literary Agency, Inc., 845 Third Ave., New York, NY 10022; David Higham Associates, 5-8 Lower John St., Golden Square, London W1R 4HA, England.

■ Career

British Civil Service, His Majesty's Exchequer and Audit Department, London, England, auditor, 1936-41; Institution of Electrical Engineers, *Science Abstracts,* London, assistant editor, 1949-50; freelance writer, 1951—. Underwater explorer and photographer, in partnership with Mike Wilson, on Great Barrier Reef of Australia and coast of Sri Lanka, 1954-64. Has appeared on television and radio numerous times, including as commentator with Walter Cronkite on *Apollo* missions, CBS-TV, 1968-70, and as host of television series *Arthur C. Clarke's Mysterious World,* 1980, and *Arthur C. Clarke's World of Strange Powers,* 1984. Acted role of Leonard Woolf in Lester James Peries's film *Beddagama* (based on Woolf's *The Village in the Jungle*), 1979.

Director of Rocket Publishing Co., United King-dom; founder, director, and owner, with Hector Ekanayake, of Underwater Safaris (a scuba-diving business), Sri Lanka; founder and patron, Arthur C. Clarke Centre for Modern Technologies, Sri Lanka, 1984—. Chancellor of University of Moratuwa, Sri Lanka, 1979—; Vikram Sarabhai Professor, Physical Research Laboratory, Ahmeda-bad, India, 1980; trustee, Institute of Integral Edu-cation, Sri Lanka. Fellow, Franklin Institute, 1971, King's College, 1977, and Institute of Robotics, Carnegie-Mellon University, 1981. Lecturer, touring United States and Britain, 1957-74. Board member of National Space Institute, United States, Space Generation Foundation, United States, International Astronomical Union (Search for ExtraTerrestrial Intelligence) Commission 51, International Space University, Institute of Fundamental Studies, Sri

Lanka, and Planetary Society, United States. Chairperson, Second International Astronautics Congress, London, 1951; moderator, "Space Flight Report to the Nation," New York, 1961. *Military service:* Royal Air Force, radar instructor, 1941-46; became flight lieutenant. *Member:* International Academy of Astronautics (honorary fellow), International Science Writers Association, International Council for Integrative Studies, World Academy of Art and Science (academician), British Interplanetary Society (honorary fellow; chairperson, 1946-47, 1950-53), Royal Astronomical Society (fellow), British Astronomical Association, Association of British Science Writers (life member), British Science Fiction Association (patron), Royal Society of Arts (fellow), Society of Authors (council member), American Institute of Aeronautics and Astronautics (honorary fellow), American Astronautical Society (honorary fellow), American Association for the Advancement of Science, National Academy of Engineering (United States; foreign associate), Science Fiction Writers of America, Science Fiction Foundation, H. G. Wells Society (honorary vice president), Third World Academy of Sciences (associate fellow), Sri Lanka Astronomical Society (patron), Institute of Engineers (Sri Lanka; honorary fellow), Sri Lanka Animal Welfare Association (patron), British Sub-Aqua Club.

■ Awards, Honors

International Fantasy Award, 1952, for *The Exploration of Space;* Hugo Award, World Science Fiction Convention, 1956, for "The Star"; Kalinga Prize, UNESCO, 1961, for science writing; Junior Book Award, Boy's Club of America, 1961; Stuart Ballantine Gold Medal, Franklin Institute, 1963, for originating concept of communications satellites; Robert Ball Award, Aviation-Space Writers Association, 1965, for best aerospace reporting of the year in any medium; Westinghouse Science Writing Award, American Association for the Advancement of Science, 1969; Second International Film Festival special award, and Academy Award nomination for best screenplay with Stanley Kubrick, Academy of Motion Picture Arts and Sciences, both 1969, both for *2001: A Space Odyssey; Playboy* editorial award, 1971, 1982; D.Sc., Beaver College, 1971, and University of Moratuwa, 1979; Nebula Award, Science Fiction Writers of America, 1972, for "A Meeting with Medusa"; Nebula Award, 1973, Hugo Award, 1974, John W. Campbell Memorial Award, Science Fiction Research

Association, 1974, and Jupiter Award, Instructors of Science Fiction in Higher Education, 1974, all for *Rendezvous with Rama;* Aerospace Communications Award, American Institute of Aeronautics and Astronautics, 1974; Bradford Washburn Award, Boston Museum of Science, 1977, for "contributions to the public understanding of science"; GALAXY Award, 1979; Nebula and Hugo Awards, both 1980, both for *The Fountains of Paradise;* special Emmy Award for engineering, National Academy of Television Arts and Sciences, 1981, for contributions to satellite broadcasting; "Lensman" Award, 1982; Marconi International Fellowship, 1982; Centennial Medal, Institute of Electrical and Electronics Engineers, 1984; E. M. Emme Astronautical Literature Award, American Astronautical Society, 1984; Grand Master Award, Science Fiction Writers of America, 1986; Vidya Jyoti Medal (Presidential Science Award), 1986; Charles A. Lindbergh Award, 1987; named to Society of Satellite Professionals Hall of Fame, 1987; named to Aerospace Hall of Fame, 1988; Special Achievement Award, Space Explorers Association, 1989; Lord Perry Award, 1992; Nobel peace prize nomination, 1994; Distinguished Public Service Medal, NASA, 1995; Space Achievement Medal and Trophy, BIS, 1995; Mohamed Sabeen Award for Science, 1996; Von Karman Award, IAA, 1996. D. Sc., Beaver College, 1971, and University of Moratuwa, 1979; D.Litt., University of Bath, 1988.

■ Writings

NONFICTION

Interplanetary Flight: An Introduction to Astronautics, Temple, 1950, Harper (New York City), 1951, 2nd edition, 1960.

The Exploration of Space (U.S. Book-of-the-Month Club selection), Harper, 1951, revised edition, Pocket Books, 1979.

The Young Traveller in Space, Phoenix, 1953, published as *Going into Space,* Harper, 1954, revised edition (with Robert Silverberg) published as *Into Space: A Young Person's Guide to Space,* Harper, 1971.

The Exploration of the Moon, illustrated by R. A. Smith, Harper, 1954.

The Coast of Coral, Harper, 1956.

The Reefs of Taprobane: Underwater Adventures around Ceylon, Harper, 1957.

The Scottie Book of Space Travel, Transworld Publishers, 1957.

The Making of a Moon: The Story of the Earth Satellite Program, Harper, 1957, revised edition, 1958.

Voice across the Sea, Harper, 1958, revised edition, 1974.

(With Mike Wilson) *Boy beneath the Sea,* Harper, 1958.

The Challenge of the Spaceship: Previews of Tomorrow's World, Harper, 1959.

(With Wilson) *The First Five Fathoms: A Guide to Underwater Adventure,* Harper, 1960.

The Challenge of the Sea, Holt, 1960.

(With Wilson) *Indian Ocean Adventure,* Harper, 1961.

Profiles of the Future: An Inquiry into the Limits of the Possible, Harper, 1962, revised edition, Holt, 1984.

The Treasure of the Great Reef, Harper, 1964, new edition, Ballantine, 1974.

(With Wilson) *Indian Ocean Treasure,* Harper, 1964.

(With the editors of *Life*) *Man and Space,* Time-Life, 1964.

Voices from the Sky: Previews of the Coming Space Age, Harper, 1965.

(Editor) *The Coming of the Space Age: Famous Accounts of Man's Probing of the Universe,* Meredith, 1967.

The Promise of Space, Harper, 1968.

(With Neil Armstrong, Michael Collins, Edwin E. Aldrin, Jr., Gene Farmer, and Dora Jane Hamblin) *First on the Moon,* Little, Brown, 1970.

Report on Planet Three and Other Speculations, Harper, 1972.

(With Chesley Bonestell) *Beyond Jupiter,* Little, Brown, 1972.

The View from Serendip (autobiography), Random House, 1977.

Arthur C. Clarke's Mysterious World (also see below; television series), Yorkshire Television, 1980.

(With Simon Welfare and John Fairley) *Arthur C. Clarke's Mysterious World* (based on television series), A & W Publishers, 1980.

Ascent to Orbit, a Scientific Autobiography: The Technical Writings of Arthur C. Clarke, Wiley, 1984.

1984: Spring—A Choice of Futures, Del Rey, 1984.

(With Welfare and Fairley) *Arthur C. Clarke's World of Strange Powers* (also see below; based on television series of same title), Putnam, 1984.

(With Peter Hyams) *The Odyssey File,* Fawcett (New York City), 1985.

Arthur C. Clarke's July 20, 2019: Life in the 21st Century, Macmillan, 1986.

Arthur C. Clarke's Chronicles of the Strange and Mysterious, edited by Welfare and Fairley, Collins, 1987.

Astounding Days: A Science Fictional Autobiography, Bantam, 1989.

How the World Was One: Beyond the Global Village, Bantam, 1992.

By Space Possessed, Gollancz (London), 1993.

The Snows of Olympus: A Garden on Mars, Norton, 1995.

Front Line of Discovery, National Geographic Society, 1995.

Rogue Asteroids and Doomsday Comets, Wiley, 1997.

Arthur C. Clarke & Lord Dunsany: A Correspondence, Anamnesis Press, 1998.

(Co-editor with Ian MacAuley) *Greetings Carbon-Based Bipeds!,* St. Martin's Press, 1999.

Also author of introduction to *Inmarsat History.* Contributor to books, including *Mars and the Mind of Man,* Harper, 1973; *Frontline of Discovery: Science on the Brink of Tomorrow,* National Geographic Society, 1994; and *The Case for Mars,* Simon & Schuster, 1997.

FICTION

The Sands of Mars (also see below), Sidgwick & Jackson, 1951.

Prelude to Space (also see below), World Editions, 1951, published as *Master of Space,* Lancer Books, 1961, published as *The Space Dreamers,* Lancer Books, 1969.

Islands in the Sky, Winston, 1952, new edition, Penguin Books, 1972.

Childhood's End (also see below), Ballantine, 1953.

Against the Fall of Night (also see below), Gnome Press, 1953.

Expedition to Earth (also see below; short stories), Ballantine, 1953.

Earthlight (also see below), Ballantine, 1955.

Reach for Tomorrow (short stories), Ballantine, 1956.

The City and the Stars (also see below; based on novel *Against the Fall of Night*), Harcourt, 1956, new edition, Yestermorrow, 1999.

The Deep Range (also see below), Harcourt, 1957.

Tales from the White Hart, Ballantine, 1957.

The Other Side of the Sky (short stories), Harcourt, 1958.

Across the Sea of Stars (anthology; includes *Childhood's End* and *Earthlight*), Harcourt, 1959.

A Fall of Moondust (also see below), Harcourt, 1961, abridged edition, University of London Press, 1964.

From the Oceans, from the Stars (anthology; includes *The Deep Range* and *The City and the Stars*), Harcourt, 1962.

Tales of Ten Worlds (short stories), Harcourt, 1962.

Dolphin Island: A Story of the People of the Sea, Holt, 1963.

Glide Path, Harcourt, 1963.

Prelude to Mars (anthology; includes *Prelude to Space* and *The Sands of Mars*), Harcourt, 1965.

An Arthur C. Clarke Omnibus (contains *Childhood's End, Prelude to Space*, and *Expedition to Earth*), Sidgwick & Jackson, 1965.

(Editor) *Time Probe: The Science in Science Fiction*, Dial (New York City), 1966.

The Nine Billion Names of God (short stories), Harcourt, 1967.

A Second Arthur C. Clarke Omnibus (contains *A Fall of Moondust, Earthlight*, and *The Sands of Mars*), Sidgwick & Jackson, 1968.

(With Stanley Kubrick) *2001: A Space Odyssey* (screenplay; also see below), Metro-Goldwyn-Mayer, 1968.

2001: A Space Odyssey (novelization of screenplay), New American Library, 1968, published with a new introduction by Clarke, ROC (New York City), 1994.

The Lion of Comarre, Harcourt, 1968.

Against the Fall of Night, Harcourt, 1968.

The Lost Worlds of 2001, New American Library, 1972.

The Wind from the Sun (short stories), Harcourt, 1972.

(Editor) *Three for Tomorrow*, Sphere Books, 1972.

Of Time and Stars: The Worlds of Arthur C. Clarke (short stories), Gollancz, 1972.

Rendezvous with Rama (also see below), Harcourt, 1973, adapted edition, Oxford University Press, 1979.

The Best of Arthur C. Clarke, edited by Angus Wells, Sidgwick & Jackson, 1973, published as two volumes, Volume 1: *The Best of Arthur C. Clarke: 1937-1955*, Volume 2: *The Best of Arthur C. Clarke: 1956-1972*, 1977.

Imperial Earth: A Fantasy of Love and Discord, Gollancz, 1975, Harcourt, 1976.

Four Great Science Fiction Novels (contains *The City and the Stars, The Deep Range, A Fall of Moondust*, and *Rendezvous with Rama*), Gollancz, 1978.

The Fountains of Paradise, Harcourt, 1979.

(Editor with George Proctor) *The Science Fiction Hall of Fame*, Volume 3: *TheNebula Winners*, Avon, 1982.

2010: Odyssey Two, Del Rey, 1982.

The Sentinel: Masterworks of Science Fiction and Fantasy (short stories), Berkeley Publishing, 1983.

Selected Works, Heinemann, 1985.

The Songs of Distant Earth, Del Rey, 1986.

2061: Odyssey Three, Del Rey, 1988.

(With Gentry Lee) *Cradle*, Warner Books, 1988.

A Meeting with Medusa (bound with *Green Mars* by Kim Stanley Robinson), Tor Books, 1988.

(With Lee) *Rama II*, Bantam, 1989.

(With Gregory Benford) *Beyond the Fall of Night*, Putnam, 1990.

The Ghost from the Grand Banks, Bantam, 1990.

Tales from the Planet Earth, illustrated by Michael Whelan, Bantam, 1990.

(With Gentry Lee) *The Garden of Rama*, Bantam, 1991.

The Hammer of God, Bantam, 1993.

(With Lee) *Rama Revealed*, Bantam, 1994.

(With Mike McQuay) *Richter 10*, Bantam, 1996.

3001: The Final Odyssey, Ballantine, 1997.

Expedition to Earth, Ballantine, 1998.

Reach for Tomorrow, Ballantine, 1998.

Tales from the White Heart, Ballantine, 1998.

Arthur C. Clarke's Mysteries, Trans-Atlantic, 1998.

The Sands of Maris, Yestermorrow, 1999.

(With Paul Preuss) *Venus Prime*, Pocket Books, 2000.

OTHER

Opus 700, Gollancz, 1990.

Rama: The Official Strategy Guide, Prima Pub. (Rocklin, CA), 1996.

Also author of television series *Arthur C. Clarke's World of StrangePowers* and a movie treatment based on *Cradle*. Author of afterword to *Breaking Strain*, Avon, 1987, and *Maelstrom*, Avon, 1988, both by Paul Preuss. Contributor of more than 600 articles and short stories, occasionally under pseudonyms E. G. O'Brien and Charles Willis, to numerous magazines, including *Harper's, Playboy, New York Times Magazine, Vogue,* and *Horizon.*

Clarke's works have been translated into Polish, Russian, French, German, Spanish, Serbo-Croatian, Greek, Hebrew, Dutch, and more than twenty other languages.

■ Adaptations

2010: Odyssey Two was filmed in 1984 by Metro-Goldwyn-Mayer (Clarke has a cameo in the film); the short story "The Star" was adapted for an episode of *The New Twilight Zone* by CBS-TV in 1985. The following works have been optioned for movies: *Childhood's End*, by Universal; *The Songs of Distant Earth,* by Michael Phillips; *The Fountains of Paradise,* by Robert Swarthe; and *Cradle,* by Peter Guber. Clarke has made the following sound recordings of his works for Caedmon: *Arthur C. Clarke Reads from his 2001: A Space Odyssey,* 1976; *Transit of Earth; The Nine Billion Names of God;* and *The Star,* 1978; *The Fountains of Paradise,* 1979; *Childhood's End,* 1979; and *2010: Odyssey Two.* A full-length recording of *A Fall of Moondust* was made by Harcourt in 1976.

■ Sidelights

Arthur C. Clarke is renowned not only for his science fiction—which has earned him the title of Grand Master from the Science Fiction Writers of America and the unofficial "poet laureate of the space age," as David Brin writing in the *Los Angeles Times* dubbed him. Clarke also has a reputation for first-rate scientific and technical writing. His best known work in the latter field is "Extraterrestrial Relays," a 1945 article in which he first proposed the idea of communications satellites; Clarke has also published works on such diverse topics as underwater diving, space exploration, and scientific extrapolation. Nevertheless, it is Clarke's science fiction that has won him his reputation, with such novels as *Childhood's End* and *Rendezvous with Rama* being widely hailed as classics of the genre. In addition, his story "The Nine Billion Names of God" was named to the science fiction "Hall of Fame," while the movie *2001: A Space Odyssey,* co-written with director Stanley Kubrick, has been called the most important science fiction film ever made.

Clarke's fiction, which often deals with themes of exploration and discovery, almost always conveys to the reader a sense of wonder about the universe. Some critics, seeing the author's detailed descriptions of possible futures, have accused Clarke of ignoring the human element for the sake of science in his work. But while the development of scientific ideas and speculations plays a large role in Clarke's narratives, "what distinguishes Clarke's fictions from the usually more ephemeral examples of science fiction is his vision," Eric S. Rabkin asserted in his 1979 study *Arthur C. Clarke.* This vision, wrote Rabkin, is "a humane and open and fundamentally optimistic view of humankind and its potential in a universe which dwarfs us in physical size but which we may hope some day to match in spirit."

Born in 1917 in an English seaside town, Clarke discovered science fiction at the age of twelve, when he encountered the pulp magazine *Amazing Stories.* The encounter soon became an "addiction," as Clarke related in a 1983 article in the *New York Times Book Review:* "During my lunch hour away from school I used to haunt the local Woolworth's in search of my fix, which cost threepence a shot, roughly a quarter today." The young Clarke then began nurturing his love for the genre through the books of such English writers as H. G. Wells and Olaf Stapledon. He began writing his own stories for a school magazine while in his teens, but was unable to continue his schooling for lack of funds. He consequently secured a civil service job as an auditor, which left him plenty of free time to pursue his literary hobby. Alone in London, Clarke joined an association of several science fiction and space enthusiasts, and as he recalled in his 1977 autobiography *The View from Serendip,* "my life was dominated by the infant British Interplanetary Society [BIS], of which I was treasurer and general propagandist." As part of his involvement with the BIS, Clarke wrote several scientific articles on the feasibility of space travel for the organization's journal; the BIS also gained him contacts with several science fiction editors and writers, that led to the publication of some of his short stories.

In 1941, although his auditor's position was still a reserved occupation, Clarke engaged in "what was probably the single most decisive act of my entire life," as he described it in *Ascent to Orbit, a Scientific Autobiography: The Technical Writings of Arthur C. Clarke;* he volunteered for the Royal Air Force. En route to becoming a radar instructor in a new system called Ground Controlled Approach, Clarke taught himself mathematical and electronics theory. After the war, Clarke entered college and obtained a degree in physics as well as pure and applied mathematics. Upon graduation, he spent two years as an assistant editor for a technical journal. But with publication of the novel *Childhood's End* (1953) and *The Exploration of Space,* which in 1952 was the first science book ever chosen as a Book-of-the-Month Club selection, Clarke began earning enough money to pursue writing full-time.

Besides allowing Clarke to leave his job, the success of *The Exploration of Space* also broke ground in explaining scientific ideas to a popular audience. What enabled the book to reach such a wide audience is a "charm and magnetism" that is due to "Clarke's ability to reduce complex subjects to simple language and his steadfast avoidance of fantasy as a substitute for factual narration," observed Roy Gibbons in the *Chicago Sunday Tribune*.

Clarke applied the same speculative techniques to other areas in the 1962 book *Profiles of the Future: An Inquiry into the Limits of the Possible*. The author "has a thorough grounding in science, and, in addition has a nimble and most receptive mind," Isaac Asimov stated in the *New York Times Book Review*. "Nothing reasonable frightens him simply because it seems fantastic, and—equally important—nothing foolish attracts him simply because it seems fantastic." Asimov went on to notes that "this book offers all of us a chance to raise our eyes from the ground and to contemplate the scenery ahead. It is marvelous scenery indeed, and there could scarcely be a better guide to its landmarks than Arthur Clarke." Reviewer R. C. Cowen of the *Christian Science Monitor* expressed a similar opinion, praising *Profiles of the Future* as being "highly entertaining reading [that] also is informative, for the author is careful to adhere to the yardstick of natural laws that set the bounds of the possible." Cowen added that Clarke "helps a layman to learn the difference between rational speculation and . . . wholly baseless imaginings."

Although most speculative science texts are soon outdated, Clarke's work has withstood years of technical progress. In *The Promise of Space,* published in 1968 to "replace" *The Exploration of Space,* Clarke showed how many of his predictions have come true. Rather than simply cataloging recent discoveries, Clarke's work has incorporated them into new ideas: "All through the book Clarke not only recounts what has been done during the last two decades," wrote Willy Ley in the *New York Times Book Review,* "but has his eye on both the immediate results and the future." Similarly, *Science* contributor Eugene M. Emme asserted that the book contains "the best available summary of scientific and imaginative theory regarding space potentials. . . . Collectively they offer a most persuasive rationale." A 1984 revision of *Profiles of the Future* also withstands years of advancement: "Testing the limits of technological progress," observed David N. Samuelson in the *Los Angeles Times Book Review,* "it has remained remarkably current since its 1962 book publication." Gregory Benford, who hailed Clarke "a vindicated sage in his own time," theorized in the *Washington Post*

Book World that while "books on futurology date notoriously, this one has not, principally because Clarke was unafraid of being adventurous." And *New York Times Book Review* writer Gerald Jonas offered this reason for Clarke's success: "What makes Clarke such an effective popularizer of science is that, without bobbling a decimal point or fudging a complex concept, he gives voice to the romantic side of scientific inquiry."

Early Science Fiction Works

Although much of Clarke's early fiction reinforced the idea that space travel was an eventuality, *Childhood's End*, his first successful novel, is "Clarke's only work—fiction or nonfiction—in which 'The stars are not for Man,'" Thomas D. Clareson suggested in *Voices for the Future: Essays on Major Science Fiction Writers.* The novel relates the appearance of the Overlords, a race of devil-shaped aliens who have come to guide Earth to peace and prosperity. After eliminating all individual governments and thus ending war, the Overlords use their superior technology to solve the problems of poverty, hunger, and oppression. The cost of this utopia is that most scientific research is set aside as unnecessary, and the exploration of space is forbidden. The motives of the Overlords become clear as the youngest generation of humans develops extrasensory powers; the children of Earth are to join the Overmind, a collective galactic "spirit" that transcends physical form. The need for science, technology, and space is eliminated with humanity's maturation, and the Earth itself is destroyed as her children join the Overmind.

Some critics have viewed *Childhood's End* as the first manifestation of the theme of spiritual evolution that appears throughout Clarke's fiction. Writing in the critical anthology *Arthur C. Clarke,* John Huntington described the novel as Clarke's solution to one of the problems posed by technological progress: how spiritual development can keep pace with scientific development when by making man comfortable, science often takes away man's curiosity and drive.

Childhood's End solves the problem with a stage of "transcendent evolution," and Huntington proposed that "it is its elegant solution to the problem of progress that has rightly earned *Childhood's End* that 'classic' status it now enjoys." However,

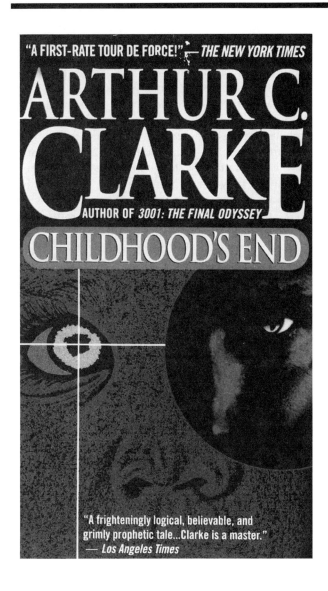

"A FIRST-RATE TOUR DE FORCE!" — *THE NEW YORK TIMES*

ARTHUR C. CLARKE

AUTHOR OF *3001: THE FINAL ODYSSEY*

CHILDHOOD'S END

"A frighteningly logical, believable, and grimly prophetic tale...Clarke is a master."
— *Los Angeles Times*

Clarke's 1953 novel concerns a race of Overlords who bring a peaceful paradise to Earth by eliminating war, poverty, and oppression—with a price.

Donald A. Wollheim, considered this solution a negative one; writing in his 1971 book *The Universe Makers* he commented that *Childhood's End* "has always seemed to me to be a novel of despair. Others critics may see it as offering hope, but this tampering with humanity always struck me as being synthetic." Nonetheless, other critics have reaffirmed the novel as one of hope; *Childhood's End* "becomes a magnificently desperate attempt to continue to hope for a future for the race in the face of mounting evidence to the contrary," John Hollow wrote in *Against the Night, the Stars: The Science Fiction of Arthur C. Clarke.*

Written in 1953 in the midst of the Cold War, "[the novel] becomes, in fact, a sometimes brilliant attempt to turn the contrary evidence to the positive," Hollow added. "It becomes nothing less than an effort to make positive the destruction of the race."

2001

Clarke's best-known novel, *2001: A Space Odyssey* was the result of four years work on both the film version and the subsequent book. The collaboration between Clarke and director Stanley Kubrick began when the late filmmaker sought a suitable basis for making the "proverbial good science fiction movie," as Kubrick described it. The two finally settledupon Clarke's 1951 short story "The Sentinel," and developed it "not [into] a script, which in [Kubrick's] view does not contain enough of the visual and emotional information necessary for filming, but a prose version, rather like a novel," Michel Ciment related in *Focus on the Science Fiction Film.* The result "was of more help to him in creating the right atmosphere because it was more generous in its descriptions," Ciment wrote.

The film and the novel have the same basic premise: a large black monolith has been sent to Earth to encourage the development of man. First shown assisting in the "dawn of man" four million years ago, a monolith is next uncovered on the moon, and upon its unveiling sends a strong radio signal toward the outer planets. As a result the spaceship *Discovery,* operated by the intelligent computer HAL 9000, is sent in the direction of the signal to investigate. However, while the human crew is kept ignorant of the ship's true assignment, the HAL 9000 begins to eliminate what it sees as obstacles in the way of the mission—including the human crew. But first-captain Dave Bowman manages to survive and upon his arrival at a moon of Saturn (Jupiter in the film) encounters yet a third monolith, which precipitates a journey through the infinite. Bowman is transformed during this journey, and subsequently arrives at a higher evolutionary plane as the Star Child.

"Clarke's *2001: A Space Odyssey* was an extraordinary development in fiction, a novel written in collaboration with the director who was simultaneously filming it," observed Colin Greenland of the *Times Literary Supplement*. Clarke himself explained in the epilogue to the 1982 edition of *2001* that during the project he "often had the strange experience of revising the manuscript *after* viewing rushes based upon an earlier version of the story—a stimulating but rather expensive way of writing a novel." Because the book appeared three months after the movie's premiere, it was inevitable that critics would draw comparisons between the two. *New Statesman* contributor Brenda Maddox found the book lacking beside the movie; the novel "has all the faults of the film and none of its virtues." The critic elaborated: "The characters still have the subtlety of comic-strip men and, lacking the film's spectacular visual gimmickry . . .

Clarke's most famous work, *2001*, is based on his story "The Sentinel" and describes humankind's first encounter with a vastly superior alien race that seeks to improve humanity.

the story must propel itself with little gusts of scientific explanation." In contrast, Eliot Fremont-Smith asserted in the *New York Times* that "the immense and moving fantasy-idea of *2001* . . . is an idea that can be *dramatically* envisioned only in the free oscillations of the delicately cued and stretched mind." The critic added that the film "is too direct for this, its wonders too unsubtle and, for all their majesty, too confining." And where the movie may have been obscure, "all of it becomes clear and convincing in the novel. It is indeed an odyssey, this story, this exhilarating and rather chilling science fiction fantasy." Nevertheless, in comparing the visual genius of the film with the clarity of the book, Clarke himself admitted in *Focus on the Science Fiction Film* that both versions "did something that the other couldn't have done."

Another Classic

"Although it lacks some of the metaphysical fireworks and haunting visionary poetry of [his earlier work]," Clarke's *Rendezvous with Rama* is nevertheless "essentially an expression of wonder in the presence of Mystery," a *Virginia Quarterly Review* contributor commented. Written in 1973, the novel is the only work to win all four major awards in its genre; writing in the *Times Literary Supplement*, Thomas M. Disch hailed it as "probably [Clarke's] most considerable work of art." The book follows the appearance of an asteroid-like object which is hurtling directly towards the inner solar system—and which turns out to be a cylindrical, obviously unnatural artifact. An Earth ship is dispatched to the object, labelled "Rama," and a team led by commander Bill Norton enters to investigate. The exploration of the many mysterious aspects of Rama is interrupted by several distractions—including the emergence of what appears to be generated life forms and the arrival of a nuclear warhead sent by paranoid colonists from nearby Mercury. The study of Rama is concluded safely, however, although Norton's team has not gathered enough information to discern a purpose to the craft. Seemingly indifferent to a meeting with intelligent life, Rama then exits the solar system and continues its journey. "This is story-telling of the highest order," Theodore Sturgeon wrote in the *New York Times Book Review*. "There are perpetual surprise, constant evocation of the sense of wonder, and occasions of the most breathless suspense."

Although classic works such as *Childhood's End* and *Rendezvous with Rama* focus on the effects of extraterrestrial visitation, Clarke's next two works concentrate more on the achievements of humanity. *Imperial Earth: A Fantasy of Love and Discord,* takes place in the quincentennial year of 2276. The novel includes demonstrations of outer planet mining operations, cloning, and spaceship propulsion systems, all woven into the story of Titan native Duncan Makenzie's visit to Earth. Duncan's trip serves many purposes; ostensibly it is to deliver an address at the quincenntenial celebration, but it is also to investigate political and scientific intrigues, as well as to procure, through cloning, an heir for the sterile Duncan. Through Duncan's eyes "Clarke not only supplies us with a fair number of technological wonders," observed Mark Rose in the *New Republic,* but the author also "makes much of such human matters as the political and psychological isolation of a distant colonial world such as Titan." Rose lauded the novel as "a literary performance conducted with genuine intelligence and grace." *National Review* contributor Steve Ownbey praised *Imperial Earth* as "a book nobody should miss. It's an utterly delightful tale, suspenseful and moving, full of unexpected chuckles and stunning surprises."

Clarke's 1979 Hugo- and Nebula-winning *The Fountains of Paradise* is even more technical in its basic premise: the construction of an orbital "space elevator" designed to make escaping the Earth's gravity a simple process. Based on actual scientific treatises, Clarke once again develops his idea"with sufficient technical detail to lend plausibility" said Gerald Jonas in the *New York Times Book Review,* "and the more plausible it sounds, the more stupendous it becomes." The novel also concerns Vannevar Morgan, the engineer obsessed with realizing the creation of his space elevator. Providing a "curious backdrop" to Morgan's enterprise is "a highly advanced galactic civilization [which] has already communicated with the human race through a robot probe," summarized Jonas. In addition, Morgan's story is paralleled by the account of Prince Kalidasa, who 2,000 years earlier challenged the gods by attempting to build a garden tower into heaven—on Taprobane, the same island that Morgan wants for his elevator. But while critics commended this parallel, they faulted Clarke for not sustaining it: "the direct interweaving of Kalidasa's story should have extended throughout the entire work rather than petering out," commented Paul Granahan in *Best*

In collaboration with Clarke, director Stanley Kubrick's *2001: A Space Odyssey* was a cutting-edge sci-fi film in 1968 that still draws acclaim today.

Sellers. Similarly, *New Republic* contributor Tim Myers criticized Clarke for ending the parallel: "The Indian king, the only character with nobility, is taken from us. We are left with Morgan, a pathetic egotist who is also hopelessly stereotyped."

The Sequels to *2001*

Although Clarke (and others) insisted for several years that it was impossible to write a sequel to *2001,* in 1982 Clarke published *2010: Odyssey Two.* Incorporating elements of both the film and novel versions, as well as new information from the *Voyager* probes of Jupiter, in *2010* "Clarke sensibly steps back down to our level to tell the story of a combined Russian and American expedition to salvage Bowman's deserted ship, the *Discovery,* and finds out what happened," related Colin Greenland in the *Times Literary Supplement.* Although the expedition finds the remains of the ship and repairs the HAL 9000, the purpose of the black monolith mystifies them. While some critics found this an adequate approach to a sequel, others chided Clarke for even attempting to follow up a "classic." *Science Fiction Review* writer Gene DeWeese argued that a key problem is that *2010* "is not so much a sequel to the original book, which was in many ways superior to the movie, but a sequel to and an explanation of the movie. Unfortunately, many of these explanations already existed [in the novel of *2001*]." *Washington Post Book World* contributor Michael Bishop noted a tendency on Clarke's part to over-explain: "Ponderous expository dialogue alternates with straightforward expository passages in which Heywood Floyd . . . or the author himself lectures the reader." And Gerald Jonas of the *New York Times Book Review* complained that *2010* "violates the mystery [of the original] at every turn."

Despite the various criticisms, *2010* still "has its share of that same sense of wonder, which means that it is one of the dozen or so most enjoyable SF books of the year," said Gene DeWeese. "Clarke deftly blends discovery, philosophy, and a newly acquired sense of play," stated *Time* contributor Peter Stoler, creating a work that will "entertain" readers. Cary Neeper presented a similar assessment in the *Christian Science Monitor*, noting that "Clarke's story drives on to an exciting finish in which the mix of fantasy and fact leaves the reader well satisfied with a book masterfully written." And in contrast to the criticisms of the sequel's worthiness, Bud Foote claimed in the *Detroit News* that with "the book's penultimate triumph [of] a new, awesome and terrifying world transformation," Clarke has created "a fine book." The critic concluded that *2010* "is better than the original book, and it illuminates and completes the original movie. It is so good, in fact, that even Clarke couldn't write a sequel to it."

Despite this assertion, 1988 brought *2061: Odyssey Three*, the next chapter in the saga of the black monolith. The year 2061 will be the next appearance of Halley's comet; *Odyssey Three* follows Heywood Floyd on a survey of the object. While en route, his survey party is redirected to rescue a ship that has crashed on the Jovian moon of Europa—the one celestial object the monoliths have warned humans against visiting. Some critics have been skeptical of a second sequel, such as the *Time* reviewer who found that "the mix of imagination and anachronism is wearing as thin as the oxygen layer on Mars." Although Gerald

Jonas of the *New York Times Book Review* also observed that "Mr. Clarke's heart is obviously not in the obligatory action scenes that advance the plot," he conceded that the author "remains a master at describing the wonders of the universe in sentences that combine a respect for scientific accuracy with an often startling lyricism." Clarke "is not to be measured by the same standards we apply to a mundane plot-smith," asserted David Brin in the *Los Angeles Times*. "He is, after all, the poet laureate of the Space Age. He is at his best making the reader feel, along with Heywood Floyd," continued Brin, "how fine it might be to

In 1997, Clarke published the final chapter of his "Odyssey" series, in which twenty-first century astronaut Frank Poole is revived to find that the monoliths may actually pose a threat to humanity.

stand upon an ancient comet, out under the stars, knowing that it is those dreams that finally come true that are the best dreams of all."

Between the publication of the two "Odyssey" sequels Clarke finished *The Songs of Distant Earth,* an elaborate revision and extension of a short story he first published in 1958. The novel takes place on the ocean world of Thalassa, where the few habitable islands there have been populated by descendants of an Earth "seedship," sent to perpetuate humanity even after the nova explosion of the Earth's sun. The Thalassan society is a type of utopia, for superstition, prejudice, and extreme violence no longer exist; the robots who raised the first generations eliminated all religion and art which might encourage these elements. The Thalassans are seemingly content with their world when the starship *Magellan* lands, bringing with it the last survivors (and witnesses) of the Earth's destruction. Although the ship is not permitted to colonize a world that has already been settled, the idyllic setting tempts the crew to a possible mutiny. Further complicating the situation is the emergence of a marine life form that appears to be intelligent, creating a possible conflict on two different fronts.

Although this dilemma "makes for an interesting novel," *Science Fiction Review* contributor Richard E. Geis faulted Clarke's plot as improbable, decrying the lack of individual conflict. Echoing previous criticisms, Geis commented that the "characters are uncomplicated, non-neurotic, with only minor problems to be solved. . . . Clarke has written a story of plausible high-tech future science and peopled it with implausible, idealized, 'nice' humans." In contrast, Dan K. Moran of the *West Coast Review of Books* maintained that "how Clarke deals with the mutiny is interesting; and his characters come alive throughout." Nevertheless, Moran noted that "the great flaw is the lack of sense-of-wonder. Nothing herein is really new, neither science nor Clarke's synthesis."

Examines the Human Spirit

The "grand theme" that runs throughout Clarke's fiction "can be stated only in the form of a paradox," Gerald Jonas of the *New York Times Book Review* suggested. "Man is most himself when he strives greatly, when he challenges the very laws of the universe; yet man is small and the universe is large, and anything he creates must, in the long run, be dwarfed by the works of others." The science in Clarke's fiction provides a good backdrop for this theme; Gregory Benford wrote in the *Washington Post Book Review* that Clarke "prefers a pure, dispassionate statement of facts and relationships, yet the result is not cold. Instead, he achieves a rendering of the scientific esthetic, with its respect for the universal qualities of intelligence, its tenacity and curiosity. His fiction neglects conflict and the broad spectrum of emotion, which gives it a curiously refreshing honesty." Although Clarke's fiction "may appear to be about science, appear to be about numbers, appear to be about ideas," Eric Rabkin wrote in his 1979 book *Arthur C. Clarke,* "in fact at bottom whatever Clarke writes is about people and that means it is about the human spirit."

Clarke's faith in the human spirit is evident in his nonfiction book *The Snows of Olympus: A Garden on Mars.* Published in 1995, at a time when NASA struggled with massive budget cutbacks, this book optimistically looks toward a future when humans will visit and colonize the Red Planet. Clarke asserts that if money were no object, human beings could walk on Mars early in the twenty-first century. He outlines a three-part mission to Mars, beginning with robot probes, which would locate needed resources on the planet and choose suitable landing sites. Unmanned space freighters would follow with equipment and supplies, intended to support the third part of the mission: the landing of a human crew. Clarke predicts that once a human colony is established, work will begin to alter the environment of Mars to make it habitable by unprotected human beings. He even believes that it is possible to create oceans and large-scale agricultural projects there. *The Snows of Olympus* is illustrated with computer-generated art depicting the transformation of Mars. Clarke created the pictures himself, beginning with maps of the planet generated by NASA's *Voyager* probe. In addition to his speculations on the years to come, Clarke's book also takes a look at past conceptions of Mars, beginning with the late nineteenth-century idea that the planet was populated by a race of intelligent beings who specialized in building canals.

Known as a futurist, Clarke turned to the past in *Astounding Days: A Science Fictional Autobiography.* Focusing on Clarke's youth and early days as a

If you enjoy the works of Arthur C. Clarke, you may also want to check out the following books and films:

David Brin, *Earth*, 1990.
Michael Crichton, *Sphere*, 1987.
Vonda M. McIntyre, *Metaphase*, 1992.
Larry Niven and Jerry Pournelle, *Lucifer's Hammer*, 1977.
Silent Running, a film starring Bruce Dern, 1971.

writer, the memoir is divided into three sections, each dedicated to one of the three editors who created the magazine *Astounding Science Fiction* (renamed *Analog* in the 1960s). Writing in *Wilson Library Bulletin*, Gene LaFaille described *Astounding Days* as a "rambling paean to the glory years of early science fiction." *Astounding Days* provides "a sweeping view of popular science and popular fiction," *Library Journal* reviewer Katherine Thorp stated.

As an octogenarian, Clarke turned once again toward the future, both immediate and distant. In *Richter 10*, written in collaboration with Mike McQuay, Clarke combines earthquakes, politics, and environmental disaster to produce a futuristic disaster novel. By the near-future year 2030, the Nation of Islam is orchestrating a civil war in California and demanding a state of its own, China is the dominant world power, southern Europe and the Middle East have been destroyed by Israel's nuclear weapons, and the ozone layer has vanished. The book's hero, Lewis Crane, is a leading authority on earth tremors and is able to predict earthquakes, but no one believes him when he predicts a giant earthquake that might wipe out the central United States. When the earthquake does not occur on time, the Nation of Islam attacks and the earth disintegrates into chaos. Crane, who has lost all credibility and support from his Chinese business sponsor, buys real estate on the moon and starts a space colony. *Booklist* praised *Richter 10* as "a taut, well-written thriller that should satisfy both Clarke's fans and the many devotees of disaster novels."

In 1997 Clarke did what he had long said was impossible: he wrote the fourth installment of his Odyssey series, *3001: The Final Odyssey*. In *3001*, another manned space voyage finds the deep-frozen Frank Poole, long presumed dead, and revives him with fourth-millennium technology. Poole masters the use of the "braincap" and other gadgets, learns about Star City, and studies the thousand years of history he has slept through. During his long sleep, a monolith has exploded Jupiter, turning it and its moons into a secondary solar system. One moon, Europa, has been colonized by a monolith that monitors human behavior and influences the plant-like beings beneath the surface to grow. Poole is alarmed to learn that his old colleague, Dave Bowman, and HAL have both become absorbed by the monolith and that the black slab's superiors are intent on doing something unthinkable to the humans that they have enslaved. Writing in the *New York Times Book Review*, John Allen Paulos observed that while the plot hangs together "reasonably well," much of the enjoyment comes from Clarke's ruminations on high technology, Freudian therapy, computer security, terrorism, and religious mania. Ian Watson of the *Times Literary Supplement* suggested that what makes *3001* compelling reading is the way in which Clarke "retrofits" earlier episodes "so that they blend with the new future and the now ex-future." While he felt that there are not many surprises to be had in the novel, Watson still praised Clarke for having "the unnerving habit of proving that whatever it is, he imagined it first." Eric Korn of the *Economist* argued that the novel begs its most interesting question: What if the monolith's part in human evolution were a bad thing? Korn wrote, "In *2001*, the monoliths were doors of transcendent perception; in *3001*, they become banal and easily dealt-with alien threats." Korn found *3001* a "disappointing end" to the Odyssey series.

"Science fiction is often called escapism—always in a negative sense," Clarke told Alice K. Turner in a 1973 *Publishers Weekly* interview. "Of course it's not true. Science fiction is virtually the only kind of writing that's dealing with real problems and possibilities; it's a concerned fiction." Clarke added that "we know so much more now that we don't have to waste time on the petty things of the past. We can use the enormous technological advances in our work. Vision is wider now, and interest has never been deeper."

Although he has been involved with the SF genre for more than half a century, Clarke's writing style and the themes he writes about have not changed greatly over the years. "I guess I'm just an old conservative," the author told Charles Platt, the author of *Dream Makers: The Uncommon Men and Women Who Write Science Fiction.* "Although, really, if I have stayed true to the original form of my writing that's simply because I have a constant commitment to science." Clarke also commented to Platt that he is proud of retaining the "sense of wonder" in his writing: "I regard it as something of an achievement not to have become cynical. . . . I do remain an optimist, especially in my fiction, because I hope it may operate as a self-fulfilling prophecy."

■ Works Cited

Asimov, Isaac, review of *Profiles of the Future*, *New York Times Book Review,* April 14, 1963, pp. 22, 24.

Benford, Gregory, review of *Profiles of the Future* (revised edition), *Washington Post Book World,* March 25, 1984, p. 6.

Bishop, Michael, review of *2010*, *Washington Post Book World,* December 26, 1982, p. 6.

Brin, David, review of *2061*, *Los Angeles Times,* December 1, 1982.

Ciment, Michael, in *Focus on the Science Fiction Film,* edited by William Johnson, Prentice Hall, 1972.

Clareson, Thomas D., editor, *Voices for the Future: Essays on Major Science Fiction Writers,* Bowling Green University Press, 1976.

Clarke, Arthur C., *2001: A Space Odyssey*, New American Library, 1968, published with new afterword, 1982.

Clarke, Arthur C., *The View from Serendip*, Random House, 1977.

Clarke, Arthur C., *New York Times Book Review,* March 6, 1983.

Clarke, Arthur C., *Ascent to Orbit, a Technical Autobiography: The Technical Writings of Arthur C. Clarke,* Wiley, 1984.

Clarke, Arthur C., *Astounding Days: A Science Fictional Autobiography,* Gollancz, 1989

Cowen, R. C., review of *Profiles of the Future*, *Christian Science Monitor,* February 26, 1963.

DeWeese, Gene, review of *2010*, *Science Fiction Review,* February, 1983.

Disch, Thomas M., review of *Rendezvous with Rama*, *Times Literary Supplement,* June 16, 1978, p. 662.

Emme, Eugene M., review of *Exploration of Space*, *Science*, August 30, 1968, pp. 874-875.

Foote, Bud, review of *2010*, *Detroit News,* November 28, 1982.

Fremont-Smith, Eliot, review of *2001*, *New York Times,* July 5, 1968.

Geis, Richard E., *Science Fiction Review,* summer, 1986.

Gibbons, Roy, *Chicago Sunday Tribune,* July 13, 1952.

Granahan, Paul, review of *Fountains of Paradise*, *Best Sellers,* May, 1979.

Greenland, Colin, review of *2010*, *Times Literary Supplement,* January 21, 1983.

Hollow, John, *Against the Night, the Stars: The Science Fiction of Arthur C. Clarke*, Harcourt, 1983, expanded edition, Ohio University Press, 1987.

Huntington, John, *Arthur C. Clarke*, Starmont House, 1979.

Jonas, Gerald, *New York Times Book Review,* October 30, 1977, p. 12.

Jonas, Gerald, review of *Fountains of Paradise*, *New York Times Book Review,* March 18, 1979, pp. 13, 25.

Jonas, Gerald, review of *2010*, *New York Times Book Review,* January 23, 1983, p. 24.

Jonas, Gerald, review of *2061*, *New York Times Book Review,* December 20, 1987, p. 18.

Korn, Eric, review of *3001*, *Economist*, April 12, 1997, p. 85.

LaFaille, Gene, review of *Astounding Days*, *Wilson Library Bulletin*, March, 1990.

Ley, Willy, review of *The Exploration of Space*, *New York Times Book Review,* August 25, 1968, p. 10.

Maddox, Brenda, review of *2001*, *New Statesman,* December 20, 1968.

Moran, Dan K., review of *Songs of the Distant Earth*, *West Coast Review of Books*, Number 1, 1986.

Myers, Tim, review of *Fountains of Paradise*, *New Republic,* March 24, 1979.

Neeper, Cary, review of *2010*, *Christian Science Monitor,* December 3, 1982, p. B3.

Olander, Joseph D., and Martin H. Greenburg, editors, *Arthur C. Clarke*, Taplinger, 1977.

Ownbey, Steve, review of *Imperial Earth*, *National Review,* May 14, 1976.

Paulos, John Allen, review of *3001*, *New York Times Book Review,* March 9, 1997.

Platt, Charles, *Dream Makers: The Uncommon Men and Women Who Write Science Fiction*, Volume II, Berkeley Publishing, 1983.

Rabkin, Eric S., *Arthur C. Clarke*, Starmont House, 1979.

Review of *Rendezvous with Rama*, *Virginia Quarterly*, winter 1974.

Review of *Richter 10*, *Booklist*, January 1-15, 1997, p. 778.

Rose, Mark, review of *Imperial Earth*, *New Republic*, March 20, 1976.

Samuelson, David N., review of *Profiles of the Future* (revised edition), *Los Angeles Times Book Review*, March 4, 1984.

Stoler, Peter, review of *2010*, *Time*, November 15, 1982.

Sturgeon, Theodore, review of *Rendezvous With Rama*, *New York Times Book Review*, September 23, 1973.

Thorp, Katherine, review of *Astounding Days*, *Library Journal*, March 1, 1990, p. 98.

Turner, Alice K., "Arthur C. Clarke," *Publishers Weekly*, September 10, 1973, pp. 24-25.

Review of *2061: Odyssey Three*, *Kirkus Reviews*, November 1, 1987.

Review of *2061: Odyssey Three*, *Time*, January 11, 1988.

Watson, Ian, review of *3001*, *Times Literary Supplement*, March 21, 1997.

Wollheim, Donald A., *The Universe Makers*, Harper, 1971.

■ For More Information See

BOOKS

Agel, Jerome, editor, *The Making of Kubrick's 2001*, New American Library, 1970.

Aldiss, Brian W., *Trillion Year Spree: The History of Science Fiction*, Atheneum (New York City), 1986.

Bleiler, E. F., editor, *Science Fiction Writers: Critical Studies of the Major Authors from the Early Nineteenth Century to the Present Day*, Scribners (New York City), 1982.

Contemporary Literary Criticism, Gale (Detroit), Volume 1, 1973, Volume 4, 1975, Volume 13, 1980, Volume 18, 1981, Volume 35, 1985.

Ketterer, David, *New Worlds for Old: The Apocalyptic Imagination, Science Fiction, and American Literature*, Indiana University Press, 1974.

Knight, Damon, *In Search of Wonder: Essays on Modern Science Fiction*, Advent, 1967, pp. 177-205.

Magill, Frank N., editor, *Survey of Science Fiction Literature*, Volumes 1-5, Salem Press, 1979.

Malik, Rex, editor, *Future Imperfect*, Pinter, 1980.

McAleer, Neil, *Arthur C. Clarke: The Authorized Biography*, Contemporary Books, 1992.

Moskowitz, Sam, *Seekers of Tomorrow: Masters of Science Fiction*, World Publishing, 1966.

Of Time and Stars: The Worlds of Arthur C. Clarke, Gollancz, 1972, pp. 7-10.

Reid, Robin Anne, *Arthur C. Clarke: A Critical Companion*, Greenwood Press, 1997.

Samuelson, David N., *Arthur C. Clarke: A Primary and Secondary Bibliography*, G. K. Hall, 1984.

Short Story Criticism, Volume 3, Gale, 1989.

Slusser, George Edgar, *The Space Odysseys of Arthur C. Clarke*, Borgo, 1978.

PERIODICALS

Algol, November, 1974.

Atlantic, April, 1963, p. 152; July, 1952.

Best Sellers, May, 1984, pp. 75-76; December 24, 1953, p. 13.

Book World, June 30, 1968, pp. 1, 3; December 19, 1971, p. 6.

Chicago Tribune, December 30, 1990, section 14, p. 6.

Christian Science Monitor, February 10, 1972, p. 10; August 8, 1973, p. 9; November 26, 1993, p. 15.

Commonweal, May 3, 1968.

Discover, May, 1997, pp. 68-69.

Extrapolation, winter, 1980, pp. 348-60; summer, 1987, pp. 105-29; spring, 1989, pp. 53-69.

Kirkus Reviews, November 1, 1987.

Library Journal, February 15, 1997, p. 164.

Locus, February, 1994, p. 75; November, 1993, p. 27.

Los Angeles Times, January 29, 1996.

Los Angeles Times Book Review, December 19, 1982; December 6, 1987; December 9, 1990, p. 10; February 3, 1991, p. 10; January 24, 1992, p. 1; August 8, 1993, p. 11; March 10, 1996.

Magazine of Fantasy and Science Fiction, September, 1979, pp. 25-26.

Nation, March 5, 1983.

National Review, November 20, 1962, pp. 403-4.

New Republic, May 4, 1968.

New Scientist, April 12, 1997, p. 44.

New Statesman, January 26, 1979.

Newsday, April 4, 1968; April 20, 1968.

Newsweek, October 30, 1961.

New Yorker, April 24, 1965; May 27, 1967; April 13, 1968; September 21, 1968; August 9, 1969, pp. 40-65; December 13, 1982; December 20, 1982.

New York Herald Tribune Book Review, July 13, 1952; August 10, 1952; August 23, 1953; March 2, 1958, p. 6.

New York Times, May 29, 1968; August 22, 1973, p. 35; December 4, 1984; February 26, 1985; April 7, 1993, p. C13, C19; November 28, 1994, p. A4; April 1, 1997; April 11, 1997.

New York Times Book Review, March 14, 1954; July 15, 1956, p. 20; January 18, 1976; May 11, 1986; May 6, 1990, p. 22; July 8, 1990, p. 22; February 3, 1991, p. 33; September 1, 1991, p. 13; June 13, 1993, p. 22; March 13, 1994, p. 30; January 28, 1996.

New York Times Magazine, March 6, 1966.

Omni, March, 1979.

People Weekly, December 20, 1982.

Playboy, July, 1986.

Publishers Weekly, June 14, 1976; January 6, 1984, p. 75; January 27, 1984, p. 72; January 22, 1996, p. 61.

Reader's Digest, April, 1969.

Saturday Review, July 5, 1952; April 20, 1968.

Science, August 30, 1968, pp. 874-875.

Science Fiction Review, March/April, 1979; August, 1981; May, 1984; fall, 1984, p. 26.

Science-Fiction Studies, July, 1979, pp. 230-31; November, 1997, pp. 441-58.

Time, July 19, 1968.

Times (London), November 25, 1982.

Times Literary Supplement, July 15, 1968; January 2, 1969; December 5, 1975; October 31, 1986.

Voice Literary Supplement, November, 1982, pp. 8-9.

Washington Post, February 16, 1982; November 16, 1982.

Washington Post Book World, November 25, 1990, p. 8; March 9, 1992, p. B1.

Western Folklore, Number 28, 1969, pp. 230-37.

World Press Review, April, 1985.*

A. C. Crispin

Personal

Born April 5, 1950, in Stamford, CT; daughter of George Arthur (a maritime management specialist) and Hope (a kindergarten teacher; maiden name, Hooker) Tickell; married Randy Lee Crispin (a pharmacist), May 9, 1973 (divorced); lives with significant other, Michael Capobianco; children: Jason Paul. *Education:* University of Maryland, B.A. (English literature), 1972. *Politics:* Democrat. *Religion:* "Universal."

Addresses

Home—Charles County, MD. *Agent*—Merrilee Heifetz, Writers House, Inc., 21 West 26th St., New York, NY 10010.

Career

Worked variously as a customer service representative, receptionist, technical librarian, and typist, 1972-74; U.S. Bureau of the Census, Suitland, MD, computer programmer, training specialist, and technical writer, 1974-83; writer, 1983—. Has taught writing workshops at Charles County Community College, Harrisburg Area Community College, Towson State University, and at many science-fiction and "Star Trek" conventions. Also worked as a horseback riding instructor, horse trainer, writing instructor, and swimming instructor. Steward of local union of American Federation of Government Employees. *Member:* Science Fiction Writers of America (Eastern Regional Director, 1990—; vice president, 1999—).

Awards, Honors

Best Books for Young Adults citation, American Library Association Young Adult Services Division, for *StarBridge* and *Silent Songs;* Best Books for the Teen Age citation, New York Public Library, for *Serpent's Gift.*

Writings

FANTASY NOVELS

(With Andre Norton) *Gryphon's Eyrie,* Tor Books, 1984.
(With Andre Norton) *Songsmith,* Tor Books, 1992.

"STAR TREK" SERIES

Yesterday's Son, Pocket Books, 1983.
Time for Yesterday, Pocket Books, 1988.
The Eyes of the Beholders, Pocket Books, 1990.
Sarek, Pocket Books, 1994.

"V" SERIES

V, Pinnacle Books, 1984.

(With Howard Weinstein) *V: East Coast Crisis*, Pinnacle Books, 1984.

(With Deborah A. Marshall) *V: Death Tide*, Pinnacle Books, 1985.

"STARBRIDGE" SERIES

StarBridge, Ace Books, 1989.

(With Kathleen O'Malley) *Silent Dances*, Ace Books, 1990.

(With Jannean Elliott) *Shadow World*, Ace Books, 1991.

(With Deborah A. Marshall) *Serpent's Gift*, Ace Books, 1992.

(With Kathleen O'Malley) *Silent Songs*, Ace Books, 1994.

(With T. Jackson King) *Ancestor's World*, Ace Books, 1996.

(With Ru Emerson) *Voices of Chaos*, Ace Books, 1997.

STAR WARS: THE "HAN SOLO" TRILOGY

The Paradise Snare, Bantam, 1997.

The Hutt Gambit, Bantam, 1998.

Rebel Dawn, Bantam, 1998.

OTHER

Sylvester (movie novelization), Tor Books, 1985.

(With Kathleen O'Malley) *Alien Resurrection* (movie novelization), Warner Books, 1997.

Also contributor to anthologies, including *Magic in Ithkar*, edited by Robert Adams and Andre Norton, Volume 3, Tor Books, 1986; *Tales of the Witch World*, edited by Andre Norton, Tor Books, Volume 1, 1987, Volume 3, 1990; *Tales from the Mos Eisley Cantina*, Bantam, 1995; and *Tales from Jabba the Hutt's Palace*, Bantam, 1996.

■ Adaptations

Some of Crispin's novels have been released on audio cassette, including *Yesterday's Son*, 1988, *Time for Yesterday*, 1989, and *Sarek*.

■ Sidelights

A. C. Crispin is the author of a number of science fiction novels, including several additions to prominent series such as "V" and "Star Trek."

Crispin also created her own series in 1989, "StarBridge," which "centers around a school for young diplomats, translators, and explorers, both alien and human, located on an asteroid far from Earth," according to the author. As Crispin once explained, "In my science fiction I enjoy the theme of 'first contact' between humans and aliens. Communication is vital in this universe. In one way or another, all my books are about communication."

Crispin's first book, *Yesterday's Son*, features characters from the original *Star Trek* television series. In this story, Mr. Spock learns that he has a son and then embarks on a mission to save him. A reviewer for *Library Journal* called the book "en-

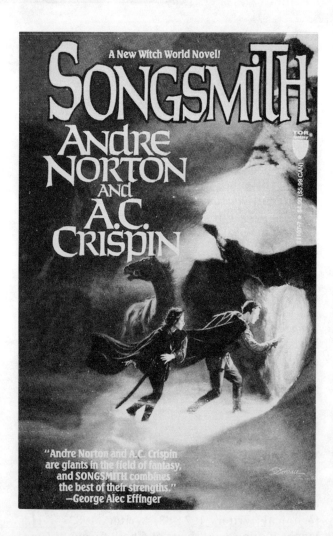

Written with Andre Norton, this 1992 fantasy novel set in the Witch World created by Norton, was one of two books that gave Crispin a chance to work with one of her favorite authors.

joyable reading," adding that Crispin "handles Vulcan psychology very well." *Sarek*, published in 1994, focuses on Spock's father, Ambassador Sarek. Sarek must decide whether to accept a dangerous mission to the Klingon Empire or keep a vigil at the deathbed of his human wife, Amanda. At stake is the future of the Federation. A *Publishers Weekly* review noted that Crispin "packed everything a die-hard Trekkie could want" into the book, which "should be roundly loved by its target audience." *Sarek* appeared on the *New York Times* hardcover best-seller list for five weeks.

Characters from television's *Star Trek: The Next Generation* take center stage in Crispin's 1990 book, *The Eyes of the Beholders*. In this story, the *Enterprise* crew is locked in a tractorbeam by a mysterious alien artifact. All the members of the crew—with the exception of the android Data—gradually become lost in private dream worlds, and Data becomes the only one who can prevent the artifact from adding the *Enterprise* to its "graveyard" of ships. Writing in *Wilson Library Bulletin*, Alan P. Mahony claimed that Crispin "brings some warmth" to the characters, though Christy Boyd of *Voice of Youth Advocates* called the book "a little stereotypical and not terribly interesting."

The "Starbridge" Series

The five books in Crispin's "StarBridge" series revolve around a futuristic school that teaches its students the skills needed to explore other worlds and promote positive relationships between different cultures. The students at StarBridge Academy include representatives of all intelligent species in the universe—ranging from giant fungi to humans—who study science and diplomacy together. The first book in the series, *StarBridge*, is told from the perspective of sixteen-year-old Mahree Burroughs. Mahree is aboard a spaceship headed for Earth when the crew receives a weak transmission that leads them to discover an unknown race, the Simiu. Mahree is able to learn the Simiu language and make friends with them, but before long a series of conflicts between the two cultures erupts into a major crisis. Mahree and two friends then must escape to the Cooperative League of Systems to get help in resolving the situation. In a review for *Booklist*, Candace Smith praised the book's "strong theme of understanding and acceptance among races."

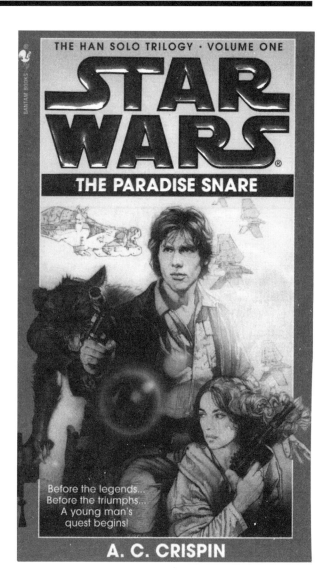

Crispin added to the Star Wars mythology with her Han Solo books, including this first book in the series, which chronicles the childhood and adolescence of the future Rebel Alliance hero.

The second book in the series, *Silent Dances*, expands this theme to include people with disabilities. Tesa, a deaf mediator, could undergo a procedure that would enable her to hear, but instead she proves that her deafness is not a handicap. *Shadow World*, the third book in the series, focuses on Mark Kenner, whose doubts about his abilities as a mediator have convinced him to resign from the academy. Instead, he embarks on a last dangerous mission to help an alien race. The Elspind's problem is that their life span has been decreasing, so that now they only live about sixteen

If you enjoy the works of A. C. Crispin, you may also want to check out the following books and films:

Joan D. Vinge, *Psion*, 1982.
Anne McCaffrey, *Crystal Singer*, 1982.
Larry Niven and Jerry Pournelle, *Footfall*, 1985.
Star Wars, a film directed by George Lucas, 1977.

years. Scientists thought they had discovered a solution, but a civil war on Elseemar, the Elspind home world, caused the experiments to be destroyed. After his ship is captured by terrorists, Mark must help negotiate a truce. In the meantime, he learns that the Elspind have come to regard death very differently than humans.

Serpent's Gift, the fourth book in the series, follows the adventures of Heather Farley, an eleven-year-old girl whose telepathic powers allow her to communicate with the school's computer system. When a series of near-disasters causes school officials to suspect computer sabotage, Heather must solve the mystery in order to avoid being blamed herself. In a review for *Booklist*, Candace Smith stated that the book "combines well-rounded, likeable characters; touches of romance; the strong but subtle theme of mutual cultural respect," and interesting technological twists. *Serpent's Gift* was recognized by the New York Public Library on its annual list of Best Books for the Teen Age.

Collaborates with Andre Norton

To Crispin, one of the benefits of becoming a science-fiction novelist was having the opportunity to meet and collaborate with author Andre Norton. Crispin once referred to Norton as "one of my favorite writers, and, as one of the first women to 'break into' the male-dominated science fiction field, she has also been a personal hero and an inspiration to me." Crispin worked with Norton to produce *Gryphon's Eyrie* in 1984 and *Songsmith* in 1992. "I get many ideas from visual images: mismatched words, pictures, and, often, dreams," Crispin once explained. "*Gryphon's Eyrie*

came about from a dream I had about Norton's characters in *The Crystal Gryphon* and *Gryphon in Glory.*" Despite the variety of her work, Crispin claimed that it has one recurring theme: "be yourself—but don't stop trying to be a better person."

Crispin returned to the "StarBridge" series with a fifth book, written with Kathleen O'Malley, in 1994; *Silent Songs* was followed by the 1996 title *Ancestor's World*, co-authored with T. Jackson King. Next, Crispin and Ru Emerson collaborated on a seventh, *Voices of Chaos*, in 1997. Set once again among the students of the StarBridge Academy, the plot centers around the potential conflict brought about by the Arrekhi, a race with feline characteristics. The Arrekhi have formally requested to be admitted into the Cooperative League, but in the application process committed a few lies of omission about their more warlike attributes. Potential for conflict flares when the Arrekhi prince at the Academy, Khyriz, falls in love with Magdalena, a dancer, and wants to bring her to his homeland. "Crispin's worlds continue to grow in complexity and interest, imaginatively 'peopled' with unique characters and events," opined Mary Arnold in a review of the work for *Voice of Youth Advocates*.

Pens Tales about Han Solo

In 1997 Crispin enjoyed further success with a trilogy of science-fiction books that serve as a prequel to the first *Star Wars* movie; her "Han Solo" series fleshes out the hitherto-unknown early life of the hero and adventurer. This series begins with *The Paradise Snare*, whose plot chronicles Solo's parentage, childhood, and adolescence. Raised by a smuggler, Solo's ambition is to enter the Imperial Naval Academy, but his encounter with a strange cult run by the Hutts brings trouble. He is forced to eliminate a dangerous Hutt overlord, and his rescue of a slave woman from the Hutt camp puts a price on his head. The second book in the series, *The Hutt Gambit*, finds Solo on the run from the Imperial Navy. Here he befriends Chewbacca, and both fear the deadly bounty hunter Boba Fett, hired by the Hutts to hunt for Solo.

Crispin's third "Han Solo" book was 1998's *Rebel Dawn*. The maturing Solo is now an acclaimed pilot who wins the Millennium Falcon race and sets a speed record. His dissatisfaction with the new Rebel Alliance sets the stage for the beginning of the actual *Star Wars* story. The book ends as Solo is about to sign on with Luke Skywalker and Ben Kenobi to take a job as their pilot in an important mission. Hugh M. Flick, writing in *Kliatt,* called the three books "an exciting and interesting part of the *Star Wars* saga."

■ Works Cited

Arnold, Mary, review of *Voices of Chaos, Voice of Youth Advocates,* June, 1998, p. 128.

Boyd, Christy, review of *The Eyes of the Beholders, Voice of Youth Advocates,* February, 1991, pp. 361-62.

Flick, Hugh M., review of *Rebel Dawn, Kliatt,* July, 1998, p. 18.

Mahony, Alan P., "Live Long and Prosper," *Wilson Library Bulletin,* January, 1994, p. 136.

Review of *Sarek, Publishers Weekly,* January 17, 1994, p. 416.

Smith, Candace, review of *StarBridge, Booklist,* September 1, 1989, pp. 41-42.

Smith, Candace, review of *Serpent's Gift, Booklist,* April 15, 1992, p. 1509.

Review of *Yesterday's Son, Library Journal,* August, 1983, p. 1507.

■ For More Information See

PERIODICALS

Booklist, December 1, 1990, p. 720; April 15, 1992, p. 1509; March 1, 1998, p. 1098.

Chattanooga News-Free Press, September 11, 1983.

Chicago Tribune, February 18, 1994.

Kirkus Reviews, February 1, 1994, p. 102.

Kliatt, July, 1997, p. 12.

Library Journal, August, 1991, p. 180; April 15, 1997, p. 123.

Locus, October, 1989; June, 1990; January, 1991, p. 63.

Publishers Weekly, August 18, 1989, p. 56.

Voice of Youth Advocates, October, 1984, p. 205; August, 1985, p. 183; June, 1991, p. 106; August, 1992, p. 172; August, 1994, p. 154.*

Lyll Becerra de Jenkins

Personal

Born November 14, 1925, in San Gil, Colombia; died May 7, 1997, in Fripp Island, SC; daughter of Luis Becerra Lopez and Teresa Breton de Becerra; married John Jenkins; children: Francesca, Marcela, Alexandra Jenkins Reed, John Jr., William. *Religion:* Catholic.

Addresses

Agent—c/o Rosemary Brosnan, Executive Editor, Morrow Junior Books, 1350 Avenue of the Americas, New York, NY 10019.

Career

Writer; served 14 years as adjunct professor of English at Fairfield University, Fairfield, CT.

Awards, Honors

Scott O'Dell Award for Historical Fiction, Scott O'Dell Foundation, 1988, for *The Honorable Prison.*

Writings

The Honorable Prison, Dutton/Lodestar, 1988.
Celebrating the Hero, Dutton/Lodestar, 1993.
So Loud a Silence, Dutton/Lodestar, 1996.

Also author of short stories appearing in periodicals, including *New Yorker, New York Times,* and *Boston Globe.*

Sidelights

A novelist and professor, Lyll Becerra de Jenkins skillfully intertwined the personal with the political in both her life and her life's work. As an author of short stories and novels for young adults, de Jenkins wanted "to awaken a political conscience in young people," as she once told *Publishers Weekly.* Contributing to de Jenkins' own political awareness was her father—a politically outspoken judge and journalist in his native country of Colombia.

Growing up in Colombia, de Jenkins had not understood the political battles that her father fought with such graveness. Her move to the United States, however, clarified de Jenkins' memories of her father's activism. The relocation, after thirty-seven years in Colombia, provided de Jenkins with distance and room to be critical, allowing the writer to recognize that her political beliefs conflicted with those of the Colombian oli-

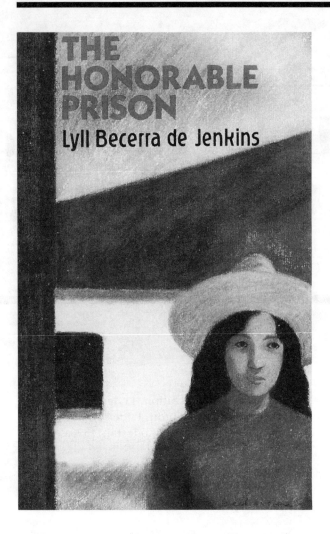

Winner of the prestigious Scott O'Dell Award, de Jenkins's debut historical novel for young adults is about a young girl who is imprisoned in a house in Columbia because of her father's editorials against the country's dictator.

garchy. In a *Booklist* interview with her editor, Rosemary Brosnan, de Jenkins commented on the impact that living in the United States had had on her writing: "I not only think that I would write differently, but I probably would never have written at all. It is precisely being in this country . . . see[ing] the contrasts between the U.S. and Colombia. . . . I understood with a new perspective the meaning of injustice and the meaning of political abuse—particularly the abuse of power." Her learned passion for politics, a respect for human rights, and love of the English language took de Jenkins on a journey from a girl who told exaggerated and theatrical true stories to a writer of political fiction based on personal truth.

Examines Life in Columbia

De Jenkins' writing career began with short stories. One of these stories, published in the *New Yorker*, evolved into the first of her three novels, *The Honorable Prison*, for which she received the Scott O'Dell Award for Historical Fiction. All three of de Jenkins' young adult books—*The Honorable Prison, Celebrating the Hero,* and *So Loud a Silence*—address issues of Colombian politics and social injustice; just as the author told Brosnan that she grew to see "with clarity the true colors and the true dimensions of the Colombian political situation," so, too, do her main characters.

It is perhaps Marta Maldonado, protagonist of *The Honorable Prison,* who is most like the author herself. Marta, the teenaged daughter of a journalist who uses his editorials to attack the military dictator of his South American homeland, is imprisoned in the mountains with her family and kept under military surveillance. Many external dangers threaten Marta and her family, including the military, the elements, illness, and starvation. Internally, Marta struggles to gain strength, freedom, and independence. At times, she must examine the conflict between her own desires and those of her family. Decisions are difficult—is friendship with a handsome young teacher daring and defiant, or life-threatening? Turmoil and despair thunder over the entire country, but when the political storm dies down, the government is overthrown, and, wrote a *Publishers Weekly* reviewer, "Marta has grown from a protected girl into a politically astute and sensitive young woman." *Horn Book* reviewer Mary M. Burns called the characters of *The Honorable Prison* "unique and unforgettable," noting that "the book achieves its stunning effects not through sensationalism but through control." Recognizing this controlled quality, Gerry Larson remarked in *School Library Journal* that the "understated narrative gives dramatic emphasis" to a "vivid and troubling portrayal of the ongoing struggle for human rights."

Celebrating the Hero, de Jenkins' second novel, also has as its protagonist an increasingly self-aware young woman. Camila Draper, a seventeen-year-old from Connecticut, is invited to a small town in Colombia for the unveiling of a memorial dedicated to the town's benefactor—her grandfather. Her mother having recently died, Camila accepts the invitation in order to learn all she can about her maternal grandparents. Camila's journey to

If you enjoy the works of Lyll Becerra de Jenkins, you may also want to check out the following books and films:

James Berry, *A Thief in the Village and Other Stories of Jamaica,* 1988.
Frances Temple, *Taste of Salt: A Story of Modern Haiti,* 1992, and *Grab Hands and Run,* 1993.
The Killing Fields, an Academy Award-winning film, 1984.

unveil the truth about the ominous shadows of her grandfather's past—the truth she had not dared to ask her mother—begins. Exposed over the course of Camila's journey are her grandfather's secrets, her feelings of alienation from both of her homelands, and her awareness of oppression. "With sudden insight," wrote *New York Times Book Review* critic Caitlin Francke, "Camila comes to a more profound understanding not only of herself and her two worlds, but also of the bittersweet nature of forgiveness." Francke suggests that de Jenkins's "eloquent contribution to . . . literature dealing with issues of dislocation and displacement" would be "especially affecting for first-generation American teen-agers searching for their identity." *Kliatt* reviewer Barbara Shepp, who particularly enjoyed the way de Jenkins "captures beautifully the details of how a Latin American town can feel, look, smell, sound and taste," praised *Celebrating the Hero* as a "sophisticated book . . . recommended for all its features, but especially for this atmospheric aspect."

■ Works Cited

Brosnan, Rosemary, "The Booklist Interview: Lyll Becerra de Jenkins," *Booklist,* September 1, 1997, pp. 10-11.
Burns, Mary M., review of *The Honorable Prison, Horn Book,* July/August, 1988, pp. 501-2.
"Flying Starts: New Faces of 1988," *Publishers Weekly,* December 23, 1988, pp. 29-30.
Francke, Caitlin, review of *Celebrating the Hero, New York Times Book Review,* January 2, 1994, p. 16.
Review of *The Honorable Prison, Publishers Weekly,* December 11, 1987, p. 67.
Larson, Gerry, review of *The Honorable Prison, School Library Journal,* February, 1988, p. 84.
Shepp, Barbara, review of *Celebrating the Hero, Kliatt,* March, 1996, p. 8.

■ For More Information See

PERIODICALS

Bulletin of the Center for Children's Books, January, 1997, p. 175.
Kirkus Reviews, August 15, 1996, p. 1236.
Voice of Youth Advocates, February, 1997, p. 328.*

Charles de Lint

■ Personal

Born December 22, 1951, in Bussum, Netherlands; immigrated to Canada, 1952, naturalized citizen, 1961; son of Frederick Charles (a navigator and survey project manager) Hoefsmit and Gerardina Margaretha (a high school teacher) Hoefsmit-de Lint; married MaryAnn Harris (an artist), September 15, 1980. *Education:* Attended Aylmer and Philemen Wright high schools. *Hobbies and other interests:* Music, fine arts.

■ Addresses

Home—Ottawa, Ontario, Canada. *Office*—P.O. Box 9480, Ottawa, Ontario, Canada K1G 3V2. *E-mail*—cdl@cyberus.ca.

■ Career

Worked in various clerical and construction positions, 1967-71, and as retail clerk and manager of record stores, 1971-83; writer in Ottawa, Ontario, 1983—. Owner and editor of Triskell Press; juror for William L. Crawford Award, Canadian SF/Fantasy Award, World Fantasy Award, Theodore Sturgeon Memorial Short Fiction Award, Horror Writers of America Award, and Nebula Short Fiction Award; member of Wickentree, a traditional Celtic folk music band in Ottawa, 1972-85, and Jump at the Sun, a Celtic/Americana folk band in Ottawa. *Member:* Science Fiction Writers of America, SF Canada.

■ Awards, Honors

William L. Crawford Award for best new fantasy author from International Association for the Fantastic in the Arts, 1984; Canadian SF/Fantasy Award ("Casper") nominations, 1986, for *Mulengro,* and 1987, for *Yarrow;* Casper Award for best work in English, 1988, for *Jack the Giant-Killer;* Readercon Small Press Award for Best Short Work, 1989, for short story, "The Drowned Man's Reel"; Reality I Commendations, Best Fantasy Author Award, 1991; New York Public Library's Best Books for the Teen Age list, and CompuServe Science Fiction and Fantasy Forum Homer Award for Best Fantasy Novel, both 1992, for *The Little Country;* Prix Ozone for Best Foreign Fantasy Short Story, 1997, for "Timeskip"; Young Adult Library Services Association of the American Library Association, Best Books for Young Adults, 1998, for *Trader.*

■ Writings

FICTION

"The Fane of the Grey Rose" (novelette), published in *Swords Against Darkness IV,* edited by Andrew J. Offutt, Zebra, 1979.

De Grijze Roos (title means "The Grey Rose"; short stories), Een Exa Uitgave, 1983.

The Riddle of the Wren, Ace Books, 1984.

Moonheart: A Romance, Ace Books, 1984.

The Harp of the Grey Rose, Starblaze, 1985.

Mulengro: A Romany Tale, Ace Books, 1985.

Yarrow: An Autumn Tale, Ace Books, 1986.

"Stick" (novella), published in *Borderland*, edited by Terri Windling and Mark Arnold, Signet, 1986.

Ascian in Rose (novella), Axolotl Press, 1987.

Jack the Giant-Killer: A Novel of Urban Faerie, Armadillo-Ace, 1987.

Greenmantle, Ace Books, 1988.

Wolf Moon, New American Library, 1988.

Westlin Wind (novella), Axolotl Press, 1988, Tor, 1993.

(Contributor) *The Annual Review of Fantasy and Science Fiction*, Meckler Publishing, 1988.

Philip Jose Farmer's The Dungeon: Book Three, Byron Preiss/Bantam, 1988.

Philip Jose Farmer's The Dungeon: Book Five, Byron Preiss/Bantam, 1988.

Svaha, Ace Books, 1989, Tor, 1994.

"Berlin" (novella), Fourth Avenue Press, 1989, reprinted in *Life on the Border*, Tor, 1991.

"The Fair in Emain Macha" (novella), *Tor SF Double #19*, Tor, 1990.

Drink Down the Moon: A Novel of Urban Faerie, Ace, 1990, Tor, 1995.

The Dreaming Place, illustrated by Brian Froud, Atheneum, 1990.

Ghostwood, illustration by Donna Gordon, Axolotl Press, 1990.

Paperjack (novella), illustrated by Judy J. King, Cheap Street, 1991.

Ghosts of Wind and Shadow (novella), Axolotl Press, 1991.

The Little Country, Morrow, 1991, Tor, 1993.

(With others) *Death Leaves an Echo* (novella) in *Cafe Purgatorium*, Tor Horror, 1991.

Spiritwalk, Tor, 1992.

Into the Green, Tor, 1993.

Dreams Underfoot: The Newford Collection, Tor, 1993.

The Wild Wood, Bantam Books , 1994.

Memory and Dream, Tor, 1994.

The Ivory and the Horn, Tor, 1995.

Jack of Kinrowan, Tor, 1995.

Trader, Tor, 1997.

Someplace to Be Flying, Tor, 1998.

Moonlight and Vines, Tor, 1999.

The Newford Stories, SF Book Club, 1999.

Forests of the Heart, Tor, in press.

FICTION, AS SAMUEL M. KEY

Angel of Darkness, Jove, 1990.

From a Whisper to a Scream, Berkley, 1992.

I'll Be Watching You, Jove, 1994.

Also author of poetry. Work represented in anthologies, including *The Year's Best Fantasy Stories:* 8, edited by Arthur W. Saha, DAW, 1982; *Dragons and Dreams* and *Spaceships and Spells,* both edited by Jane Yolen, Martin H. Greenberg, and Charles G. Waugh, Harper, 1986 and 1987. Author of columns in horror and science fiction magazines, including a monthly book review column in the *Magazine of Fantasy and Science Fiction;* "Urban Thrills: Reviews of Short Horror and Contemporary Fantasy Fiction," in *Short Form*, "Behind the Darkness: Profiles of the Writers of Horror Fiction, " in *Horrorstruck*, "Scattered Gold," in *OtherRealms*, and "Night Journeys," in *Mystery Scene*, and "The Eclectic Muse," in *Pulphouse*. Contributor to periodicals, including *Isaac Asimov's Science Fiction Magazine*.

■ Adaptations

"The Sacred Fire" from *Dreams Underfoot* is being filmed for an episode of *The Hunger* for the Showtime channel.

■ Work in Progress

A Newford novel, for Tor; short stories for various publications.

■ Sidelights

Canadian Charles de Lint is a pioneer of modern fantasy, melding Faerie with the inner city. No fey, upland greenery for him; no cavorting elves or fire-breathing dragons. De Lint blends a potent brew of contemporary realism, characters that live and breathe right off the page, fast-paced plotting, and thought-provoking messages that has captured a wide and loyal readership as well as critical raves. Gary Westfahl, in a *Los Angeles Times Book Review* piece on de Lint's *The Little Country*, warns the reader off easy assumptions vis-à-vis fantasy: "In a genre choking to death on regurgitated Tolkien, de Lint does research and imbues his story with an unusual, authentic atmosphere." Westfahl continued, "In a genre of elaborately mapped Neverlands," de Lint's tales take place in a "contemporary world" that is "no less magical." No Neverland for de Lint, but he has created an intricately mapped region of his own, described in the Newford books; not dew-filled nature, but an urban environment peopled by folks like us, and others not quite like us—crow people, shape-changers, tricksters and grifters gussied up in fantastical finery.

"If . . . Charles de Lint didn't create the contemporary fantasy," announced Tanya Huff in *Quill and Quire*, "he certainly defined it. . . . Unlike most fantasy writers who deal with battles between ultimate good and evil, de Lint concentrates on smaller, very personal conflicts." This may be the reason he appeals to all types of readers, both devoted fans and other audiences. Descriptives like "master of the genre" and "gifted storyteller" pepper reviews of de Lint's work, but de Lint himself is low-key about his achievements. In an interview with *Authors and Artists for Young Adults,* he described himself simply as a "writer of mythic fiction. It's basically mainstream writing, but with elements of myth and folktale. Not the more usual secondary-world fantasy. Some reviewers have described me as a writer who creates fantasy for people who don't normally read fantasy."

From his first publication in 1979, the novelette "The Fane of the Grey Rose," through the 1999 publication of his Newford collection of short stories, *Moonlight and Vines,* de Lint has proven himself to be a versatile and most prolific author, with over 40 books to his credit and an arm's-length list of awards and honors to his credit, including a Canadian SF/Fantasy Award, the Prix Ozone from France, and a YALSA for Best Book in 1998. Apart from a few early books in the standard high fantasy format, de Lint's output has been mainly in urban fantasy or mythic fiction, bringing quotidian magic to the streets of contemporary North America. Folk tale and myth—local variants of same, including Amerindian and Celtic (from that group of early settlers to Canada)—inform his novels and short stories, forming a bass line for a higher melody line that often includes themes of music (de Lint himself is a musician) and artists and other creative people as bridges to a deeper insight into the world. Many of de Lint's tales are set in his freshly minted city of Newford: the novels such as *Someplace to Be Flying, Trader,* and *Memory and Dream,* and the interconnected short story collections *Dreams Underfoot, The Ivory and the Horn,* and *Moonlight and Vines.* De Lint is also known for such titles as the cult classic *Moonheart,* as well as for *Yarrow* and *The Little Country,* books that, as de Lint puts it, "convey a sort of everyday magic, that show the inexplicable connectedness we sometimes experience with places, people, works of art. I believe in

these sorts of daily magic that most of us overlook in the hurried pace of modern urban life. We take these magics for granted, such as the bonds of friendship that connect us with other people and places. We have words for magic and explain it away: synchronicity, coincidence, déjà vu. But it's magic nonetheless. That's really what I'm attempting to do with my books, to show simple magics in everyday life. To make us remember, observe, see the world again."

Coming of Age in Canada

Born in Bussum, Netherlands, on December 22, 1951, de Lint immigrated with his family to Canada when he was four months old. His father worked with a surveying company, a job that took the family from Ontario to Western Canada to Quebec and on to Turkey and Lebanon until they finally settled near Ottawa. During these years of uprootedness, de Lint found stability in books, reading widely in myth and folklore. He lists Mallory, E. B. White, Tolkien, Dunsany, Lovecraft, William Morris, and Mervyn Peake among other authors whom he delighted in reading. But though he loved books, he never thought of becoming a writer. For the young de Lint, it was music that beckoned, and growing up he formed a love for Celtic music long before it became a fashionable address on the world beat map. Leaving high school two credits short of graduation, de Lint took a variety of jobs to support his music, primary among them working as a clerk at a record store.

"I don't advise my academic route to young kids," de Lint told *AAYA,* "but it is important that they know there are many paths you can take in this world. Now it is increasingly difficult to get ahead without an education, but I'm the sort who learns on his own. It is ironic though that now I do for a living all those things I hated doing in school. I loved to write back then, but not the prescribed compositions and book reports. Now I write columns and book reviews in several magazines. I hated history and geography; now I research all my novels thoroughly."

Increasingly, especially on his days off from the record store, de Lint began concentrating on fiction, writing fantasy short stories that a friend illustrated. Initially this was a pastime; when a writer saw those and recommended submission,

De Lint's groundbreaking 1984 novel was one of the earliest to combine fantasy with a modern, urban environment in a tale about an Ottawa mansion that is a battleground between good and evil.

avocation quickly turned to vocation. "I sold these first stories for the princely sum of $10.00 each and the proverbial light went on in my head," de Lint wrote on his Web site. "Here was something that I loved to do and people would actually pay me to do it." Over the next six or seven years de Lint continued to play gigs on the weekend and write stories that he submitted to small magazines. His first success with a larger market was publication of "The Fane of the Grey Rose" in a Zebra collection. De Lint later expanded this short story into the novel, *The Harp of the Grey Rose.*

Married in 1980 to Mary Ann Harris, de Lint continued clerking, playing music—in part with his

wife—and writing. When he lost his job at the record shop in 1983, his wife encouraged him to write full time. In the event, it was wise advice: de Lint sold three manuscripts that first year of full-time writing.

Toward a Mythic Fiction

One of these early books was *Riddle of the Wren,* a title that won de Lint much critical attention despite the fact that it plows the Tolkien furrow, as did his re-worked short story, *The Harp of the Grey Rose.* Writing in *Twentieth-Century Science Fiction Writers,* Maureen Speller commented that in these derivative novels "de Lint's fascination for the humbler creatures of folktale and legend, and for the darker side of magic, is also evident, and this mitigates against the more sentimental aspects. . . ." But with publication of *Moonheart,* de Lint was already moving away from the typical imaginary landscape of fantasy to an urban environment. Working on further advice from his wife, he decided to set his fantasy fiction in a realistic environment, opting for modern Ottawa, as it was the locale he knew best. With this novel de Lint began also his peculiar blending of Canadian mythologies, using traditions found in Native Indian shamanism and in Welsh Druidism. Called "a milestone of modern fantasy writing" by Speller, *Moonheart* also blends suspense, horror, and romance in the tale of an Ottawa mansion that proves to be linked to an old battle between good and evil. Tamson House is actually a gate between our world and a magical realm. De Lint's cast of characters ranges from a mage's apprentice, a reformed biker, and an Inspector for the Canadian Mounted Police, to the magical little people called manitous and legendary figures out of Welsh and Celtic myth.

Writing in *Voice of Youth Advocates,* David Snider called *Moonheart* "a fascinating and enthralling work that should be in every YA collection," while *Booklist*'s Roland Green commented that the book was "[a] very good and distinctly unconventional fantasy novel." De Lint had found his territory and his voice. "This was really my first successful blend of mythic fiction and fantasy," de Lint told *AAYA.* Over the next several years he wrote several more loosely linked novels and stories in the "Moonheart" series: *Ascian in Rose, Westlin Wind,* and *Ghostwood,* later collected in *Spiritwalk.* Reviewing that collection in *Quill and Quire,*

Michelle Sagara noted that de Lint explores not only the "brightness of magic," but also "its shadow," and that with his multi-layered characters thrown into the mix, "magic becomes choice and consequence, an echo of reality, not an escape from it." Sagara concluded that "there are very few fantasists today who write with such poetic simplicity and skill."

De Lint turned his fictional eye to Romany culture for *Mulengro*, a book that is a hybrid of horror and fantasy genres. Set among Canada's modern-day gypsy communities, the book tells the story of a series of bizarre murders that have police baffled. The gypsies, however, know that they are dealing with the mythic Mulengro, "He

CHARLES de LINT
A Modern Classic of Urban Myth and Magic
YARROW

"In de Lint's capable hands, modern fantasy becomes something other than escapism. It becomes folk song, the stuff of urban myth."
—The Phoenix Gazette

In this 1986 fantasy, Cat Midhir is a popular author whose stories, set in the Otherworld, are actually based on a real place.

Who Walks with Ghosts." It is up to a reclusive gypsy man and a young woman to get to the heart of this mythic threat and eliminate it. Gary Farber commented in *S.F. Chronicle* that *Mulengro* is "[s]uspenseful, original, and extremely well written." While some other critics did not find the novel to be as successful in blending magic with urban reality as was *Moonheart*, *Booklist*'s Green noted that de Lint "deserves high marks for his research, storytelling," and for his character descriptions.

Other early books in de Lint's development of his mythic fiction include *Yarrow* and *Jack the Giant Killer*. The former deals with a young fantasy writer whose work comes from her nightly dreamscape. But when her dreams are increasingly being stolen by a telepathic vampire-type creature, she loses the ability to create. Nancy Choice noted in *Voice of Youth Advocates* that "*Yarrow* is filled with suspense and tension from beginning to end." The protagonist of the novel, Cat, is one of a long line of appealing female characters de Lint has created, a "just plain nice person you would like to have living next door," according to Choice. *Jack the Giant Killer* continues this two-fold trend of strong female characters and a blend of urban setting with Faerie legend. Part of a series of modern retellings of fairy tales, the novel centers on Jacky Rowan, who develops magical powers through the domain of a red cap. She can see the giant in the city park and the elves in the oaks. Faerie has come to the city. And soon she learns that the good elves are dwindling in number, the bad ones prospering. The only way to stop this process is to set the princess free and recapture the Horn for the forces of good. Identifying with the elves as part of the Kinrowan clan, Jacky takes on the task with a little help from her friends, in a "very satisfying" tale, according to Tom Easton of *Analog Science Fiction/Science Fact*, who also dubbed de Lint "one of Canada's modern masters of fantasy." De Lint reprised Jacky in *Drink Down the Moon*, another blend of fairytale motifs and modern settings; both books were later published in the omnibus *Jack of Kinrowan*.

De Lint's intricately plotted and crafted novels are not the result of equally intricate plot outlines, but of a hit-and-miss organic approach to writing, as the author described it to *AAYA*. "I like to start out with a sense of theme—basic things like let's treat each other better, or do unto others, or be loyal and true to your friends, or we should pay attention to the world around us, to really see it for the magic it contains. Those are the sorts of messages I deal in. And I also like to have the sense of a few scenes in my head, and of course a few characters that I get to know in the process of writing about them. I don't like writing from an outline; it bores me and it too often makes the writing dead, without spontaneity. Of course this method can lead to dead ends. I sometimes get a hundred or two hundred pages into a novel and then discover that I took a wrong turn ten, twenty, maybe a hundred pages earlier. Then I have to throw it all out and start from where it stopped working."

De Lint once again combined Native American mythology with Celtic in his 1990 novel, *The Dreaming Place,* with illustrations by Brian Froud. Featuring teenage cousins, Nina and Ashley, and an emphasis on realism, this book "might . . . encourage some realistic fiction fans to give . . . fantasy a try," according to Kathryn Pierson in *Bulletin of the Center for Children's Books.*

De Lint's next novel, *The Little Country,* is one of his "most complex," as de Lint himself describes it. It is also one of his favorites, a story within a story and a loving exposition of de Lint's own affection for folk music. Set in modern Cornwall, the novel tells the story of Janey Little, a successful musician, who comes back to the village of Mousehole in England. Apart from her music, another major thing that has influenced her life are the writings of Billy Dunthorn, and she soon discovers an unpublished manuscript of Dunthorn's in the family attic. This manuscript tells the story of Jodi and her friend Denzil in the fictional village of Bodbury. As Janey gets further into the book, parallels develop between real life and that of the story in the found manuscript. Outside forces conspire in the form of John Madden of the Order of the Grey Dove who must have the magical Dunthorn manuscript, which can provide the possessor with ultimate power. The reader is soon swept along following two storylines that ultimately converge. As Peter Crowther noted in *St. James Guide to Fantasy Writers,* the book is filled with "charm, excitement, and above all, complete believability." According to Crowther, "it is [de Lint's] unerring knack of concentrating on his characters and filling them out, making them so real, that places his work at the forefront of the field." *Publishers Weekly* commented that de Lint's "rendering of the small Cornish town of

The land of Faerie is blended again with modern Ottawa in this story about a young woman who the elves believe to be a trickster hero come to save them from an evil power.

Mousehole and the life of a folk musician rings true."

The World of Newford

One of de Lint's most popular fictional conceits has been his creation of a fantasy world for an ensemble cast of characters. But true to de Lint form, this imaginary world is a compilation of urban settings, from London to Los Angeles. "The derivation of Newford was accidental," de Lint told *AAYA.* "It just grew over the course of several stories. I suddenly realized that I had created a new setting all my own with its own geography, commerce, and population. There are a lot of advantages to such a fictional place: I don't have to go out and do research to make sure I've got the right store on the right corner, for example. But Newford has its own headaches for me. It's getting so complex that I need a map and concordance to keep things straight. And I don't have those. It's all in my head."

The first collection of Newford tales, *Dreams Underfoot,* gathered stories published in magazines over several years, and began the building of the ensemble cast of characters that flow in and out of all the Newford stories. There is Jilly, the artist; Lorio, part gypsy and part punk; Lesli, who sets free the Faerie with her music; and a rich assortment of other urban types. One of the outstanding stories in *Dreams Underfoot,* "Timeskip," won France's Prix Ozone. Elizabeth Hand, in the *Washington Post Book World,* called this "a genuinely chilling ghost story as poignant as it is creepy." Further story collections in the Newford series include *The Ivory and the Horn,* a "fanciful and moving collection," according to *Publishers Weekly,* and *Moonlight and Vines,* stories which demonstrated de Lint to be, according to *Booklist*'s Green, "the most literate and ingenious purveyor of urban fantasy."

De Lint has also used his fictional Newford as the setting for four novels: *Memory and Dream, Trader, Someplace to Be Flying,* and *Forests of the Heart.* In the first of these, the painter, Isabelle, learns to paint amazing creatures that unleash ancient spirits into the modern world. "It is hard to imagine urban fantasy done better than it is by de Lint at his best," remarked *Booklist*'s Green. Jodi L. Israel, writing in *Kliatt,* commented that "Charles de Lint is a master of contemporary fantasy," and that his "literate and flowing style makes his words a pleasure to read." Trading places is at the heart of de Lint's 1997 *Trader,* in which a man named Trader awakes to discover he has traded bodies with a reprobate named Johnny Devlin. Trying to reclaim his own life, Trader becomes involved in the lives of all those whom Devlin has injured. Along the way, readers are re-introduced to stock characters out of Newford, including Jilly Coppercorn and street musician Geordie Riddell, as well as the shaman, Bones. "Readers familiar with de Lint's work know that he is a master of imagery and trenchant detail," wrote Donna Scanlon in a *Voice of Youth Advocates* review of *Trader.* "He continues to demonstrate his remarkable ability here," Scanlon

If you enjoy the works of Charles de Lint, you may also want to check out the following books and films:

Steven Brust, *Agyar,* 1993.
Esther Friesner, *Elf Defense,* 1988.
Robert Holdstock, Mythago Wood, 1984.
Jennfier Roberson, Sword-Singer, 1988.
Will Shetterly, *Elsewhere,* 1991.
Nancy Springer, *Larque on the Wing,* 1994.
12 Monkeys, a film starring Bruce Willis and Brad Pitt, 1995.

concluded, "never los[ing] control of his myriad plot threads or deftly drawn characters."

One of the most popular Newford novels, and de Lint's personal favorite, is *Someplace to Be Flying,* featuring freelance photographer Lily Carson and a gypsy cab driver, Hank Walker. Once again, de Lint draws the reader into a parallel otherworld, a city beneath the city in the Tombs, and into the realm of shape-shifting animal people, who were the original inhabitants of the earth. The original animal people, as de Lint has it, ultimately turned into the separate animals and people we know today, and in his book, the author focuses specifically on corvids—crows and ravens. *Library Journal*'s Jackie Cassada praised de Lint's "elegant prose and effective storytelling" and his "unique" blend of "magical realism" and "multicultural myths." Brian Jacomb concluded a laudatory *Washington Post Book World* review by noting that "*Someplace to Be Flying* is . . . a solid thriller, full of suspense and peppered with villains of various talents and their adversaries, the decent folk who constantly try to thwart their evil intentions." "As a writer, my first obligation is to entertain," de Lint concluded to *AAYA.* "But as an artist, I know that I first have to please myself, to entertain myself. I try to write the sort of book I want to read but have not been able to find. There has to be that sort of energy in the book, or it won't work for others. Along the way, I hope to remind readers about how much everyday magic there is all around us in the world, if we only will take the time to really see." For de Lint, the very process of writing reinforces the overriding theme of his work. "Making things up for a living is a very magical occupation."

■ Works Cited

Cassada, Jackie, review of *Someplace to Be Flying,* *Library Journal,* January, 1998, p. 148.

Choice, Nancy, review of *Yarrow, Voice of Youth Advocates,* February, 1987, p. 291.

Crowther, Peter, *St. James Guide to Fantasy Writers,* St. James Press, 1996, pp. 153-55.

De Lint, Charles, interview with *Authors and Artists for Young Adults,* conducted July 23, 1999.

De Lint, Charles, excerpt from author's Web site, located at http://www.cyberus.ca/~cdl/bio.htm.

Easton, Tom, "The Reference Librarian," *Analog Science Fiction/Science Fact,* August, 1988, pp. 137-38.

Farber, Gary, review of *Mulengro, S.F. Chronicle,* July, 1986, p. 41.

Green, Roland, review of *Moonheart, Booklist,* December 15, 1984, p. 558.

Green, Roland, review of *Mulengro, Booklist,* November 15, 1985, p. 468.

Green, Roland, review of *Memory and Dreams, Booklist,* October 1, 1994, p. 246.

Green, Roland, review of *Moonlight and Vines, Booklist,* December 1, 1998, p. 655.

Hand, Elizabeth, review of *Dreams Underfoot, Washington Post Book World,* May 30, 1993, p. 9.

Huff, Tanya, "Rising Stars in Fantasy Worlds," *Quill and Quire,* May, 1993, p. 26.

Israel, Jodi L., review of *Memory and Dreams, Kliatt,* January, 1996, p. 14.

Review of *The Ivory and Horn, Publishers Weekly,* March 27, 1995, p. 77.

Jacomb, Brian, review of *Someplace to Be Flying, Washington Post Book World,* March 15, 1998, p. 9.

Review of *The Little Country, Publishers Weekly,* December 7, 1990, p. 74.

Pierson, Kathryn, review of *The Dreaming Place, Bulletin of the Center for Children's Books,* January, 1991, p. 114.

Sagara, Michelle, review of *Spiritwalk, Quill and Quire,* July, 1992, pp. 37-38.

Scanlon, Donna, review of *Trader, Voice of Youth Advocates,* August, 1997, p. 192.

Snider, David, review of *Moonheart, Voice of Youth Advocates,* February, 1985, pp. 335-36.

Speller, Maureen, essay on de Lint in *Twentieth-Century Science Fiction Writers,* third edition,St. James Press, 1991, pp. 196-98.

Westfahl, Gary, "Orange County Apple and Other Aberrations," *Los Angeles Times Book Review,* February 3, 1991, p. 11.

■ For More Information See

BOOKS

Clute, John and Peter Nicholls, editors, *The Encyclopedia of Science Fiction,* St. Martin's Press, 1993.

Science Fiction and Fantasy Literature, 1975-1991, Gale, 1992.

PERIODICALS

Analog Science Fiction/Science Fact, September, 1987, pp. 159-62; November, 1993, pp. 162-69.

Booklist, May 15, 1992, p. 1666; February 1, 1995, p. 993; January 1, 1997, p. 826; December 1, 1998, p. 655.

Library Journal, May 15, 1992, p. 123; February 15, 1999, p. 188.

Locus, October, 1993, p. 33; November, 1994, pp. 52, 68.

Publishers Weekly, October 3, 1994, p. 54; January 26, 1998, p. 74; December 21, 1998, p. 60.

Quill and Quire, January, 1995, p. 35; January, 1997, p. 18; February, 1997, p. 49; February, 1998, p. 35.

School Library Journal, February, 1991, p. 93; December, 1993, pp. 29, 149.

Voice of Youth Advocates, April, 1994, p. 36; April, 1998, pp. 12, 36.

—Sketch by J. Sydney Jones

Gabriel García Márquez

agency, Bogotá, 1959, and worked as its correspondent in Havana, Cuba, and New York City, 1961; writer, 1965—. Fundación Habeas, founder, 1979, president, 1979—. *Member:* American Academy of Arts and Letters (honorary fellow).

■ Awards, Honors

Colombian Association of Writers and Artists Award, 1954, for story "Un dia despues del sabado"; Premio Literario Esso (Colombia), 1961, for *La mala hora*; Chianciano Award (Italy), 1969, Prix de Meilleur Livre Étranger (France), 1969, and Rómulo Gallegos prize (Venezuela), 1971, all for *Cien años de soledad*; LL.D., Columbia University, 1971; Books Abroad/Neustadt International Prize for Literature, 1972; Nobel Prize for literature, 1982; *Los Angeles Times* Book Prize nomination for fiction, 1983, for *Chronicle of a Death Foretold*; *Los Angeles Times* Book Prize for fiction, 1988, for *Love in the Time of Cholera*; Serfin Prize, 1989.

■ Writings

FICTION

La hojarasca (novella; title means "Leaf Storm"; also see below), Ediciones Sipa, 1955, reprinted, Bruguera, 1983.
El coronel no tiene quien le escriba (novella; title means "No One Writes to the Colonel"; also see below), Aguirre Editor, 1961, reprinted, Bruguera, 1983.

■ Personal

Surname pronounced Gar-*see*-a Mar-*kez*; born March 6, 1928, Aracataca, Colombia; son of Gabriel Eligio Garcia (a telegraph operator) and Luisa Santiaga Márquez Iguarán; married Mercedes Barcha, March, 1958; children: Rodrigo, Gonzalo. *Education:* Attended National University of Colombia, 1947-48, and University of Cartagena, 1948-49.

■ Addresses

Agent—Agencia Literaria Carmen Balcells, Diagonal 580, Barcelona 08021, Spain.

■ Career

Began career as a journalist, 1947; reporter for *Universal*, Cartegena, Colombia, late 1940s, *El Heraldo,* Baranquilla, Colombia, 1950-52, and *El Espectador,* Bogotá, Colombia, until 1955; freelance journalist in Paris, London, and Caracas, Venezuela, 1956-58; worked for *Momento* magazine, Caracas, 1958-59; helped form Prensa Latina news

La mala hora (novel; also see below), Talleres de Graficas "Luis Perez", 1961, reprinted, Bruguera, 1982, English translation by Gregory Rabassa published as *In Evil Hour,* Harper, 1979.

Los funerales de la Mamá Grande (short stories; title means "Big Mama's Funeral"; also see below), Editorial Universidad Veracruzana, 1962, reprinted, Bruguera, 1983.

Cien años de soledad (novel), Editorial Sudamericana, 1967, reprinted, Catedra, 1984, English translation by Rabassa published as *One Hundred Years of Solitude,* Harper, 1970, with a new foreword by Rabassa, Knopf, 1995.

Isabel viendo llover en Macondo (novella; title means "Isabel Watching It Rain in Macondo"; also see below), Editorial Estuario, 1967.

No One Writes to the Colonel and Other Stories (includes "No One Writes to the Colonel," and stories from *Los Funerales de la Mamá Grande*), translated by J. S. Bernstein, Harper, 1968.

La increíble y triste historia de la cándida Eréndira y su abuela desalmada (short stories; also see below), Barral Editores, 1972.

El negro que hizo esperar a los ángeles (short stories), Ediciones Alfil, 1972.

Ojos de perro azul (short stories; also see below), Equisditorial, 1972.

Leaf Storm and Other Stories (includes "Leaf Storm," and "Isabel Watching It Rain in Macondo"), translated by Rabassa, Harper, 1972.

El otoño del patriarca (novel), Plaza & Janés Editores, 1975, translation by Rabassa published as *The Autumn of the Patriarch,* Harper, 1976.

Todos los cuentos de Gabriel García Márquez: 1947-1972 (title means "All the Stories of Gabriel García Márquez: 1947-1972"), Plaza & Janés Editores, 1975.

Innocent Erendira and Other Stories (includes "Innocent Erendira and Her Heartless Grandmother" and stories from *Ojos de perro azul*), translated by Rabassa, Harper, 1978.

Dos novelas de Macondo (contains *La hojarasca* and *La mala hora*), Casa de las Americas, 1980.

Crónica de una muerte anunciada (novel), La Oveja Negra, 1981, translation by Rabassa published as *Chronicle of a Death Foretold,* J. Cape, 1982, Knopf, 1983.

Viva Sandino (play), Editorial Nueva Nicaragua, 1982, 2nd edition published as *El asalto: el operativo con que el FSLN se lanzo al mundo,* 1983.

El rastro de tu sangre en la nieve: El verano feliz de la señora Forbes, W. Dampier Editores, 1982.

El secuestro: Guion cinematografico (unfilmed screenplay), Oveja Negra, 1982.

Erendira (filmscript; adapted from his novella *La increíble y triste historia de la cándida Eréndira y su abuela desalmada*), Les Films du Triangle, 1983.

Collected Stories, translated by Rabassa and Bernstein, Harper, 1984.

El amor en los tiempos del cólera, Oveja Negra, 1985, English translation by Edith Grossman published as *Love in the Time of Cholera,* Knopf, 1988.

A Time to Die (filmscript), ICA Cinema, 1988.

Diatribe of Love against a Seated Man (play; first produced at Cervantes Theater in Buenos Aires, 1988), Arango Editores, 1994.

El general en su labertino, Mondadori, 1989, English translation by Grossman published as *The General in His Labyrinth,* Knopf, 1990.

Collected Novellas, HarperCollins, 1990.

Doce cuentos peregrinos, Mondadori, 1992, English translation by Grossman published as *Strange Pilgrims: Twelve Stories,* Knopf, 1993.

The Handsomest Drowned Man in the World: A Tale for Children, translated by Rabassa, Creative Education, 1993.

Del amor y otros demonios, Mondadori, 1994, English translation by Grossman published as *Of Love and Other Demons,* Knopf, 1995.

NONFICTION

(With Mario Vargas Llosa) *La novela en América Latina: Diálogo,* Carlos Milla Batres, 1968.

Relato de un náufrago (journalistic pieces), Tusquets Editor, 1970, English translation by Randolph Hogan published as *The Story of a Shipwrecked Sailor,* Knopf, 1986.

Cuando era feliz e indocumentado (journalistic pieces), Ediciones El Ojo de Camello, 1973.

Crónicas y reportajes (journalistic pieces), Oveja Negra, 1978.

Periodismo militante (journalistic pieces), Son de Maquina, 1978.

De viaje por los países socialistas: 90 días en la "Cortina de hierro" (journalistic pieces), Ediciones Macondo, 1978.

(Contributor) *Los sandanistas,* Oveja Negra, 1979.

(Contributor) Soledad Mendoza, editor, *Asi es Caracas,* Editorial Ateneo de Caracas, 1980.

Obra periodística (journalistic pieces), edited by Jacques Gilard, Bruguera, Volume 1: *Textos constenos,* 1981, Volumes 2-3: *Entre cachacos,* 1982, Volume 4: *De Europa y América (1955-1960),* 1983.

El olor de la guayaba: Conversaciones con Plinio Apuleyo Mendoza (interviews), Oveja Negra, 1982, English translation by Ann Wright published as *The Fragrance of Guava,* Verso, 1983.

(With Guillermo Nolasco-Juarez) *Persecución y muerte de minorías: dosperspectivas,* Juárez Editor, 1984.

(Contributor) *La Democracia y la paz en América Latina,* Editorial El Buho, 1986.

La aventura de Miguel Littin, clandestino en Chile: Un reportaje, Editorial Sudamericana, 1986, English translation by Asa Zatz published as *Clandestine in Chile: The Adventures of Miguel Littin,* Holt, 1987.

Primeros reportajes, Consorcio de Ediciones Capriles, 1990.

(Author of introduction) Mina, Gianni, *An Encounter with Fidel: An Interview,* translated by Mary Todd, Ocean Press, 1991.

Notas de prensa, 1980-1984, Mondadori, 1991.

Elogio de la utopia: Una entrevista de Nahuel Maciel, Cronista Ediciones, 1992.

Noticia de un secuestro, Mondadori, 1996, translated from the Spanish by Grossman as *News of a Kidnapping,* Knopf, 1997.

(With Reynaldo Gonzales) *Cubano 100%,* photographs by Gianfranco Gorgoni, Charta, 1998.

■ Adaptations

Several of García Márquez's works have been adapted into motion pictures: the title story of the collection *Innocent Erendira and Other Stories* was adapted for the film *Erendira,* Les Films du Triangle, 1984; *Chronicle of a Death Foretold* was adapted in 1987; and the short story "The Saint" was adapted for a film under the title of *Milagro in Roma.* A play, *Blood and Champagne,* has been based on García Márquez's *One Hundred Years of Solitude.*

■ Sidelights

Nobel Prize-winning, Colombian author Gabriel García Márquez has influenced an entire generation of writers around the world. Popularizing the genre of magic realism, García Márquez built upon the work of such writers as the Cuban Aléjo Carpentier and that master of the short story, Jorge Louis Borges, to concoct an entertaining, accessible brew of realism and fancy. "When characters now levitate or fly away," noted the García Márquez scholar Regina Janes in *Contemporary World Writers,* "move surrounded by butterflies, bleed strange colors, marry their aunts, watch dead birds rain from the skies, or suffer from the winds of disillusion, García Márquez's spirit has touched the page, directly or indirectly." Such influences can be readily seen in the work of international authors such as Isabelle Allende, Alice Walker, Mark Helprin, and Salman Rushdie, to name but a few.

This revolution in writing can be traced to García Márquez's most influential book, *One Hundred Years of Solitude,* published in the Spanish original in 1967, a family saga which follows the fortunes and misfortunes of the Buendía family over a century of compressed time. "Violating the Aristotelian precept that a probable impossibility is preferable to an improbable possibility, the novel set out to restore a sense of wonder relative both to the objects or representation and to the surface of the text," Janes observed. In so doing, García Márquez provided a new way of portraying Latin America and Latin Americans, a mode that did not condescend to so-called "fringe" cultural areas as so much mainstream Western literature had, which neither pitied such characters nor made them quaint in some folk tale manner. Instead, García Márquez's colorful and fanciful creation of the Buendía clan and the imaginary town of Macondo illuminated not only the life of the people of Latin American, but also the history of the region. His magic often comes from close and reawakened viewing of rational events which the modern world takes for granted, as well as from a juxtaposition of the noble and banal.

García Márquez's *One Hundred Years of Solitude* was an immediate bestseller, translated into more than thirty languages and selling in excess of twentymillion copies worldwide. It put Latin American literature onto the map, and made García Márquez's name known from Bombay to Boston. In further novels and short stories, García Márquez perfected the new genre of magic realism and then moved beyond it. Often he returns to his beloved Macondo to tell stories of various imagined people of the imaginary locale, like a South American Faulkner (one of García Márquez's self-proclaimed masters) mining the resources of a Latin American Yoknapatawpha County. *The Autumn of the Patriarch* again employs the fantastic and impossible to develop a seemingly realistic tale of the power of dictators, but with much of his later fiction, García Márquez left this device behind. In novels such as the anti-mystery, *Chronicle of a Death Foretold,* which follows the pattern of a Greek tragedy, or *Love in the Time of Cholera*, which deals with a love that has a second chance, or *The General in His Labyrinth*, which employs the devices of historical fiction to tell of Simón Bolívar's final trip down the Magdalena River, García Márquez has provided his readers with new and varying literary perspectives.

With his 1992 short story collection, *Strange Pilgrims*, García Márquez abandoned Latin America for European settings, relating tales of expatriates far from home. And in his 1995 *Of Love and Other Demons*, he returned once again to the world of Macondo to reconstruct the life of one Sierva Maria in a somber tone of magic realism. García Márquez, who began his literary career as a journalist, has also published several notable nonfiction works, prominent among them the 1997 tale of Colombian kidnappings and drug kingpins, *News of a Kidnapping.*

Throughout both his fiction and nonfiction, García Márquez has remained true to his own political nature, viewing events with a leftist perspective, but one that never gets in the way of his story. His themes are large: love, death, power, and human freedom. His blend of striking and unexpected detail, exaggeration, episodic narratives, impossibility, and incongruity continue to amaze and attract new readers. Honoring García Márquez for his work with the 1982 Noble Prize for Literature, the Swedish Academy remarked: "With his stories Gabriel García Márquez has created a world of his own which is a microcosmos. In its tumultuous, bewildering yet graphically convincing authenticity, it reflects a continent and its human riches and poverty."

Aracataca as Microcosmos

Born on March 6, 1928, to Gabriel Elegio García and Luisa Santiaga Márquez de García, García Márquez spent the first eight years of his life in the small town of Aracataca, on Colombia's Caribbean coast. His father, a telegrapher and amateur poet, moved the family to a new post at a smaller village shortly after the arrival of his first born, but García Márquez was left behind with the maternal grandparents, Colonel Nicolás García and Tranquilina Iguarán de Márquez. Such a practice was common in the region with poor young parents getting a start in life, and where grandparents were an integral part of the extended family. However, in this case, García Márquez's grandparents had been against the marriage of their daughter to the poor telegraph operator. Thus, such an event was life shaping for García Márquez, and he would return to his parents only upon the death of his grandfather.

Young García Márquez grew up listening to the local myths and legends as recounted by his grandfather, as well as to his stories of the civil war at the turn of the century, the so-called Thousand Days War, in which he was a young officer. García Márquez also heard more fantastical tales as recounted by his grandmother in a deadpan manner. The boy took as given the fact that his grandparents' rambling old house was home to a wide assortment of ghosts. The old couple, especially the grandmother, were very superstitious and imparted a sense of the supernatural in everyday life to the impressionable youngster under their care. García Márquez has noted that you did not leave your room after six in the evening in order to avoid the fantastic terrors the house held. "The style of my books is almost entirely that of my grandmother," García Márquez noted in an article in *Atlas World Press Review.* "Whenever she did not want to answer a question, she would invent fantasies so that I wouldn't be saddened by the truth of things. It was almost impossible for me to distinguish where reality left off and imagination took over; my head was full of images. The world of my childhood caused me to lose fear of doing some things in literature, because anything is possible—just as it had been in my childhood."

The setting of Aracataca, with its steamy Caribbean climate and blend of African and Hispanic cultures, also played a role in García Márquez's future development. Colombians look upon the region as somewhat unique and exotic: males there might support several households, for example, and sire dozens of children. A medieval code of honor still existed when García Márquez was a youngster. Banana had been king for a time in the region, and the North Americans were represented in the form of the United Fruit Company. But Aracataca was an outpost of civilization, far from the center of Colombian life. There García Márquez remained while his parents lived in another village, and even when they moved back to Aracataca, he remained with his grandparents, going to his parents only for visits or if he was sick.

This childhood time capsule burst with the colonel's death. García Márquez was sent to his parents in Sucre; child and parents were strangers to each other, and García Márquez barely knew his numerous siblings born in the meantime. However, he soon developed a close bond to his mother, and from his father García Márquez felt he owed the vocation of literature. Both an amateur poet and lover of music, the elder Márquez was an avid reader who inspired the activity in his son. García Márquez took to writing and illustrating comics during this time, but also saw that the family was struggling financially. He decided to take things into his own hands at age twelve, and applied for a scholarship for high school. The family scraped enough money together to send him to Bogotá where the scholarship exams were held. García Márquez managed to win one at the Jesuit school in Zipaquirá, high in the Andes near Bogotá. During these years, he earned the reputation of being a writer, even though he in fact wrote little. But he always thought of himself as one and knew that was what he wanted to do with his life. Receiving his high school degree in 1946, he went on to the National University in Bogotá with the intention of working for a law degree.

A Literary Apprenticeship

However, something more vital than law happened to García Márquez at the university. He fell in with a group of like-minded literary youths and began talking books late into the night. Discovering Franz Kafka's *Metamorphosis* was a revelation for him. Reading the opening about a character who changes into an insect overnight, he knew he had found his home. "When I read the line I thought to myself that I didn't know anyone was allowed to write things like that," García Márquez commented in a 1984 *Paris Review* interview. "If I had known, I would have started writing a long time ago. So I immediately started writing short stories." The first of these were published in the literary pages of a Bogotá newspaper, *El Espectador.*

He began reading everything he could get his hands on, beginning with the Bible, a book where fantastic things happen with regularity. García Márquez's incipient literary life in Bogotá came to an end in 1949 with the assassination of a liberal candidate for president; the country was thrown into turmoil for the next decade, a period known as *la violencia.* Violence in the capital led García Márquez to leave Bogotá and enroll in the University of Cartagena on the coast. His years in Cartagena were vital to his apprenticeship; falling in with another group of literary types, he alsocontinued his wide reading: from Sophocles to Faulker, and from Hemingway to Woolf. These became his new masters, and he continued producing short stories, publishing them in newspapers.

In 1950, García Márquez gave up on university and took a newspaper job in nearby Barranquilla at *El Heraldo.* He continued his frenzied reading

gabriel garcía márquez

Nobel Prize Winner

PERENNIAL

one hundred years of solitude

CLASSICS

Translated into English in 1970, Garcia Marquez's 1967 novel about the Buendia family and the history of the fictional town of Macondo is credited with popularizing Latin American literature in North America.

and writing, and his nighttime book chats. By day, García Márquez honed his word skills on the day-to-day tasks of journalism. During this period, he also returned to Aracataca with his mother to sell the ancestral house. This journey back to his roots was also a reawakening of the past for the budding writer. He saw everything in the new light of his readings, saw how he could use material from his childhood in an entirely original way, almost Faulknerian in tone. "From that trip to the village I came back to write *Leaf Storm*, my first novel," García Márquez told *Paris Review*. "What really happened to me in that trip to Aracataca was that I realized that everything that had occurred in my childhood had a literary value that I was only now appreciating."

Journalist and Young Novelist

In 1954, García Márquez returned to Bogotá as a journalist for *El Espectador*. Here he did several features a week, daily editorial notes, and movie reviews. At night he worked on his novel. His diligence finally paid off with the 1955 publication of *Leaf Storm*, as well as a national award for a short story. Though its publication caused little literary stir in Colombia, *Leaf Storm* is important in that it introduces García Márquez's fictional town, Macondo, and the novel takes place there in the early years of the twentieth century when the region was transformed by the leaf storm of the arrival of an American banana company. Progress in all its forms is portrayed with the new money brought in by the Americans; the village is transformed overnight. Characters that appear in later fiction are introduced in this episodic novel, including an unnamed colonel modeled after his grandfather and destined to become Colonel Aureliano Buendía in *One Hundred Years of Solitude*. But boom is followed by bust in Macondo as the banana company leaves and by 1928—the year García Márquez was born, the town was drained and tired.

Told from multiple points of view and dealing with themes of decadence and the past, *Leaf Storm* has been compared to Faulkner's *As I Lay Dying*. Raymond L. Williams, writing in his critical study *Gabriel García Márquez*, noted that this first novel "is a remarkably successful venture in the creation of an 'other reality.' This success is due to the ability to fictionalize a reader who experiences a myth, rather than having to have it explained."

Though employing primarily realistic elements, this debut novel provides a foreshadowing of magical things to come.

The same year his debut novel was published, García Márquez was sent to Geneva as the correspondent of *El Espectador*. Soon thereafter, the Colombian military government closed the newspaper and García Márquez was stranded in Europe. From Geneva he went to Rome, and then to Paris where he worked as a freelance writer and at times collected bottles on the streets to buy food. His European years, as difficult as they were financially, allowed him to concentrate on his writing full time. During this period he worked on the manuscripts of the novels *In Evil Hour* and *No One Writes to the Colonel*, as well as on the short story collection, *Big Mama's Funeral*. Additionally, as a freelance journalist, García Márquez traveled throughout Eastern Europe. In 1958, he returned to Colombia, and married his childhood sweetheart, Mercedes Barcha. The couple settled in Caracas, Venezuela, where García Márquez worked for the newspaper *Momento* and continued working on the stories in *Big Mama's Funeral*.

With the coming of the Cuban revolution in 1959, García Márquez, like many other Latin American intellectuals, felt that times were finally changing. He began working for the Cuban press agency, Prensa Latina, in Bogotá, then in Cuba, and finally in New York. While in the United States, García Márquez made a pilgrimage by bus through Faulkner's South. In 1961 came publication of *No One Writes to the Colonel*, the story of an aging colonel who spends fifteen years waiting for his pension check. The colonel in question is originally from the mythical Macondo; the book is somber in tone, a reflection of the repressive years of military dictatorship in Colombia. As critics have noted, the novel is important primarily in its further development of the Macondo universe, as is the novel *In Evil Hour*, published in 1962. In this book, anonymous notes begin to appear on the doors of homes in an unnamed village, notes revealing secrets and accusing various people of misdeeds. Again inspired by the political atmosphere of *la violencia*, this third novel brings forward characters who have appeared in the earlier novels and short stories. Employing an episodic montage technique, García Márquez tells his tale in some forty brief sections. The notes inspire acts of revenge that soon get out of control, precipitating a return of political oppression.

As William Logan wrote in *Washington Post Book World*: "García Márquez's preoccupations with the texture of humanity and with individual guilt manifested socially, so evident in this biting novel, needed only the ingredient of the fabulous, a sense of dream hardened into life, to blossom the luxuriant and majestic fiction of *One Hundred Years of Solitude* and *The Autumn of the Patriarch*."

That missing ingredient, "the fabulous," was served up in García Márquez's short story collection, *Big Mama's Funeral*, also published in 1962. For the first time, García Márquez employed hyperbolic humor, an element that became integral to his later work. The first sentence of the title story begins: "This is, for all the world's unbelievers, the true account of Big Mama, absolute sovereign of the Kingdom of Macondo, who lived for ninety-two years, and died in the odor of sanctity one Tuesday last September, and whose funeral was attended by the Pope." This and other stories in the collection play with humor and hyperbole verging on the fantastical.

Though his early fiction earned several Colombian literary awards for García Márquez, he still had not made a breakthrough with his writing. Living abroad, in Mexico, he continued his journalism. From 1962 to 1965 it seemed he had given up literature, working only on some film scripts. But these years were an incubation period as the world of Macondo gestated and grew in García Márquez's imagination. In 1965, he gave up journalism for full-time writing. García Márquez worked in isolation for the next two years, living in his make-believe Kingdom of Macondo.

One Hundred Years of Solitude

"*One Hundred Years of Solitude* is an utter joy to read yet, paradoxically, an elusive book to write about," noted Williams in his critical study of the author. "What we most enjoy reading is not necessarily the same as what we can most comfortably explain or analyze." The story of the Buendía family, this 1970 novel is also the story of the fictional Macondo, and by extension an epic but oblique look at the development of Colombia and of Latin American countries in general. Simply put, as García Márquez is fond of doing, the novel tells the story of this family, united initially by the marriage of cousins, and of its fears—because of this quasi-incestuous beginning—of engender-

ing an offspring born with the tail of a pig. All of their efforts are in vain, however. As García Márquez himself told Rita Guibert for her book *Seven Voices,* "and just because of their very efforts to avoid having one they ended up by doing so. Synthetically speaking, that's the plot of the book, but all this about symbolism . . . not at all."

The novel begins with a descendant of the original couple, and is told in episodic, telescoping flashback and flash-forward sections: "Many years later, as he faced the firing squad, Colonel Aureliano Buendía was to remember thatdistant afternoon when his father took him to discover ice. At that time Macondo was a village of twenty adobe houses, built on the bank of a river of clear water that ran along a bed of polished stones, which were white and enormous, like prehistoric eggs. The world was so recent that many things lacked names, and in order to indicate them it was necessary to point." Thus, within two sentences, García Márquez sets the dual threads of his tale: the Buendía clan and Macondo. And with a few more strokes sets the magical tone, as well. This is a mythical time, the beginning of all things, Eden perhaps.

The Buendías are the original founders of Macondo, having set off from the interior of Colombia to forge a new life in the wilderness. A family curse lies over the Buendías: the birth of a child with a pig's tail because cousins have once married. Thus when José Arcadio Buendía takes as his bride his cousin Úrsula Iguarán, it is feared the same might happen again and the line might end. Úrsula refuses to consummate the marriage and one of the men of the village jokes that José Arcadio is impotent, whereupon José kills the man and takes Úrsula. The resulting child is born normal, but the couple is forced to flee, pursued by the dead man's ghost. Guilt and inescapable fate are built into the novels earliest sections.

José Arcadia thus acts as a sort of biblical Moses, leading a small band into the jungle to some promised land. It is then that they found the village of Macondo. José Arcadio is something of the village patriarch, but is continually tempted by the traveling gypsy, Melquíades, into inventing schemes that go awry. There is a magnet which it is hoped will extract gold ore; a telescope that can be used as a weapon. The gypsies come every March, bringing inventions from the outside world to the remote village. Finally José Arcadio goes insane, is tied to a chestnut tree, and dies, but he continues to babble in Latin even after his death. The wife, Úrsula, the matriarch of the novel, survives into succeeding generations.

Soon not only civilization but also government comes to Macondo, and the new magistrate has a beautiful daughter, Remedios, with whom the second son of José Arcadio and Úrsula, who is called Aureliano, falls desperately in love. He finally marries her, after scribbling over all the walls of his home love poems to her. The outside world intrudes ever more in Macondo, involving the reluctant Aureliano in the endless battles between Liberals and Conservatives—a reflection of the actual history of Colombia. A colonel now, but more happily a dreamer who spends his free time making little golden fish, Aureliano leads his Liberals in thirty-two rebellions against the Conservatives. Defeated, Aureliano threatens to sometime incite his seventeen illegitimate sons to revolt again; all his sons are killed in a single night, but for one who escapes, like Moses, hidden among the bulrushes.

The arrival of a banana company from the United States transforms Macondo, but its ruthless practices inflame one of José Arcadio's grandsons. He organizes a strike which is brutally suppressed, with several thousand dead—a hyperbolic reference to an actual occurrence. The bodies are all spirited away by train and no one remembers the incident. Bizarre events overcome the village of Macondo: at one time the people are afflicted with an insomnia which leads to a collective loss. Signs have to be put on everything, for no one can remember the names for the most common objects. After the massacre of the workers, torrential rains come to Macondo, lasting four years, eleven months, and two days. Macondo's civilization— what there is of it—is destroyed by the resulting Great Flood. However, with this cleansing rain, the town is reborn fresh and pure.

In the end, such a rebirth can not hold true for the Buendía line: an illegitimate heir to the clan, Aureliano Babilonia, lives unknowingly with his aunt. She dies giving birth to their child, born with a pig's tail. The child is carried away by ants, ending the history of the Buendías. It is also left to Aureliano Babilonia to turn the novel in on itself, discovering that the gypsy Melquíades, has already written this entire tale, inventing

This 1975 work of magical realism, told from the viewpoint of a fictional dictator of a Caribbean nation, is Garcia Marquez's polemic against societies that allow monstrous dictators to take them over.

Macondo just as he has the Buendías. In the final pages Aureliano Babilonia finally deciphers this mysterious parchment manuscript left behind by the enigmatic gypsy only to discover that everything—including himself—is a fiction. Every action of the family has been foretold and was merely a fulfilment of fictional destiny.

To say that the critical reception of *One Hundred Years of Solitude* was enthusiastic would be understatement. Something new had come into the literature of the 1960s. Paul West, writing in the *Chicago Tribune Book World*, commented that García Márquez "feeds the mind's eye non-stop, so much so that you soon begin to feel that never has what we superficially call the surface of life had so many corrugations and configurations." West went on to conclude, "It's not often that you find a Technicolor tableau of fools which, got up as a family saga, stretches the mind by cramming it and reenacts paradise found and lost as a version of Latin America's own history. . . . Like the jungle itself, this novel comes back again and again, fecund, savage and irresistible." Reviewer John Leonard termed García Márquez's work a "marvelous novel," in the *New York Times,* noting that "Macondo is Latin America in microcosm." Leonard continued, "Family chronicle, then, and political *tour de force,* and metaphysical speculation, a cathedral of words, perceptions, and legends that amounts to the declaration of a state of mind. . . . With a single bound Gabriel García Márquez leaps onto the stage with Günter Grass, Vladimir Nabokov, his appetite as enormous as his imagination, his fatalism greater than either. Dazzling."

In a lengthy review in the *New York Review of Books,* Jack Richardson, like other critics, drew attention to the element of magic in *One Hundred Years of Solitude:* "At the heart [of the novel] is its magic, a magic that moves from the simply phenomenal—a levitating priest, a flock of yellow butterflies that flit ominously about a young seducer, plants that bleed when cut, countless ghosts that are accepted as part of the natural landscape—to the core of Márquez's world. In this world . . . beings shuffle back and forth in time, and the ordinary has been so clearly seen and relentlessly followed to its conclusion that the world itself becomes more than natural, becomes instead, a wild conjuring of things which may seem to be set in reality but which slide imperceptibly into the fantastic." Richardson concluded, "Márquez forces upon us at every page the wonder and extravagance of life . . . and when the book ends with its sudden self-knowledge and its intimations of holocaust, we are left with that pleasant exhaustion which only very great novels seem to provide."

Though other writers—Borges and Carpentier, for example—had employed this magical element before, García Márquez's consistent use in an otherwise realistic format prompted the phrase "magic realism" to describe the new genre. As Thor Vilhjálmsson noted in *Books Abroad,* "It seems to me that García Márquez marries realism and objectivity with a most singular sense of the fantas-

tic and delicious fabulating gifts, often employing surrealistic clairvoyance to paint frescoes full of moral indignation and anger protesting against oppression and violence, degradation and deceit. . . . In juxtaposing the twin elements of humor and tragedy, García Márquez often achieves contrapuntal heights where language and image are thoroughly fused." Robert Kiely also remarked on the author's eloquent use of language and juxtaposition, writing in the *New York Times Book Review* that García Márquez "creates a continuum, a web of connections and relationships. However bizarre or grotesque some particulars may be, the large effect is one of great gusto and good humor, and even more, of sanity and compassion. . . . He has written a novel so filled with humor, rich detail and startling distortion that it brings to mind the best of Faulkner and Günter Grass. It is a South American Genesis, an earthy piece of enchantment."

Other critics have also mentioned the biblical aspects of *One Hundred Years of Solitude,* from the Eden-like descriptions of Macondo, to the Moses-like role that José Arcadio plays, to the flood at the end of the novel. The themes of guilt and power, of destiny, as well as the Sophoclean tragedy as the result of incest are also key elements to a reading of the novel. And as Williams noted, the novel is also "a unique social document in that it captures a wide gamut of Colombia's social, political, and economic realities." The battle between Liberals and Conservatives, the exploitation at the hands of the United Fruit Company, these are historical facts which García Márquez wove into his fiction, sometimes with hyperbole, sometimes with understatement. But as García Márquez noted in his *Paris Review* interview, "It always amuses me that the biggest praise for my work comes for the imagination while the truth is that there's not a single line in all my work that does not have a basis in reality."

Despite the enormous worldwide success of his novel, García Márquez has consistently refused to sell the film rights, refusing an offer of $2 million at one point. "I don't want to see it turned into a movie, because I want readers to go on imagining the characters as they see them," García Márquez told Claudia Dreifus in an interview for *Playboy.* "That isn't possible in the cinema. In movies, the image is so definite that the spectator can no longer imagine the character as he wants to, only as the screen imposes it on him."

Themes of Power, Love, and Destiny

García Márquez's success gave him the luxury of time; journalism now became something he did only by choice. It was eight years before García Márquez published another novel. His next publication was the collection, *The Incredible and Sad Tale of Innocent Erendira and Her Heartless Grandmother,* which moves away from the Macondo of his early fiction. But the author was at work on another project that had occupied him off-and-on for many years. It was the story of a dictator. Such a work would allow him to voice many of his own anti-rightist sentiments. Published in 1975, *The Autumn of the Patriarch* was hungrily awaited by readers and critics alike. Told from multiple viewpoints, it is "a stunning portrait of the archetype: the pathological fascist tyrant," according to William Kennedy writing in the *New York Times Book Review.* Once again, García Márquez employed fabulist techniques. "The book is . . . mystical, surrealistic, Rabelaisian in its excesses, its distortions and its exotic language," continued Kennedy.

The General, an unnamed dictator of an unnamed Caribbean country, lives to be somewhere between 107 and 232 years and fathers some 5,000 children. Told largely from the General's mind, the narrative skips over time as if it were a compressed mountain range. In the episodic telling of his life, the General is revealed as a monster. "The book is a supreme polemic," remarked Kennedy, "a spiritual expose, an attack against any society that encourages or even permits the growth of such a monstrosity." John Sturrock remarked in the *Times Literary Supplement* that "*The Autumn of the Patriarch* is the desperate, richly sustained hallucination of a man rightly bitter about the present state of so much of Latin America." Some critics, while praising the theme and style, found the novel problematic for its very Rabelaisian abundance and exaggeration. Ronaldo De Feo writing in the *National Review* hailed the novel as "García Márquez's most intense and extreme vision of isolation; "a unique, remarkable novel" despite its "overabundance of riches." Raymond Williams, writing in his critical study of García Márquez, noted that *The Autumn of the Patriarch*, while a disappointment to some, "is a major book for both García Márquez and the field of the contemporary Latin-American novel," and "is a continuation of the transcendent regionalism so evident in García Márquez's previous work."

In 1982, García Márquez was honored with the Nobel Prize for Literature, an award which only confirmed what readers around the world had already determined by their numbers and loyalty. This period in the author's life also led to new directions. Tackling more polemic and political issues with plays, journalism, and film scripts, his fiction also broke new ground. Leaving Macondo behind with *The Autumn of the Patriarch,* García Márquez also began to leave magic realism—an increasingly overcrowded genre—behind with his next novels, including *Chronicle of a Death Foretold* and *Love in the Time of Cholera.* In the former, a young woman is returned on her wedding night for not being a virgin, and her brothers set out to avenge this stain on their reputation and her purity. A classic tale of Latin machismo, *Chronicle of a Death Foretold* is something of a mystery told backward, for the brothers announce to the town their intention of killing the lover, Santiago Nasar. Everyone knows about it but the condemned man who is, in the end, brutally murdered.

Writing in the *Washington Post Book World,* Jonathan Yardley called the short novel "a virtuoso performance . . . ingeniously and impeccably constructed," which offers "a sobering, devastating perspective on the system of male 'honor'." Reviewer Gregory Rabassa noted in *World Literature Today* that despite telling the reader that Nasar is going to be killed, García Márquez manages "to maintain the suspense at a high level by never describing the actual murder until the very end." Several reviewers commented on García Márquez's use of journalistic technique in the telling. *Chicago Tribune Book World* editor John Blades noted that the book was "a straight-faced parody of conventional journalism," but "at the same time, this is precision-tooled fiction; the author subtly but skillfully manipulates his chronology for dramatic effect." Told in a more realistic style than his other books, *Chronicle of a Death Foretold* announced a departure in style for García Márquez. As Christopher Lehmann-Haupt commented in the *New York Times,* "I found *Chronicle of a Death Foretold* by far the author's most absorbing work to date. I read it through in a flash, and it made the back of my neck prickle." Placing the work in a broader perspective, Raymond Williams concluded that the short novel "is not a book of profound resonance, but a superb entertainment."

García Márquez has said that the two years spent writing *Love in the Time of Cholera* were the hap-

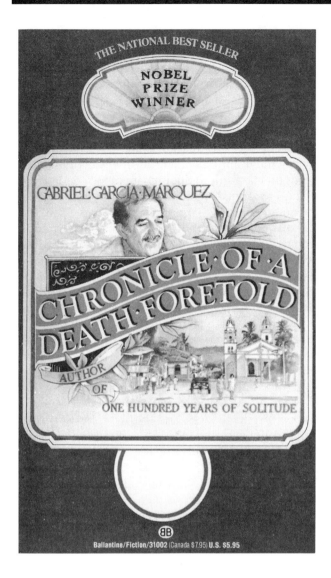

In this anti-mystery, the brothers of a woman who has been rejected on her wedding night for not being a virgin tell the entire town that they will kill the husband, who becomes the only one ignorant of the plan.

piest of his life. Fable and fact are also blended in that 1988 novel, which is "an amazing celebration of the many kinds of love between men and women," according to Elaine Feinstein writing in the *Times* of London. The novel was in part inspired by the love between García Márquez's parents, his father a poor telegraph operator, poet, violinist, and liberal, and his mother from a well-to-do family. In this regard, they somewhat resemble Fermina and Florentino of the novel. At the outset of the story, Fermina is left a widow when her husband, Dr. Juvenal Urbino, dies try-

ing to rescue a parrot from a tree. Not long thereafter, Florentino Ariza, the suitor she gave up half a century before, appears to try and woo this woman he has loved for all those years. The rest of the novel recounts the courtship struggles as well as the years of the Fermina's marriage and Florentino's life without her. Reviewing the novel in *New York Times Book Review*, the writer Thomas Pynchon remarked that García Márquez "writes with impassioned control, out of a maniacal serenity," and that his voice "has matured, found and developed new resources, been brought to a level where it can at once be classical and familiar, opalescent and pure. . . ." Pynchon called the book a "shining and heartbreaking novel." Paul Bailey writing in the *Listener* called *Love in the Time of Cholera* "the best, in my view, that Márquez has written," while reviewer S. M. J. Minta remarked in *Times Literary Supplement* that "it is a novel in praise of spontaneity, sexual passion, disorder and vitality, a triumph of the uncertain, sprawling confusion of life over the comforting, dull precision of authority, a victory of the indigenous over the imported, old age over death, the popular over the learned." Minta went on to note, "Wittily, the novel also celebrates the sheer joy of reading." Galen Strawson concluded in the *Observer*, "The book is rich and brilliant with emotion—an extraordinary poeticisation of old age."

The Last Days of the Great Liberator

With *The General in his Labyrinth,* García Márquez told yet another type of story: historical fiction. The novel relates the story of the final months in the life of the great Simón Bolívar, who gained independence for the northern colonies of South America. Attempting to write a fictional piece about this man is akin to writing about the final days of George Washington. García Márquez's labyrinth of the title is the tangle of scandals and gossip which surrounded Bolívar's final days. Focusing on the last months of the man's life, *The General in His Labyrinth* details Bolívar's renouncing of the Colombian presidency and his final long journey down the Magdalena River to his death near the Caribbean coast in 1830. During this time Bolívar also supported a military coup in hopes of uniting the country. Applauded for its research, the novel was dubbed "a fascinating literary tour de force and a moving tribute to an extraordinary man," by the novelist Margaret Atwood in the

If you enjoy the works of Gabriel Gabriel García Márquez, you may also want to check out the following books:

Isabelle Allende, *The House of the Spirits*, 1985, and *Of Love and Shadows*, 1987.
Julia Alvarez, *In the Time of the Butterflies*, 1994.
Jorge Luis Borges, *Fictions*, 1984.

New York Times Book Review. Alicia Borinsky noted in the *Dictionary of Literary Biography*, "In writing this historical fiction, García Márquez has joined the contemporary Latin-American writers who think of the novel as an ideal medium for critical interpretation of the past. In this case, the persona of the reader, who has the task of rethinking the terms of Bolívar's cult, is parallel to the persona of Bolívar himself, coming to terms with his career and associates."

García Márquez revisited the short story format in his *Strange Pilgrims*, a dozen stories set in Europe, and then in 1994 returned to his fictional Macondo for the novel *Of Love and Other Demons*. Inspired by a story he covered as a young journalist, the novel recreates the fabulous life of one Sierva Maria, daughter of wealthy parents who grows up with the African slaves on her family's plantation. Bitten by a rabid dog, the girl undergoes an exorcism, but the presiding priest is bitten as well—with love for young Sierva. Told in a somewhat watered-down version of his old magic realism, the novel won guarded praise from critics. Reviewer Jonathan Yardley noted in *Washington Post Book World* that the author's mood "is almost entirely melancholy and his manner is, by contrast with his characteristic ebullience, decidedly restrained." *Time* magazine's R. Z. Sheppard was more positive, declaring that García Márquez "demonstrates once again the vigor of his own passion: the daring and irresistible coupling of history and imagination."

Such a coupling also takes place in García Márquez's journalistic endeavors, including the 1997 *News of a Kidnapping*, which recounts the edge-of-the-seat tale of a series of kidnappings mounted by the drug lords of Colombia in their attempts to avoid U.S. extradition. Ten prominent Colombians, some television personalities, journalists, or relatives of judges and politicians, were kidnapped and held as hostages in the early 1990s by Colombian drug traffickers, including the infamous Pablo Escobar. This was the apotheosis of a long reign of drug terror which claimed the lives of twenty-five journalists from 1983 to 1991. The traffickers hoped to blackmail the government into giving them imprisonment inside Colombia (instead of extradition) in exchange for the release of the kidnapped people. *Booklist*'s Bonnie Smothers noted that this complex situation is "just the sort of human snakepit that García Márquez finds a home in," while Robert Stone commented in the *New York Times Book Review* that García Márquez displays "a quick eye for the illuminating detail and a capacity for assembling fact." *Kirkus Reviews* concluded, "García Márquez's consummate rendering of this hostage-taking looms as the symbol of an entire country held hostage to invisible yet violently ever-present drug lords." John Leonard praised García Márquez's sense of history, sense of morality, and sense of story in a *Nation* review of *News of a Kidnapping:* "With his alert sympathy, perfect awareness and capacity for surprise, the greatnovelist reminds us that there is no redemption in contempt, nor any community."

Spoken truly about his journalism, these same words can also describe García Márquez's approach to all his work. His sense of humanity and humor blend sometimes in magic realism, sometimes in social realism. As the Nobel Prize committee noted, "Gabriel García Márquez has created a world of his own which is a microcosmos." For the committee, and for readers around the world, this is not so much a location as a destination, "a cosmos in which the human heart and the combined forces of history time and again burst the bounds of chaos—killing and procreation."

■ **Works Cited**

"Announcement by the Swedish Academy," as quoted in *Dictionary of Literary Biography Yearbook: 1982*, Gale, 1983, p. 4.

Atwood, Margaret, review of *The General in His Labyrinth*, *New York Times Book Review*, September 16, 1990, pp. 1, 30.

Bailey, Paul, "The Loved One," *Listener*, June 30, 1988, p. 29.

Blades, John, review of *Chronicle of a Death Foretold*, *Chicago Tribune Book World*, April 3, 1983.

Borinsky, Alicia, "Gabriel García Márquez," *Dictionary of Literary Biography,* Volume 113: *Modern Latin-American Fiction Writers,* Gale, 1992, pp. 168-72.

De Feo, Ronald, "The Solitude of Power," *National Review,* May 27, 1977, pp. 620, 622.

Dreifus, Claudia, "Playboy Interview: Gabriel García Márquez," *Playboy,* February, 1983.

Feinstein, Elaine, review of *Love in the Time of Cholera, Times,* June 30, 1988.

García Márquez, Gabriel, "Big Mama's Funeral," collected in *No One Writes to the Colonel and Other Stories,* Harper and Row, 1968.

García Márquez, Gabriel, *One Hundred Years of Solitude,* Avon, 1971, p. 11.

García Márquez, Gabriel, "The Making of a Classic," *Atlas World Press,* July, 1979.

Guibert, Rita, *Seven Voices: Seven Latin American Writers Talk to Rita Guibert,* Vintage Books, 1973.

Janes, Regina, "García Márquez, Gabriel," *Contemporary World Writers,* 2nd edition, edited by Tracy Chevalier, St. James Press, 1993, pp. 192-94.

Kennedy, William, "The Author of the Patriarch," *New York Times Book Review,* October 31, 1976, p. 1.

Kiely, Robert, review of *One Years of Solitude, New York Times Book Review,* March 8, 1970, pp. 5, 24.

Lehmann-Haupt, Christopher, review of *Chronicle of a Death Foretold, New York Times,* March 25, 1983, p. 21.

Leonard, John, "Myth Is Alive in Latin America," *New York Times,* March 3, 1970, p. 39.

Leonard, John, review of *News of a Kidnapping, Nation,* June 16, 1997, p. 23.

Logan, William, "The Writings on the Wall," *Washington Post Book World,* November 25, 1977, pp. 5-6.

Minta, S. M. J., "In Praise of the Popular," *Times Literary Supplement,* July 1-7, 1988, p. 730.

Review of *News of a Kidnapping, Kirkus Reviews,* May 1, 1997, p. 693.

Plimpton, George, editor, *Writers on Their Work: The Paris Review Interviews,* 6th series, Viking, 1984.

Pynchon, Thomas, "The Heart's Eternal Vow," *New York Times Book Review,* April 10, 1988, pp. 1, 47, 49.

Rabassa, Gregory, review of *Chronicle of a Death Foretold, World Literature Today,* Winter, 1983.

Richardson, Jack, "Master Builder," *New York Review of Books,* March 26, 1970, pp. 3-4.

Sheppard, R. Z., review of *Of Love and Other Demons, Time,* May 22, 1995, p. 73.

Smothers, Bonnie, review of *News of a Kidnapping, Booklist,* May 1, 1997, p. 1458.

Stone, Robert, review of *News of a Kidnapping, New York Times Book Review,* August 16, 1998, p. 24.

Strawson, Galen, "Sixty Years of Celibacy," *Observer,* July 3, 1988, p. 42.

Sturrock, John, "The Unreality Principle," *Times Literary Supplement,* April 15, 1977, p. 451.

Vilhjálmsson, Thor, "Presenting Gabriel García Márquez," *Books Abroad,* Winter, 1973, pp. 10-11.

West, Paul, "A Green Thought in a Green Shade," *Chicago Tribune Book World,* February 22, 1970, pp. 4-5.

Williams, Raymond L., *Gabriel García Márquez,* Twayne, 1984, pp. 39, 69, 85, 140.

Yardley, Jonathan, review of *Chronicle of a Death Foretold, Washington Post Book World,* March 27, 1983.

Yardley, Jonathan, review of *Of Love and Other Demons, Washington Post Book World,* May 14, 1995, p. 3.

■ For More Information See

BOOKS

Bell, Michael, *Gabriel García Márquez: Solitude and Solidarity,* St. Martin's Press (New York City), 1993.

Bell-Villada, Gene H., *García Márquez: The Man and His Work,* University of North Carolina Press, 1990.

Brotherson, Gordon, *The Emergence of the Latin American Novel,* Cambridge University Press, 1979.

Contemporary Literary Criticism, Gale, Volume 2, 1974; Volume 3, 1975; Volume 8, 1978; Volume 10, 1979; Volume 15, 1980; Volume 27, 1984; Volume 47, 1988; Volume 55, 1989, Volume 68, 1991.

Dolan, Sean, *Gabriel García Márquez,* Chelsea House, 1994.

Fiddian, Robin W., *García Márquez,* LonGarcía Márquezan. 1995.

Gabriel García Márquez, nuestro premio Nobel, La Secretaria de Informacion y Prensa de la Presidencia de la Nacion, 1983.

Gonzalez, Nelly S., *Bibliographic Guide to Gabriel García Márquez, 1986-1992,* Greenwood Press, 1994.

Janes, Regina, *Gabriel García Márquez: Revolutions in Wonderland,* University of Missouri Press, 1981.

McGuirk, Bernard, and Richard Cardwell, editors, *Gabriel García Márquez: New Readings,* Cambridge University Press, 1988.

Pritchett, V. S., *The Myth Makers,* Random House, 1979.

Vargas Llosa, Mario, *García Márquez: Historia de un deicido,* Barral Editores, 1971.

Wood, Michael, *Gabriel García Márquez: One Hundred Years of Solitude,* Cambridge University Press, 1990.

PERIODICALS

Antioch Review, winter, 1991, p. 154.

Books Abroad, Summer, 1973; Spring, 1976.

Book World, June 29, 1997.

Chicago Tribune, March 6, 1983; October 31, 1993.

Chicago Tribune Book World, November 11, 1979; November 7, 1982; November 18, 1984; April 27, 1986.

Detroit News, October 27, 1982; December 16, 1984.

Globe and Mail (Toronto), April 7, 1984; September 19, 1987; May 21, 1988.

Harper's, July, 1997, p. 32.

Hispania, September, 1976; September, 1993, pp. 439-45; March, 1994, pp. 80-81; April, 1999, p. 13.

London Magazine, April/May, 1973; November, 1979.

Los Angeles Times, October 22, 1982; January 25, 1987; August 24, 1988; June 1, 1997.

Los Angeles Times Book Review, April 10, 1983; November 13, 1983; December 16, 1984; April 27, 1986; June 7, 1987; April 17, 1988; October 24, 1993, pp. 3, 10; May 14, 1995, pp. 3, 5; June 1, 1997, p. 10.

Maclean's, July 24, 1995, p. 50; September 1, 1997, p. 56.

Nation, December 2, 1968; May 15, 1972; May 14, 1983; June 12, 1995, pp. 836-40.

National Observer, April 20, 1970.

National Review, June 10, 1983.

New Republic, April 9, 1977; October 27, 1979; May 2, 1983.

New Statesman, June 26, 1970; May 18, 1979; February 15, 1980; September 3, 1982.

Newsweek, March 2, 1970; November 8, 1976; July 3, 1978; December 3, 1979; November 1, 1982; October 8, 1990, p. 70.

New York Review of Books, January 24, 1980; April 14, 1983; January 11, 1996, p. 37; October 9, 1997, p. 19.

New York Times, July 11, 1978; November 6, 1979; October 22, 1982; December 7, 1985; April 26, 1986; June 4, 1986; April 6, 1988.

New York Times Book Review, September 29, 1968; February 20, 1972; July 16, 1978; September 16, 1978; November 11, 1979; November 16, 1980; December 5, 1982; March 27, 1983; April 7, 1985; April 27, 1986; August 9, 1987; May 28, 1995, p. 8; June 15, 1997, p. 16.

Paris Review, Winter, 1981.

People Weekly, July 24, 1995, p. 26; September 15, 1997, p. 56.

Publishers Weekly, May 13, 1974; December 16, 1983; March 27, 1995, pp. 72-73; June 10, 1996, p. 45.

Review, number 24, 1979; September/December, 1981.

Spectator, October 16, 1993, pp. 40-41.

Time, March 16, 1970; November 1, 1976; July 10, 1978; November 1, 1982; March 7, 1983; December 31, 1984; April 14, 1986; June 2, 1997.

Times (London), November 13, 1986.

Times Literary Supplement, February 1, 1980; September 10, 1982; July 14-20, 1989, p. 781; July 7, 1995; July 11, 1997; May 15, 1998, p. 22.

Tribune Books (Chicago), June 28, 1987; April 17, 1988.

UNESCO Courier, February, 1996, p. 4; August 10, 1997, p. 3.

Variety, March 25, 1996, p. 55.

Washington Post, October 22, 1982; April 10, 1994, p. F1.

Washington Post Book World, November 14, 1976; November 25, 1979; November 7, 1982; November 18, 1984; July 19, 1987; April 24, 1988; October 31, 1993, p. 7; June 29, 1997, p. 5.*

—Sketch by J. Sydney Jones

Allen Ginsberg

■ Personal

Born June 3, 1926, in Newark, NJ; died April 5, 1997, in New York, NY; son of Louis (a poet and teacher) and Naomi (Levy) Ginsberg; partner of Peter Orlovsky. *Education:* Columbia University, A.B., 1948. *Politics:* "Space Age Anarchist." *Religion:* "Buddhist-Jewish."

■ Career

Poet. Brooklyn Naval Yard, Brooklyn, NY, spot welder, 1945; Bickford's Cafeteria, New York City, dishwasher, 1945; worker on various cargo ships, 1945-56; literary agent, reporter for New Jersey union newspaper, and copy boy for *New York World Telegram,* 1946; May Co., Denver, CO, night porter, 1946; market research consultant in New York City and San Francisco, 1951-53; University of British Columbia, Vancouver, instructor, 1963; Committee on Poetry Foundation, founder and treasurer, 1966-97; Gathering of the Tribes for a Human Be-In, San Francisco, organizer, 1967; Jack Kerouac School of Disembodied Poetics, Naropa Institute, Boulder, CO, co-founder, co-director, and

teacher, 1974-97. Gave numerous poetry readings at universities, coffee houses, and art galleries in the United States and elsewhere; addressed numerous conferences, including Group Advancement Psychiatry Conference, 1961, Dialectics of Liberation Conference, 1967, LSD Decade Conference, 1977, and World Conference on Humanity, 1979. Appeared in numerous films, including *Pull My Daisy,* 1960; *Guns of the Trees,* 1962; *Couch,* 1964; *Wholly Communion, Chappaqua,* and *Allen for Allen,* all 1965; *Joan of Arc* and *Galaxie,* both 1966; *Herostratus, The Mind Alchemists,* and *Don't Look Back,* all 1967; *Me and My Brother,* 1968; *Dynamite Chicken,* 1971; *Renaldo and Clara,* 1978; *It Doesn't Pay to Be Honest,* 1984; *It Was Twenty Years Ago Today,* 1987; *Heavy Petting,* 1988; *John Bowles: The Complete Outsider* and *Jonas in the Desert,* both 1994; and as narrator of *Kaddish* (television film), 1977. Performer on numerous recordings, including *San Francisco Poets,* Evergreen Records, 1958, *Howl and Other Poems,* Fantasy, 1959, and *Holy Soul Jelly Roll: Poems and Songs, 1949-1993,* Rhino/Word Beat, 1995. *Member:* National Institute of Arts and Letters, P.E.N., New York Eternal Committee for Conservation of Freedom in the Arts.

■ Awards, Honors

Woodbury Poetry Prize; Guggenheim fellow, 1963-64; National Endowment for the Arts grant, 1966, and fellowship, 1986; National Institute of Arts and Letters award, 1969; National Book Award for Poetry, 1974, for *The Fall of America*; National Arts Club Medal of Honor for Literature, 1979; Poetry Society of America gold medal, 1986; Golden Wreath, 1986; Before Columbus Foundation award, 1990, for lifetime achievement; Harriet Monroe Poetry Award, University of Chicago, 1991; American Academy of Arts and Sciences fellowship, 1992.

■ **Writings**

POETRY

Howl and Other Poems, introduction by William Carlos Williams, City Lights (San Francisco), 1956, revised edition, Grabhorn-Hoyem, 1971, 40th-anniversary edition, City Lights, 1996.

Siesta in Xbalba and Return to the States, privately printed, 1956.

Kaddish and Other Poems, 1958-1960, City Lights, 1961.

Empty Mirror: Early Poems, Corinth Books (Chevy Chase, MD), 1961, new edition, 1970.

A Strange New Cottage in Berkeley, Grabhorn Press, 1963.

Reality Sandwiches: 1953-1960, City Lights, 1963.

The Change, Writer's Forum, 1963.

Kral Majales (title means "King of May"), Oyez (Kensington, CA), 1965.

Wichita Vortex Sutra, Housmans (London), 1966, Coyote Books (Brunswick, ME), 1967.

TV Baby Poems, Cape Golliard Press, 1967, Grossman, 1968.

Airplane Dreams: Compositions from Journals, House of Anansi (Toronto), 1968, City Lights, 1969.

(With Alexandra Lawrence) *Ankor Wat*, Fulcrum Press, 1968.

Scrap Leaves, Tasty Scribbles, Poet's Press, 1968.

Wales—A Visitation, July 29, 1967, Cape Golliard Press, 1968.

The Heart Is a Clock, Gallery Upstairs Press, 1968.

Message II, Gallery Upstairs Press, 1968.

Planet News, City Lights, 1968.

For the Soul of the Planet Is Wakening . . . , Desert Review Press, 1970.

The Moments Return: A Poem, Grabhorn-Hoyem, 1970.

Ginsberg's Improvised Poetics, edited by Mark Robison, Anonym Books, 1971.

New Year Blues, Phoenix Book Shop (New York City), 1972.

Open Head, Sun Books (Melbourne), 1972.

Bixby Canyon Ocean Path Word Breeze, Gotham Book Mart (New York City), 1972.

Iron Horse, Coach House Press (Chicago), 1972.

The Fall of America: Poems of These States, 1965-1971, City Lights, 1973.

The Gates of Wrath: Rhymed Poems, 1948-1952, Grey Fox (San Francisco), 1973.

Sad Dust Glories: Poems during Work Summer in Woods, 1974, Workingman's Press (Seattle), 1975.

First Blues: Rags, Ballads, and Harmonium Songs, 1971-1974, Full Court Press (New York City), 1975.

Mind Breaths: Poems, 1972-1977, City Lights, 1978.

Poems All over the Place: Mostly Seventies, Cherry Valley (Wheaton, MD), 1978.

Mostly Sitting Haiku, From Here Press (Fanwood, NJ), 1978, revised and expanded edition, 1979.

Careless Love: Two Rhymes, Red Ozier Press, 1978.

(With Peter Orlovsky) *Straight Hearts' Delight: Love Poems and Selected Letters*, Gay Sunshine Press (San Francisco), 1980.

Plutonian Ode: Poems, 1977-1980, City Lights, 1982.

Collected Poems, 1947-1980, Harper (New York City), 1984, expanded edition published as *Collected Poems: 1947-85*, Penguin (New York City), 1995.

Many Loves, Pequod Press, 1984.

Old Love Story, Lospecchio Press, 1986.

White Shroud, Harper, 1986.

Cosmopolitan Greetings: Poems, 1986-1992, Harper-Collins (New York City), 1994.

Illuminated Poems, illustrated by Eric Drooker, Four Walls Eight Windows (New York City), 1996.

Selected Poems, 1947-1995, HarperCollins, 1996.

Also author, with Kenneth Koch, of *Making It Up: Poetry Composed at St. Mark's Church on May 9, 1979*.

OTHER

(Author of introduction) Gregory Corso, *Gasoline* (poems), City Lights, 1958.

(With William Burroughs) *The Yage Letters* (correspondence), City Lights, 1963.

(Contributor) David Solomon, editor, *The Marijuana Papers* (essays), Bobbs-Merrill (New York City), 1966.

Prose Contribution to Cuban Revolution, Artists Workshop Press, 1966.

(Translator with others) Nicanor Parra, *Poems and Antipoems*, New Directions (Newton, NJ), 1967.

(Contributor) Charles Hollander, editor, *Background Papers on Student Drug Abuse,* U.S. National Student Association, 1967.

(Author of introduction) John A. Wood, *Orbs: A Portfolio of Nine Poems,* Apollyon Press, 1968.

(Contributor) Bob Booker and George Foster, editors, *Pardon Me, Sir, but Is My Eye Hurting Your Elbow?* (plays), Geis, 1968.

(Author of introduction) Louis Ginsberg, *Morning in Spring* (poems), Morrow (New York City), 1970.

(Compiler) *Documents on Police Bureaucracy's Conspiracy against Human Rights of Opiate Addicts and Constitutional Rights of Medical Profession Causing Mass Breakdown of Urban Law and Order,* privately printed, 1970.

(Contributor of commentary) Jean Genet, *May Day Speech,* City Lights, 1970.

Indian Journals: March 1962-May 1963; Notebooks, Diary, Blank Pages, Writings, City Lights, 1970.

Notes after an Evening with William Carlos Williams, Portents Press, 1970.

Declaration of Independence for Dr. Timothy Leary, Hermes Free Press, 1971.

(Author of introduction) William Burroughs Jr., *Speed* (novel), Sphere, 1971.

(Author of foreword) Ann Charters, *Kerouac* (biography), Straight Arrow Books, 1973.

(Contributor of interview) Donald M. Allen, editor, *Robert Creeley, Contexts of Poetry: Interviews 1961-1971,* Four Seasons Foundation (San Francisco), 1973.

The Fall of America Wins a Prize (text of speech), Gotham Book Mart, 1974.

Gay Sunshine Interview: Allen Ginsberg with Allen Young, Grey Fox, 1974.

The Visions of the Great Rememberer (correspondence), Mulch Press (San Francisco), 1974.

Allen Verbatim: Lectures on Poetry, Politics, and Consciousness, edited by Gordon Ball, McGraw (New York City), 1975.

Chicago Trial Testimony, City Lights, 1975.

The Dream of Tibet, City Moon, 1976.

To Eberhart from Ginsberg (correspondence), Penmaen Press (Great Barrington, MA), 1976.

Journals: Early Fifties, Early Sixties, edited by Gordon Ball, Grove (New York City), 1977.

(Contributor) Jonathan Williams, editor, *Madeira and Toasts for Basil Bunting's 75th Birthday,* Jargon Society (East Haven, CT), 1977.

(And author of afterword) *As Ever: Collected Correspondence of Allen Ginsberg and Neal Cassady,* Creative Arts, 1977.

(Author of introduction) Anne Waldman and Marilyn Webb, editors, *Talking Poetics from Naropa Institute: Annals of the Jack Kerouac School of Disembodied Poetics,* Volume I, Shambhala (Boulder, CO), 1978.

Composed on the Tongue (interviews), edited by Donald Allen, Grey Fox, 1980.

(With others) *Nuke Chronicles,* Contact Two (Bowling Green, NY), 1980.

Your Reason and Blake's System, Hanuman Books, 1989.

Allen Ginsberg: Photographs, Twelvetrees Press (Pasadena, CA), 1991.

(Author of introduction) Ernesto Cardenal, *Ergo! The Bumbershoot Literary Magazine,* Bumbershoot, 1991.

(Author of foreword) Anne Waldman, editor, *Out of This World: The Poetry Project at the St. Mark's Church in the Bowery, an Anthology, 1966-1991,* Crown (New York City), 1991.

(Author of introduction) Andy Clausen, *Without Doubt,* Zeitgeist Press, 1991.

(Author of introduction) Jack Kerouac, *Poems All Sizes,* City Lights, 1992.

(Author of introduction) Sharkmeat Blue, *King Death: And Other Poems,* Underground Forest/ Selva Editions, 1992.

(Author of afterword) Louis Ginsberg, *Collected Poems,* edited by Michael Fournier, Northern Lights, 1992.

Snapshot Poetics: Allen Ginsberg's Photographic Memoir of the Beat Era, introduction by Michael Kohler, Chronicle Books (San Francisco), 1993.

(Editor with Peter Orlovsky) *Francesco Clemente: Evening Raga 1992,* Rizzoli International (New York City), 1993.

Honorable Courtship: From the Author's Journals, January 1-15, 1955, edited and illustrated by Dean Bornstein, Coffee House Press (Minneapolis), 1994.

(Author of introduction) Edward Leffingwell, *Earthly Paradise,* Journey Editions, 1994.

Journals Mid-Fifties, 1954-1958, edited by Gordon Ball, HarperCollins, 1995.

(Contributor and author of foreword) Anne Waldman, editor, *The Beat Book: Poems and Fiction of the Beat Generation,* Shambhala (Boston), 1996.

(Author of foreword) Ko Un, *Beyond Self: 108 Korean Zen Poems,* Parallax Press (Berkeley, CA), 1997.

Work appears in numerous anthologies, including *The Beat Generation and the Angry Young Men,* edited by Gene Feldman and Max Gartenberg, Citadel Press, 1958; and *The New Oxford Book of American Verse*, edited by Richard Ellmann, Oxford University Press, 1976. Contributor of poetry and articles to periodicals, including *Evergreen Review, Journal for the Protection of All Beings, Playboy, Nation, New Age, New Yorker, Atlantic Monthly, Partisan Review*, and *Times Literary Supplement*. Book reviewer, *Newsweek*, 1950; correspondent, *Evergreen Review*, 1965; former contributing editor, *Black Mountain Review*; former advisory guru, *Marijuana Review*.

Ginsberg's papers are housed at Stanford University.

■ **Adaptations**

"Kaddish" was adapted as a film, with Ginsberg as narrator, and broadcast by National Educational Television in 1977.

■ **Sidelights**

Gaining notoriety for both his highly profiled activities in the social and political movements of the mid- to late twentieth century as well as for his poetry, Allen Ginsberg came to represent, to many critics, the poetic voice of an entire generation. With the 1956 publication of *Howl and Other Poems*, Ginsberg threw down the gauntlet of counterculture youth, going on to become first a prominent member of the Beat movement and then one of the first hippies as he helped spearhead the anti-war movement of the 1960s. Citing numerous incidents of Ginsberg's attempts to shatter social decorum and break with tradition, Bruce Bawer noted in his review of Ginsberg's *Collected Poems, 1947-1980* in *New Criterion*: "What is remarkable is not that Ginsberg . . . advertised himself with such arrogance and audacity, but that it . . . worked like a charm; thanks to such shameless scene-stealing antics, he . . . attained a measure of fame that he could never have secured by his poetry alone. He is, unarguably, the only poet in America who is not just a member of the August American Academy of Arts and Letters but a bona fide celebrity. . . . He is truly famous."

With works such as his *Howl and Other Poems*, Ginsberg gave voice to a force intent upon fighting, with words, what were perceived to be destructive, oppressive "social norms." Referring to "Howl" as expressed with a "Hebraic-Melvillian bardic breath"—a reference to Ginsberg's own religious background—the thirty-year-old poet used the raw, honest language of the streets rather than conform to the accepted standard: a refined language couched in literary tradition and classical references. The title poem of *Howl* shocked some critics: as Walter Sutton wrote in his *American Free Verse: The Modern Revolution in Poetry*, "Howl" served as "a tirade revealing an animus directed outward against those who do not share the poet's social and sexual orientation." However, others viewed the new poet as a welcome voice in a stale, oppressive literary tradition. As Mark Ford noted in a review of Ginsberg's work in the *London Review of Books*: "From the first "Howl" had a kind of totemic significance . . . because it drew so clearly and cleverly the lines of battle between the hips and the squares, the holy bums and the Establishment's 'scholars of war' and 'fairies of advertising' with their 'mustard gas of sinister intelligent editors.'"

Ginsberg's poetry has its roots in a complex lifeview that evolved as a result of a difficult-to-navigate childhood. Born in 1926 in Newark, New Jersey, he was raised by a Russian-born Jewish mother who suffered from paranoia and who, during her son's adolescence, would be institutionalized a number of times. The emotional instability caused by Naomi Ginsberg's mental illness, coupled with her political radicalism as a member of the Communist Party, would greatly influence both her son's own compulsion to shatter tradition and his need for attention and recognition. In a vain attempt to provide his family with some structure, Louis Ginsberg treated his son, Allen, with a strict hand. Despite being resented by Allen as a severe disciplinarian, Louis proved to be an influence equally as strong as Naomi. A teacher at a New Jersey high school and a respected poet, Louis Ginsberg provided to his son, by his own example and encouragement, an outlet for Allen's emotional turmoil through poetry. However, Louis would have been less accepting of Allen's growing awareness of his own homosexuality; as Ginsberg traversed his high school years he hid his attraction to members of the same sex from both his parents and his friends.

Ginsberg had always been a voracious reader, and through his family library he was exposed to the

After being banned from reading his uncensored poems to a live audience, a court decision in New York permitted Ginsberg to read to fans at Washington Square Park in 1966.

works of Edgar Allan Poe, Emily Dickinson, and other Romantic and Metaphysical poets. As he began to seriously pursue his interest in poetry, a new influence appeared in the form of the poet William Carlos Williams, whose works Ginsberg was first introduced to while attending high school in Patterson, New Jersey. Williams, a fellow Paterson, New Jersey resident, was not highly thought of as a poet by Ginsberg's teachers, who considered his poems unrefined and amateur. However, what Ginsberg heard within Williams' work was not an unschooled voice but an attempt by the poet to capture the rough-edged street talk in the blue-collar neighborhoods where Ginsberg lived. Williams' influence would be pivotal in Ginsberg's development as a poet—with a nod to Williams, Allen rewrote several of his finished poems, changing them to incorporate the rough-edged speech that would come to characterize his more mature work.

Birth of the Beats

After graduating from high school at age sixteen, Ginsberg left home and enrolled at New York's Columbia University, where he kept company with fellow-students Jack Kerouac and Lucien Carr, as well as William S. Burroughs, an older man who had an apartment near the Columbia campus. The men had several things in common: in addition to coming from relatively comfortable middle-class surroundings (except for Burroughs, who was an heir to the vast Burroughs Corporation fortune), they each rejected the stifling academic atmosphere at Columbia, embedded as it was in a tradition of regimentation, routinization, and classical learning. Instead, they embraced a belief that true genius is born of madness with a dash of poverty; that poets such as nineteenth-century British writer William Blake, who broke with the accepted path and allowed himself to be led by his own internal emotional chaos, were the true geniuses. It was this philosophy that would characterize the Beats, as they and other like-minded writers soon became known.

Reflecting the Beats' identification with the underclasses as well as with his own need to reject the sheltered, middlebrow life of the Columbia campus—and gain money to indulge in another Beat characteristic: drug use—Ginsberg went outside the school confines and took several jobs, including stints as a spot welder in a shipyard, a dishwasher, and a worker on cargo ships. Not surprisingly, the teachings of such Columbia educators as Lionel Trilling were endured but ultimately rejected by Ginsberg, although the young Beat nonetheless managed to graduate in 1948. Unfortunately, his graduation would coincide with a stint in the Columbia Psychiatric Institute after he was found guilty of aiding fellow Beat member Herbert Huncke in a burglary.

With the cachet of his prestigious college degree negated by a criminal record, Ginsberg knew that following his father into a career such as teaching was now out of the question. During his junior year he had gained his first taste of life as a professional writer while serving a stint as a reporter on a newspaper published by a local labor union. Along with a college degree from Columbia, that job experience counted for enough to land Ginsberg a position as copy boy for the *New York World Telegram,* although he resumed his more arduous but better-paying shipyard work by the end of the year. Ginsberg remained on the East Coast for the next few years, working and developing his poetic voice.

1950 could be considered the start of Ginsberg's "professional" literary career, as he began a succession of writing jobs. After a stint as book reviewer for *Newsweek* magazine, he moved to the West Coast, where he worked as a market research consultant. By 1953, deciding to make the San Francisco Bay area his new home, Ginsberg rekindled his friendships with fellow Beat writers Kerouac and Burroughs, fell in love with Neal Cassady—who rejected Ginsberg's love and whose death in the mid-1960s would devastate the poet—and began a long-term romantic relationship with Peter Orlovsky. Kerouac had begun to write novels in a style that he called "spontaneous prose." This style, which involved putting a roll of white paper into a typewriter and typing con-

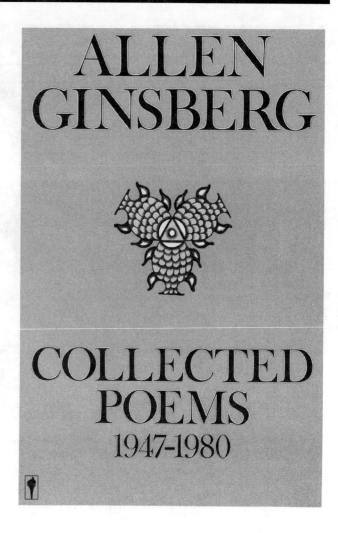

This 1980 collection of Ginsberg's works offers a prime sampling of his often erotic and socially critical verses.

tinuously using a "stream of consciousness" technique, was immediately adopted by Ginsberg, who scribbled lines as the muse struck and refused to rewrite or refine what resulted from this spontaneous effort. Ginsberg would later describe the process during an interview with Kenneth Koch in the *New York Times Book Review:* "I write a little bit every other day. I just write when I have a thought. Sometimes I have big thoughts, sometimes little thoughts. The deal is to accept whatever comes. Or work with whatever comes. Leave yourself open."

Kerouac's invention, as well as Ginsberg's increasing view of himself as a transcendental poet on the order of Walt Whitman led the two Columbia transplants to influence their compatriots—a growing cadre of West Coast writers that now included Lawrence Ferlinghetti, Gregory Corso, and Kenneth Rexroth–to form the San Francisco Beats. The group emphasized a writer's emotions and natural mode of expression over traditional literary structures, citing as their literary predecessors William Blake, Walt Whitman, Herman Melville, Henry David Thoreau, and Ralph Waldo Emerson. In *American Poetry Review* Fred Moramarco described Ginsberg's desire "to be perceived as a divinely inspired, gifted Dionysian spirit, yoking the poles of the romantic sensibility, the luminous visions of [William] Blake with the Democratic Vistas of Whitman."

Howl Shocks Literary Establishment

In 1956, with the publication of *Howl and Other Poems,* Ginsberg expanded his notoriety beyond the confines of the San Francisco Bay Area. First read aloud at the Six Gallery in San Francisco, the poems collected in *Howl* were published by fellow poet Ferlinghetti's City Lights bookstore. "Howl" reflects the Beat concept of genius, describing the insanity of Ginsberg's generation, as it opens: "I saw the best minds of my generation destroyed by madness, starving hysterical naked/ dragging themselves through the negro streets at dawn looking for an angry fix,/angelheaded hipsters burning for the ancient heavenly connection to the starry dynamo in the machinery of night." Focusing on criminals and deviates, and on sexual deviance, drug use, and self-destructive behavior, the work also invokes Moloch, an ancient god of fire to whom children were given in sacrifice. Moloch's name is repeated, chantlike, as Ginsberg allies him with man's predilection for war and suppression of cultural and sexual diversity. "The movement of 'Howl,'" explained Gregory Stevenson in his *The Daybreak Boys: Essays on the Literature of the Beat Generation,* ". . . is from protest, pain, outrage, attack, and lamentation to acceptance, affirmation, love and vision— from alienation to communion. The poet descends into an underworld of darkness, suffering, and isolation and then ascends into spiritual knowledge . . . and a sense of union with the human community and with God."

In addition to stunning its audience, Ginsberg's reading of *Howl* also stunned the San Francisco Police Department. Because of the graphic sexual language of the poem, authorities declared Ginsberg's book obscene, banned it, and arrested publisher Ferlinghetti. The trial that followed attracted national attention, as prominent literary critics, including friend Rexroth, defended Ginsberg's work and the book's publication. The trial propelled Ginsberg to national celebrity, and the outcome—that *Howl* was not obscene—was his vindication. *Howl* became the manifesto of the anti-bourgeois Beats and a rallying point of a growing counterculture movement across the United States. The ideas and art of the Beats would greatly influence popular culture during the 1950s and 1960s.

Develops Self-Identity as Visionary

Having made a name for himself with *Howl,* Ginsberg's next work was *Kaddish and Other Poems,* published in 1961. "Kaddish", similar in format and style to "Howl", has as its basis the traditional Hebrew prayer for the dead after which it is named. Within its long lines, it recounts the life and death of Ginsberg's mother, a tale reflecting the chaos that, while hurtful to Ginsberg as a younger man, he now embraced as a Beat. The poet's complex feelings for Naomi Ginsberg, an affection colored by his mother's struggle with the mental illness that took her life in 1956, form the basis for "Kaddish," considered by critics to be among Ginsberg's best work. Describing "Kaddish" in the *Dictionary of Literary Biography,* John Ower noted that the work, abrupt and powerful, "is one of the poet's most important and powerful works. . . . While 'Kaddish' is moving primarily as a poem of psychological revelation and elemental human emotion, the piece gains added depth and force by its connection of the personal to both social and . . . metaphysical concerns."

Kaddish would be among the first of several collected works deliberately exploring Ginsberg's experiences writing poetry under the influence of mind-altering drugs. A continuing preoccupation reflected throughout all of Ginsberg's poetry is a concern with the spiritual realm. Indeed, Ginsberg believed himself to be a visionary of sorts, a belief stemming from a series of visions—sparked, perhaps by an indulgence in marijuana and accompanied by what Ginsberg believed was the voice of the long-dead poet William Blake—he had while reading Blake's poetry shortly after leaving

Columbia. These "visions" were embraced by his fellow Beats, for whom he became a sort of spiritual guru. They also prompted Ginsberg to experiment, for a time, with using various drugs as a means of furthering his art. In fact, according to the poet, some of his best work was written while under the influence of various mind-altering substances: peyote fueled Ginsberg's efforts for portions of "Howl"; heroin for "I Hate America"; amphetamines for "Kaddish"; LSD for "Wales Visitation"; and codeine for "Death to Van Gogh's Ear." "The Blake vision and the taking of hallucinogenics had at least two lasting consequences for Ginsberg's poetic development," according to *Dictionary of Literary Biography* essayist Laszlo K. Gefin. "First, they strengthened his sense of alienation from mainstream notions of selfhood and being. . . . Second, writing under the influence of drugs helped loosen the bonds of customary language usage, not only in scrambling grammar and getting rid of what the poet termed 'syntactical sawdust,' but also in encouraging . . . his free association and juxtaposition of disparate words and phrases."

Ginsberg's experimentation with mind-altering drugs continued until he took a trip to India in 1962. There he encountered meditation and yoga, which he embraced as more conducive to literary output, and which he began to promote in place of marijuana and heroin. Ginsberg's fascination with Eastern religions also began at this point, and he was encouraged by his discovery of mantras— rhythmic chants used to induce a heightened connection with the spiritual realm. The rhythm, breath, and elemental sounds incorporated into these mantras quickly found their way into Ginsberg's poetry: mantras were woven into the body of some works, while others contained a sustained breathiness. One form of meditation used by Ginsberg, called *shamatha*, allows one to concentrate on one's own breathing. Shamatha would be used by Ginsberg as a way of writing several poems in his *Mind Breaths: Poems, 1972-1977*, a 1978 collection that marked a transition from the raw anger of his earlier works to a more tranquil life-view. During the many poetry readings he was now requested to conduct around the country, Ginsberg would often begin by chanting a mantra, thereby creating the mood he desired for his recitation.

Ginsberg's interest in Eastern religions eventually led him to the Venerable Chogyam Trungpa,

Rinpoche, a business-minded Buddhist abbot from Tibet. In the early 1970s he attended classes at Trungpa's Colorado-based Naropa Institute, and also taught some poetry classes there, the purpose of which was to make Buddhists more articulate. By 1974 Ginsberg and fellow poet Anne Waldman had founded their Jack Kerouac School of Disembodied Poetics at the Naropa Institute, attracting such prominent poets as Diane di Prima, Ron Padget, and William H. Burroughs to lecture. In 1972 Ginsberg also took the Refuge and Boddhisattva vows, formally committing himself to the Buddhist faith.

From Visionary to Political Dissident

While spirituality influenced Ginsberg's manner of writing, politics and social issues continued to be the main subject matter of both his life and art. The poet's political philosophy was strongly libertarian in nature: he supported individual expression over traditional structure. Mirroring his mother's radicalism, several of his early poems focus on the labor union struggles of the 1930s, popular radical figures, the Communist purges of Senator Joseph McCarthy, and other leftist touchstones. In "Wichita Vortex Sutra," the title poem of his 1966 collection, he attempts to end the Vietnam War through a kind of mantra-like evocation, while "Plutonian Ode" performs the same magic upon nuclear power. Even works such as "Howl," although not overtly political, are still considered by many critics to contain strong social criticisms.

In the mid-1960s Ginsberg became closely associated with the Hippie movement, as well as with opposition to U.S. involvement in the war in Vietnam. Many of his poems, such as those collected in *Empty Mirror: EarlyPoems* and *The Fall of America: Poems of These States, 1965-1971*, reflect this activity. He advocated a strategy in which antiwar demonstrators extolled peace and love while demonstrating their disaffection for the war, using mantras, flowers, bells, and incense in their public protests for peace. Ginsberg coined this strategy "flower power." In 1967 he helped organize one of the first hippie festivals, the "Gathering of the Tribes for a Human Be-in," modeling it after a Hindu religious festival called a *mela*. The Gathering of the Tribes served as an inspiration for hundreds of other hippie gatherings to follow, infuriating the middle classes while inspiring many college-age students to embrace the counterculture. Ginsberg also testified for the defense during the notorious "Chicago Seven" conspiracy trial, in which several antiwar activists were charged with conspiracy to cross state lines to promote a riot.

Not surprisingly, or perhaps intentionally, Ginsberg's politics sometimes drew the attention of law enforcement and other authorities. He was among those arrested at an antiwar demonstration in New York City in 1967; a year later he was teargassed at the Democratic National Convention in Chicago. In 1972 his active, vocal demonstration against then-President Richard M. Nixon at the Republican National Convention in Miami again landed Ginsberg in jail. In 1978 Ginsberg and long-time companion Orlovsky were arrested for sitting on train tracks in order to stop a trainload of radioactive waste coming from the Rocky Flats Nuclear Weapons Plant in Colorado.

Ginsberg's political activism was not confined to the United States. To the chagrin of the Communist Cuban government, during his 1965 visit to that country as a correspondent for *Evergreen Review,* he complained about the treatment of gays at the University of Havana. The government asked Ginsberg to leave the country. Shortly thereafter, the scruffy, bearded, drug-promoting poet traveled to Czechoslovakia, where he was elected "King of May" by thousands of cheering Czech citizens. The next day the Czech government extended an invitation for him to go elsewhere, ostensibly because he was "sloppy and degenerate." Ginsberg viewed the situation differently, noting later that the Czechs were embarrassed by the popularity of a bearded, drug-using, homosexual poet.

The 1980s brought with it a more open environment for gays and lesbians in the United States,

Ginsberg reads from his most famous collection, *Howl,* outside the U.S. Court of Appeals in 1994, protesting a policy that restricted the broadcast of "indecent material" over the airwaves.

and many of Ginsberg's poetry written during this period tends toward the erotic. As Gefin noted, the poet "combines explicit sexuality with a rueful and gently self-ironic recognition of growing old." During his later career Ginsberg also authored 1986's "White Shroud," which some critics have praised as on the same level as "Kaddish" and "Howl" in the Ginsberg pantheon. Inspired by a dream Ginsberg had in which his mother appeared as a bag-lady on the streets of New York's Lower East Side, "White Shroud" "traces a poet-hero's archetypal search for guidance," explained Gefin. In the work Naomi appears as a wise woman who, despite her poverty, remains fierce and independent and proud. By the 1990s Ginsberg had moved from the playful eroticism of the 1980s to the musical verse of *Collected Poems*, which contains such works as "Do the Meditation Rock," "Put down Your Cigarette Rag (Don't Smoke)," and "Airplane Blues."

Continues to Fascinate Critics

From his early days as a disaffected Columbia student attempting to conform standards of genius to his own mindset, to his role as a long-haired, "dirty," drug-using hippie role-model, to his position as a political agitator embracing numerous leftist causes and expressing his disdain for what he perceived as a fat, complacent middle-class America, to his still more recent establishment within the very legion he once sought to denigrate—the academia-approved pantheon of the most notable writers of the twentieth century—Ginsberg's poetic career has been one of the most influential and controversial of his generation. According to James Campbell in the *Times Literary Supplement*, "No one has made his poetry speak for the whole man, without inhibition of any time, more than Ginsberg." Even after Ginsberg's poetic statement had become more a commodity itself, partly through his redundancy as a poet, and partly through his appearance on talk shows and other mass-audience "celebrity" vehicles, Ginsberg remains the object of much scholarly attention. Three years before Ginsberg's death in April of 1997, a documentary directed by Jerry Aronson, *The Life and Times of Allen Ginsberg*, was released. The same year, Stanford University paid Ginsberg a reported $1 million for the poet's personal archives. Even the poet's photographs of fellow Beats, collected and published as *Allen Ginsberg: Photographs* in 1991, have given

In this final collection of his verses, Ginsberg contemplates his own death while continuing to berate America's sacrosanct political and cultural beliefs.

critics and scholars new insights into the poet's life and legacy.

Collections of Ginsberg's previously published works continue to remain in continuous publication, while his letters and journals have also regularly made their way to bookstore shelves. Works such as *Honorable Courtship: From the Author's Journals*, and *Journals Mid-Fifties: 1954-1958*, published in 1994 and 1995 respectively, reflect the public's continued fascination with Ginsberg's legacy, as well as the author's continued need to obsess upon himself. Jim Krusoe, reviewing *Journals Mid-Fifties* in the *Los Angeles Times Book Review*, maintains that the work "provides plenty of food for thought about genius in general and about

If you enjoy the works of Allen Ginsberg, you may also want to check out the following:

William S. Burroughs, *Naked Lunch,* 1959.
Lawrence Ferlinghetti, *A Coney Island of the Mind,* 1958.
Jack Kerouac, *On the Road,* 1957.
The Source, a documentary about the Beats featuring readings by Johnny Depp and Dennis Hopper, 1999.

Ginsberg's development in particular." For other reviewers, however, these journals shed less light on the poet than they do on his written works and the development of his oeuvre. As a reviewer noted in the *Economist:* "In most writers self-pre-occupation is usually mortal. But Mr. Ginsberg has the balancing gifts of promiscuous curiosity and an almost sappy, American optimism." For Krusoe, in the end, "the brilliance of these journals is exactly the brilliant persistence of a man who will not quit until his dream life, his love life and his poems are melded into a single whole."

During his lifetime Ginsberg was compared by critics most often with writers Robert Lowell, Frank O'Hara, and Charles Olson, each of whom broke with tradition in establishing a new, uniquely American verse in the mid-twentieth century. Of Ginsberg's position within this group, *Dictionary of Literary Biography* essayist Paul Christiensen commented that "Each of these major writers gave to the main currents of verse his own unique voice and intelligence, but it was Ginsberg especially who seems to have awakened America's youth to the powers of poetry to make stirring prophecies and to reinvigorate the spheres of politics and ideology. Perhaps more than any other poet of his time or since, Ginsberg is the bard of disaffected youth in America, the single most potent lyric voice discoursing on national crises in ways that arouse and stimulate the young to take part in the political process." In an essay in *Journal of Popular Culture,* critic George W. Lyon Jr. compared Ginsberg to nineteenth-century British poet Lord Byron, and noted: "We often speak of 'fine arts' and 'popular arts' as though there existed an absolute distinction between the two. Occasionally a figure will link both worlds. So it is with Allen Ginsberg."

■ Works Cited

Bawer, Bruce, "The Phenomenon of Allen Ginsberg," *New Criterion,* February, 1985, pp. 1-14.

Campbell, James, review of *Cosmopolitan Greetings, Times Literary Supplement,* September 9, 1995, p. 22.

Christiensen, Paul, "Allen Ginsberg," *Dictionary of Literary Biography,* Volume 16: *The Beats: Literary Bohemians in Postwar America,* Gale, 1983, pp. 214-41.

Ford, Mark, "I Am Prince Mishkin," *London Review of Books,* April 23, 1987, pp. 22-23.

Gefin, Laszlo K., "Allen Ginsberg," *Dictionary of Literary Biography,* Volume 169: *American Poets since World War II, Fifth Series,* Gale, 1996, pp. 116-36.

Ginsberg, Allen, interview with Kenneth Koch, *New York Times Book Review,* October 23, 1977, pp. 9, 44-46.

Review of *Journals Mid-Fifties, 1954-1958, Economist,* November 11, 1995, p. 8.

Krusoe, Jim, review of *Journals Mid-Fifties, Los Angeles Times Book Review,* September 3, 1995, p. 4.

Lyon, George W., Jr., "Allen Ginsberg: Angel Headed Hipster," *Journal of Popular Culture,* winter, 1969, pp. 391-403.

Moramarco, Fred, "Moloch's Poet: A Retrospective Look at Allen Ginsberg's Poetry," *American Poetry Review,* September/October, 1982, pp. 10-18.

Ower, John, "Allen Ginsberg," in *Dictionary of Literary Biography,* Volume 5: *American Poets since World War I,* Gale, 1980, pp. 269-86.

Stevenson, Gregory, "Allen Ginsberg's 'Howl': A Reading," in *The Daybreak Boys: Essays on the Literature of the Beat Generation,* Southern Illinois Press, 1990, pp. 50-58.

Sutton, Walter, *American Free Verse: The Modern Revolution in Poetry,* New Directions, 1973.

■ For More Information See

BOOKS

Carroll, Paul, *The Poem in Its Skin,* Follett, 1968.

Charters, Ann, *Scenes along the Road,* Gotham Book Mart, 1971.

Charters, Ann, *Kerouac,* Straight Arrow Books, 1973.

Charters, Samuel, *Some Poems/Poets: Studies in American Underground Poetry since 1945,* Oyez, 1971.

Concise Dictionary of American Literary Biography: 1941-1968, Gale (Detroit), 1987.

Contemporary Literary Criticism, Gale, Volume 1, 1973, Volume 2, 1974, Volume 3, 1975, Volume 4, 1975, Volume 6, 1976, Volume 13, 1980, Volume 36, 1986, Volume 69, 1992, Volume 109, 1999.

Contemporary Poets, sixth edition, St. James Press (Detroit), 1996.

Cook, Bruce, *The Beat Generation,* Scribner (New York City), 1971.

Erlich, J. W., editor, *Howl of the Censor,* Nourse Publishing, 1961.

Faas, Ekbert, editor, *Toward a New American Poetics: Essays and Interviews,* Black Sparrow Press (Santa Barbara, CA), 1978.

Fielder, Leslie A., *Waiting for the End,* Stein & Day (Briarcliff Manor, NY), 1964.

Gay and Lesbian Biography, St. James Press, 1997.

Gay and Lesbian Literature, St. James Press, 1994.

Gay Sunshine Interview: Allen Ginsberg with Allen Young, Grey Fox Press, 1974.

Gross, Theodore L., editor, *Representative Men,* Free Press (New York City), 1970.

Kramer, Jane, *Allen Ginsberg in America,* Random House (New York City), 1969, new edition, Fromm International Publishing, 1997.

Lipton, Lawrence, *The Holy Barbarians,* Messner (New York City), 1959.

McNally, Dennis, *Desolate Angel: Jack Kerouac, the Beats, and America,* Random House, 1979.

Merrill, Thomas F., *Allen Ginsberg,* Twayne (New York City), 1969.

Mersmann, James F., *Out of the Vietnam Vortex: A Study of Poets and Poetry against the War,* University Press of Kansas, 1974.

Miles, Barry, *Two Lectures on the Work of Allen Ginsberg,* Contemporary Research Press (Dallas), 1993.

Morgan, Bill, *The Works of Allen Ginsberg, 1941-1994: A Descriptive Bibliography,* Greenwood Press (Westport, CT), 1995.

Morgan, Bill, *The Response to Allen Ginsberg, 1926-1994: A Bibliography of Secondary Sources,* foreword by Ginsberg, Greenwood Press, 1996.

Mottram, Eric, *Allen Ginsberg in the Sixties,* Unicorn Bookshop, 1972.

Parkinson, Thomas F., *A Casebook on the Beats,* Crowell (New York City), 1961.

Poetry Criticism, Volume 4, Gale, 1992.

Portuges, Paul, *The Visionary Poetics of Allen Ginsberg,* Ross-Erikson (Santa Barbara, CA), 1978.

Rather, Lois, *Bohemians to Hippies: Waves of Rebellion,* Rather Press (Oakland, CA), 1977.

Reference Guide to American Literature, third edition, St. James Press, 1994.

Rexroth, Kenneth, *American Poetry in the Twentieth Century,* Herder, 1971.

Rosenthal, Mocha L. *The Modern Poets: A Critical Introduction,* Oxford University Press, 1960.

Rosenthal, Mocha L., *The New Poets: American and British Poetry since World War II,* Oxford University Press, 1967.

Roszak, Theodore, *The Making of a Counter Culture,* Doubleday (Garden City, NY), 1969.

Schumacher, Michael, *Dharma Lion,* St. Martin's Press (New York City), 1994.

Shaw, Robert B., editor, *American Poetry since 1960: Some Critical Perspectives,* Dufour (Chester Springs, PA), 1974.

Simpson, Louis, *A Revolution in Taste,* Macmillan (New York City), 1978.

Stepanchev, Stephen, *American Poetry since 1945,* Harper, 1965.

Tyrell, John, *Naked Angels,* McGraw, 1976.

Widmer, Kingsley, *The Fifties: Fiction, Poetry, Drama,* Everett/Edwards (DeLand FL), 1970.

PERIODICALS

Advocate, February 22, 1994.

American Poetry Review, September, 1977.

Antioch Review, spring, 1994, p. 374.

Ariel, October, 1993, pp. 21-32.

Art Press, Number 188, 1994, pp. E24-26.

Atlanta Journal and Constitution, November 19, 1994, p. WL23.

Best Sellers, December 15, 1974.

Black Mountain Review, autumn, 1957.

Bloomsbury Review, March, 1993, p. 5.

Booklist, April 15, 1994, p. 1503; April 15, 1995, p. 1468.

Book World, May 25, 1969.

Bulletin of Bibliography, December, 1993, pp. 279-293.

Carolina Quarterly, spring/summer, 1975.

Chicago Review, summer, 1975.

Denver Post, July 20, 1975.

Detroit News, April 18, 1997.

Dionysos, winter, 1993, pp. 30-42.

East West Journal, February, 1978.

Encounter, February, 1970.

Entertainment Weekly, October 11, 1996, p. 92.

Esquire, April, 1973.

Evergreen Review, July/August, 1961.

Globe and Mail (Toronto), February 23, 1985.

Harper's, October, 1966.

Hudson Review, autumn, 1973.

Interview, June, 1994, p. 16.

Journal of American Culture, fall, 1993, pp. 81-88.

Lambda Book Report, July, 1993, p. 42; July, 1994, p. 47; September, 1994, p. 34.

Library Journal, June 15, 1958; February 1, 1987; May 1, 1994; August, 1995, p. 79.

Life, May 27, 1966.

Los Angeles Times, April 18, 1985; February 16, 1994, p. F1; February 17, 1994, p. F3.

Los Angeles Times Book Review, January 2, 1994, p. 12; May 29, 1994, p. 8.

Michigan Quarterly Review, spring, 1994, pp. 350-359.

Nation, February 25, 1957; November 11, 1961; November 12, 1977; May 20, 1991.

National Observer, December 9, 1968.

National Review, September 12, 1959; May 19, 1997, p. 54.

National Screw, June, 1977.

New Age, April, 1976.

New Republic, July 25, 1970; October 12, 1974; October 22, 1977.

New Statesman, May 12, 1995, p. 38; October 27, 1995, p. 47.

New Times, February 20, 1978.

New Yorker, August 17, 1968; August 24, 1968; May 28, 1979.

New York Times, February 6, 1972; May 21, 1994, p. A13; September 20, 1994, p. C15; September 25, 1994, sec. 2, p. 34; October 29, 1994, p. A19; September 29, 1995, p. C18.

New York Times Book Review, September 2, 1956; May 11, 1969; August 31, 1969; April 15, 1973; March 2, 1975; March 19, 1978; May 29, 1994, p. 14.

New York Times Magazine, July 11, 1965.

Observer (London), June 11, 1995, p. 16.

Parnassus, spring/summer, 1974.

Partisan Review, number 2, 1959; number 3, 1967; number 3, 1971; number 2, 1974.

People, July 3, 1978; November 25, 1996, p. 27.

Philadelphia Bulletin, May 19, 1974.

Playboy, April, 1969; January, 1995, p. 24.

Plays and Players, April, 1972.

Poetry, September, 1957; July, 1969; September, 1969.

Progressive, May, 1994, p. 48; August, 1994, pp. 34-39.

Salmagundi, spring/summer, 1973.

San Francisco Oracle, February, 1967.

Saturday Review, October 5, 1957.

Small Press Review, July/August, 1977.

Stand, autumn, 1995, p. 77.

Thoth, winter, 1967.

Time, February 9, 1959; November 18, 1974; March 5, 1979.

Times Literary Supplement, July 7, 1978; September 1, 1995, p. 22.

Tribune Books (Chicago), June 11, 1995, p. 5.

Unmuzzled Ox, Volume 3, number 2, 1975.

USA Today, July, 1995, p. 96.

Vanity Fair, March, 1994, p. 186.

Village Voice, April 18, 1974.

Washington Post, March 17, 1985.

Washington Post Book World, March 20, 1994, p. 12.

Western American Literature, spring, 1995, pp. 3-28.

Whole Earth Review, fall, 1995, p. 90.

World Literature Today, winter, 1995, p. 146.

OTHER

The Life and Times of Allen Ginsberg (film), First Run Features, 1994.

■ Obituaries

PERIODICALS

Economist, April 12, 1997, p. 87.

Entertainment Weekly, April 18, 1997, p. 18.

Los Angeles Times, April 6, 1997, p. A1.

Maclean's, April 14, 1997, p. 11.

Nation, April 28, 1997, p. 8.

National Review, May 5, 1997.

Newsweek, April 14, 1997, p. 60.

New York Times, April 7, 1997, pp. A1, A42; April 7, 1997, pp. B1, B3; April 8, 1997, p. B10.

Observer (London), April 6, 1997, p. 4.

People, April 21, 1997, p. 169.

Progressive, May, 1997, p. 10.

Rolling Stone, May 29, 1997, p. 34.

Time, April 14, 1997, p. 31.

Times (London), April 7, 1997.

Washington Post, April 6, 1997, p. B8.*

—Sketch by Pamela L. Shelton

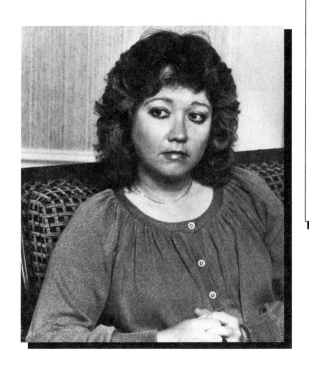

S. E. Hinton

■ Personal

Born in 1950, in Tulsa, OK; married David E. Inhofe (in mail order business), September, 1970; children: Nicholas David. *Education:* University of Tulsa, B.S., 1970.

■ Addresses

Home—Tulsa, OK.

■ Career

Writer. Consultant on film adaptations of her novels; minor acting roles in some film adaptations of her novels.

■ Awards, Honors

New York Herald Tribune best teenage books citation, 1967, *Chicago Tribune Book World* Spring Book Festival Honor Book, 1967, *Media & Methods* Maxi Award, American Library Association (ALA) Best Young Adult Books citation, both 1975, and Massachusetts Children's Book Award, 1979, all for *The Outsiders;* ALA Best Books for Young Adults citation, 1971, *Chicago Tribune Book World* Spring Book Festival Award Honor Book, 1971, and Massachusetts Children's Book Award, 1978, all for *That Was Then, This Is Now;* ALA Best Books for Young Adults citation, 1975, *School Library Journal* Best Books of the Year citation, 1975, and Land of Enchantment Book Award, New Mexico Library Association, 1982, all for *Rumble Fish;* ALA Best Books for Young Adults citation, 1979, *School Library Journal* Best Books of the Year citation, 1979, New York Public Library Books for the Teen-Age citation, 1980, American Book Award nomination for children's paperback, 1981, Sue Hefly Award Honor Book, Louisiana Association of School Libraries, 1982, California Young Reader Medal nomination, California Reading Association, 1982, and Sue Hefly Award, 1983, all for *Tex;* Golden Archer Award, 1983; Recipient of first ALA Young Adult Services Division/*School Library Journal* Margaret A. Edwards Award, 1988, for body of work.

■ Writings

YOUNG ADULT NOVELS

The Outsiders, Viking (New York City), 1967.
That Was Then, This Is Now, illustrated by Hal Siegel, Viking, 1971.

Rumble Fish (also see below), Delacorte (New York City), 1975.

Tex, Delacorte, 1979.

Taming the Star Runner, Delacorte, 1988.

CHILDREN'S BOOKS

Big David, Little David, illustrated by Alan Daniel, Doubleday, 1995.

The Puppy Sister, illustrated by Jacqueline Rogers, Delacorte, 1995.

OTHER

(With Francis Ford Coppola) *Rumble Fish* (screenplay; adapted from her novel), Universal, 1983.

■ Adaptations

Film adaptations of Hinton's novels include *Tex,* starring Matt Dillon, Walt Disney Productions, 1982; *The Outsiders,* starring C. Thomas Howell and Matt Dillon, Warner Bros., 1983; and *That Was Then, This Is Now,* starring Emilio Estevez and Craig Sheffer, Paramount, 1985. *The Outsiders* was adapted as a television series by Fox-TV, 1990. Current Affairs and Mark Twain Media adapted *The Outsiders* and *That Was Then, This Is Now* as filmstrips with cassettes, both 1978. *Rumble Fish* was adapted as a record and cassette, Viking, 1977.

■ Sidelights

Ponyboy. Greasers vs. Socs. For millions of fans around the world, these few words will instantly call up the world of *The Outsiders,* S. E. Hinton's classic novel about teen gangs and the troubled process of fitting in. Since publication of this first novel in 1967, "the world of young adult writing and publishing [has] never [been] the same," according to Jay Daly in the critical study, *Presenting S. E. Hinton.* Daly went on to note that "*The Outsiders* has become the most successful, and the most emulated, young adult book of all time." Ironically, this quiet revolution in book writing and publishing was wrought by a seventeen-year-old girl, who by all rights should have been one of the intended readers of the novel, not its author.

Susan Eloise Hinton was a high school sophomore at Tulsa's Will Rogers High School when she be-

gan her novel. At the time she had not the slightest dream in the world that her manuscript would be published, let alone that it would sell millions of copies worldwide, spawn a motion picture, and start a trend in publishing toward gritty realism for younger readers. At the time, young Susie was simply working out private concerns. Firstly, she was reacting to divisions apparent in her own high school, and secondly she was filling a void in subject matter that she herself wanted to read. At the time when Hinton began writing, young adult titles were mostly pure as corn and sweetly innocent; tales in which the major problem was which dress to wear to the prom or whether such-and-such a boy would be the date. "Into this sterile chiffon-and-orchids environment then came *The Outsiders,*" observed Daly. "Nobody worries about the prom in *The Outsiders;* they're more concerned with just staying alive till June."

If Hinton turned the world of publishing upside down with her youthful title, its publication did the same for her life. As word of mouth slowly made the book a classic (it now has eight million copies in print), Hinton was attempting to develop a normal life, studying education at the University of Tulsa, marrying, and having a family. Writing block settled in and it was four years before her second title, *That Was Then, This Is Now,* came out, another edgy story of teen angst. Two further books were published in four-year intervals: *Rumble Fish* in 1975, and *Tex* in 1979. Then nearly a decade passed before publication of her fifth YA title, *Taming the Star Runner.* Since that time, Hinton has published two titles for younger readers. Small in output, Hinton has nonetheless made a major impact on children's literature, a fact confirmed by the 1988 presentation to her of the first annual Margaret A. Edwards Award for career achievement. Her books now have over ten million copies in print; four of her five YA titles have been filmed; and Hinton still receives bushels of mail from enthusiastic fans for all her books, but especially for *The Outsiders,* now over three decades old, but with a message that continues to speak across the generations.

The Tulsa Outsider

Hinton was born in 1948, in Tulsa, Oklahoma, but little more is known about her early years, as Hinton herself is a very private public person. Indeed, confusion reins around aspects of her life,

The 1983 film adaptation of *The Outsiders* had an all-star cast, including Emilio Estevez, Rob Lowe, C. Thomas Howell, Matt Dillon, Ralph Macchio, Patrick Swayze, and Tom Cruise.

such as her year of birth as well as her inspiration for beginning to write. What is known is that she grew up a voluntary tomboy in love with horses. That passion has not diminished over the years, and Hinton is still an avid horsewoman. She was able to use her horse lore in the novel, *Taming the Star Runner*. Hinton's tomboy status also brought her closer to male friends than female. She identified more with active males than with the passive role females of the day were encouraged to project.

A self-confessed outsider as a youngster, Hinton did not belong to any one clique in school, but was friends with a wide variety of types. Along with horses Hinton also developed an early love of reading. "I started reading about the same time everyone else did," Hinton wrote in *Fourth Book of Junior Authors*, "and began to write a short time later. The major influence on my writing has been my reading. I read everything, including Comet cans and coffee labels." Her first writing efforts dealt with horses, and her stories were generally told from a boy's point of view. By the time she reached high school, she was ready to tackle a larger subject, namely the rivalry between two groups in the school, the "greasers" and the affluent "socs" (short for "socials").

In the wake of school shootings across the nation during the 1990s, all Americans have become more sensitive to the outsider groups at school, to the cruel pecking orders established in the microcosm of schools. In Hinton's day, peer pressure was no less severe and oppressive. "I felt the greasers were getting knocked when they didn't deserve it," Hinton told an interviewer for *Seventeen* shortly after publication of her novel. "The custom for instance, of driving by a shabby boy and screaming 'Greaser!' at him always made me boil. But it was the cold-blooded beating of a friend of mine that gave me the idea of writing a book."

Hinton began the writing in her sophomore year, during the time her father, Grady P. Hinton, was diagnosed with a brain tumor. As Daly put it, "It is not something she talks about, but one gets the impression that his hospitalization, and the inevitable, unavoidable conclusion that his illness promised, were factors in her withdrawing into herself." While her mother spent more and more time at the hospital, Hinton spent more time in her room or at the dining room table working on her novel. "Susie was very close to her father," Hinton's mother told Yvonne Litchfield of the *Tulsa Daily World*, "and I noticed that the sicker he became the harder she worked." Hinton's father died in her junior year, about the time she completed her book.

Hinton worked through four drafts of her story before she was happy with it, but still she gave no thought to publication until the mother of one of her school friends—a professional children's writer—took a look at the manuscript. This reader

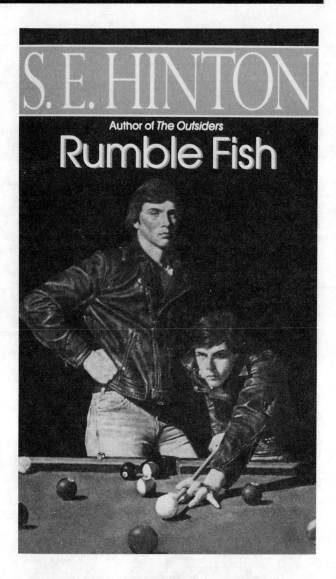

In 1975's *Rumble Fish* young Rusty-James wants to be like his tough, older brother, Motorcycle Boy, but a series of tragic events lead to Motorcycle Boy's death and land Rusty-James in reform school.

immediately saw commercial possibilities to the book and urged Hinton to get in touch with her own New York agent. The Oklahoma teenager did just that, and the rest is publishing history.

The Outsiders

Hinton's novel was, as Hinton myth has it, accepted for publication the night of her highschool graduation, and it appeared in bookstores the spring of her freshman year at college at the University of Tulsa. As the book was written from the male perspective, Hinton's publisher, Viking, prompted her to adapt the more genderless author name of S. E. Hinton. Such a publication was an enormous gamble for a prestigious New York house, but Hinton's book was no overnight success. Slowly and by word of mouth sales grew and continued growing. Letters started arriving at the Hinton household from teenagers all over the country confessing that they never imagined somebody else felt like they did, that they were solaced by the fact that others felt like outsiders just as they did. It was soon apparent that Hinton had touched a raw nerve in American culture.

Hinton's novel deals with a matter of days in the lives of a small group of Tulsa teenagers, loosely modeled after Hinton's own classmates. The book begins and ends with the same lines: "When I stepped out into the bright sunlight from the darkness of the movie house, I had only two things

on my mind: Paul Newman and a ride home." In fact the entire book is a composition that the narrator, Ponyboy Curtis, must complete for English class. Trailed home from the movie by a group of Socs (pronounced "soshes" for Socials), Ponyboy is jumped by these rivals, and is saved by his older brothers, Darry and Sodapop, along with other members of his gang, the greasers. These others include the tough guy, Dallas Winston, and the joker who carries a switchblade, Two-Bit Matthews.

Later that night, Ponyboy, Dallas, and another gang member, Johnny, sneak into the drive-in and meet up with two Socs girls, Cherry and Marcia. Confronted after the movie by more Socs, led by Bob Sheldon, their most dangerous fighter, Cherry avoids an altercation by leaving with the Socs. Ruminating about their situation in a vacant lot, Ponyboy and Johnny fall asleep and by the time

Matt Dillon (center) plays Rusty-James and Mickey Rourke (right) plays Motorcycle Boy in the 1983 film adaptation of *Rumble Fish*.

Ponyboy gets home, he has a run-in with Darry, who has been waiting up for him. Orphaned, the three brothers take care of each other. But Ponyboy has had enough, and decides to run away. Heading off with Johnny, they get only as far as the park before Sheldon and the Socs meet up with them again. In the ensuing fight, Johnny kills Sheldon with a knife.

Heading out is not merely optional now, but vital. Dallas tells the duo of a church hideout in a nearby town, and for the next five days they hole up, reading *Gone with the Wind*, talking about the Robert Frost poem, "Nothing Gold Can Stay," appreciating sunsets and dawns, and munching on baloney sandwiches. When Dally, or Dallas, comes to visit, Johnny says he's through with running; he's going to turn himself in. On the way home, they go by the church and see that it is burning. Perhaps this is a result of the cigarettes they left inside, but whatever the cause they know that children are trapped inside. Without thinking, both Ponyboy and Johnny rush inside to save them. Though they rescue the children, Johnny is badly hurt when a timber falls on his back. Ponyboy and Dallas are also both badly burned.

Cast in the uncommon role of hero, Ponyboy goes to visit Johnny in critical condition at the hospital. Later that evening there is a big rumble between rival gangs, and even the injured Dallas shows up. Victorious, the greasers are jubilant, and Ponyboy and Dallas rush to the hospital to tell Johnny, only to discover him near death. With his dying words, Johnny tells Ponyboy to "Stay gold," referring to the Frost poem about youth and lost innocence. Johnny's death pushes the edgy Dallas over the line. He robs a grocery store and goes down in a hail of police bullets, an unloaded gun in his hands, his death a rather blindly foolish martyrdom.

Suffering from a concussion incurred at the big rumble, Ponyboy collapses, confined to bed for days. He gets it in his head that he killed Sheldon, not Johnny, and is set to confess at the hearing about the death, but he is acquitted before he has a chance to confess. He remains numb inside, until he discovers another exhortation from Johnny to stay gold, this time in a note left in their copy of *Gone with the Wind*. This breaks through to him and he picks up his pen to start his term paper, writing the first lines of the novel once again.

Critical reception of this publishing phenomenon was mostly laudatory; those with reservations mostly found the book erred on the side of over-sentimentality and cliched writing. "Can sincerity overcome cliches?" asked Thomas Fleming in the *New York Times Book Review.* Fleming answered his own question mostly in the positing: "In this book by a now 17-year-old author, it almost does the trick. By almost any standard, Miss Hinton's performance is impressive." Fleming's view was reflected by other reviewers, both then and now. Writing in *Horn Book,* Jane Manthorne called Hinton's work a "remarkable novel … a moving, credible view of the outsiders from inside." Lillian N. Gerhardt, reviewing the novel in *School Library Journal,* drew attention to the rare fact in juvenile novels of "confronting the class hostilities which have intensified since the Depression." Gerhardt noted that "Ponyboy . . . tells how it looks and feels from the wrong side of the tracks." Reviewing the book in *Atlantic Monthly,* Nat Hentoff lamented the sometimes "factitious" plot, but declared that Hinton, "with an astute ear and a lively sense of the restless rhythms of the young, also explores the tenacious loyalties on both sides of the class divide." Hentoff concluded that the book was so popular among the young "because it stimulates their own feelings and questionings about class and differing life-styles." An English reviewer for the *Times Literary Supplement* cut to the chase when noting that it was largely irrelevant whether adult reviewers found the novel dull, contrived, over-sentimentalized, too violent, or just plain implausible. "Young readers will waive literary discrimination about a book of this kind and adopt Ponyboy as a kind of folk hero for both his exploits and his dialogue," the reviewer concluded.

In the event, this critic was dead on. Once word of mouth was established regarding the youth and gender of the writer of *The Outsider*, sales continued to grow and grow. It was apparent that Hinton and Viking had struck an entirely untapped readership; young kids aching for their stories to be told from their point of view with their voice. Little matter that Hinton's supposed stark realism was really "mythic" as the critic Michael Malone pointed out in an extended piece on the author in *Nation*. "Far from strikingly realistic in literary form," Malone remarked, "[Hinton's] novels are romances, mythologizing the tragic beauty of violent youth. . ." Malone and others have rightly pointed out that the vast ma-

Matt Dillon plays Tex McCormick in the 1982 adaptation of Hinton's *Tex*, about troubled teen brothers who are largely abandoned by their rodeo rider father.

jority of teenagers personally experience nothing close to the violence of Hinton's characters, nor do they suffer the vacuum of parental supervision of her Peter Pan-like cast of orphans and near orphans who must look after themselves or watch out that alcoholic, abusive parents do not do them harm.

Never mind, either, the fact of Hinton's sometimes "mawkish and ornate" prose, according to Malone who noted that Ponyboy "fling[s] adjectives and archaic phrases ('Hence his name,' 'Heaven forbid') around like Barbara Cartland." Ponyboy, through whose eyes the action is viewed, describes characters with an elevated language that is often inappropriate to his spoken thought; he is also prone to quoting Frost. But never mind any of this; Ponyboy and his cast of friends and foes alike, are romantic representations, not the viscerally realistic depictions they are usually labeled.

Gene Lyons, writing in *Newsweek,* got it right: "The appeal of Hinton's novels is obvious. . . . The narrator-hero of each is a tough-tender 14- to 16-year-old loner making his perilous way through a violent, caste-ridden world almost depopulated of grownups. 'It's a kid's fantasy not to have adults around,' says Hinton. While recklessness generally gets punished, her books are never moralistic—all manner of parental rules are broken with impunity."

"I Couldn't Even Write a Letter"

Royalties from *The Outsider* helped to finance Hinton's education at the University of Tulsa where she studied education and where she met her husband, David Inhofe. But for several years Hinton suffered from writer's block so severe that, as she told Carol Wallace in the *Daily News,* "I couldn't even write a letter." In an interview with Linda Plemons in the *University of Tulsa Annual,* Hinton confessed that "I couldn't write. I taught myself to type in the sixth grade, and I couldn't even type or use my typewriter to write a letter. Things were pretty bad because I also went to college and started reading good writers and I thought, 'Oh, no.' I read *The Outsiders* again when I was 20, and I thought it was the worst piece of trash I'd ever seen. I magnified all its faults."

Finally, after she decided that teaching was not for her, and with encouragement from Inhofe, Hinton sat down to write a second novel. Setting herself the goal of two pages a day, Hinton had, after a few months, a rough draft of the novel, *That Was Then, This Is Now.* Once again Hinton sets her action in the same Tulsa-like surroundings, and focuses on an orphan, Mark, who has lived with the narrator, Bryon, and Bryon's mother since his own parents killed each other in a fight. It is now over a year since the ending of *The Outsiders,* and the old gang and social rivalries are not as clear-cut as they once were. The days of hippies are at hand; drugs are part of the teen landscape. One of the characters, M&M, is a proto-hippy whose LSD overdose tips the balances between Bryon and Mark. No angel himself, Bryon turns in his foster brother for supplying M&M with drugs. There is gang violence aplenty, teens on the prowl and on their own—Ponyboy Curtis even makes an appearance. Overall the book is more disciplined than Hinton's first title, but as Daly and other critics pointed out, "it lacks something." For Daly, it was the inspirational "spark" missing that kept it from breathing true life as had *The Outsiders.*

Other reviewers, however, found Hinton's second novel a moving and heartfelt cry from yet another teenager in pain. For Michael Cart, writing in the *New York Times Books Review,* Bryon's struggles with his future and with those he loves form the core of the book. "The phrase, 'if only' is perhaps the most bittersweet in the language," Cart noted, "and Miss Hinton uses it skillfully to underline her theme: growth can be a dangerous process." Though Cart had problems with Bryon's ultimate "life-denying self-pity," turning against his love and life, he concluded that Hinton created "a mature, disciplined novel, which excites a response in the reader. Whatever its faults, her book will be hard to forget." Reviewing the novel in *School Library Journal,* Brooke Anson remarked that

the book was an "excellent, insightful mustering of the pressures on some teen-agers today, offering no slick solutions but not without hope, either." *Horn Book*'s Sheryl B. Andrews found that this "disturbing" and "sometimes ugly" book "will speak directly to a large number of teen-agers and does have a place in the understanding of today's cultural problems." Selected a Best Books for Young Adults, *That Was Then, This Is Now* confirmed Hinton as more than a one-book author.

Another four years passed between publication of *That Was Then, This Is Now* and Hinton's third novel, *Rumble Fish.* Hinton's narrator, Rusty-James, is another classic sensitive outsider type, who begins his narrative with the blunt declaration: "I was hanging out at Benny's, playing pool, when I heard Biff Wilcox was looking to kill me." Rusty-James's older brother, Motorcycle Boy, something of a Dallas Winston clone, meets a violent death in the novel, echoes of Dallas's demise in *The Outsiders.* And like Hinton's other novels, *Rumble Fish* takes place in compressed time, focusing on incidents which change the life of the narrator forever. Dubbed Hinton's "most ambitious" novel by Geoff Fox and George Walsh writing in *St. James Guide to Children's Writers,* the novel deals with Rusty-James's attempts to make some meaning of life after the passing of the gang conflicts that made his brother such a hero. Now, however, Motorcycle Boy is disenchanted, without hope, and virtually commits suicide, gunned down breaking into a pet store. By the end of the novel Rusty-James is left on his own, having lost his brother, his reputation, and his girl, and is without direction. As Jane Abramson noted in *School Library Journal,* "it is Rusty-James, emotionally burnt out at 14, who is the ultimate victim." Abramson concluded that the "[s]tylistically superb" *Rumble Fish* "packs a punch that will leave readers of any age reeling." Some reviewers, such as Anita Silvey in *Horn Book,* found the novel unsatisfying and Hinton's further writing potential "unpromising."

Rumble Fish did have admirers both in the United States and abroad. *Publishers Weekly* declared that "Ms. Hinton is a brilliant novelist," and Margery Fisher, writing in England's *Growing Point,* commented that "once more is the American urban scene in a book as uncompromising in its view of life as it is disciplined." While others complained of too blatant symbolism in the form of Motorcycle Boy and the fighting fish that give the book its title, Fisher concluded that "Of the three striking books by this young author, *Rumble Fish* seems the most carefully structured and the most probing." Exploring themes from aloneness to biological necessity, *Rumble Fish* tackles large questions in a small package. As Daly concluded about this third novel, "In the end we respond to *Rumble Fish* in a much deeper way than we do to *That Was Then, This Is Now.* It's an emotional, almost a physical response, as opposed to the more rational, intellectual reaction that the other book prompted." Daly went on to note that despite its defects in too-obvious symbolism, it "works as a novel. . . . And there is a name usually given to this kind of success. It is called art."

Hinton herself noted that she had been reading a lot about color symbolism and mythology when writing *Rumble Fish,* and that such concerns crept into the writing of the novel, especially in the character of Motorcycle Boy, the alienated, color-blind gang member looking for meaning. Hinton begins with character, as she has often noted in interviews, but in *Production Notes* for *Rumble Fish,* the screenplay of which she co-wrote with Francis Ford Coppola, she remarked that the novel "was a hard book to write because Rusty-James is a simple person, yet the Motorcycle Boy is the most complex character I've ever created. And Rusty-James sees him one way, which is not right, and I had to make that clear. . . . It's about over-identifying with something which you can never understand, which is what Rusty-James is doing. The Motorcycle Boy can't identify with anything."

Of Books and Movies

The standard four years passed again before publication of Hinton's fourth title, *Tex,* which was, according to Daly, "Hinton's most successful effort" to date. Once again the reader is on familiar ground with near-orphan protagonists, and troubled youths. With *Tex,* however, Hinton opts for a more sensitive and perhaps less troubled narrator than before. Tex McCormick is, as Hinton noted in Delacorte Press's notes from the author, "perhaps the most childlike character I've ever done, but the one who makes the biggest strides toward maturity. I have to admit he's a favorite child." Of course this was several years before the birth of Hinton's own son, Nick.

Another fourteen-year-old lacking parental supervision, Tex has his older brother Mason to look after him while their father is on the rodeo circuit. A story of relationships, Hinton's fourth title focuses on the two teenagers at a time when Mason has had to sell off the family horses to pay bills, as no money has come from their father. This includes Tex's own horse, Negrito. Straining already strained relations between the brothers, this loss of a favored animal sets the plot in motion. Tex tries to run off and find the animal. Neither his friend Johnny nor Johnny's sister Jamie (the romantic attachment) is able to talk Tex out of it, but Mason drags him home in the pickup. Johnny and Tex are forever getting in trouble and things get rougher between Mason and Tex by the time the two brothers are kidnapped by a hitchhiker (Mark from *That Was Then, This Is Now,* who has busted out of jail). Tex's presence of mind saves them, but gets Mark, the hitchhiker, killed by the police. Notoriety at this brings the father home, but disappointment follows when he fails to track down Negrito as he promised. More trouble in company with Johnny and then with a former friend of Mason's who now deals drugs, lands Tex in hospital with a bullet wound. He learns that his real father was another rodeo rider, gets a visit from Johnny and Jamie, and once recovered and reconciled with Mason, convinces his older brother that he should go on to college as he's wanted to. Tex tells him he's lined up a job working horses and can take care of himself.

"Hinton's style has matured since she exploded onto the YA scene in 1967," noted Marilyn Kaye in a *School Library Journal* review of *Tex.* Kaye felt that Hinton's "raw energy . . . has not been tamed—its been cultivated." The outcome, said Kaye, "is a fine, solidly constructed, and well-paced story." *Growing Point*'s Fisher once again had high praise for Hinton, concluding that "In this new book Susan Hinton has achieved that illusion of reality which any fiction writer aspires to and which few ever completely achieve."

Hinton's re-created reality was strong enough to lure Hollywood. Disney productions bought the rights to *Tex,* filming a faithful adaptation of the novel with young Matt Dillon in the lead role, and introducing actors Meg Tilly and Emilio Estevez. Shot in Tulsa, the movie production used Hinton as an advisor, introducing Dillon to her own horse, Toyota, which played the role of Negrito, and teaching the young actor how to ride. It was the beginning of a long and continu-

---

If you enjoy the works of S. E. Hinton, you may also want to check out the following books and films:

Sue Ellen Bridgers, *Permanent Connections*, 1987.
Alden R. Carter, *Up Country*, 1989.
Lynn Hall, *Flying Changes*, 1991.
Rebel without a Cause, a film starring James Dean, 1955.

---

ing friendship between Hinton and Dillon, who played in three of the four adaptations of her novels. The movie also started a trend of introducing young actors on their way up in her movies.

Next to get a film treatment was *The Outsiders*, though not from Disney this time but from Francis Ford Coppola of *Godfather* fame. Somewhat operatic in its effect, the movie cast Dillon as Dallas Winston, and also starred such future luminaries as Patrick Swayze, Rob Lowe, Tom Cruise, and Estevez. Coppola also filmed *Rumble Fish*, shooting it in black and white to resonate with Motorcycle Boy's color blindness. Once again Dillon starred, with Micky Rourke as Motorcycle Boy. Dennis Hopper, Tom Waits, and Nicolas Cage rounded out the cast. The script was co-written by Hinton and Coppola. In both the Coppola adaptations, Hinton played bit parts as well as worked closely as an advisor during production. However, with the fourth movie adaptation, from a screenplay by Estevez and starring him, Hinton remained on the sidelines. Thus, within a few short years—from 1982 to 1985—all of Hinton's novels were turned into movies and her popularity was at an all-time high, with movie sales driving up book sales. Hinton had the added plus in that her experience with movies was a very positive one. "I really have had a wonderful time and made some very good friends," Hinton told Dave Smith of the *Los Angeles Times* regarding her work with Coppola. "Like a lot of authors, I'd heard the horror stories about how they buy the property and then want the author to disappear and not meddle around worrying about what they're doing to the book. But that didn't happen at all. They invited me in right from the start, and I helped with the screenplays."

Throughout the early 1980s, then, Hinton was busy with movie adaptations and with her son, born in 1983. It was not until 1988 that she brought out another novel, *Taming the Star Runner*. Earlier that year Hinton became the first recipient of the Young Adult Services Division/ *School Library Journal* Author Achievement Award, otherwise known as the Margaret A. Edwards Award, for career achievement in YA literature. It had been nine years since publication of *Tex*; it was thus fitting that she would have a new title out after receiving such an award. Those first four books had a rough sort of unity to them: a portrayal of the difficult process of sorting through problems of alienation and belonging, with a kind of synthesis if not solution presented by the ending of *Tex*. In other words, that youthful furrow had been plowed, and Hinton was ready, it seemed, to move on to new acreage.

Taming the Star Runner, while dealing with some of the old themes, does set off in new directions. Hinton moves from first- to third-person narration in the story of fifteen-year-old Travis Harris who is sent off to his uncle's Oklahoma ranch in lieu of juvenile hall. He has nearly killed his stepfather with a fireplace poker, an attack not unprovoked by the abusive stepfather. What follows is the classic city-boy-come-to-the-country motif. Unwillingly, Travis learns hard lessons on the ranch, but the change from urban to rural is not a Technicolor idyll. Travis arrives in the middle of his uncle's divorce, and the man is distant from him. He takes to hanging out at a barn on the property which is rented to Casey Kincaid, three years older than Travis and a horse trainer. She is in the process of taming the eponymous stallion, Star Runner. It is the relationship which grows between this unlikely pair that forms the heart of the book. Another major element—a tip of the hat to Hinton's own history—is the acceptance by a New York publisher of a book that young Travis has written. But there are no easy solutions: the stepfather refuses to give permission for publication, as he comes off less than noble in the pages of the manuscript. Finally Travis's mother stands up to the stepfather and signs permission for him. He has grown closer to Casey, as well as his uncle, but there are no completely happy endings for Hinton, either. Star Runner is killed in an electrical storm and Travis and his uncle are forced to move off the ranch to town, but he is now a published author and has made a real friend in Casey.

Reviews of the novel were largely positive. Nancy Vasilakis commented in *Horn Book* that it "has been generally agreed that no one can speak to the adolescent psyche the way S. E. Hinton can," and now with her fifth novel, Vasilakis felt that the author "hasn't lost her touch." In a lengthy critique in the *New York Times Book Review,* Patty Campbell noted that "Hinton has produced another story of a tough young Galahad in black T-shirt and leather jacket. The pattern is familiar, but her genius lies in that she has been able to give each of the five protagonists she has drawn from this mythic model a unique voice and a unique story." Campbell also commented on the "drive and the wry sweetness and authenticity" of the authorial voice, concluding that "S. E. Hinton continues to grow in strength as a young adult novelist." *Kirkus Reviews* also found much to praise in the novel, remarking that "Hinton continues to grow more reflective in her books, but her great understanding, not of what teenagers are but of what they can hope to be, is undiminished." Daly, in his critical study, *Presenting S. E. Hinton,* called this fifth novel "Hinton's most mature and accomplished work."

Since publication of *Taming the Star Runner,* Hinton's work has traveled light miles away from her cast of outsiders and bad boys. The year 1995 saw publication of two Hinton titles, both for younger readers. *Big David, Little David* is a picture book based on a joke she and her husband played on their son Nick when the boy was entering kindergarten. In the book, a boy named Nick wonders if a classmate who resembles his father and has the same name could possibly be the same person as his father. Another title inspired by her son is *The Puppy Sister,* about a sibling rivalry between a puppy and an only child, a situation complicated when the puppy slowly changes into a human sister.

Hinton has focused on family in recent years, and on her hobby of horseback riding. She is reportedly at work on another YA novel, though there are no indications whether or not she will return to her outsider themes. "I don't think I have a masterpiece in me," Hinton once told Smith in the *Los Angeles Times,* "but I do know I'm writing well in the area I choose to write in. I understand kids and I really like them. And I have a very good memory. I remember exactly what it was like to be a teenager that nobody listened to or paid attention to or wanted around." In the three-plus decades since Hinton herself was a teenager, things have changed very little out there. The street kids, the gangs, the cliques at school that drive kids to extremes: these are all still at play, and Hinton's novels speak to teens as strongly now as they did at the time of their publication.

■ Works Cited

Abramson, Jane, review of *Rumble Fish, School Library Journal,* October, 1975, p. 106.

Andrews, Sheryl B., review of *That Was Then, This Is Now, Horn Book,* July-August, 1971, p. 338.

Anson, Brooke, review of *That Was Then, This Is Now, Library Journal,* June 15, 1971, p. 2138.

Campbell, Patty, review of *Taming the Star Runner, New York Times Book Review,* April 2, 1989, p. 26.

Cart, Michael, review of *That Was Then, This Is Now, New York Times Book Review,* August 8, 1971, p. 8.

Daly, Jay, *Presenting S. E. Hinton,* Twayne, 1987.

de Montreville, Doris, and Elizabeth J. Crawford, editors, *Fourth Book of Junior Authors,* H. W. Wilson, 1978, p. 176.

"Face to Face with a Teen-Age Novelist," *Seventeen,* October, 1967.

Fisher, Margery, review of *Rumble Fish, Growing Point,* May, 1976, p. 2894.

Fisher, Margery, review of *Tex, Growing Point,* May, 1980, pp. 3686-87.

Fleming, Thomas, review of *The Outsiders, New York Times Book Review,* May 7, 1967, part 2, pp. 10-12.

Gerhardt, Lillian N., review of *The Outsiders, School Library Journal,* May 15, 1967, pp. 2028-29.

Hentoff, Nat, review of *The Outsiders, Atlantic Monthly,* December, 1967.

Hinton, S. E., "S. E. Hinton: On Writing and *Tex,"* publicity release from Delacorte Press, winter, 1979/spring, 1980.

Hinton, S. E., "Rumble Fish," *Production Notes,* No Weather Films, 1983.

Kaye, Marilyn, review of *Tex, School Library Journal,* November, 1979, p. 88.

Litchfield, Yvonne, "Her Book to Be Published Soon, But Tulsa Teen-Ager Keeps Cool," *Tulsa Daily World,* April 7, 1967, p. 20.

Lyons, Gene, "On Tulsa's Mean Streets," *Newsweek,* October 11, 1982, pp. 105-06.

Malone, Michael, "Tough Puppies," *Nation,* March 8, 1986, pp. 276-78, 280.

Manthorne, Jane, review of *The Outsiders, Horn Book,* August, 1967, p. 475.

Review of *The Outsiders, Times Literary Supplement,* October 30, 1970.

Plemons, Linda, "Author Laureate of Adolescent Fiction," *University of Tulsa Annual, 1983-84,* p. 62.

Review of *Rumble Fish, Publishers Weekly,* July 28, 1975, p. 122.

Silvey, Anita, review of *Rumble Fish, Horn Book,* November-December, 1975, p. 601.

Smith, Dave, "Hinton, What Boys Are Made Of," *Los Angeles Times,* July 15, 1982.

St. James Guide to Young Adult Writers, St. James Press, 1999, pp. 454-55.

Review of *Taming the Star Runner, Kirkus Reviews,* August 15, 1988, p. 1241.

Vasilakis, Nancy, review of *Taming the Star Runner, Horn Book,* January-February, 1989, pp. 78-79.

Wallace, Carol, "In Praise of Teenage Outcasts," *Daily News,* September 26, 1982.

■ For More Information See

BOOKS

Children's Literature Review, Gale, Volume 3, 1978, Volume 23, 1991.

Contemporary Literary Criticism, Volume 30, Gale, 1984.

Stanek, Lou Willett, *A Teacher's Guide to the Paperback Editions of the Novels of S. E. Hinton,* Dell, 1980.

St. James Guide to Young Adult Writers, St. James Press, 1999.

PERIODICALS

American Film, April, 1983.

Book World, May 9, 1971.

Booklist, April 1, 1994, p. 1463; October 15, 1994, p. 413; January 15, 1995, p. 936; June 1, 1995, p. 1760.

Bulletin of the Center for Children's Books, February, 1995, p. 200; November, 1995, p. 92.

Children's Book Review, December, 1971.

Daily News, September 26, 1982.

English Journal, September, 1989, p. 86.

Kirkus Reviews, April 15, 1967, pp. 506-07; October 15, 1975, p. 1193; January 1, 1980, p. 9.

Los Angeles Times, October 14, 1983.

New York Times, March 20, 1983; March 23, 1983; October 7, 1983; October 23, 1983.

New York Times Book Review, August 27, 1967, pp. 26-29; November 19, 1995, p. 37; November 16, 1997, p. 26.

Publishers Weekly, December 12, 1994, p. 62; July 17, 1995, p. 230; July 28, 1997, p. 77.

Quill & Quire, April, 1995, p. 37.

Record, November, 1967, pp. 201-02.

Saturday Review, May 13, 1967; January 27, 1968.

School Library Journal, December, 1993, p. 70; April, 1995, p. 102; October, 1995, p. 104; May, 1996, p. 76.

Signal, May, 1980, pp. 120-22.

Times Literary Supplement, October 22, 1971, p. 1318; April 2, 1976; March 20, 1980.

Village Voice, April 5, 1983.

Washington Post, October 8, 1982; October 18, 1983.

Washington Post Book World, February 12, 1989.

—Sketch by J. Sydney Jones

Edward Hopper

Gallery of Art and the Library of Congress (Washington), the Metropolitan Museum of Art, Museum of Modern Art, and the Whitney Museum of American Art (New York City), and the Victoria and Albert Museum (London).

■ Personal

Born July 22, 1882, in Nyack, NY; died May 15, 1967, in New York; married Josephine Verstille Nivison (a painter), July 9, 1924. *Education:* Studied at the Correspondence School of Illustrating; studied painting under Robert Henri, Kenneth Hayes Miller, and William Merritt Chase at the New York School of Art, 1900-06.

■ Career

Painter. Visited Paris, 1906-07, 1909, and 1910; associated with the Ashcan group, and worked as commercial artist and illustrator, New York City, until 1924; spent summers in South Truro, MA, from 1930. *Exhibitions:* The Armory Show, New York City, 1913; Whitney Studio Club, New York City, 1920, 1922; Whitney Museum of American Art, 1932, 1960, 1964, 1980, 1989, 1995; Museum of Modern Art, New York City, 193; Arts Club of Chicago, 1934. Hopper's works are in the permanent collections of the Museum of Fine Arts, (Boston), the Art Institute of Chicago, the Corcoran

■ Awards, Honors

U.S. Shipping Board, Poster Prize, 1918; Logan Medal, Chicago Society of Etchers, 1923; Clark Prize, Corcoran Gallery of Art, 1937; Ada S. Garrett prize, Art Institute of Chicago, 1942, for *Nighthawks*; honorary doctorate in fine arts, School of the Art Institute of Chicago, 1950; Edward MacDowell Medal, 1966.

■ Sidelights

Edward Hopper was one of the quieter revolutionaries of twentieth-century American painting. He used flat, boxy lines, somber tones, and a uniquely idiosyncratic attention to detail to depict scenes that ranged from the modern urban landscapes of New York City in the 1930s to vintage rural structures in New England. Another favorite subject for Hopper's brush was interior scenes marked by an unusual tension; how he managed to portray such acres of silence between two figures—usually a man and a woman—remains one of the mysteries of his artistry.

Hopper's 1942 painting, *Nighthawks*, is one of the most-recognized works of twentieth-century American art.

Hopper's very surname has lent itself to the term "Hopper-esque," an adjective used to tag a scene that looks vintage American and feels oppressive or desolate in some subtle way. "No American painter has influenced popular culture more deeply," declared *Time*'s Robert Hughes. Hopper's 1942 view of an all-night city diner, *Nighthawks*, remains one of contemporary American art's most enduring images. "We think of Hopper as a realist, a figurative painter who gives us a faithful rendition of the physical world, yet this does little to explain the aura of mystery in his work, the sense of detachment combined with almost spiritual intensity," wrote Morris Dickstein in *Dissent*. "He has often been acclaimed as the poet of the ordinary, the nondescript—the forerunner of photographers like Walker Evans—conferring unprecedented attention on gas stations, motel rooms, movie theaters, city streets and buildings, bare offices, late-night diners, clapboard houses, railroad tracks, empty fields, and deserted country roads."

Early Influences

Born in 1882, Hopper was the son of a dry-goods merchant, Garrett Henry Hopper, and his wife Elizabeth Griffiths Smith Hopper. The second of their two children, "Eddie," as he was called as a child, and his sister Marion grew up in Nyack, New York, a mid-sized town situated on the banks of the Hudson River. Though the Hoppers were earnest Baptists—his maternal great-grandfather was the founder of the Baptist congregation in Nyack—they were also lovers of art and literature. The books of French and Russian authors such as Victor Hugo and Ivan Turgenev were present in his house, while Elizabeth Hopper instilled in both children an appreciation for the visual arts. Books of reproductions from the Old Masters, how-to drawing books, and art supplies were plentiful in the household. Hopper began drawing at the age of five, and was already signing his drawings by the age of ten.

Though he enjoyed enthusiastic encouragement from a family that recognized his early talent, Hopper nevertheless had a difficult adolescence. At the age of twelve he was already six feet tall, and because of his gangly appearance, his classmates nicknamed him "Grasshopper." As a result, he spent even more time alone, and simply devoted his hours to honing his drawing skills. After graduating from Nyack High School in 1899,

Hopper began taking both the train and ferry to commute to New York City, where he enrolled in a rather shabby school of commercial illustration. His desire to study art was tempered by his father's worries about the financial opportunities of such a risky career, and so as a compromise his father agreed to pay tuition for classes at the Correspondence School of Illustrating. A year later, Hopper convinced his parents to allow him to transfer to the New York School of Art, founded by a well-regarded painter named William Merritt Chase.

After a year further in commercial illustration, Hopper began taking courses in painting, and in 1902 began studying with Robert Henri, an established painter who would greatly challenge Hopper as an artist. Henri was iconoclastic and enthusiastic, and encouraged his young students to look at the world around them and paint from that, in contrast to the still lifes that other instructors at the school emphasized. Hopper rented a room on Fourteenth Street and was able to stop commuting to his parents' home after a time; the residence also allowed him to remain much later in the city to attend plays and concerts. Hopper blossomed during these years, and won both acclaim for his early works and several student

prizes before graduation in 1906. He was believed to have a promising career ahead of him.

Travels to Paris

Between the years 1906 and 1910 Hopper made three extended trips to Paris for further study and inspiration. Like the French Impressionists, whose work—along with many other young artists of this era—he found revolutionary, he began working out of doors. Over the next few years, Hopper created a body of work that depicted Paris's bridges, parks, and denizens "en plein air," the term for painting outside of the studio. The people and architecture of Paris, and its heady sense of life lived on the street, fascinated him. He returned to New York twice, exhibited some of his works to only minor success, and began to work as a commercial illustrator. After a final stay in France in 1910, he sailed for America. "It seemed awfully crude and raw here when I got back," Hopper later told an interviewer, according to Gail Levin's 1995 *Edward Hopper: An Intimate Biography.* "It took me ten years to get over Europe."

Hopper was twenty-eight years old at the time, and his early artistic promise seemed to have abated. He had not sold any of his works at the exhibitions and galleries to which he was invited to show. He took a studio on East 59th Street and began looking for freelance jobs as a commercial illustrator, a career that he soon came to loathe. But he also began to earn a regular income through this, though he refused to work more than three days a week in order to continue painting, and was relieved to have found a way to support himself. He did a great deal of work for *System* magazine, the forerunner of *Business Week,* and in his scenes of office interiors and commercial enterprises, Hopper became skilled in depicting commonplace objects such as furniture and product displays. This training would lend realistic detail to his later paintings.

In 1913 Hopper submitted two works to the Domestic Exhibition Committee for the International Exhibition of Modern Art, the groundbreaking event that literally introduced the work of contemporary European painters to Americans. One was accepted: an oil he had done in 1911, an image of a sloop in which the mainsail and jib take up much of the picture plane. An offer was made for *Sailing* by a Manhattan textile manufac-

A self portrait of Edward Hopper.

Hopper's 1954 work *Ryder's House* was painted during his later years, which were spent happily and frugally with his beloved wife, Josephine.

turer and art collector for $250, and Hopper readily accepted it. Despite the success he found with this, one of the few of his works that did not depict a European scene, he continued to work with French themes and settings for the next few years.

After 1913 Hopper moved into rooms at 3 Washington Square North in Greenwich Village, where he would remain for the remainder of his life; he would eventually purchase additional space in the building as finances and vacancies permitted. To escape the city in the summer, he began sojourning with other artists at the casual colonies they were establishing on the New England coast. He spent his first summer in Gloucester, Massachusetts, and also visited Monhegan Island, Maine,

and the Cape Cod enclave of South Truro, among other seaside communities.

Finding Success

Around 1918 Hopper, still a commercial illustrator and part-time drawing instructor, finally began to gain a modicum of success, especially when his 1918 anti-war poster (*Smash the Hun*), created for the United States Shipping Board, took first prize among a large field of contenders. A friend from art school helped engineer Hopper's admittance into the Whitney Studio Club, an arts group and gallery space founded by heiress Gertrude Vanderbilt Whitney. The Whitney gave Hopper his first solo show in January of 1920, and from there he began to exhibit elsewhere and sell more of his paintings. In the summer of 1923, he met his future wife Josephine Verstille Nivison at the summer artists' colony in Gloucester. A former actress and painter in her own right, Nivison was forty years old and summering there with her beloved cat, Arthur, the presence of whom provided a conversational opener for the shy, reserved Hopper. He was then forty-one years old.

Almost immediately Hopper began working in a looser style, fueled by competition with Nivison. After Gloucester, they dated in New York and often dined at a Chinese restaurant on Columbus Circle that Hopper would immortalize in *Chop Suey* (1927). They were married in July of 1924. That fall, Hopper enjoyed great success with a series of paintings shown at the Frank K. M. Rehn Gallery on Fifth Avenue, and he sold sixteen works in all. Critics praised his works as original and decidedly new and American. With the largesse, Hopper was finally able to abandon his career as a commercial illustrator.

During the rest of the 1920s, Hopper's reputation as an artist grew exponentially. His works now concentrated on a very American landscape of images: the lighthouses of New England, the New York skyline, or interior scenes of flappers in restaurants such as *Chop Suey* or *Automat,* also from 1927. Jo Nivison Hopper sat for this work, and after their marriage was the only female model he ever used. In *Automat,* a woman in a cloche hat sits alone inside one of New York City's new all-night, electric-lit cafeterias. Hopper also won acclaim for his 1925 painting *House by the Railroad,* which would be acquired by New York's Museum of Modern Art. The stark setting offers only an imposing Victorian house and railroad track horizontally bisecting the landscape. It reportedly became the very model for the spooky dwelling in the 1959 Alfred Hitchcock thriller *Psycho.* "This solitary house seems to recall America's more innocent past—a simpler moment that has been left behind by modern urban life and its complexities," remarked Levin in another book, her 1980 tome *Edward Hopper: The Art and the Artist.* "*House by the Railroad* seems to embody the very character of America's rootless society."

During the 1930s Hopper found increasing professional success, winning prizes from juried exhibitions and an invitation to participate in the first Whitney Museum of American Art Biennial

in 1932; the museum had been founded by Gertrude Whitney, and Hopper would have close ties with it for the remainder of his long career. In 1934 the Arts Club of Chicago gave a retrospective of his work. Hopper and his wife continued to spend summers on Cape Cod, and that same year they built a house on land they had purchased on South Truro, Massachusetts. During these warm months he painted seascapes, lighthouses, and sailboats. In New York, he and Jo loved to attended the cinema and theater, which was their only real extravagance. They saw the work of many young modernist American playwrights, Maxwell Anderson and Elmer Rice among them, and critics have often remarked upon the stagy or cinematic quality of Hopper's paintings. "More than any artist in our history—more than [George] Inness or [Thomas] Eakins or [Winslow] Homer—Hopper found a way of showing not just how America looks but how America is, lived under illuminations so harsh and unforgiving they feel like moral searchlights, punctuating the bleakness," wrote Arthur C. Danto in *Nation.*

Hopper's long career in commercial illustration also provided a distinct element to his work. In many paintings, the imagery of advertising is featured prominently. Kate Rubin, writing in *Antiques,* cited two works as particularly reflective of this: the plate-glass storefront in *Drug Store* (1927), in which the corner shop, closed for the night, is nevertheless brightly lit and dominated by a display for the digestive remedy Ex-Lax. The 1940 oil *Gas* depicts a solitary, oddly besuited man at a row of filling station pumps in an obviously rural area. "The world of advertising and trademarks is here transformed into a mysterious, beckoning vision brightly lit in the dark shadows of the city," Rubin observed. "In *Gas,* Pegasus—the trademark of the Mobil Corporation and the symbol of poetic inspiration—hovers over the edge of the forest like a sign marking the boundary between nature and civilization."

In New York, Hopper would often take the elevated train through Manhattan and the boroughs in search of inspiration. From these trips came his "office" paintings, which were a somewhat unusual subject matter for an artist to portray at the time. But Hopper had executed so many scenes of American business interiors during his commercial career that he remained fascinated by it as a serious artist. In *Office at Night* (1940) a man is seated at a desk, a woman stands at the file cabinet behind him, she is looking at him, but he ignores her; this, coupled with the nightfall evident from the window, creates an atmosphere of sexual tension inside the painting. Hopper once said that his "el" train rides provided him with brief scenes he could later explore on canvas. *Office at Night* was prompted by one such trip, with its "glimpses of office interiors that were so fleeting as to leave fresh and vivid impressions on my mind," Hopper wrote in a 1948 letter to a museum official, quoted by Levin in her 1980 book. "My aim was to try to give the sense of an isolated and lonely office interior rather high in the air, with the office furniture which has a very definite sense of meaning for me."

Nighthawks

"In a great Hopper there is always the moment of frozen time, literally a tableau, as though the curtain had just gone up but the narrative hasn't begun," declared *Time*'s art critic Hughes. "It gives images of ordinary things their mystery and power." Such evocative drama was famously apparent in what would become Hopper's signature work, *Nighthawks*, which he finished in 1942 and sold that same year to a major museum, the Art Institute of Chicago. The canvas, over five feet in length, depicts an all-night diner viewed from the outside of its large plate-glass corner window. Inside are a couple, a lone man in a fedora, and a restaurant employee; it is clearly late, judging from the empty sidewalk outside, and the scene is bathed in red, green, and yellow hues. The Hoppers often ate at such places, and this one in particular was based on one in their neighborhood, a diner on Greenwich Avenue near the intersection of Seventh Avenue and Eleventh Street. "Hopper," wrote Levin in her 1995 biography, "made the couple look straight ahead, as if lost in separate reveries, raked by the harsh light that

Though he never returned to Europe, Hopper did spend his final years traveling America and capturing its scenes, as in 1960's *People in the Sun*.

also picks out the man, yet reduces his bulk and emphasizes his isolation and posture of indifference, while the counterman cocks his head upward, in a gaze not connecting with the others."

Hopper himself said of *Nighthawks,* a title suggested by his wife, that he "didn't see it as particularly lonely," according to Levin's biography. "I simplified the scene a great deal and made the restaurant bigger. Unconsciously, probably, I was painting the loneliness of a large city." The sense of desolate solitude that pervades the work helps explain why it achieved such a place in American iconography, and as a work of art *Nighthawks* and his other images from this period dovetailed perfectly with a nation that was only then recognizing its uniqueness as a cultural and economic force. "To the American viewer the paintings have an almost aching familiarity, of scenes viewed through passed windows along barren metropolitan streets, or at daybreak or sunset driving past houses standing at the edges of upstate villages, isolated amid their shadows," remarked Danto in *Nation.* "They instantly convey an oppressive sense of a loneliness so palpable that one feels it as the American soul objectified, the spareness of American spiritual life made visible, as if our light, our trees, our houses, our very garments are an inner emptiness translated into the language of commonplace objects, postures, and perspectives."

In *Time,* Hughes also wrote about Hopper's place in the pantheon of American artists. "He saw an America no one else had got right," declared Hughes, "and now you can't see it without seeing him. His baking New York rooftops and rows of stumpy brownstones, his blue vistas of the sea at Wellfleet where yachts lean with plump sails into the light, his isolated people gazing from the windows of dull apartments or seedy motels, have become part of the very grain and texture of American's self-image."

A Simple Life

Hopper and his wife, who also continued to paint and draw, lived at the Washington Square apartment for the remainder of their lives; it had no elevator and they negotiated the 74 stairs even when in their eighties and in poor health. They lived frugally, and always drove a secondhand car. His wife shopped for their clothes at Woolworth's and Sears and hooked rag rugs. Hopper never

If you enjoy the works of Edward Hopper, you may also want to check out the following:

The portraits of the great Dutch painter Rembrandt van Rijn, one of Hopper's favorite artists.
The works of American painters Winslow Homer and Thomas Eakins.

returned to Europe, but did make cross-country trips that inspired such works as *Carolina Morning* (1955) and *Western Motel* (1957). The Whitney feted him with a major retrospective in 1964, but declining health curtailed his efforts in the studio during these years.

Hopper's last work was a touching tribute to his wife, but also managed to hearken back to his days as a young man in Paris. *Two Comedians* (1965) shows two white-garbed *commedia dell'arte* figures taking their stage bow, viewed from the orchestra pit, "their free hands poised as if about to gesture in deference to each other," wrote Levin in her 1995 biography. Hopper died in his studio on May 15, 1967, and was buried in the family cemetery plot in Nyack. Jo Nivison Hopper died just ten months later, and left a bequest of 2,500 works by her late husband to the Whitney Museum.

The Whitney, with its extensive archival materials, remains the repository of visual and written information detailing Hopper's long and illustrious career. The institution once again honored Hopper with a 1995 show, "Edward Hopper and the American Imagination," which exhibited nearly five dozen of his best-known works. Reviews of the retrospective spoke eloquently of Hopper's place in American art. "Enough of Hopper's America survives beneath the Americanization that has overtaken our country, along with the rest of the world, that we can project Hopper's vision onto McDonald's and Wal-Mart, Victoria's Secret and The Gap, were we to imagine him as having painted these, and realize how little Americanization has to do with being American," stated Danto in *Nation.* "Hopper infused gasoline pumps and Ex-Lax signs with the same unredeemed pathos he gave to railroad tracks and hotel lobbies, so the Golden Arches and the shopping cart would hardly have daunted him."

■ Works Cited

Danto, Arthur C., review of *Edward Hopper: An Intimate Biography, Nation,* October 2, 1995, p. 355.

Dickstein, Morris, "Looking at Hopper: An Art of Subtraction," *Dissent,* winter, 1997, pp. 93-97.

Hughes, Robert, "Under the Crack of Reality," *Time,* July 17, 1995, pp. 54-56.

Levin, Gail, *Edward Hopper: The Art and the Artist,* Norton, 1980.

Levin, Gail, *Edward Hopper: An Intimate Biography,* Alfred A. Knopf, 1995.

Rubin, Kate, "Edward Hopper and the American Imagination," *Antiques,* August, 1995, p. 166.

■ For More Information See

BOOKS

Levin, Gail, *Edward Hopper,* Norton, 1986.

Levin, Gail, *Hopper's Places,* University of California Press, 1998.

Lyons, Deborah, editor, *Edward Hopper: A Journal of His Work,* Norton, 1997.

Rodman, Selden, *Conversations with Artists,* Devin-Adair, 1957.

Spring, Justin, *The Essential Edward Hopper,* Andrews McMeel, 1998.

PERIODICALS

American Artist, January, 1976, pp. 70-75, 103-6.

Art in America, Number 1, 1960; Spring, 1980, pp. 60-63.

Arts Digest, April, 1955.

Art Journal, Summer, 1981, pp. 150-60.

Arts Magazine, September, 1974, pp. 29-33; May, 1981; March, 1980, pp. 156-60; May, 1981, pp. 154-61.

Economist, August 12, 1995, p. 70.

Harper's Bazaar, June, 1995, p. 76.

New England Quarterly, September, 1988.

New Leader, October 12, 1964, pp. 28-29.

New Republic, December 5, 1995, p. 29.

Smithsonian, September, 1980, pp. 126-33.

Time, December 24, 1956, pp. 28, 36-39.*

Robin McKinley

Personal

Born November 16, 1952, in Warren, OH; daughter of William (in the U.S. Navy and Merchant Marines) and Jeanne Carolyn (a teacher; maiden name, Turrell) McKinley; married Peter Dickinson (an author), January 3, 1992. *Education:* Attended Dickinson College, 1970-72; Bowdoin College, B.A. (summa cum laude), 1975. *Politics:* "Few affiliations, although I have strong feelings pro-ERA and pro-freedom—anti-big business and anti-big government. I grow more cynical all the time, and am now more likely to belong to countryside-saving charities." *Religion:* "You could call me a lapsed Protestant." *Hobbies and other interests:* Gardening, horses, walking, travel, many kinds of music, and life as an expatriate and the English-American culture chasm.

Addresses

Home—Maine and Hampshire, England. *Agent*—Merrilee Heifetz, Writers House, Inc., 21 West 26th St., New York, NY 10010.

Career

Writer, 1975—. Ward and Paul (stenographic reporting firm), Washington, DC, editor and transcriber, 1972-73; Research Associates, Brunswick, ME, research assistant, 1976-77; bookstore clerk in Maine, 1978; teacher and counselor at private secondary school in Natick, MA, 1978-79; Little, Brown, Inc. (publisher), Boston, MA, editorial assistant, 1979-81; barn manager on a horse farm, Holliston, MA, 1981-82; Books of Wonder, New York City, clerk, 1983; freelance reader, copy- and line-editor, general all-purpose publishing dogsbody, 1983-91. *Member:* Many gardening and garden societies, Phi Beta Kappa (lapsed).

Awards, Honors

Horn Book honor list citation, 1978, for *Beauty: A Retelling of the Story of Beauty and the Beast*, 1985, for *The Hero and the Crown*; Best Books for the Teen Age citation, New York Public Library, 1980, 1981, 1982, all for *Beauty: A Retelling of the Story of Beauty and the Beast*; Best Young Adult Books citation, American Library Association, 1982, and Newbery Honor citation, 1983, both for *The Blue Sword*; Newbery Medal, 1985, for *The Hero and the Crown*; D.H.L., Bowdoin College, 1986, Wilson College, 1996; World Fantasy Award for best anthology, 1986, for *Imaginary Lands*; *Horn Book* Honor List, 1988, for *The Outlaws of Sherwood*, 1995, for *Knot in the Grain*; Best Books for the Teen

Age and Best Adult Book for the Teen Age, American Library Association, 1994, for *Deerskin;* notable book selection, Association for Library Service to Children, American Library Association, for The Hero and the Crown.

■ Writings

Beauty: A Retelling of the Story of Beauty and the Beast, Harper, 1978.

The Door in the Hedge (short stories), Greenwillow, 1981.

The Blue Sword, Greenwillow, 1982.

The Hero and the Crown, Greenwillow, 1984.

(Editor) *Imaginary Lands* (short stories; includes McKinley's "The Stone Fey"), Greenwillow, 1985.

(Adapter) Rudyard Kipling, *Tales from the Jungle Book,* Random House, 1985.

(Adapter) Anna Sewell, *Black Beauty,* illustrated by Susan Jeffers, Random House, 1986.

(Adapter) George MacDonald, *The Light Princess,* illustrated by Katie Thamer Treherne, Harcourt, 1988.

The Outlaws of Sherwood, Greenwillow, 1988.

My Father Is in the Navy (picture book), illustrated by Martine Gourbault, Greenwillow, 1992.

Rowan (picture book), illustrated by Donna Ruff, Greenwillow, 1992.

Deerskin (adult fantasy), Putnam, 1993.

A Knot in the Grain and Other Stories (includes some of the stories published in Terri Windling's collections), Greenwillow, 1994.

Rose Daughter, Greenwillow, 1997.

The Stone Fey, illustrated by John Clapp, Harcourt, 1998.

Robin Hood, Greenwillow, 1999.

Author of a sequel to *The Hero and the Crown,* to be published by Greenwillow; contributor to anthologies, including *Elsewhere II,* edited by Terri Windling and Mark Arnold, Ace Books, 1982; *Elsewhere III,* edited by Terri Windling and Mark Arnold, Ace Books, 1984; and *Faery,* edited by Terri Windling, Ace Books, 1985. Also contributor of book reviews to numerous periodicals. Author of column, "In the Country," for *New England Monthly,* 1987-88.

■ Adaptations

Random House recorded *The Hero and the Crown* (1986) and *The Blue Sword* (1994) on cassette.

■ Sidelights

Robin McKinley has been described by her friends Terri Windling and Mark Alan Arnold in *Horn Book* as a "person who approaches every instant and event with such boisterousness, energy, and vehemence that even the most mundane aspects of her life are infused with vibrancy." According to Windling and Arnold, McKinley is "special and extraordinary," an "important writer of our generation." Yet McKinley has recalled that she was an awkward adolescent who spent her time alone, reading, riding horses, thinking about horses, and wishing she could have the kind of adventures boys seemed to be having.

"I despised myself for being a girl," she once stated, "and ipso facto being someone who stayed at home and was boring, and started trying to tell myself stories about girls who did things and had adventures." Just after graduating summa cum laude from Bowdoin College with a degree in English literature, McKinley began to have adventures of her own. She became the woman Windling and Arnold know, and a hero to young women readers in search of strong, honorable role models. McKinley's retellings of traditional fairy tales and completely original, contemporary fantasies portray girls "who do things."

Although feminism is not the sole force driving McKinley's creativity, it is a cause she consciously promotes. She once commented, "I am obsessed with the idea of freedom, especially because I'm a WASP female of limited imagination. I'm preoccupied with the notion of a woman's ability, or inability, to move within her society. I am not so purblind as to think that the only thing seriously wrong with our civilization is that men have more freedom of choice than women, but I strongly believe that that is one important thing wrong, and that it must be changed. Nor will I give up the idea that men and women can cope with each other in some relaxed and affectionate fashion—under this crabby exterior there beats the squashy heart of a romantic. . . . But meanwhile there are no princesses who wring their hands and stand around in ivory towers waiting for princes to return from the wars in my stories."

McKinley's stories include short retellings of classics from Anna Sewell's *Black Beauty* to George MacDonald's *The Light Princess* and Rudyard Kipling's *The Jungle Book.* She has also published a number of short stories and edited *Imaginary Lands,* a collection of fantasies that includes her own "The Stone Fey." McKinley has insisted that her work is written for those who want to read it, not just for young people. Yet she has also written some original picture books for children. *Rowan* is a story about a girl selecting and loving a pet dog. *My Father Is in the Navy* portrays a young girl whose father has been away for some time: as he is about to return, she tries to remember what her father looks like. McKinley is perhaps best known, however, for her novel-length retellings, and for the books set in a world she created called Damar.

The Damarian Cycle

McKinley began writing the work that generated the Damarian cycle just after she graduated from college. She explained, "I had begun—this would be about '76—to realize that there was more than one story to tell about Damar, that in fact it seemed to be a whole history, volumes and volumes of the stuff, and this terrified me. I had plots and characters multiplying like mice and running in all directions." McKinley decided to take a break from the Damar story after she viewed an adaptation of "Beauty and the Beast" on television. McKinley was so disappointed with what she saw that she began to write a version of the classic fairy tale herself.

The resulting novel, *Beauty: A Retelling of the Story of Beauty and the Beast,* was immediately published and won praise from readers and critics alike. According to Michael Malone in the *New York Times Book Review,* the novel is "much admired not only for its feminism but for the density of detail in the retelling." "It's simply a filling out of the story, with a few alterations," wrote a *Kirkus Reviews* critic. McKinley's Beauty, or Honour, as she is named in this version, is an awkward child, not a beauty, and her "evil sisters" are caring and kind. Critics have also praised McKinley's handling of fantasy in the medieval setting. "The aura of magic around the Beast and his household comes surprisingly to life," commented a *Choice* critic.

McKinley resumed work on her Damar stories, and a collection of stories called *The Door in the Hedge,* during the late 1980s. *The Blue Sword,* McKinley's second novel, was published in 1982.

The hero in this novel is Harry Crewe, an adolescent woman who must forge her identity and battle an evil force at the same time. The plot takes off when Harry is kidnapped and learns (from her kidnappers) how to ride a horse and battle as a true warrior. While she struggles in the tradition of the legendary female hero of Damar, Aerin, Harry becomes a hero in her own right. Although the story is set in the fantastic world of Damar (which Darrell Schweitzer characterizes as "pseudo-Victorian" in *Science Fiction Review*), critics have noted that Harry is a heroine contemporary readers may well understand.

Newbery Comes Calling

Like the retelling, *Beauty, The Blue Sword* earned McKinley recognition and praise. *The Blue Sword,* however, provided critics with an understanding of McKinley's ability to create entirely original plots, characters, and fantastic worlds. Moreover, critics and readers alike enjoyed the richness and excitement of the book. *Booklist* contributor Sally Estes, for example, described *The Blue Sword* as "a zesty, romantic heroic fantasy with . . . a grounding in reality that enhances the tale's verve as a fantasy." For *The Blue Sword* McKinley was awarded a Newbery honor.

In *The Hero and the Crown,* the next Damar novel, readers are taken back in time to learn about the legendary warrior woman Harry so revered. McKinley explained, "I recognized that there were specific connections between Harry and Aerin, and I deliberately wrote their stories in reverse chronological order because one of the things I'm fooling around with is the idea of heroes: real heroes as opposed to the legends that are told of them afterwards. Aerin is one of her country's greatest heroes, and by the time Harry comes along, Harry is expected—or Harry thinks she is—to live up to her. When you go back and find out about Aerin in *Hero,* you discover that she wasn't this mighty invincible figure. . . . She had a very hard and solitary time of her early fate."

At first, Aerin is graceless and clumsy; it takes her a long time to turn herself into a true warrior, and she suffers many traumas. Yet she is clever and courageous, bravely battling and killing the dragons that are threatening Damar. Merri Rosenberg asserted in the *New York Times Book Review* that McKinley "created an utterly engrossing fantasy, replete with a fairly mature romantic subplot as well as adventure." In the opinion of Mary M. Burns in *Horn Book, The Hero and the Crown* is "as richly detailed and elegant as a medieval tapestry. . . . Vibrant, witty, compelling, the story is the stuff of which true dreams are made." *The Hero and the Crown* earned McKinley the coveted Newbery Medal in 1985 for the best American children's book of the year. McKinley shared her mixed feelings about winning the award: "The Newbery award is supposed to be the peak of your career as a writer for children or young adults. I was rather young to receive it; and it is a little disconcerting to feel—okay, you've done it; that's it, you should retire now." Fortunately for her fans, McKinley continued to write retellings of traditional favorites and original stories and novels.

Gives New Life to Classic Works

The Outlaws of Sherwood provides one example of McKinley's penchant for revising and reviving a traditional tale. Instead of concentrating on Robin Hood—or glorifying him—McKinley's novel focuses on other characters in the band of outlaws and provides carefully wrought details about their daily lives: how they get dirty, and sick, and how they manage their outlaw affairs. Robin is not portrayed as the bold, handsome marksman and sword handler readers may remember from traditional versions of the "Robin Hood" story. Instead, he is nervous, a poor shot, and even reluctant to form his band of merry men. Not surprisingly, the band of merry men in *The Outlaws of Sherwood* is a band of merry men and *women*. "The young women are allowed to be angry, frankly sexual, self willed—and even to outshoot the men, who don't seem to mind," related *Washington Post Book World* reviewer Michele Landsberg. Maid Marian stands out as a brilliant, beautiful leader and amazingly talented archer. *The Outlaws of Sherwood* is "romantic and absorbing . . . [and] the perfect adolescent daydream where happiness is found in being young and among friends," concluded Shirley Wilton of *Voice of Youth Advocates.*

McKinley's *Deerskin* also demonstrates her talent for creating new tales out of the foundations of old ones. As Betsy Hearne of *Bulletin of the Center for Children's Books* noted, *Deerskin* is an "adult fantasy" for mature readers; it presents a "darker side of fairy tales." Based on Perrault's "Donkey-

Originally published as a short story in the fantasy collection *Imaginary Tales*, McKinley later expanded this tale, *The Stone Fey*, into a full-length novel published in 1998.

skin," a story in which a king desires his own daughter after his queen dies, McKinley's novel relates how a beautiful princess is raped by her father after the death of her mother. This "is also a dog story," Hearne reminded readers: Princess Lissar survives the brutal attack, and her emotional trauma afterwards, because of her relationship with her dog, Ash. "Written with deep passion and power, *Deerskin* is an almost unbearably intense portrait of a severely damaged young woman. . . . [T]here is also romance, humor, and sheer delight," commented Christy Tyson in *Voice of Youth Advocates.* "*Deerskin* is a riveting and relentless fairy tale, told in ravishing prose," concluded *School Library Journal* critic Cathy Chauvette.

While McKinley has asserted that "Damar has never been a trilogy" and doesn't want to close off her own mental access to Damar by embedding it completely in text, she has facilitated her readers' access to Damar. Some of the stories in

A Knot in the Grain and Other Stories are set in Damar and include familiar characters. All of these stories, according to Betsy Hearne in *Bulletin of the Center for Children's Books,* bear "McKinley's signature blend of the magical and the mundane in the shape of heroines" who triumph and find love despite the obstacles they face. The stories demonstrate McKinley's "remarkable ability to evoke wonder and belief," asserted *Horn Book* contributor Ann A. Flowers.

McKinley felt that she could flesh out the "Beauty and the Beast" tale even further than she had done in 1978 with the acclaimed *Beauty,* and did so in 1997 with *Rose Daughter.* Over three hundred pages in length, this novel is filled with complex narrative elements. Readers learn about the early family life and personalities of the three sisters: the acerbic Jeweltongue; Lionheart, a physically daring girl; and the title character, Beauty. Their mother has died, and as the book begins they are living with their wealthy father in a city. When he loses his business, they relocate to a cottage in the countryside, where new hardships bring the family closer together.

One central element to McKinley's *Rose Daughter* is the flower of the title: in their world, roses are extremely difficult to cultivate, and need a great deal of actual love; Beauty discovers, in her country garden, that she possesses just such a talent. Yet she is plagued by recurring, disturbing dreams of a dark corridor, a memory of her mother, and the scent of roses. The Beast is a legendary local figure, a tragic hero who is only half-man; Beauty journeys to his castle and begins tending the magic roses in his garden; soon other flora and fauna return to the former wasteland. A romance develops between the two, and her tenderness toward the Beast eventually unlocks the curse that has beset him. "As before, McKinley takes the essentials of the traditional tale and embellishes them with vivid and quirky particulars," declared a *Publishers Weekly* review. Jennifer Fakolt, reviewing the book for *Voice of Youth Advocates,* asserted that "McKinley has captured the timelessness of the traditional tale and breathed into it passion and new life appropriate to the story's own 'universal themes' of love and regeneration."

McKinley once remarked why she considered her work important: "As a compulsive reader myself, I believe that you are what you read. . . . My books are also about hope—I hope. Much of mod-

ern literature has given up hope and deals with anti-heroes and despair. It seems to me that human beings by their very natures need heroes, real heroes, and are happier with them. I see no point in talking about how life is over and it never mattered anyway. I don't believe it."

If you enjoy the works of Robin McKinley, you may also want to check out the following books:

Lois McMaster Bujold, *The Spirit Ring,* 1992.
Ellen Datlow and Terri Windling, *Snow White, Blood Red,* 1993.
Lisa Goldstein, *Walking the Labyrinth,* 1996.
Robert Holdstock, *The Bone Forest,* 1992.
Jane Yolen, *Tales of Wonder,* 1983.

■ Works Cited

Review of *Beauty: A Retelling of the Story of Beauty and the Beast, Kirkus Reviews,* December 1, 1978, p. 1307.

Review of *Beauty: A Retelling of the Story of Beauty and the Beast, Choice,* July and August, 1979, p. 668.

Burns, Mary M., review of *The Hero and the Crown, Horn Book,* January-February, 1985, pp. 59-60.

Chauvette, Cathy, review of *Deerskin, School Library Journal,* September, 1993, p. 261.

Estes, Sally, review of *The Blue Sword, Booklist,* October 1, 1982, p. 198.

Fakolt, Jennifer, review of *Rose Daughter, Voice of Youth Advocates,* February, 1998, p. 394.

Flowers, Ann A., review of *A Knot in the Grain, Horn Book,* July-August, 1994, pp. 458-59.

Hearne, Betsy, review of *Deerskin, Bulletin of the Center for Children's Books,* September, 1993, p. 16.

Hearne, Betsy, review of *A Knot in the Grain and Other Stories, Bulletin of the Center for Children's Books,* June, 1994, p. 327.

Landsberg, Michele, review of *The Outlaws of Sherwood, Washington Post Book World,* November 6, 1988, p. 15.

Malone, Michael, review of *The Outlaws of Sherwood, New York Times Book Review,* November 13, 1988, p. 54.

Review of *Rose Daughter, Publishers Weekly,* June 16, 1997, p. 60.

Rosenberg, Merri, review of *The Hero and the Crown, New York Times Book Review,* January 27, 1985, p. 29.

Schweitzer, Darrell, review of *The Blue Sword, Science Fiction Review,* August, 1983, p. 46.

Tyson, Christy, review of *Deerskin, Voice of Youth Advocates,* August, 1993, p. 168.

Wilton, Shirley, review of *The Outlaws of Sherwood, Voice of Youth Advocates,* April, 1989, p. 44.

Windling, Terri, and Mark Alan Arnold, "Robin McKinley," *Horn Book,* July-August, 1985, pp. 406-9.

■ For More Information See

BOOKS

Authors and Artists for Young Adults, Volume 4, Gale, 1990, pp. 193-202.

Pringle, David, editor, *St. James Guide to Fantasy Writers,* St. James Press, 1996, pp. 399-401.

Dictionary of Literary Biography, Volume 52: *American Writers for Children since 1960: Fiction,* Gale, 1986, pp. 262-66.

St. James Guide to Young Adult Writers, St. James Press, 1999.

PERIODICALS

Best Sellers, January, 1985, p. 399.

Booklist, August, 1997, p. 1898.

Bulletin of the Center for Children's Books, October, 1997, p. 58.

Growing Point, November, 1983, p. 4160.

Horn Book, July-August, 1985, pp. 395-405; March-April, 1989, p. 218.

Junior Bookshelf, June, 1984, pp. 141-42.

Los Angeles Times Book Review, May 22, 1988, pp. 10-11.

School Library Journal, May, 1986, p. 106; December, 1986, p. 108; May, 1992, p. 91; October, 1992, p. 93.

Voice of Youth Advocates, October, 1994, p. 225.*

L. E. Modesitt, Jr.

■ Personal

Born Leland Exton Modesitt, Jr., on October 19, 1943, in Denver, CO; son of Leland Exton (an attorney) and Nancy Lila (Evans) Modesitt; married Christina Alma Gribben (an educator), October 22, 1977 (divorced 1991); married Carol Ann Hill (a singer and professor of voice; maiden name, Janes), January 4, 1992; children: (first marriage) Leland Exton III, Susan Carnall, Catherine Grant, Nancy Mayo, Elizabeth Leanore, Kristen Linnea; (step-children) Lara Beth Hill, Kevin Lawrence Hill. *Education:* Williams College, B.A., 1965; graduate study at University of Denver, 1970-71. *Politics:* Republican. *Religion:* Episcopalian.

■ Addresses

Home—255 South Sunny View Rd., Cedar City, UT 84720.

■ Career

C. A. Norgren Co. (industrial pneumatics company), Littleton, CO, market research analyst, 1969-70; Koelbel & Co. (real estate and construction firm), Denver, CO, sales associate, 1971-72; legislative assistant to U.S. Representative Bill Armstrong, 1973-79; administrative assistant and staff director for U.S. Representative Ken Kramer, 1979-81; U.S. Environmental Protection Agency, Washington, DC, director of Office of Legislation and Congressional Affairs, 1981-83, special assistant, Office of External Affairs, 1984-85; Multinational Business Services, Inc., Washington, DC, regulatory/communications consultant, 1985-89; independent regulatory and communications consultant, 1989—; writer. Lecturer in science fiction writing at Georgetown University, 1980-81; lecturer in English and writing, Plymouth State College (New Hampshire), 1990-93. *Military service:* U.S. Navy, 1965-69; became lieutenant.

■ Writings

SCIENCE FICTION

The Fires of Paratime, Timescape (New York City), 1982.
Hammer of Darkness, Avon, 1985.
(With Bruce Scott Levinson) *The Green Progression,* Tor Books, 1992.
Timedivers' Dawn, Tor Books, 1992.
The Timegod, Tor Books, 1993.
Of Tangible Ghosts, Tor Books, 1994.
The Parafaith War, Tor Books, 1996.
Adiamante, Tor Books, 1996.
The Ghost of the Revelator, Tor Books, 1998.
Gravity Dreams, Tor Books, 1999.

Contributor to science fiction magazines, including *Analog Science Fiction/Science Fact, Galaxy,* and *Isaac Asimov's Science Fiction Magazine.*

SCIENCE FICTION; "ECOLITAN MATTER" SERIES

The Ecologic Envoy, Tor Books, 1986.
The Ecolitan Operation, Tor Books, 1989.
The Ecologic Secession, Tor Books, 1990.
The Ecolitan Enigma, Tor Books, 1997.

SCIENCE FICTION; "FOREVER HERO" TRILOGY

Dawn for a Distant Earth, Tor Books, 1987.
The Silent Warrior, Tor Books, 1987.
In Endless Twilight, Tor Books, 1988.
The Forever Hero (contains *Dawn for a Distant Earth, The Silent Warrior,* and *In Endless Twilight*), Tor Books, 1999.

FANTASY; "RECLUCE" SERIES

The Magic of Recluce, Tor Books, 1991.
The Towers of the Sunset, Tor Books, 1992.
The Magic Engineer, Tor Books, 1994.
The Order War, Tor Books, 1995.
The Death of Chaos, Tor Books, 1995.
Fall of Angels, Tor Books, 1996.
The Chaos Balance, Tor Books, 1997.
The White Order, Tor, 1998.
Colors of Chaos, Tor, 1999.

The Magic of Recluce, The Towers of the Sunset, and *The Magic Engineer* have also appeared in British editions published by Orbit. Some of the books in the "Recluce" series are scheduled to be published in German.

FANTASY; "THE SPELLSONG CYCLE"

The Soprano Sorceress, Tor, 1997.
The Spellsong War, Tor, 1998.
Darksong Rising, Tor, 1999.

■ **Sidelights**

The environmentally focused science fiction and fantasy novels of L. E. Modesitt, Jr. have been praised for their finely crafted plots, which are rich in technological detail. In both his "Forever Hero" trilogy and the nine-book (and counting) series about the island kingdom of Recluce, as well as his other novels, Modesitt has woven diverse ecological theories and technologies into his storylines. From ghosts reenacting their untimely deaths to the adventures of the scattered survivors of a post-nuclear holocaust earth, Modesitt's novels boast intriguing characters and imaginative plots in tales that entertain and enlighten readers.

Categorized under the science fiction subgenre referred to as "hard" science fiction, works such as Modesitt's "Forever Hero" trilogy and 1996's *The Parafaith War* and *Adiamante,* stress intricately devised plots. In the "Forever Hero" novels, the earth has been destroyed by nuclear war. Modesitt's epic revolves around the adventures of MacGregor Corson Gerswin, a strong, resourceful, and seemingly indestructible loner who manages to survive on what little the earth's surface still produces. He, and others like him, join as trainees for the army of a powerful intergalactic empire that has added the weakened Earth to its collection of colonial outposts.

The Reformation of Earth

In *Dawn for a Distant Earth,* which opens the "Forever Hero" trilogy, the surface of the earth has degenerated into poisoned oceans and barren deserts, its unwholesome atmosphere broken by violent climatic outbursts that include hail and tornadoes. Survivors of the nuclear holocaust are divided between the suspicious "shambletowners," whose small, tattered communities dot the landscape, and "devilkids" who, like Gerswin, live in isolation, stealing what they cannot glean from the land. Now a lieutenant with the Imperial Army and stationed back on planet Earth, Gerswin dedicates himself to terraforming his home planet—reworking the atmospheric conditions to allow Earth to support life again—while also attempting to stop the Empire from using the earth as a dump-site for sub-standard life-forms from other worlds.

In *Endless Twilight,* the second book in the series, Modesitt recounts Gerswin's attempts to break the grip of the powerful Empire and continue to restore the ecology of planet Earth. The protagonist draws upon his knowledge of genetic engineering to help the people of several worlds dominated by the ruthless intergalactic superpower to create sufficient food and shelter for themselves. Meanwhile, through his creative genius he finds a way

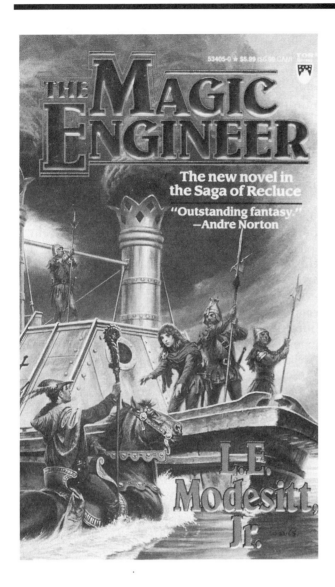

Ambitious wizard's apprentice Dorrin is exiled for dreaming about metallurgy and creating fantastic machines, and then he must decide whether to defend his home and those who punished him from White Wizards.

to undermine the greedy Empire's network for robbing each of these worlds of their riches. While a broad technological knowledge provides the series with an intricate plotline, some critics contended that Gerswin, the Forever Hero, is too invulnerable. Comparing *In Endless Twilight* to the popular "Star Wars" books, Tom Pearson notes in *Voice of Youth Advocates* that "Gerswin would be more interesting and believable if, like Luke Skywalker, he had a sense of humor or some interesting friends, or a superhuman villain like Darth Vader to oppose him."

Modesitt's *The Parafaith War* finds Trystin Desoll, an officer in the Eco-Tech army, involved in a long-standing racially based interstellar battle with opposing Revenant forces. He is also fighting the prejudice of his own people because, due to his fair complexion and blue eyes, he looks more Revenant than Eco-Tech. A man of great intelligence and perception, Desoll is eventually ordered to infiltrate the Revenant stronghold of Wystuh and assassinate that group's leader; instead, he devises a way to end the war peacefully, using the Revenants' fanatical religious beliefs as the means.

Addresses Environmental Concerns

Washington, D.C., where Modesitt once served as director of legislation for the Environmental Protection Agency (EPA), represents one wellspring of ideas for his diverse science fiction novels. While works like the "Forever Hero" trilogy have loose ties to his EPA experiences, 1992's *The Green Progression* is a direct outgrowth of his career as an environmental consultant. Coauthored with consultant Bruce Scott Levinson, the novel is a science fiction thriller concerning a Soviet effort to sap the power of the U.S. industrial base by trapping it within a web of regulatory bureaucracy. Jack McDarvid and Jonnie Black, consultants to an international chemical company known as JAFFE, become savvy to the Russian plot after their boss is murdered on the job. The two consultants soon discover that environmental restrictions against pesticides and other industrial technologies have been pushed into law with the backing of Soviet agents who use U.S. environmental lobbyists as puppets in a covert Cold War battle plan.

Modesitt's other forays into the world of ecological science fiction include the four books he has written in the "Ecolitan Matter" series: *The Ecologic Envoy* (1986), *The Ecolitan Operation* (1989), *The Ecologic Secession* (1990), and *The Ecolitan Enigma* (1997), as well as *Of Tangible Ghosts*, (1994) and its sequel *The Ghost of the Revelator* (1998). Taking place in an alternate world where ghosts and psychic phenomenon exist, *Of Tangible Ghosts* sets forth an alternative history of our own planet. Northeast Columbia (which represents the United States and Canada) is a Dutch-based culture (the British never won colonial control of North America in Modesitt's version of history) that features a quiet, dedicated workforce with a love of hot chocolate. It is one of two competing super-powers; the other is the power-hungry Austro-Hungarian Empire. The great psychic energy of the spirit world is the only thing preventing these powerful governments from going to war over world domination; ghosts haunting the sites of their untimely deaths and replaying the means of their murder has made the thought of creating battlefields—sites of mass death—untenable.

Doktor Johan Eschbach, a teacher of environmental economics who formerly worked as an agent

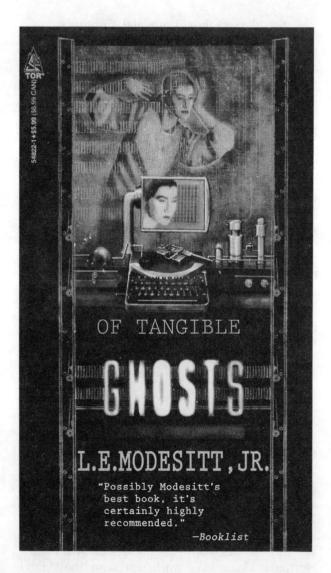

In this 1994 alternate-world novel, ghosts really do exist, and their powers are about to be harnessed by an evil Austro-Hungarian empire intent on world domination.

for the Columbian government, is drawn into the struggle for world domination when a colleague is murdered and Eschbach encounters her ghost, who demands justice. As he seeks his friend's murderer, the hero discovers that a computer-driven technology able to harness the power of ghosts and channel it to serve human interests has been developed; this frightening technology is being fought over by Northeast Columbia and the sinister Austro-Hungarian Empire.

Modesitt "excels in using subtle details to enhance the credibility of an imaginary parallel world," notes one *Library Journal* reviewer. And Jennifer D. Kubenka adds her praise for the novel in *Voice of Youth Advocates*: "an engaging and all-too-human protagonist, a finely realized world, and misused technology that is vaguely familiar yet exotic and different makes for a reading experience that will linger in the reader's mind and sense long after the last page has been turned."

In *The Ghost of the Revelator*, his sequel to *Of Tangible Ghosts*, the author relates the further adventures of spy-turned-professor Eschbach as he and his diva wife Llysette battle the evil bureaucracy in contemporary, alternative North America. Reviews for this novel were mixed. "Intriguing ethical issues of ghost raising and zombie-izing seem to evaporate here, because Modesitt gets bogged down in environmentalism, two-career marriage angst, the eternal professorial woes of apathetic students and conniving administrators and the perils of an alternative Latter Day Saint theocracy," a *Publishers Weekly* reviewer writes. However, Roland Green of *Booklist* praises *The Ghost of the Revelator* as "intelligent alternate history" and comments, "This is all quicker paced than much of Modesitt's other work, and the alternate world in which it is set remains a most originally conceived and intelligently executed melding of history and fantasy." A *Library Journal* reviewer also applauded the book, writing that "Modesitt's lucid prose and careful attention to detail lend substance to this tale of occult intrigue."

Delves Into Fantasy

The fantasy genre has also proved to be a fertile ground for Modesitt's storytelling abilities. In his nine-part "Recluce" series, which includes such novels as *The Magic Engineer* and *The Death of Chaos*, and *Colors of Chaos*, the author recounts the history of an otherworldly island called Recluce, where a balance exists between the forces of Order and those of Chaos: if chaotic activity increases, then order must also increase to restore the lost equilibrium. The wellspring of this world's "magic" increases as such balances are struck; White Wizards promote Chaos, while Black Wizards work to promote Order, and both fight the natural balance of nature. In *The Magic of Recluce*, which introduces readers to the series, a woodworker's apprentice named Lerris is forced to leave his home in a test that moves him from childhood to maturity after he criticizes the island's laws. Temporarily exiled from Recluce, Lerris seeks the help of a grey wizard in coming to terms with Order-dominated island culture. He also encounters Antonin, the master of the laws of Chaos, who uses his power to disrupt and destroy law, thereby increasing his own supply of chaotic magic. Lerris eventually grows up and begins to both understand and appreciate the importance of laws in preserving the stability of his island home.

Published five years after *The Magic of Recluce, Fall of Angels* is the "prequel" to the saga of the battle between Order and Chaos. A spaceship full of female angels, who are involved in a battle against demons, enters an alien universe. There they land on a planet where all but the highest elevations are hot enough to kill them. To make matters worse, some of the planet's inhabitants already wield the magic of Chaos, against which the order of these Amazonian warriors and one male engineer must prevail. Other "Recluce" novels recount various other segments of the saga. *The Towers of the Sunset* describes the island's founding, as Creslin, son of a powerful female military leader and himself a Black Storm Wizard able to control the heavens, flees from an arranged marriage in order to find himself. Pursued by his distraught and slightly annoyed fiance, Megaera, with whom he shares an empathic bond (when he feels pain, she does as well, and vice versa), as well as by the White Wizards of Chaos who feel threatened by his growing power, Creslin finds refuge upon a desolate island and vows to start a new life. "The concept of a necessary maintenance between Order and Chaos is an interesting departure from most SF and fantasy ideas," writes Diane Yates in a *Voice of Youth Advocates* review of the second "Recluce" novel.

As in *The Magic of Recluce, The Magic Engineer* also centers around a young man. But this time, rather than a bored youth, the young man is Dorrin, the ambitious son of a Black Wizard. Fascinated by the forbidden art of metallurgy—an orderly process that unfortunately generates chaos through its by-products, air and water pollution—he is exiled to the land of Chaos. There he continues to dream of building machinery. Recluce eventually is threatened by White Wizards, and Dorrin must choose between following his dream of practicing Chaotic arts or defending his Order-driven island home. The battle between controlled technological

Part of the nine-novel series that includes *The Magic Engineer*, this 1995 installment also involves the history of the island world of Recluce and its battle between Order and Chaos.

If you enjoy the works of L. E. Modesitt, you may also want to check out the following books and films:

Poul Anderson, *The Game of Empire*, 1985.
Emma Bull, *Falcon*, 1989.
C. J. Cherryh, *The Paladin*, 1988.
Paula Volsky, *Illusion*, 1992.
Star Wars: Episode 1—The Phantom Menace, a film directed by George Lucas, 1999.

advancement and chaos continues in *The Order War* as yet another metalworker, Justen, engages in direct battle with the armies of Chaos, who have taken over much of the world in the wake of the steam engine's development. "Modesitt is as clever as his blacksmith heroes," notes Tom Easton in a review of *The Order War* for *Analog*, "finding ways to discuss today's environmental concerns and technological hubris in ways that can reach a public that prefers wish-fulfillment fantasy to more hard-nosed SF."

Colors of Chaos, the ninth installment of the "Recluce" series, is written from the "other side," as Chaos battles the forces of Order. "[Modesitt's] skill in portraying the humanity of characters who possess the power to destroy others with a thought adds a level of verisimilitude and immediacy rarely found in grand-scale fantasy," writes reviewer Jackie Cassada of *Library Journal*.

Modesitt once commented: "One of my motivations in writing fantasy was to create 'real' places with 'real' people, economics, and politics, not pale copies of might-have-been medieval societies that once existed on earth. Some of the 'Recluce' books have technology, and that technology impacts and is impacted by order/chaos magic. Both technology and magic have an impact on their users, and often a high price to pay. One reason for that is my observation that talented individuals, whatever their field, usually pay a high price for their talent, and I felt that would be true of talented magicians as well."

"Writers write," Modesitt once explained. "They have to, or they would not be writers. I am a writer who worked at it long enough to become an author. Virtually all of my early and formal training in writing was devoted to poetry—where I had a choice! I did not write my first science fiction story for publication until I was twenty-nine, and my first novel was published just before my thirty-ninth birthday." Modesitt commented that the motivation for his fiction comes from several sources. "Although the various aspects of power and how it changes people and how government systems work and how they don't are themes underlying what I write, I try to concentrate on people—on heroes in the true sense of the word. A man who has no fear is not a hero. He's a damned fool. A hero is a man or woman who is shivering with fear and who conquers that fear to do what is right. I also believe that a writer simultaneously has to entertain, educate, and inspire. If he or she fails in any of these goals, the book will somehow fall flat."

■ Works Cited

Cassada, Jackie, Review of *Colors of Chaos*, *Library Journal*, January, 1999, p. 166.

Easton, Tom, review of *The Order War*, *Analog Science Fiction/Science Fact*, June, 1995, pp. 167-68.

Review of *The Ghost of the Revelator*, *Library Journal*, September 15, 1998, p. 117.

Review of *The Ghost of the Revelator*, *Publishers Weekly*, August 10, 1998, p. 374.

Green, Roland, Review of *The Ghost of the Revelator*, *Booklist*, September 1, 1998, p. 73.

Kubenka, Jennifer D., review of *Of Tangible Ghosts*, *Voice of Youth Advocates*, April, 1995, pp. 37-38.

Review of *Of Tangible Ghosts*, *Library Journal*, September 15, 1994.

Pearson, Tom, review of *In Endless Twilight*, *Voice of Youth Advocates*, December, 1988, p. 247.

Yates, Diane, review of *The Towers of the Sunset*, *Voice of Youth Advocates*, February, 1991, pp. 354-55.

■ For More Information See

PERIODICALS

Analog Science Fiction/Science Fact, August, 1994, pp. 161-62.

Booklist, May 1, 1991, p. 1698; March 1, 1994, p. 1185; October 1, 1994, p. 245; January 1995, p. 803; September 1, 1995, p. 48.

Environmental Forum, October, 1982; April, 1983.

Kirkus Reviews, December 1, 1995, p. 1673.

Library Journal, March 14, 1994, p. 104; December 1994, pp. 138-39; September 15, 1995, p. 97.

Los Angeles Times Book Review, December 19, 1982.

Publishers Weekly, November 22, 1991, p. 38; January 2, 1995, p. 63; August 28, 1995, p. 106; December 20, 1999, p. 61.

Voice of Youth Advocates, August/September, 1987, p. 132; August, 1995, p. 174; February, 1996, p. 385.

Washington Times, February 3, 1988.

Louise Moeri

Personal

Surname rhymes with "story"; born November 30, 1924, in Klamath Falls, OR; daughter of Clyde (a farmer) and Hazel (Simpson) Healy; married Edwin Albert Moeri (a civil servant), December 15, 1946; children: Neal Edwin, Rodger Scott, Patricia Jo Ann. *Education:* Stockton Junior College, A.A., 1944; University of California, Berkeley, B.A., 1946. *Religion:* Protestant.

Addresses

Home—18262 South Austin Rd., Manteca, CA 95336.

Career

Manteca Branch Library, Manteca, CA, library assistant, 1961-78; writer.

Awards, Honors

Literary Award, outstanding children's book by western writer, PEN Center U.S.A. West, 1990, for *The Forty-third War*.

Writings

FOR YOUNG ADULTS

The Girl Who Lived on the Ferris Wheel, Dutton, 1979.
Save Queen of Sheba, Dutton, 1981.
First the Egg, Dutton, 1982.
Downwind, Dutton, 1984.
Journey to the Treasure, Scholastic, 1986.
The Forty-third War, Houghton, 1989.

FOR CHILDREN

Star Mother's Youngest Child, illustrated by Trina Schart Hyman, Houghton, 1975.
A Horse for X. Y. Z., illustrated by Gail Owens, Dutton, 1977.
How the Rabbit Stole the Moon, illustrated by Marc Brown, Houghton, 1977.
The Unicorn and the Plow, illustrated by Diane Goode, Dutton, 1982.

Sidelights

Adolescents confronted with adult-sized challenges are a special concern of fiction writer Louise Moeri. The author of several young adult novels that show how teens can come to terms with personal and family problems, Moeri tries to instill in her readers a sense of hope at life's possibilities. Hollis Lowery-Moore wrote in *Twentieth-*

Century Young Adult Writers, "Cynical readers may scoff at the happy endings achieved in Moeri's chronicles of adverse conditions and unthinkable hardships, but the careful construction of credible characters and the tense plots ensure that most readers are cheering for these stalwart youngsters and will be dissatisfied with anything less than favorable resolutions."

The "adverse conditions" and "tense plots" that characterize Moeri's novels are familiar to the author, who follows the cardinal rule, "Write what you know." Born in Klamath Falls, Oregon, in 1924, Moeri grew up during the Great Depression. Lack of work and money forced her family to move several times during those difficult years. Like many working-class Americans, Moeri's parents were poor, and life for her family was difficult. "I was born into a troubled generation and into troubled times," the writer once explained. "My childhood was lived against a background of fear and worry, the scars of which are still very evident in me today. It was many years before I realized that life without scars is not possible, and that the important thing is not what happens to you, but what you do with it."

The Outsider

Despite their impoverished circumstances, Moeri's parents managed to provide their daughter with a good education "at the cost of such effort as I can only guess about now." Young Moeri particularly enjoyed her hours spent at school. "Writing was at first just a curious and effortless adventure, and I was surprised to find that people thought I did it well," she recalled. Because she and her family moved frequently, Moeri often found herself in the role of outsider, the new kid in class—"the last one to find a friend, the last one to be chosen for any team," as she admitted, "And yet, in a family that utterly lacked stability and peace, I was taught some of the most valuable lessons. I learned that one's first commitment was to those human souls—parents, husband or wife, children, friends—with whom one had been entrusted. I learned that once I began something I must finish it. I learned to view myself, my actions, and the world around me through a framework of Christian principles. And I learned that any returns one might expect from life depended upon the amount of effort [one] put into it, taking also as my first obligation the need to

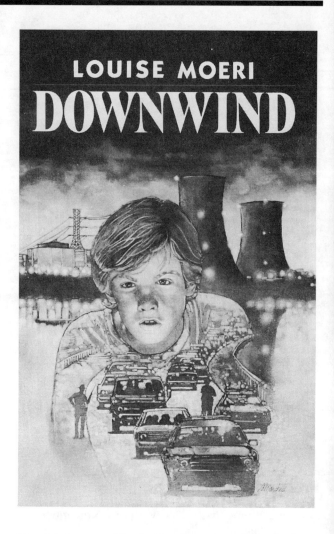

Moeri brings to life the horrors of an industrial disaster in this 1984 novel of a boy who must flee his home during a nuclear plant meltdown.

locate whatever opportunities lay at hand and make the best possible use of them."

Moeri married and became the mother of three children, but she continued to write for enjoyment, poetry and short stories being her favorite forms. Writing for children was "the direct outgrowth of my good fortune in getting a job in our local public library," she explained. "I shared these wonderful books with my own three children, and before long was caught up in the desire to write some of my own. Most of them failed to find a market, but *Jack and Jill* magazine finally purchased one, which they printed under the title 'A Shaggy Dog Story,' and I had the joy of seeing my work in print for the first time." Four picture books and several young adult novels would later follow Moeri's print debut.

First Efforts

Moeri's first published book was *Star Mother's Youngest Child*, an illustrated Christmas story about a lonesome elderly woman who finds an unkempt young child on her doorstep one Christmas Eve morning. Moeri followed this initial success with several more picture books for young children: *A Horse for X. Y. Z.*, *How the Rabbit Stole the Moon*, and *The Unicorn and the Plow*. She began writing fiction for older children with *The Girl Who Lived on the Ferris Wheel*, published four years after *Star Mother's Youngest Child*. In this novel eleven-year-old Til (Clothilde) fears her mentally disturbed mother's repeated abuse, but feels helpless to save herself. Her greatest happiness is in her Saturday visits with her father, divorced from her mother. Her father's favorite pastime is for them to ride together on the Ferris wheel, but he is unaware that Til is secretly frightened of the ride because it symbolizes for her an endless, repetitive journey over which she has no control. Gradually Til realizes that her mother's increasingly violent behavior is becoming life-threatening, but her out-of-touch father is slower to understand or accept the dangerous situation in which he has left his daughter. In a review in *Horn Book*, Kate M. Flanagan contended that while Til's dilemma is convincing, Moeri "creates the feeling of a movie thriller rather than an understanding of a prevalent social problem." A review in *Publishers Weekly*, however, said, "Moeri's realistic characters and situations emphasize the need for urgent attention to a serious social problem."

Moeri's next novel, *Save Queen of Sheba*, a survival story set in the old American West, was well-received. In this tale, twelve-year-old King David and his little sister, Queen of Sheba, survive an Indian attack on their wagon train, but are left to fend for themselves in the wilderness as they search for other survivors. Zena Sutherland of the *Bulletin of the Center for Children's Books* found *Save Queen of Sheba* to be, "on the whole a deft sustaining of suspense and mood, impressive in a book that has so stark a setting and so sparse a cast." *Horn Book* reviewer Ann A. Flowers agreed that the children were intriguing characters, and the story was "believable and human."

First the Egg, Moeri's 1982 novel about California high school senior Sarah Webster, depicts a more subtle form of survival. Cast in the role of "mother hen" during her Marriage and Family class, Sarah is paired with fellow student David Hanna and told by their teacher to "parent" a raw egg for an entire week as if it were their own infant. Sarah finds herself gaining a more mature outlook about both her family and herself through the course of the project. She also finds herself falling in love with David, a handsome but angry young man, who acts out his distaste for the assignment by leaving the bulk of the work to Sarah. In the *Bulletin of the Center for Children's Books*, Zena Sutherland called *First the Egg* "a remarkably discerning story," praising Moeri's "sub-

This award-winning novel realistically details what life might be like for a twelve-year-old rebel fighter experiencing war in a Central American country.

stantial characterization and dialogue." *Voice of Youth Advocates* contributor Carole A. Barham similarly maintained that "Moeri presents, within a bare-bones skeleton, an engaging, intriguing story about growing up."

Lives in Crisis

Moeri focused once again on themes of courage and survival amid crisis in her novels *Downwind* and *The Forty-third War*, both featuring contemporary settings. *Downwind* relates the plight of a boy who must look after his two younger siblings during a frenzied mass-exodus from their hometown when an accident at a local nuclear power plant threatens a meltdown. "This is a graphic look at a response to an emergency situation by the ill-prepared," noted *School Library Journal* contributor Wanna M. Ernst, adding that because Moeri's characters are the focus of the story, "the emergency precipitating the evacuation could be any type of disaster."

Moeri's award-winning adventure tale *The Forty-third War* takes place in an unnamed, yet familiar, area of Latin America. The novel finds twelve-year-old Uno Ramirez caught up in the throes of revolution in his politically unstable country when he is captured, along with several other young boys from his village, by a party of raiding soldiers and forced to join the guerrilla forces of the charismatic Captain Mendoza. After a week's training, Uno joins a rebel patrol in the jungle. He is wounded, but his compadres rescue him, and Uno's loyalty to the rebels deepens after the pro-government soldiers rape his sister, kill his father, and terrorize a nearby village. Praising Moeri for her well-researched and vivid portrayal of life among the rebel forces of such countries as El Salvador and Nicaragua, Ethel R. Twichell commented in *Horn Book*, "The unending wars in Central America are described with devastating accuracy in the microcosm of twelve-year-old Uno Ramirez's experiences." Betsy Hearne of the *Bulletin of the Center for Children's Books* said, "The scenes of conflict are taut and the protagonists' fears vividly projected."

In the years since she began her writing career, Moeri has watched her children, grandchildren, and great-grandchildren grow up—"the most terrifying and joyous experience I could imagine," she once commented. "The family now ranges

---

If you enjoy the works of Louise Moeri, you may also want to check out the following books:

Avi, *The Fighting Ground*, 1984.
Omar S. Castaneda, *Among the Volcanoes*, 1991.
Carol Matas, *Code Name Kris*, 1990.

---

from a toddler barely plus one year old to a tall teenager facing adulthood. I have taken part in school visits, trips to the dentist, frantic late-night phone calls for help with homework ('Grandma, quick! What was the Edict of Nantes?'), and moments when 'nobody understands me.' I've loved every minute of it."

Outside of her immediate family, Moeri continues to be concerned with the lot of young people everywhere. "I am appalled at the way the world treats its children," she stated. "Fragile human lives are swept aside by armies on the march to some sought-for victory which, having lost the children along the way, can be no kind of victory. Even in the relatively stable societies, we have much to answer for in the way of ignorance, cruelty, and one of the greatest sins of all—indifference. I hope to carry on my small part of this struggle with books that shine some light on the lives of children."

■ Works Cited

Barham, Carole A., review of *First the Egg*, *Voice of Youth Advocates*, April, 1983, p. 38.

Ernst, Wanna M., review of *Downwind*, *School Library Journal*, September, 1984, pp. 120-21.

Flanagan, Kate M., review of *The Girl Who Lived on the Ferris Wheel*, *Horn Book*, February, 1980, p. 64.

Flowers, Ann A., review of *Save Queen of Sheba*, *Horn Book*, October, 1981, pp. 536-37.

Review of *The Girl Who Lived on the Ferris Wheel*, *Publishers Weekly*, December 24, 1979, p. 58.

Hearne, Betsy, review of *The Forty-third War*, *Bulletin of the Center for Children's Books*, November, 1989, pp. 66-67.

Lowery-Moore, Hollis, "Louise Moeri," *Twentieth-Century Young Adult Writers*, St. James Press (Detroit), 1994, pp. 463-64.

Sutherland, Zena, review of *Save Queen of Sheba*, *Bulletin of the Center for Children's Books*, September, 1981, p. 13.

Sutherland, Zena, review of *First the Egg*, *Bulletin of the Center for Children's Books*, January, 1983, p. 93.

Twichell, Ethel R., review of *The Forty-third War*, *Horn Book*, January-February, 1980, pp. 69-70.

■ For More Information See

BOOKS

Something about the Author Autobiography Series, Volume 10, Gale Research, 1990, pp. 165-81.

PERIODICALS

Bulletin of the Center for Children's Books, March, 1976, p. 115; December, 1977, p. 63; April, 1980, p. 158; September, 1982, p. 16; April, 1984, p. 152.

Horn Book, October, 1977, p. 533; October, 1982, p. 521.

Kirkus Reviews, June 15, 1977, p. 626; April 1, 1982, p. 419; September 1, 1989, pp. 1130-31.

Publishers Weekly, February 5, 1982, p. 387; November 19, 1982, p. 77; February 17, 1984, p. 90.

Harry Turtledove

■ Personal

Born June 14, 1949, in Los Angeles, CA; married Laura Frankos (a writer); children: Alison, Rachel, Rebecca. *Education:* University of California at Los Angeles, Ph.D. in Byzantine history, 1997.

■ Addresses

Agent—Scott Meredith, 845 Third Ave., New York, NY 10022.

■ Career

Science fiction novelist and short story writer. Worked as a technical writer for Los Angeles County Office of Education.

■ Awards, Honors

HOMer Award for Short Story, 1990, for "Designated Hitter;" John Esthen Cook Award for Southern Fiction, 1993, for *The Guns of the South*; Hugo Award for best novella, 1994, for "Down in the Bottomlands;" Sidewise Award honorable mention, 1995, Nebula Award and Hugo Award nomina-

tions, 1996, both for "Must and Shall;" Sidewise Award honorable mention, 1995, for *The Two Georges*, and 1996, for the "Worldwar" series; Premio Italia, 1996, for *Worldwar: In the Balance*; Sidewise Award for Long Form, 1997, for *How Few Remain*; *Publishers Weekly* Top Ten SF Books list, 1998, for *The Great War: American Front*; Nebula Award nomination, 1999, for *How Few Remain*.

■ Writings

NOVELS

A Different Flesh, Congdon & Weed (New York), 1988.
Noninterference, Ballantine (New York), 1988.
A World of Difference, Ballantine, 1990.
The Guns of the South: A Novel of the Civil War, Ballantine, 1992.
The Case of the Toxic Spell Dump, Ballantine, 1994.
(With Richard Dreyfuss) *The Two Georges*, Tor (New York), 1996.
Thessalonica, Baen, 1997.
Between the Rivers, St. Martin's Press, 1998.
(With Judith Tarr) *Household Gods*, Tor, 1999.

FANTASY NOVELS: "GERIN THE FOX" SERIES

(As Eric G. Iverson) *Wereblood*, Belmont Tower, 1979.

(As Iverson) *Werenight*, Belmont Tower, 1979.
Prince of the North, Baen (New York), 1994.
King of the North, Baen, 1996.
Fox and Empire, Baen, 1998.

FANTASY NOVELS: "VIDESSOS CYCLE" SERIES

The Misplaced Legion, Ballantine, 1987.
An Emperor for the Legion, Ballantine, 1987.
The Legion of Videssos, Ballantine, 1987.
Swords of the Legion, Ballantine, 1987.
Krispos Rising, Ballantine, 1991.
Krispos of Videssos, Ballantine, 1991.
Krispos the Emperor, Ballantine, 1994.
The Stolen Throne, Ballantine, 1995.
Hammer and Anvil, Ballantine, 1996.
The Thousand Cities, Ballantine, 1997.
Videssos Besieged, Ballantine, 1998.

SCIENCE FICTION NOVELS: "WORLDWAR" SERIES

Worldwar: In the Balance, Ballantine, 1994.
Worldwar: Tilting the Balance, Ballantine, 1995.
Worldwar: Upsetting the Balance, Ballantine, 1996.
Worldwar: Striking the Balance, Ballantine, 1996.
Colonization: Second Contact, Del Rey, 1999.
Colonization: Down to Earth, Del Rey, 2000.

SCIENCE FICTION NOVELS: "THE GREAT WAR" SERIES

How Few Remain, Del Rey, 1997.
The Great War: American Front, Del Rey, 1998.
The Great War: Walk in Hell, Del Rey, 1999.
The Great War: Breakthroughs, Del Rey, 2000.

FANTASY NOVELS: "DARKNESS" SERIES

Into the Darkness, Tor, 1999.
Darkness Descending, Tor, 2000.

SHORT STORIES

Agent of Byzantium, Congdon & Weed, 1987, revised edition, 1994.
Kaleidoscope, Ballantine, 1990.
Earthgrip, Ballantine, 1991.
Departures, Ballantine, 1993.
(Editor) *Alternate Generals*, Pocket Books, 1998.

Also contributor of short stories to *Magazine of Fantasy and Science Fiction* and *Analog*.

Collaborated with Susan Schwartz, S. M. Stirling, and Judith Tarr on "War World" series.

OTHER

(Translator) *The Chronicle of Theophanes: An English Translation of Anni Mundi 6095-9305 (A.D. 602-813)*, University of Pennsylvania Press (Philadelphia, PA), 1982.
(As H. N. Turtletaub) *Justinian* (historical novel), Forge, 1998, Tor, 1999.

■ Work in Progress

Novels in the following series: "The Great War," *Settling Accounts*; "Worldwar," *Aftershocks*; "Darkness," *Through the Darkness*, and "perhaps three or four more in the same series."

■ Sidelights

Harry Turtledove is "the standard-bearer for alternate history," according to Tom Squitieri writing in *USA Today*. A sub-genre of science fiction, alternate history has fast become one of the hottest new genres of the 1990s, and Turtledove is, as Russell Letson noted in *Locus*, the "best practitioner of the classic alternate-history story since L. Sprague de Camp domesticated it for American SF over a half-century ago." Letson went on to list Turtledove's virtues as an alternate history guru: "meticulous research and thorough knowledge of his period, an understated but firm way with storytelling, and a sense of the exotic appeal of the past combined with a recognition of the ordinariness of ordinary life."

Turtledove has served up fantasy versions of the Roman Empire and Byzantium in his fictions, reworked the Civil War so that the South wins, allied Nazis and Jews against an unearthly power, constructed trench warfare in the United States, and rewritten the history of early man. Quite brazenly creating alternate universes, turning history on its head, and perennially making the reader ask the question, "What if?" Turtledove's alternate history takes shape not in individual novels, but in series of novels. His popular "Videssos Cycle," in which Caesar's legions are transported from ancient Gaul to a world of wizards, comprises eleven-books; his "Worldwar" series began as a tetralogy and has since sprouted a further trilogy in the "Colonization" extension; his "Great War" series is planned to include five books; and "Darkness," set in a fantastical middle ages, may stretch to seven. His breakthrough, however, was not in a series, but in the stand-alone title, *The Guns of the South*, his account of how the Civil War might have progressed if South African time travelers had handed over a modern arsenal to General Lee.

As Turtledove told Jeremy Bloom in the *Chicon 2000 Progress Report*, "The way I do it, I use the standard SF technique. Because one of the things SF does is postulate—if we changed this, what happens next?—most of those changes are set in the present and then you examine the future, or set in the future and then you examine the farther future. I say, all right, what if we make that change and set it in the past? With as rigorous an extrapolation as I can make." Rigor is something Turtledove can appreciate in things historical: he earned a Ph.D. in Byzantine history from UCLA before becoming a mainstay of the alternate history book section.

"This Is So Cool"

Born in Los Angeles, California, on June 14, 1949, Turtledove grew up in nearby Gardena. Turtledove is descended from Romanian immigrants who first settled in Winnipeg, Canada before moving on to California. A major turning point in his young life came when Turtledove was fourteen and discovered a copy of L. Sprague de Camp's *Lest Darkness Fall* in a second-hand bookstore. "I read it," Turtledove told Bloom, "and thought 'This is so cool,' and started trying to find out what Sprague was making up and what was real. I was hooked."

History also hooked him, though he was slow to realize it. He began college as an engineering major at Cal Tech, but flunked out in his freshman year. This was not simply an academic tragedy; those were the days when a college deferment kept one out of Vietnam, so Turtledove subsequently spent a year at California State in Los Angeles improving his grade point average "to the point where it was visible to the naked eye," as he told Bloom, and then entered UCLA where he ultimately—in 1977—earned a doctorate. His dissertation was on *The Immediate Successors of Justinian*, a look at late sixth-century Byzantium. "If it hadn't been for Sprague I wouldn't have the degree I have—I wouldn't have gotten interested in Byzantine history any OTHER way. I wouldn't

have written a lot of what I've written, because I wouldn't know the things I happen to know." Turtledove has his own private list of what-ifs.

Turtledove's doctorate made him eminently unemployable. He quickly turned to writing, publishing his first two novels, *Wereblood* and *Werenight*, in 1979 under the pseudonym Eric G. Iverson because his editor thought that no one would believe his real name. He continued to publish as Iverson until 1985. These were lean years for Turtledove as a creative writer, and he earned his

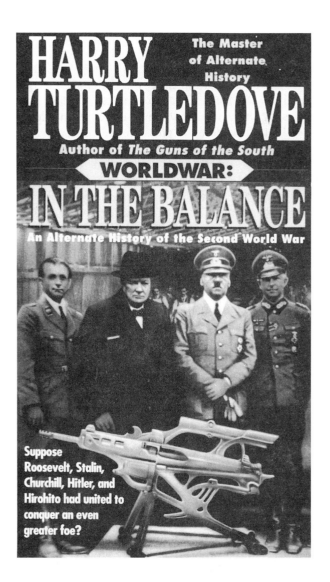

In the first of his "Worldwar" alternate history novels, Turtledove poses this question: What if all the leaders of the Axis and Allied powers had to cooperate in the middle of World War II to defeat an alien invader?

living as a technical writer for the Los Angeles County of Education. It was not until 1991 that he could leave technical writing and devote himself full-time to alternate history.

A Man of Many Worlds

Turtledove's writing has included many genres. As he noted to Bloom, he has written SF that is not alternate history—pure or hard SF—and he has written fantasy, "historically-based fantasy, high fantasy, funny fantasy," but ultimately it is Turtledove's reworking of history that influences most of his work. His first publication initiated this peculiar blending of fantasy and history. The "Gerin the Fox" novels, the first two of which were published under his Iverson pen name, deal with an empire in decline. As Peter T. Garratt noted in *St. James Guide to Fantasy Writers*, the books in the series deal with a theme and location that "resembles a cross between Rome and medieval Europe." The hero is a baron of a border province that remains aloof from central authority, paying no taxes, but when it is menaced by a powerful wizard, the province and its baron are left to themselves in a battle for survival. The first novels of this cycle were also Turtledove's first novels; since that time the series has grown to encompass five titles. Turtledove returned to the series fifteen years after the first title, to expand on Gerin's life and his attempts to make peace for his families, and to explore the concept of a universe containing multiple gods. *Prince of the North*, *King of the North*, and *Fox and Empire* fill out this mythical Empire of Elabon.

He began a more ambitions cycle of novels in 1987, the "Videssos Cycle." The cycle is made up of three separate series of books, as well as a few short stories. The core of the cycle includes four books published in 1987: *The Misplaced Legion*, *An Emperor for the Legion*, *The Legion of Videssos*, and *Swords of the Legion*. The hero of this quartet of books is Marcus Scaurus, a well-educated Roman officer of the late republic era who receives a mysterious sword while campaigning near Gaul. During a battle with an enemy chieftain who has an identical sword, the sword blades touch, and Scaurus, the chieftain, and all the Roman soldiers are magically transported to another world. This alternate world, the Empire of Videssos, resembles eleventh-century Byzantium, and the enemy chieftain joins forces with the Romans to make con-

tact with the locals. Scaurus and his men become involved in palace intrigue and adventures that almost bring about the downfall of the Empire. According to Garratt, the second and third volumes of the tetralogy "are among the best things Turtledove has written." The empire is in chaos. Scaurus has married the widow of a powerful mercenary and tries valiantly to bring civil wars within Videssos to an end. Ultimately, Scaurus's wife must choose between loyalty to him or to her own kin, a long line of mercenaries.

Turtledove wrote a three-book series of prequels to the "Videssos Cycle": *Krispos Rising*, *Krispos of Videssos*, and *Krispos the Emperor*. Set several centuries before the main cycle, these books feature the protagonist Krispos, born a lowly farmer, but destined to become an emperor. He accomplishes this in the course of the trilogy. Turtledove returned to Videssos again in the four volume "The Time of Troubles" cycle.

Early in his career, Turtledove wrote stand-alone novels, one of the most popular being the 1987 *Agent of Byzantium*, a collection of seven interrelated stories about the adventures of secret agent Basil Argyros. The tales rest upon a tweaking of history: in Turtledove's cosmology, the young Mohammed was converted to Christianity by a Nestorian priest instead of founding his own powerful religion. Turtledove then follows the historical revisions that would follow upon such a change, one of them being still powerful Byzantine and Persian empires in the early fourteenth century. Argyros is at the center of the plots and counter-plots of the time, and helps introduce many inventions to the empire: the telescope, gunpowder, and printing among them. "The narrative carries the reader along," commented M. Hammerton in *Twentieth-Century Science-Fiction Writers*, also saying "If we are not deeply saddened by the death from smallpox of Basil's family, we at least believe that he was." Letson reported in *Locus* that the "greatest pleasure in these stories for me . . . is the evocation of the past."

Although, other stand-alone novels by Turtledove have achieved success, it was *The Guns of the South: A Novel of the Civil War*, published in 1992, that connected his name to the genre of alternate history and brought him attention from the mainstream press as well as the SF community. The story begins in January, 1864 with General Lee's Confederate Army suffering from shortages of

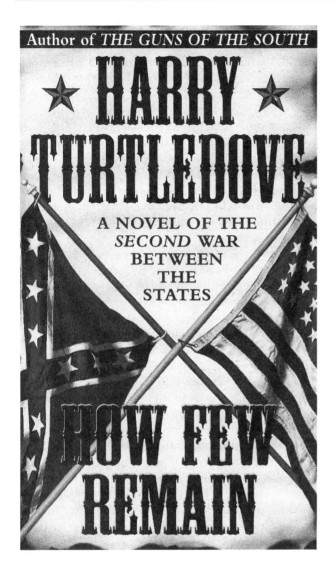

Author of *THE GUNS OF THE SOUTH*

★ HARRY ★ TURTLEDOVE

A NOVEL OF THE *SECOND* WAR BETWEEN THE STATES

HOW FEW REMAIN

Years after the South has won the Civil War and declared independence from the United States, the two sides begin to war again over the annexation of Mexican territory in Turtledove's 1997 novel.

viewing the title in *Booklist*, called Turtledove's re-creation an "exceptionally riveting and innovative narrative that successfully straddles the gulf between fact and fantasy." Discussing his own personal fascination with the Civil War period, as well as its popularity as a theme for alternate history, Turtledove told Bloom, "There is a general fascination with that period because it's a key period in the history of the United States. We are what we are now, for better and for worse, because of what happened during those four crowded years."

Other popular individual titles include his humorous take on the environment, *The Case of the Toxic Spell Dump*, and another volume set in the same universe thirteen centuries earlier, *Thessalonica*. A similar novel is his 1998 *Between the Rivers*, related to *The Case of the Toxic Spell Dump* by the shared theme of henotheism, or the belief that many gods exist and that their strength is based on the number of adherents and worshippers they attract. Set in a fantasy world similar to ancient Mesopotamia, the gods of this universe are not only manifold, but also manifest. Their actions are all too visible as they constantly meddle in human affairs. A trio of protagonists scheme to cripple the power of some of these gods as Turtledove examines the classic SF theme of reason versus faith. *Publishers Weekly* said that Turtledove "uses all of his historiographical and narrative skills, plus his inimitable wit, to elevate his version of [this] theme to the same high level occupied by (among others) L. Sprague de Camp." Jackie Cassada, writing in *Library Journal*, said that Turtledove's "cadenced prose imparts an epic feel to this tale of humanity's attempt to forge its own destiny," and *Kirkus Reviews* called the book "[h]istorically intriguing, splendidly textured, and full of stimulating ideas. . . ."

both arms and supplies. Lee, despondent that the war may be lost, receives an interesting visitor, Andries Rhoodie, a time traveler from South Africa, who offers the General a supply of futuristic armaments, including the AK-47. This weaponry allows the South to win the war and changes history. When the Confederacy later begins to relax its slave laws, however, the South African time travelers become nervous because their purpose in helping Lee was to create a future white supremacist culture. As Lee continues his reforms, he and his men are suddenly faced with a new threat—Rhoodie and his soldiers. Margaret Flanagan, re-

Another popular book is *Justinian*, straight history from Turtledove, writing under the pen name H. N. Turtletaub. The choice of pseudonym was once again an editor's choice out of the fear that a straight historical fiction would not sell well and affect the author's future sales. In the event, his portrait of Justinian II, the wily Byzantine emperor, proved quite successful and saleable. *Booklist*'s Flanagan called it an "artfully styled narrative," noting Turtledove's "painstaking attention to historical details" that combine to "vivify this mesmerizing account of one of history's most remarkable rulers." Turtledove also collaborated with the

actor Richard Dreyfuss on a speculative novel, *The Two Georges*, about the American colonies, in which England never lost control of its North American relatives. Featuring King George of England and George Washington, the novel has been optioned by Britain's Granada Television.

Cycles of War

Turtledove, for all his success with individual titles, still seems to prefer the grand sweep of cycles and series. With his "Worldwar" series he

In this second novel in the "Great War" series, the United States sides with Germany and the Confederate States fight with France and Britain during World War I.

explored what might have happened had an external menace confronted Earth at the time of the Second World War. Employing an old SF theme, Turtledove creates new meanings for it. In his tale, it is late 1942, and the world is at war. Nazis are busy trying to eliminate Jews, and in America, scientists are trying to unlock the secrets of the atom, when, suddenly, the skies overhead are filled with spaceships full of alien invaders. These reptilian invaders call themselves the Race, but earthlings name them the Lizards. Earth-bound enemies form odd alliances to battle this new and devastating menace that seeks to enslave the people of this world.

Turtledove's canvas for this four-part epic is the entire planet Earth. The huge cast of characters includes real people from history such as Generals Marshall and Patton, scientists Leo Szilard and Enrico Fermi, and the political figures of Churchill, Roosevelt, and Molotov. Settings include the United States, England, Germany, the Soviet Union, China, and Japan. Reviewing the first novel in the quartet, *Worldwar: In the Balance*, Thomas Pearson of *Voice of Youth Advocates* called the series "promising." *Booklist*'s Roland Green, in a starred review, dubbed Turtledove "one of alternate history's authentic modern masters," and the first novel of the series an "engrossing volume." Letson, reviewing the initial title in *Locus*, commented that the novel delivers excitement "in the form of interesting characters responding to conditions both new and unchanged. . . . It is this ground-level . . . view of the world at war that I find gripping, the lives of individuals as they are affected by the macrohistorical military-economic-political forces represented by the wargames layer of the book." *Publishers Weekly* called Turtledove's *Worldwar: In the Balance* an "intelligent speculative novel" which "gives a surprisingly convincing flavor to the time-worn story of warring nations uniting to repel extraterrestrials."

Turtledove continued the story with *Worldwar: Tilting the Balance*, in which earthlings begin to fight back using ginger, addictive to the Lizards. Pearson commented in *Voice of Youth Advocates* that "[r]eal historical characters intermingle with Turtledove's fictional creatures in a wild 600-page blend of soap opera, carefully drawn character studies, and slam-bang action." *Upsetting the Balance* and *Striking the Balance* complete the tetralogy, ending with an uneasy truce declared between earthlings and the Race. Reviewing the final volume, a *Kirkus Reviews* critic said that Turtledove had created a huge opus. "A cast of thousands with a plot to match, well-drawn if unoriginal aliens, a wealth of fascinating speculation—and scope for any number of sequels."

Turtledove's sequel was not long in coming. Set sixteen years after the end of the "Worldwar" books, the "Colonization" series begins with the arrival of a flotilla of Lizard starships carrying a cargo of forty million sleep-frozen Lizard colonists. The first of a projected three-book series, *Colonization: Second Contact* is "Outstanding entertainment," according to *Booklist*'s Roberta Johnson. "In high fashion, the master of alternative SF launches a sequel series to his acclaimed 'Worldwar' tetralogy," according to a reviewer for *Publishers Weekly*. The same reviewer said that Turtledove, "[w]ith his fertile imagination running on overdrive . . . develops an exciting, often surprising story that will not only delight his fans but will probably send newcomers back to the 'Worldwar' saga to fill in the backstory."

War on a global scale also serves as the backdrop for Turtledove's "Great War" series, which had its inception in another Civil War novel, *How Few Remain*. This time, Turtledove changes history with the Confederacy winning the Battle of Antietam, and going on to win the Civil War in an alliance with the French and British. When the United States declares war on the Confederate States in 1881 over its purchase of northern territories from Mexico, the Confederacy again wins the conflict with the support of the French and British. This is the setting for the alternate history Turtledove explores in subsequent novels about the First World War. "The novel displays the compelling combination of rigorous historiography and robust storytelling that readers have come to expect from Turtledove," noted a reviewer for *Publishers Weekly*, who added, "Turtledove delivers his most gripping novel since 1992's *The Guns of the South*."

In *The Great War: American Front*, Turtledove employs the same historical world. It is 1914 and there is a world war between Germany, an ally of the United States, and the alliance of France, England, and the Confederate States. "Turtledove sustains high interest throughout the lengthy narrative," commented *Publishers Weekly*. "With shocking vividness, Turtledove demonstrates the extreme fragility of our modern world. . . . This is state-of-the-art alternate history, nothing less." Turtle-

---

If you enjoy the works of Harry Turtledove, you may also want to check out the following books and films:

Brian W. Aldiss, *The Year before Yesterday,* 1987.
Terry Bisson, *Fire on the Mountain,* 1988.
Orson Scott Card, *Alvin Journeyman,* 1995.
Mike Resnick, *Alternate Presidents,* 1992.
Planet of the Apes, a film starring Charlton Heston, 1968.

---

dove extends his saga in *The Great War: Walk in Hell*, the second volume of a planned tetralogy. This book covers the year 1915 that includes a Negro rebellion in the Confederacy and a United States invasion of Canada where the horrors of trench warfare occur on the American continent instead of in Europe. According to *Booklist*'s Roland Green, "This is not alternate history intended to give readers the warm fuzzies; it is a remorseless working out of the consequences of greater follies producing even worse results than the ones we may read about in actual history."

Turtledove is busy working on another cycle of novels, projected to be a five or six volume series, named "Darkness." These fantasies utilize technology of the 1930s and 1940s, but sets them in an imaginary world where technological advances are achieved through magic. *Into the Darkness*, the first novel in the series, opens in a fantasy world reminiscent of medieval Europe, Derlavai, where sorcery has been harnessed to create military power. This sprawling saga begins with the forces of Algarve invading the kingdom of Forthweg.

Turtledove, married to a novelist—the mystery writer Laura Frankos—spends most of his time writing. One interviewer estimated that Turtledove writes 350 days per year, hardly surprising given his prodigious output over the last two decades. In the 1990s alone he has written over two dozen action-packed and bookspine-imperiling epics. He does not simply regurgitate history; he absorbs all relevant facts about a period, throws in a what-if, and then follows the trail as it leads to a completely new history. Summing up the difference between writing history and fiction, Turtledove told Bloom, "Fiction has to be plausible. All history has to do is happen."

■ Works Cited

Review of *Between the Rivers*, *Kirkus Reviews*, January 1, 1998, p. 28.

Review of *Between the Rivers*, *Publishers Weekly*, January 26, 1998, p. 73.

Bloom, Jeremy, "Da Toastmaster Guest of Honor," *Chicon 2000 Progress Report 2*, http://www.sfsite.com/~silverag/toastmaster.html.

Cassada, Jackie, review of *Between the Rivers*, *Library Journal*, January, 1998, p. 149.

Review of *Colonization: Second Contact*, *Publishers Weekly*, November 30, 1998, p. 53.

Flanagan, Margaret, review of *The Guns of the South*, *Booklist*, November 1, 1992, p. 490.

Flanagan, Margaret, review of *Justinian*, *Booklist*, August 19, 1998, p. 1971.

Garratt, Peter T., "Turtledove, Harry (Norman)," *St. James Guide to Fantasy Writers*, edited by David Pringle, St. James Press, 1996, pp. 562-64.

Review of *The Great War: American Front*, *Publishers Weekly*, April 27, 1998, p. 50.

Green, Roland, review of *Worldwar: In the Balance*, *Booklist*, December 1, 1993, p. 678.

Green, Roland, review of *The Great War: Walk in Hell*, *Booklist*, June 1, 1999.

Hammerton, M., "Turtledove, Harry," *Twentieth-Century Science-Fiction Writers*, 3rd edition, edited by Noelle Watson and Paul E. Schellinger, St. James Press, 1991, pp. 809-10.

Review of *How Few Remain*, *Publishers Weekly*, August 16, 1997, p. 390.

Johnston, Roberta, review of *Colonization: Second Contact*, *Booklist*, January 1, 1998, p. 842.

Letson, Russell, review of *Worldwar: In the Balance*, *Locus*, February, 1994, pp. 31-32.

Letson, Russell, review of *Agent of Byzantium*, *Locus*, April, 1994, pp. 23-24.

Pearson, Thomas, review of *Worldwar: In the Balance*, *Voice of Youth Advocates*, August, 1995, pp. 160-61.

Pearson, Thomas, review of *Worldwar: Tilting the Balance*, *Voice of Youth Advocates*, August, 1996, p. 172.

Squitieri, Tom, "Author Loves to Shake Up History," *USA Today*, October 13, 1998.

Review of *Worldwar: In the Balance*, *Publishers Weekly*, December 6, 1993, p. 60.

Review of *Worldwar: Striking the Balance*, *Kirkus Reviews*, October 1, 1996, p. 1434.

■ For More Information See

BOOKS

The Encyclopedia of Science Fiction, edited by John Clute and Peter Nicholls, St. Martin's Press, 1993.

Reginald, Robert, *Science Fiction and Fantasy Literature, 1975-1991*, Gale, 1992.

PERIODICALS

Booklist, February 15, 1987, p. 878; May 1, 1987, p. 1336; June 15, 1987, p. 1565; August, 1987, p. 1722; October 1, 1987, p. 222; May 1, 1990, p. 1688; May 15, 1990, p. 1785; January 1-15, 1996, p. 799; February 1, 1996, p. 899; March 1, 1999, p. 1104.

Kirkus Reviews, May 1, 1987, p. 682; March 15, 1988, p. 417; August 1, 1992, p. 947; January 1, 1995, p. 34; August 15, 1997, p. 1265.

Library Journal, April 15, 1988, p. 98; September 1, 1992, p. 217; November 15, 1993, p. 102; December, 1995, p. 163; June 15, 1998, p. 110; January, 1999, p. 165.

Locus, June, 1990, p. 33; March, 1991, p. 60; October, 1991, pp. 31, 56.

Publishers Weekly, January 23, 1987, p. 66; May 22, 1987, p. 69; March 18, 1988, p. 76; March 16, 1990, p. 66; January 11, 1991, p. 98; August 24, 1992, p. 63; February 20, 1995, p. 200; January 22, 1996, p. 61; February 5, 1996, p. 80; March 22, 1999, p. 74; August 23, 1999, p. 54.

Science Fiction Chronicle, October, 1987, p. 41; January, 1988, p. 49; April, 1988, p. 52.

Voice of Youth Advocates, June, 1992, p. 116; October, 1996, pp. 221-22.

Washington Post Book World, June 27, 1993, p. 12.*

—Sketch by J. Sydney Jones

Jean Ure

Personal

Surname sounds like "Ewer"; born January 1, 1943, in Surrey, England; daughter of William (an insurance officer) and Vera (Belsen) Ure; married Leonard Gregory (an actor and writer), 1967. *Education*: Attended Webber-Douglas Academy of Dramatic Art, 1965-67. *Religion*: None. *Hobbies and other interests*: Reading, writing letters, walking dogs, playing with cats, music, working for animal rights.

Addresses

Home—88 Southbridge Rd., Croydon, Surrey CR0 1AF, England. *Agent*—Maggie Noach, 21 Redan St., London W14 0AB, England.

Career

Writer. Worked variously as a waitress, cook, washer-up, nursing assistant, newspaper seller, shop assistant, theater usherette, temporary shorthand-typist, translator, secretary with NATO and UNESCO, and television production assistant. *Member*: Society of Authors, Vegan Society, Animal Aid.

Awards, Honors

American Library Association Best Book for Young Adults citation, 1983, for *See You Thursday*; *See You Thursday* and *Supermouse* were Junior Literary Guild selections.

Writings

FOR YOUNG ADULTS

A Proper Little Nooryeff, Bodley Head, 1982, published in the United States as *What If They Saw Me Now?*, Delacorte, 1984.
If It Weren't for Sebastian, Bodley Head, 1982, Delacorte, 1985.
You Win Some, You Lose Some, Bodley Head, 1984, Delacorte, 1987.
The Other Side of the Fence, Bodley Head, 1986, Delacorte, 1988.
One Green Leaf, Bodley Head, 1987, Delacorte, 1989.
Play Nimrod for Him, Bodley Head, 1990.
Dreaming of Larry, Doubleday, 1991.
Always Sebastian, Bodley Head, 1993.
A Place to Scream, Doubleday, 1993.
Has Anyone Seen This Girl?, Bodley Head, 1996.
Dance with Death, Scholastic, 1996.

"PLAGUE" TRILOGY

Plague 99, Methuen, 1990, published in the United States as *Plague*, Harcourt, 1991.
Come Lucky April, Methuen, 1992.
Watchers at the Shrine, Methuen, 1992

FOR CHILDREN

Ballet Dance for Two, F. Watts, 1960, published in England as *Dance for Two*, illustrated by Richard Kennedy, Harrap, 1960.
Hi There, Supermouse!, illustrated by Martin White, Hutchinson, 1983, published in the United States as *Supermouse*, illustrated by Ellen Eagle, Morrow, 1984.
You Two, illustrated by Eagle, Morrow, 1984, published in England as *The You-Two*, illustrated by White, Hutchinson, 1984.
Nicola Mimosa, illustrated by White, Hutchinson, 1985, published in the United States as *The Most Important Thing*, illustrated by Eagle, Morrow, 1986.
Megustar, Blackie, 1985.
Swings and Roundabouts, Blackie, 1986.
A Bottled Cherry Angel, Hutchinson, 1986.
Brenda the Bold, illustrated by Glenys Ambrus, Heinemann, 1986.
Tea-Leaf on the Roof, illustrated by Val Sassoon, Blackie, 1987.
War with Old Mouldy!, illustrated by Alice Englander, Methuen, 1987.
Who's Talking?, Orchard, 1987.
Frankie's Dad, Hutchinson, 1988.
(With Michael Lewis) *A Muddy Kind of Magic*, Blackie, 1988.
(With Lewis) *Two Men in a Boat*, Blackie, 1988.
Cool Simon, Orchard, 1990.
Jo in the Middle, Hutchinson, 1990.
The Wizard in the Woods, illustrated by David Anstley, Walker, 1990, Candlewick Press, 1992.
Fat Lollipop, Hutchinson, 1991.
William in Love, Blackie, 1991.
Wizard in Wonderland, illustrated by David Anstley, Walker, 1991, Candlewick Press, 1993.
Spooky Cottage, Heinemann, 1992.
The Unknown Planet, Walker, 1992.
Wizard in the Woods, Walker, 1992.
The Ghost That Lives on the Hill, Methuen, 1992.
Bossyboots, Hutchinson, 1993.
Captain Cranko and the Crybaby, Walker, 1993.
Phantom Knicker Nicker, Blackie, 1993.
Star Turn, Hutchinson, 1994.
The Children Next Door, Scholastic, 1996.

"WOODSIDE SCHOOL" SERIES

The Fright, Orchard Books, 1987.
Loud Mouth, Orchard Books, 1988.
Soppy Birthday, Orchard Books, 1988.
King of Spuds, Orchard Books, 1989.
Who's for the Zoo?, Orchard Books, 1989.

"THURSDAY" TRILOGY

See You Thursday, Kestrel, 1981, Delacorte, 1983.
After Thursday, Kestrel, 1985, Delacorte, 1987.
Tomorrow Is Also a Day, Methuen, 1989.

"VANESSA" TRILOGY

Trouble with Vanessa, Transworld, 1988.
There's Always Danny, Transworld, 1989.
Say Goodbye, Transworld, 1989.

"WE LOVE ANIMALS" SERIES

Foxglove, Barron's Educational Series, 1999.
Snow Kittens, Barron's Educational Series, 1999.
Daffy Down Donkey, Barron's Educational Series, 1999.
Muddy Four Paws, Barron's Educational Series, 1999.

FOR ADULTS

The Other Theater, Transworld, 1966.
The Test of Love, Corgi, 1968.
If You Speak Love, Corgi, 1972.
Had We but World Enough and Time, Corgi, 1972.
The Farther Off from England, White Lion, 1973.
Daybreak, Corgi, 1974.
All Thy Love, Corgi, 1975.
Marriage of True Minds, Corgi, 1975.
No Precious Time, Corgi, 1976.
Hear No Evil, Corgi, 1976.
Curtain Fall, Corgi, 1978.
Masquerade, Corgi, 1979.
A Girl Like That, Corgi, 1979.
(Under pseudonym Ann Colin) *A Different Class of Doctor*, Corgi, 1980.
(Under pseudonym Ann Colin) *Doctor Jamie*, Corgi, 1980.
(Under name Jean Gregory) *Love beyond Telling*, Corgi, 1986.

"RIVERSIDE THEATER ROMANCE" SERIES

Early Stages, Corgi, 1977.

Dress Rehearsal, Corgi, 1977.
All in a Summer Season, Corgi, 1977.
Bid Time Return, Corgi, 1978.

GEORGIAN ROMANCES; UNDER PSEUDONYM SARAH MCCULLOCH

Not Quite a Lady, Corgi, 1980, Fawcett, 1981.
A Most Insistent Lady, Corgi, 1981.
A Lady for Ludovic, Corgi, 1981.
Merely a Gentleman, Corgi, 1982.
A Perfect Gentleman, Corgi, 1982.

TRANSLATOR

Henri Vernes, *City of a Thousand Drums*, Corgi, 1966.
Vernes, *The Dinosaur Hunters*, Corgi, 1966.
Vernes, *The Yellow Shadow*, Corgi, 1966.
Jean Bruce, *Cold Spell*, Corgi, 1967.
Bruce, *Top Secret*, Corgi, 1967.
Vernes, *Treasure of the Golcondas*, Corgi, 1967.
Vernes, *The White Gorilla*, Corgi, 1967.
Vernes, *Operation Parrot*, Corgi, 1968.
Bruce, *Strip Tease*, Corgi, 1968.
Noel Calef, *The Snare*, Souvenir Press, 1969.
Sven Hassel, *March Battalion*, Corgi, 1970.
Hassel, *Assignment Gestapo*, Corgi, 1971.
Laszlo Havas, *Hitler's Plot to Kill the Big Three*, Corgi, 1971.
Hassel, *SS General*, Corgi, 1972.
Hassel, *Reign of Hell*, Corgi, 1973.

OTHER

Contributor of articles to periodicals, including *Vegan, Writers' Monthly, Books for Keeps,* and *School Librarian.*

■ Sidelights

Jean Ure's young adult books combine her lively sense of humor with unique stories that often contain off-beat situations and characters. Ure is a vegetarian who is avid about animal rights, and while her books make references to these tendencies among her characters, they are never preachy. Class struggles, homosexuality, sexual awakenings, and feminism are also among her topics, all of which she discusses with freshness and immediacy.

Ure does not remember a time when she did not want to be a writer. Born in Surrey, England, as a young girl she would steal notebooks from her school to fill them with imaginative stories. "I was brought up, in a tradition of writing, inasmuch as my father's family were inveterate ode writers, sending one another long screeds of poetry on every possible occasion," Ure recalled in an essay for *Something About the Author Autobiography Series (SAAS).* She was also happy to read poetry or dance in front of a room of adoring relatives.

"The reason I turned to writing for young adults was, basically, that it offered a freedom which 'genre' writing does not allow."

—Jean Ure

Going to school, however, was painful for Ure. She constantly felt that she did not fit in. Ure humorously speculated in *SAAS* on the reasons why she never felt a part of the crowd. "The more I think about it, the more it seems to me that hair was the root cause of all my problems," she said, citing limp and unmanageable locks. "I am almost seriously persuaded that had it not been for hair, I would have gone to the party along with everyone else."

Being outside of the popular crowd caused Ure to fantasize about many things, including being in love and dancing. Being a compulsive writer, Ure wrote down these fantasies. She sent the manuscript off to a publisher, and at the age of sixteen she became a published writer. "Writing *Dance for Two* was a very cathartic exercise and brought me great solace," she told *SAAS.* "I almost managed to believe that . . . I really *did* have a sweetheart called Noel, that I really *was* a ballet dancer."

Ambition and not wanting to continue with the pain of school-life were reasons why Ure chose to try writing as a profession rather than go to college. She spent a long time doing menial jobs while trying to get her work published. Discouraged by her lack of success, Ure enrolled in a drama class and found she had a talent for entertaining. While attending drama school, she met her husband, Leonard Gregory, at one of the few parties she attended, and he became a major influence in her life. Shortly afterward, her writing career suddenly took off, and she started writing romantic novels and translating books. While these did not stimulate her intellectually, they helped her learn her craft and earn a living at the same time. After a few years, however, she began to feel like she was compromising herself by writing these books.

See You Thursday Marks Turning Point

The year 1980 was a turning point for Ure. She wrote in *SAAS*, "I really emerged as myself, with a book for young adults called *See You Thursday*." It focuses on a blind pianist named Abe and a sixteen-year-old rebel named Marianne. Although Abe is eight years older, wiser, and from a different background than Marianne, the pair become attracted to each other, and the relationship blossoms as Marianne sheds her shyness and finds a new maturity. In *After Thursday*, the sequel that followed this popular book, the romance of Abe and Marianne is further tested by their differing perspectives on independence. Ure was extremely happy to have found this fresh audience for her writing. "The reason I turned to writing for young adults was, basically, that it offered a freedom which 'genre' writing does not allow," she related to *SAAS*. Ure used her instinctive talent for writing to create these books. She commented, "When I created Abe, my blind pianist, I did the very minimum of research into blindness, but was able to gain direct knowledge, albeit to a severely limited extent, of how it would be to be blind by tying a scarf about my eyes and blundering around the house." *See You Thursday* won the American Library Association's Best Book for Young Adults citation in 1983.

Ure returned to the themes of autonomy and awakening sexuality in the "Vanessa" trilogy, which includes *Trouble with Vanessa*, *There's Always Danny*, and *Say Goodbye*, as well as in *The Other Side of the Fence*. Describing the first two books of the "Vanessa" trilogy as more than a romantic tale, Stephanie Nettell in the *Times Literary Supplement* labeled Ure's novels "intelligent, spiky and imaginative." Similarly enthusiastic about *The Other Side of the Fence*, reviewers such as *Bulletin of the Center for Children's Books* contributor Zena Sutherland praised the novel as "mature and sen-

sitive. . . . [It is] told with both momentum and nuance." This romance is unusual, however, because it concerns a young homosexual, Richard, who meets and finds friendship with Bonny, a girl who is attracted to him but cannot understand, until the end, why her sexual interest is not returned. Although one critic, *School Library Journal* writer Karen K. Radtke, questioned Bonny's "naiveté" regarding Richard (when she is otherwise street-smart), Radtke admitted that the story may be satisfying to teenagers who "harbor secret fantasies about . . . flaunting parental authority."

Ure's sensitive treatment of relationships is often the focus of critical reviews. The special rivalry among sisters is explored in *Supermouse* when a shy but talented girl, Nicola, is offered a dancing role over her more favored younger sister, Rose. Mary M. Burns in *Horn Book* wrote that even though the story is told from the point of view of an eleven-year-old, "the author has managed to suggest subtle emotions which underlie the family's values and actions." The story is continued in *The Most Important Thing* when Nicola, now fourteen, must decide whether her future career will include ballet, or whether she should concentrate instead on science and maybe become a doctor. Cynthia K. Leibold concluded in the *School Library Journal* that "Ure is skillful at creating colorful characters . . . and her characters execute their roles perfectly."

Examines Ethical and Moral Issues

Using insight and sometimes humor, Ure's novels often question values and touch upon subjects such as social standards. In one such book, *What If They Saw Me Now?*, an athletic young man is caught in an amusing dilemma when he is asked to dance the male lead in a ballet. Described by Sutherland in the *Bulletin of the Center for Children's Books* as "a funny and liberating" novel, Ure's treatment of the subject may appeal to both boys and girls as they appreciate Jamie's predicament—to overcome his own and others' "macho" stereotypes.

Coping with illness is the theme of two of Ure's contemporary works, *If It Weren't for Sebastian* and *One Green Leaf*, the first focusing on mental illness, and the latter on a fatal physical sickness. In *If It Weren't for Sebastian* the title character is

If you enjoy the works of Jean Ure, you may also want to check out the following books:

Ann Benson, *The Plague Tales*, 1997.
Ben Mikaelsen, *Countdown*, 1996.
Jill Paton Walsh, *A Parcel of Patterns*, 1983.
WarGames, a film starring Matthew Broderick, 1983.

an intense, but peace-loving, young man whose "strangeness" is an object of scorn and misunderstanding to others. Maggie becomes his friend and soon discovers that Sebastian is being treated as an out-patient at a mental health clinic. Ure "explores the borderline psychotic and his relationships with great sensitivity and understanding," declared Sutherland in a *Bulletin of the Center for Children's Books* review. Fatal illness is treated with similar sympathy and skill in *One Green Leaf*. After an unsuccessful surgery, it becomes obvious that David's cancer is terminal. Ure's emphasis, however, is on how David copes, and on the affection of his friends during his illness. According to Tess McKellen in the *School Library Journal*, the author "dramatizes successfully the effect of unexpected tragedy on young minds and emotions" in the novel.

Other topics for Ure's creative energy often center around her current passions: music, vegetarianism, animal rights, books, and theater. Her main motive is not to convert people, but to stimulate them. She told *SAAS* that, when writing, she sets out "to make people think: to make them examine their motives and question their assumptions." She concluded by summing up her reasons for writing, explaining that "it will always be my characters who interest me the most; and my aim, if conscious aim I have . . ., will still be to stimulate and entertain."

The 1993 novel *Always Sebastian* brought back the unique title character of Ure's previous novel. Its plot follows the relationship between Sebastian, now deeply involved in the animal-rights movement, and Maggie, a single parent with two daughters. That same year, Ure also authored a science-fiction thriller for teens, *A Place to Scream*. The work is set in the year 2015, and it is a fu-

ture in which social problems caused by incautious economic policies have worsened immensely. Its protagonist is the teenage Gillian, who has been fortunate enough to grow up in an affluent household, but feels overwhelmed by the world outside. Her involvement with a maverick new friend brings both romance and a sense of purpose to her life.

The "Plague" Series

Ure won critical plaudits for her next series, "Plague," which includes the post-apocalyptic tales *Plague 99* (published in the United States as *Plague*), *Come Lucky April*, and *Watchers at the Shrine*. All were published between 1990 and 1992, and set in Ure's native England. *Plague 99* opens in the twentieth century in a world where nuclear catastrophe has triggered a contagious and deadly illness. Returning from camp, Fran Latimer finds both of her parents dead and her best friend ill. She teams up with Shahid, a schoolmate, and as the plague worsens in their hometown, with death seemingly everywhere, they journey to Shahid's brother's home, only to find the family there decimated as well. When Shahid becomes sick, Fran nurses him as they hide out in an old bookstore, and he recovers enough for them to once more begin their journey to safety. As *Plague 99* concludes, they are on their way to distant Cornwall, where Fran's grandmother lives.

Plague 99 proved such a popular book with teens that Ure decided to continue the story. *Come Lucky April* follows the story of Fran and Shahid's great-grandson, Daniel. A hundred years after the fateful flight to Cornwall, Daniel learns of the existence of Fran's fascinating journal, which she wrote during the plague. He travels to Croydon where it was left behind, but the London suburb is now an entirely feminist-governed community in which new births are the result of artificial insemination. Male offspring in Croydon are likely castrated, though Ure only hints the practice is part of their legal system. A virtual outlaw in this community by reason of his gender, Daniel falls in love with one of its members, April, and she must choose between remaining in her progressive, nonviolent society or leaving with him and entering a harshly ordered, retrogressive outside world.

Watchers at the Shrine, Ure's third installment in the "Plague" series, reveals that in the year 2099

April did not leave Croydon, but remained behind and gave birth to a son, Hal. When the boy nears puberty, he is sent to Cornwall to escape castration, but he has trouble adjusting to the vastly different patriarchal community. A large number of birth defects occur in Cornwall since an abandoned nuclear power plant nearby is still emitting radiation. Hal is shocked to discover that both people in the greater Cornwall community and inside the odd religious sect known as the Watchers, with whom he is sent to live, display an ignorance of history and science, and, in contrast to Croydon, women are treated quite brutally. He falls in love with a Watchers' daughter, who was born with a birth defect, and as a result, will soon be relegated to the community's brigade of officially sanctioned prostitutes. Instead, the pair escape to Croydon where a crisis has brought some positive changes to the feminist community's system of social order. A reviewer for *Junior Bookshelf* commended Ure's powers of description in creating a desolate, post-plague Britain, termed here "intriguing as well as shocking and forbidding, and she contrives associations for Hal which increase the horror of societies which have lost their way."

Ure is also the author of the 1996 teen novel *Has Anyone Seen This Girl?* Told in diary form, the book begins with fourteen-year-old Caroline riding in a train to her new boarding school. Aboard the train, she meets Rachel, and the two become fast friends. At school, however, the quirky Rachel is an outcast, and Caroline is torn between peer pressure to reject her and a sense of loyalty to her first friend. Rachel makes friendship difficult, however, as she proves to be a demanding, asocial friend, and Caroline suffers tremendous guilt when Rachel runs away from the school. "Jean Ure once again writes with a sympathetic understanding of young people," said Maggie Bignell in *Quill & Quire*.

■ Works Cited

Bignell, Maggie, review of *Has Anyone Seen This Girl?*, *Quill & Quire*, August, 1996, p. 121.

Burns, Mary M., review of *Supermouse*, *Horn Book*, June, 1984, p. 334.

Leibold, Cynthia K., review of *The Most Important Thing*, *School Library Journal*, May, 1986, p. 110.

McKellen, Tess, review of *One Green Leaf*, *School Library Journal*, May, 1989, p. 128.

Nettell, Stephanie, review of *Trouble with Vanessa* and *There's Always Danny*, *Times Literary Supplement*, June 9, 1989, p. 648.

Radtke, Karen K., review of *The Other Side of the Fence*, *School Library Journal*, April, 1988, p. 114.

Sutherland, Zena, review of *What If They Saw Me Now?*, *Bulletin of the Center for Children's Books*, June, 1984, p. 195.

Sutherland, Zena, review of *If It Weren't for Sebastian*, *Bulletin of the Center for Children's Books*, June, 1985, p. 197.

Sutherland, Zena, review of *The Other Side of the Fence*, *Bulletin of the Center for Children's Books*, February, 1988, p. 127.

Ure, Jean, essay in *Something about the Author Autobiography Series*, Volume 14, Gale, 1992.

Review of *Watchers at the Shrine*, *Junior Bookshelf*, October, 1994, p. 191.

■ For More Information See

BOOKS

Children's Literature Review, Volume 34, Gale, 1994.

PERIODICALS

Books for Keeps, July, 1993, p. 28; November, 1993, p. 29; October, 1994, p. 28; May, 1996, p. 16.

Bulletin of the Center for Children's Books, December, 1983, p. 79; May, 1984, p. 176; October, 1984, p. 36; April, 1986, p. 160; June, 1986, p. 198; May, 1987, p. 180; May, 1989, p. 238; October, 1991, p. 52.

Horn Book, December, 1983, p. 720; August, 1984, p. 479; March, 1988, p. 212.

Junior Bookshelf, August, 1993, pp. 163-164; June, 1996, p. 127.

Publishers Weekly, November 25, 1983, p. 64; April 13, 1984, p. 72; February 8, 1985, p. 77; May 30, 1986, p. 68; June 12, 1987, p. 86.

School Librarian, November, 1993, p. 168; November, 1994; February 1, 1995, p. 6.

School Library Journal, August, 1984, p. 87; October, 1984, p. 163; August, 1985, p. 82; August, 1986, p. 108; October, 1991, p. 150; October, 1992, pp. 122-123; July, 1993, p. 87.

Times Literary Supplement, July 16, 1985, p. 910; November 28, 1986, p. 1347; September 1, 1989, p. 957.

Voice of Youth Advocates, August-October, 1986, p. 152; October, 1989, p. 218.*

Rachel Vail

for Children's Books, 1992, for *Do-Over;* Books for the Teen Age, New York Public Library, 1992, for *Do- Over,* and 1994, for *Ever After;* Best Books citation, School Library Journal, 1996, for *Daring to Be Abigail.*

■ Personal

Born July 25, 1966, in New York, NY; daughter of an attorney and a school psychologist; married, husband's name Mitchell (a physician); children: Zachary. *Education:* Georgetown University, B.A., 1988.

■ Addresses

Home—New York, NY. Office—c/o Writers House, 21 West 26th Street, New York, NY 10010.

■ Career

Writer. *Member:* Authors Guild.

■ Awards, Honors

Editor's Choice, Booklist, 1991, for *Wonder,* and 1992, for *Do-Over;* Pick of the List designation, American Booksellers Association, 1991, for *Wonder;* Blue Ribbon designation, *Bulletin of the Center*

■ Writings

Wonder, Orchard (New York City), 1991.
Do-Over, Orchard, 1992.
Ever After, Orchard, 1994.
Daring to Be Abigail, Orchard, 1996.
Over the Moon (picture book), illustrated by Scott Nash, Orchard, 1998.

"FRIENDSHIP RING" SERIES

If You Only Knew, Scholastic, Inc., 1998.
Please, Please, Please, Scholastic, Inc., 1998.
Not That I Care, Scholastic, Inc., 1999.
What Are Friends For?, Scholastic, Inc., 1999.

■ Sidelights

The author of several novels for young teens, Rachel Vail brings to life the sometimes exciting, sometimes scary, but always perplexing passage from childhood to the world of adults. In novels like *Do-Over* and *Daring to Be Abigail,* Vail successfully captures what it means to be a pre-teen, often drawing critical comparisons between her work and that of popular young adult novelist Judy Blume. "Vail has the measure of this vulnerable age and its painful concern about identity within the group," noted a critic in *Kirkus Reviews,* commenting on Vail's debut novel, *Wonder,* and her depiction of the gawkiness of seventh grade. Equally adept at portraying the fumbling steps of both girls and boys in their halting progress along the path toward adulthood, Vail had been commended for her efforts by such organizations as the New York Public Library, the American Bookseller's Association, and a number of periodicals. Her four-novel "Friendship Ring" series caused *Horn Book* contributor Christine Heppermann to dub Vail "an author who's been there, done that, and, most importantly, *remembers how it felt* . . . to live through the self-esteem crash that everyone knows girls experience around adolescence but no one can quite explain."

Born in Manhattan, Vail grew up in New Rochelle, New York. In her youth she never intended to be a writer; instead, Vail was entranced by the stage and took every opportunity to appear in school and community productions. But her writing abilities drew the encouragement of various teachers, both in high school and later at Georgetown University, who helped her to develop her talent. In an autobiographical sketch for *Horn Book,* Vail recalled one instructor in particular named Doc Murphy. A theater professor, Murphy encouraged her to focus on the essentials of character. Vail observed, "I think writing would be so much more exciting and less daunting to children if the emphasis were put on the details, the questions that propel the writer to create astonishing, unique characters who, by their juxtaposition with other astonishing, unique characters, make stories happen."

Characters a Reflection of Teen Readers

Vail's emphasis on character is apparent in her first novel for children, a coming-of-age story titled *Wonder.* As twelve-year-old Jessica enters seventh grade she finds that she has suddenly become unpopular. Sheila, her former best friend, and five other girls succeed in ostracizing Jessica, giving her the humiliating nickname "Wonder" after one of the girls describes her new polka-dot dress as "a Wonder Bread explosion." With a determination fuelled by the welcome attentions of Conor O'Malley, the object of her first crush, Jessica per-

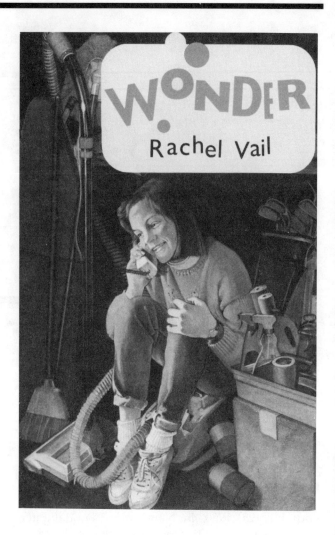

Jess Gauche muddles through seventh grade despite the cruel jokes and unpleasant name calling bestowed upon her by former friends in this 1991 work.

severes. Lauded by critics for its skillful rendering of character, *Wonder* proved to be a highly successful debut novel for its author. A *Kirkus Reviews* commentator found Jess "Gauche, likable . . . a character to remember," and *School Library Journal* contributor Debra S. Gold also spoke favorably of Vail's characterization of her central protagonist. "Jessica's first- person account reveals a three-dimensional character with whom readers will laugh and empathize," according to Gold. Deborah Abbott of *Booklist* asserted: "Piercing and funny, Vail's breezy story describes the hazards of junior high, sketched with the emotional chasms universal to the age."

One of Jessica's schoolmates, Whitman Levy, becomes the hero of Vail's next story, Do-Over.

Eighth-grader Whitman is faced with some severe family problems, including his parents' imminent break-up, while struggling with his first real boy-girl relationships and a part in the school play. Vail balances the comical tale of his various escapades with other thorny issues, including Whitman's discovery that his best friend Doug is a bigot. Eventually the self-conscious and somewhat bewildered Whitman comes to understand how to deal with all that confronts him, in a moment of self-realization while on stage: "I could screw up or I could be amazing, and there's no turning back, no do-overs."

Several reviewers of Vail's *Do-Over* commented on the author's ability to form believable characters and create interesting dialog. *School Library Journal* contributor Jacqueline Rose asserted: "Vail is a master at portraying adolescent self-absorption, awkwardness, and fickleness, all with freshness and humor." In the *Bulletin of the Center for Children's Books,* Roger Sutton cited the reason's for Vail's popularity among teen readers as "her natural ear for teenaged talk, and partly because she never, ever preaches. This is the real thing." Stephanie Zvirin of *Booklist* likewise spoke of the "sharp and genuine" dialog in *Do-Over,* commending Vail's "remarkable talent for capturing so perfectly the pleasure and pain of being thirteen—in a real kids' world."

Experiments with New Format in Third Novel

In her third novel, 1994's *Ever After,* Vail employed a new narrative technique, presenting much of her story in the form of diary entries written by fourteen-year-old Molly. Best friends Molly and Vicky live year-round on a small Massachusetts island. The presence of a new friend, summer visitor Grace, causes Vicky to feel insecure and puts a strain on her relationship with Molly. Vicky's possessiveness begins to disturb Molly, and eventually destroys the girls' friendship when Molly learns that Vicky has been reading her personal journal without permission. "That Vicky and Molly's rift is likely to be permanent . . . is just one hallmark of the authenticity of this carefully conceived story," noted a *Publishers Weekly* reviewer. A *Kirkus Reviews* commentator praised *Ever After* as "an unusually immediate portrayal of a thoughtful teen finding her balance among her peers while making peace with her own capabilities." *School Library Journal* contributor Ellen Fader characterized the book as "a breezy, smart-talking novel that explores the ever-fascinating arena of young teen friendship," while Hazel Rochman of *Booklist* expressed a common critical refrain when noting that "the contemporary teenage voice is exactly right."

Daring to be Abigail features a narrative format similar to the one that Vail employs in *Ever After.* The story unfolds in the letters of Abby Silverman, an eleven-year-old girl who has decided to "reinvent herself" while away at Camp Nashaquitsa for the summer. Her new-found boldness wins the acceptance of her fellow campers, but it also seems to require that Abby, now Abigail, forsake Dana, an unpopular girl bunking in her cabin. Although she likes Dana, Abigail succumbs to

Whitman Levy, an eighth-grader plagued with personal problems, suddenly realizes how to face his conflicts while performing in a school play.

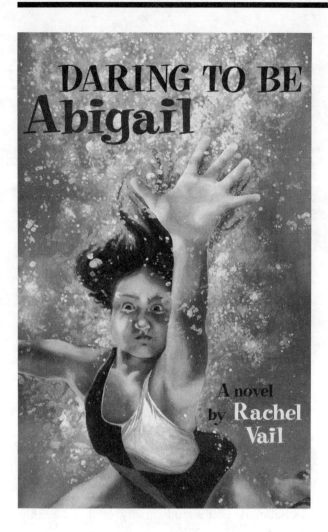

While at summer camp, Abby Silverman tries out a new personality but soon discovers that the old one wasn't so bad in this 1996 novel.

peer pressure by accepting a dare to urinate in Dana's mouthwash. Unable to stop Dana before she uses the rinse, Abigail is thrown out of the camp, and addresses a final, poignant letter to her dead father, whose apparent disappointment with Abby was what initially inflamed her crisis of identity and prompted her efforts at "reinvention." Deborah Stevenson of the *Bulletin of the Center for Children's Books* noted that Abigail's "vulnerability and her poignantly, desperately upbeat letters home will engender reader sympathy and understanding." *Booklist* reviewer Stephanie Zvirin praised Vail for once again being "right on target when it comes to the reality of preadolescent girls, catching how they act and what they say, their nastiness and envy and sweetness, and how confusing it is to long for independence, yet be afraid

of the freedom and responsibility that come with it." Lauren Adams, reviewing *Daring to Be Abigail* for *Horn Book,* commented: "As in her other books, Vail displays her talent for capturing the humor and angst of early adolescence; this latest novel . . . is her most sophisticated yet."

Even Best Friends See Things Differently

In her "Friendship Ring" series, Vail takes her characteristic focus on middle school by following a group of four girls through the seventh grade. Zoe Grandon, the youngest of five sisters, loves sports but realizes that her relationship with the boys she hangs out with and plays sports with is beginning to change. CJ Hurley is Zoe's best friend, even though her small size makes her more suited to the ballet studio (where she has spent most of her free time) instead of the gym. Blessed with a delicate frame and abundant, curly—maybe too curly—hair, CJ realizes that her concentration on dancing has resulted more from her mother's childhood dreams of becoming a prima ballerina that CJ's own passion. But how can CJ tell mom that she'd rather play soccer with Zoe?

Morgan Miller's problems stem more from her parents that even CJ's do; her father decided to leave the family to become an actor, and his wife's anger over his abandonment has settled on Morgan's shoulders as well. While she likes her friends Zoe and CJ, she is also jealous of her friends and their seemingly close-knit families, and that jealousy sometimes expresses itself in hurtful remarks. Olivia, the fourth member of the group, is the brainy one, and fitting in in sports and social life is difficult. Reluctant to leave her solitary pursuits, she is pursued by the other girls to enlarge their group.

As critic Christine Heppermann remarked in her review of the "Friendship Ring" books for *Horn Book,* Vail is an expert chronicler of "the transition from taking your personality and place in life for granted to suddenly having everything you say and do and think seem hopelessly wrong." Each of the series' titles—*If You Only Knew, Please, Please, Please, Not That I Care,* and *What Are Friends For?,* views the sequence of events from a different perspective. Through this technique, Vail shows readers that everyone has the same kind of concerns and insecurities in middle school, whether or not they are popular or appear to be

If you enjoy the works of Rachel Vail, you may also want to check out the following books and films:

Judy Blume, *Just as Long as We're Together,* 1987.
Phyllis Reynolds Naylor, *All but Alice,* 1992.
Susan Wojciechowski, *Promises to Keep,* 1991.
The Man in the Moon, a film starring Reese Witherspoon, 1991.

---

self-confident and in control of the situation. As reviewer Linda Binder noted in *School Library Journal* of the third novel in the series: Vail's "gritty, terse prose and complex characters keep readers engrossed. The questions of what makes a friend, . . . and how to be true to yourself make for an appealing story line."

If You Only Knew finds Zoe suddenly feeling self-conscious about her athletic ability, as well as the way she looks and what she wears. Comparisons with graceful CJ and streetwise Morgan on the social front find Zoe severely lacking, in her mind, and she decides to do something about it. But what? "Vail's perceptive portrayals of Zoe's stumbling attempts to win CJ as her best friend and to capture the affections of one of her [boy] pals . . . are simultaneously poignant and humorous— and sometimes painful," according to a *Publishers Weekly* contributor. In *Not That I Care,* Morgan panics over an upcoming presentation about the ten most important things in her life, in front of her English class, and regrets that a recent falling out with friend CJ has left her with no one to bolster her courage. In *Please, Please, Please* we see the falling out from another side, and realize that CJ's family isn't as perfect as jealous Morgan thinks it is. In fact, CJ feels that her need to please her mother by devoting herself to dancing is taking away from her chance to be herself, and miss out on school trips and fun times with her friends as well. As Rebecca O'Connell maintained in a *School Library Journal* review of *Please, Please, Please,* while CJ is a "complex" character, "Vail gets her protagonist's voice just right."

■ Works Cited

Abbott, Deborah, review of *Wonder, Booklist,* September 1, 1991, p. 54.

Adams, Lauren, review of *Daring to Be Abigail, Horn Book,* May-June, 1996, pp. 337-39.

Binder, Linda, review of *Not That I Care, School Library Journal,* December, 1998, p. 130.

Review of *Ever After, Kirkus Reviews,* April 1, 1994, pp. 486.

Review of *Ever After, Publishers Weekly,* February 21, 1994, pp. 255-56.

Fader, Ellen, review of *Ever After, School Library Journal,* May, 1994, p. 136.

Gold, Debra S., review of *Wonder, School Library Journal,* August, 1991, p. 196.

Heppermann, Christine, "Three Rounds in 'The Friendship Ring,'" in *Horn Book,* January/February, 1999, pp. 95-99.

Review of *If You Only Knew, Publishers Weekly,* June 8, 1998, p. 61.

O'Connell, Rebecca, review of *Please, Please, Please, School Library Journal,* December, 1998, p. 130.

Rochman, Hazel, review of Ever After, Booklist, March 1, 1994, p. 1254.

Rose, Jacqueline, review of *Do-Over, School Library Journal,* September, 1992, p. 282.

Stevenson, Deborah, review of *Daring to Be Abigail, Bulletin of the Center for Children's Books,* February, 1996, p. 207.

Sutton, Roger, review of *Do-Over, Bulletin of the Center for Children's Books,* December, 1992, pp. 125-26.

Vail, Rachel, "Making Stories Happen," *Horn Book,* May-June, 1994, pp. 301-4.

Review of *Wonder, Kirkus Reviews,* August 8, 1991, p. 1095.

Zvirin, Stephanie, review of *Do-Over, Booklist,* August, 1992, p. 2013.

Zvirin, Stephanie, review of *Daring to Be Abigail, Booklist,* March 1, 1996, p. 1184.

■ For More Information See

BOOKS

Seventh Book of Junior Authors and Illustrators, H. W. Wilson, 1996.

PERIODICALS

Bulletin of the Center for Children's Books, September, 1991, p. 24; December, 1998, pp. 148-49.

Horn Book, November-December, 1992, p. 731.

Kirkus Reviews, July 15, 1992, p. 927; November 15, 1998, p. 1673.

Publishers Weekly, August 9, 1991, p. 58; December 20, 1991, p. 24; July 20, 1998, p. 218.
School Library Journal, March, 1996, p. 198.

ON-LINE

"About Rachel Vail," located at http://place.scholastic.com/tradebks/friendshipring/index.htm (February 9, 1999).

Alice Walker

■ Personal

Born February 9, 1944, in Eatonton, GA; daughter of Willie Lee and Minnie Tallulah (maiden name, Grant) Walker; married Melvyn Rosenman Leventhal (a civil rights lawyer), March 17, 1967 (divorced, 1976); children: Rebecca. *Education:* Attended Spelman College, 1961-63; Sarah Lawrence College, B.A., 1965.

■ Addresses

Home—San Francisco, CA. *Office*—Harcourt Brace Jovanovich, 111 5th Ave., New York, NY 10003-1005.

■ Career

Writer. Wild Trees Press, Navarro, CA, co-founder and publisher, 1984-88. Has been a voter registration worker in Georgia, a worker in Head Start program in Mississippi, and on staff of New York City welfare department. Writer-in-residence and teacher of black studies at Jackson State College, 1968-69, and Tougaloo College, 1970-71; lecturer in literature, Wellesley College and University of Massachusetts—Boston, both 1972-73; distinguished writer in Afro-American studies department, University of California, Berkeley, spring, 1982; Fannie Hurst Professor of Literature, Brandeis University, Waltham, MA, fall, 1982. Lecturer and reader of own poetry at universities and conferences. Member of board of trustees of Sarah Lawrence College. Consultant on black history to Friends of the Children of Mississippi, 1967. Co-producer of film documentary, *Warrior Marks*, directed by Pratibha Parmar with script and narration by Walker, 1993.

■ Awards, Honors

Bread Loaf Writer's Conference scholar, 1966; first prize, *American Scholar* essay contest, 1967; Merrill writing fellowship, 1967; McDowell Colony fellowship, 1967, 1977-78; National Endowment for the Arts grant, 1969, 1977; Radcliffe Institute fellowship, 1971-73; Ph.D., Russell Sage College, 1972; National Book Award nomination and Lillian Smith Award from the Southern Regional Council, both 1973, both for *Revolutionary Petunias and Other Poems*; Richard and Hinda Rosenthal Foundation Award, American Academy and Institute of Arts and Letters, 1974, for *In Love and Trouble: Stories of Black Women*; Guggenheim fellowship, 1977-78; National Book Critics Circle Award nomination, 1982, and Pulitzer Prize and American Book Award, both 1983, all for *The Color Purple*; Best Books for Young Adults citation, American Library Association, 1984, for *In Search of Our Mother's Gardens: Womanist Prose*; D.H.L., University of Massachusetts, 1983; O. Henry Award, 1986, for "Kindred Spirits"; Langston Hughes Award, New York City College, 1989; Nora Astorga Leadership award, 1989; Fred Cody Award for Lifetime Achievement, Bay Area Book Reviewers Association, 1990; Freedom to Write award, PEN West, 1990; California Governor's Arts Award, 1994; Literary Ambassador Award, University of Oklahoma Center for Poets and Writers, 1998.

■ Writings

POETRY

Once: Poems (also see below), Harcourt, 1968.
Five Poems, Broadside Press, 1972.
Revolutionary Petunias and Other Poems (also see below), Harcourt, 1973.
Goodnight, Willie Lee, I'll See You in the Morning (also see below), Dial, 1979.
Horses Make a Landscape Look More Beautiful, Harcourt, 1984.
Alice Walker Boxed Set—Poetry: Good Night, Willie Lee, I'll See You in the Morning; Revolutionary Petunias and Other Poems; Once, Poems, Harcourt, 1985.
Her Blue Body Everything We Know: Earthling Poems, 1965-1990 Complete, Harcourt, 1991.

FICTION; NOVELS EXCEPT AS INDICATED

The Third Life of Grange Copeland, Harcourt, 1970.
In Love and Trouble: Stories of Black Women, Harcourt, 1973.
Meridian, Harcourt, 1976.
You Can't Keep a Good Woman Down (short stories), Harcourt, 1981.
The Color Purple, Harcourt, 1982.
Alice Walker Boxed Set—Fiction: The Third Life of Grange Copeland; You Can't Keep a Good Woman Down; In Love and Trouble, Harcourt, 1985.
The Temple of My Familiar, Harcourt, 1989.
Possessing the Secret of Joy, Harcourt, 1992.
Everyday Use, edited by Barbara Christian, Rutgers University Press, 1994.
The Complete Stories, Women's Press, 1994.
By the Light of My Father's Smile, Random House, 1997.

FOR CHILDREN

Langston Hughes: American Poet (biography), Crowell, 1973, revised edition, HarperCollins, in press.
To Hell with Dying, illustrations by Catherine Deeter, Harcourt, 1988.
Finding the Green Stone, Harcourt, 1991.

NONFICTION

In Search of Our Mothers' Gardens: Womanist Prose, Harcourt, 1983.
Living by the Word: Selected Writings, 1973-1987, Harcourt, 1988.
(With Pratibha Parmar) *Warrior Marks: Female Genital Mutilation and the Sexual Blinding of Women*, Harcourt, 1993, reprinted, 1996.
The Same River Twice: Honoring the Difficult, Scribner, 1996.
Alice Walker Banned, with introduction by Patricia Holt, Aunt Lute Books, 1996.
Anything We Love Can Be Saved: A Writer's Activism, Random House, 1997.

OTHER

(Editor) *I Love Myself When I'm Laughing . . . and Then Again When I Am Looking Mean and Impressive: A Zora Neale Hurston Reader*, introduction by Mary Helen Washington, Feminist Press, 1979.

Contributor to anthologies, including *Voices of the Revolution*, edited by Helen Haynes, E. & J. Kaplan, 1967; *The Best Short Stories by Negro Writers from 1899 to the Present: An Anthology*, edited by Langston Hughes, Little, Brown, 1967; *Afro-American Literature: An Introduction*, Harcourt, 1971; *Tales and Stories for Black Folks*, compiled by Toni Cade Bambara, Zenith Books, 1971; *Black Short Story Anthology*, compiled by Woodie King, New American Library, 1972; *The Poetry of Black America: An Anthology of the Twentieth Century*, compiled by Arnold Adoff, Harper, 1973; *A Rock against the Wind: Black Love Poems*, edited by Lindsay Patterson, Dodd, 1973; *We Be Word Sorcerers: Twenty-five Stories by Black Americans*, edited by Sonia Sanchez, Bantam, 1973; *Images of Women in Literature*, compiled by Mary Anne Ferguson, Houghton, 1973; *Best American Short Stories: 1973*, edited by Margaret Foley, Hart-Davis, 1973; *Best American Short Stories, 1974*, edited by M. Foley, Houghton, 1974; *Chants of Saints: A Gathering of*

Afro-American Literature, Art and Scholarship, edited by Michael S. Harper and Robert B. Stepto, University of Illinois Press, 1980; *Midnight Birds: Stories of Contemporary Black Women Authors,* edited by Mary Helen Washington, Anchor Press, 1980; and *Double Stitch: Black Women Write about Mothers and Daughters,* edited by Maya Angelou, HarperCollins, 1993.

Contributor to numerous periodicals, including *Negro Digest, Denver Quarterly, Harper's, Black World, Essence, Canadian Dimension,* and the *New York Times.* Contributing editor, *Southern Voices, Freedomways,* and *Ms.*

■ Adaptations

The Color Purple was made into a feature film directed by Steven Spielberg, Warner Brothers, 1985.

■ Sidelights

Best known for her Pulitzer Prize-winning novel, *The Color Purple,* as well as for its adaptation as a motion picture by Steven Spielberg, Alice Walker has become a totem for black feminism, what she calls "womanism." An outspoken proponent for causes ranging from civil and women's rights to environmentalism, Walker has taken her one-woman campaign worldwide, agitating for an end to female genital mutilation in Africa, as well as for religious and racial understanding in the United States. Daughter of Southern sharecroppers, a one-time voter registration worker in the South, and a woman of color, Walker knows firsthand about the pernicious effects of oppression. Mere survival is not what Walker is about: she desires that black men and women, as well as citizens of the globe in general, learn how to survive whole, to carry human dignity along with them.

Much of Walker's work is polemic; the best of it manages to incorporate message with strong characters such as Celie in *The Color Purple,* Meridian in the novel of the same name, or Tashi in *Possessing the Secret Joy.* A renowned poet, essayist, children's author, and short story writer, in addition to being a novelist, Walker explores the human condition and predicament in all genres. As Mary Lystad noted in *Twentieth-Century Young Adult Writers,* Walker is primarily known to young

adult readers for her novels, "powerful, strident stories principally set in America's rural and poor South." Lystad went on to note, "But Walker cannot be labeled as a southern writer, a black writer, a feminist writer. Her works speak of universal struggles for dignity and meaning and connectedness in life."

Walker views African American women as symbols of hope; not merely nurturing matriarchs who keep the hearth warm, but creative individuals who are at the very center of communal life. Barbara T. Christian commented in *Dictionary of Literary Biography:* "[Walker's] works confront the pain and struggle of black people's history, which for her has resulted in a deeply spiritual tradition. And in articulating that tradition, she has found that the creativity of black women, the extent to which they are permitted to exercise it, is a measure of the health of the entire society." Employing a lyrical prose style, Walker sets her stories and novels in the rural South, in Africa, or in Mexico, and often uses a historical time frame, be it the Depression, the era of civil rights marches, or the last half million years of human history, as she attempted in her 1989 novel, *The Temple of My Familiar.* But whatever the time, it is certain that a novel or short story from the pen of Alice Walker will be a mixture of struggle and faith. Ultimately hopeful and optimistic, Walker's works have become part of the American literary canon, taught in schools, discussed in review columns, and read eagerly by people of all ages.

Three Gifts

Alice Malsenior Walker was born on February 9, 1944, the youngest child of Willie Lee and Minnie Tallulah Grant Walker. Seven other children had preceded her, born to her sharecropper parents. Growing up poor in the rural South was not easy; as Walker recollected in her *In Search of Our Mother's Gardens,* "I can recall that I hated it, generally. The hard work in the fields, the shabby houses, the evil greedy men who worked my father to death and almost broke the courage of that strong woman, my mother." Indeed, it was the strong bond between mother and daughter that allowed Alice Walker to finally escape the boundaries of such a life whole. Minnie Lou Walker was a fighter and a believer in education. By the time Alice Walker was born, her older sisters were mostly out in the world, and she was the lone girl in a family of men. One older sister had already gone on to win scholarships and explore the world. Young Alice began school at age four, when she was too big for her mother to take with her to the fields or when she worked as a domestic servant.

When Alice showed creative talents, these were closely protected and nurtured by her mother. She was never made to leave a book to do chores; when she started to write poetry, her mother encouraged her. Minnie Lou Walker herself was

THE WONDROUS PULITZER PRIZE-WINNING NOVEL

ALICE WALKER

AUTHOR OF *THE SAME RIVER TWICE*

THE COLOR PURPLE

POCKET BOOKS

Winner of the Pulitzer Prize and American Book Award, Walker's 1982 novel is about an emotionally and physically abused woman named Celie who finds the power to love herself with the unexpected help of her husband's lover, Shug Avery.

something of a domestic artist, coming home after a hard day's work to tend her garden, made up of more than fifty varieties of plants. As Walker noted in *Gardens,* "Because of her creativity with her flowers, even my memories of poverty are seen through a screen of blooms—sunflowers, petunias, dahlias, forsythia, spirea, delphiniums, verbena . . . and on and on." And such work transformed Minnie Lou Walker, providing a lesson for her young daughter. Beautifying every chink and cranny of an otherwise drab sharecropper's cabin with her flowers, Walker's mother became "radiant, almost to the point of being invisible—except as Creator: hand and eye."

When Walker was eight, a game of cowboys and Indians led to an accidental shooting with a BB gun. Walker was injured in her right eye, but because of their isolated location, she did not see a doctor for several days. By then scar tissue had formed and she was left blind in that eye. Though a later operation removed the scar tissue, Walker remained sensitive about her looks for years thereafter until her own daughter finally liberated her from this burden by telling her how lovely she was.

Walker attended local schools, excelling at her work at Eatonton High School. During these years, Minnie Walker gave her daughter three gifts that have always remained with her, at least symbolically. First was a sewing machine that Alice Walker received when she was fifteen or sixteen. With that, she was able to sew her own clothes, even creating a prom dress for herself. Second was a typewriter, a gift that came with the implied message that told the girl to pursue her dreams. And for graduation, Minnie Walker gave her daughter a suitcase, a tacit form of permission to travel, to become part of a larger world than Georgia. All these her mother was able to buy while working in the fields or making $20 a week as a domestic.

Walker used the last of these gifts when she went away to college. Valedictorian of her class, she won a "rehabilitation scholarship" because of her injured eye to Spelman College, a black woman's college in Atlanta. Her father, Willie Lee Walker, was less encouraging about education than her mother. He found an educated daughter challenging; going to college virtually ended what had been at best a tenuous relationship between father and daughter. These dynamics—the support-

Whoopi Goldberg stars as Celie, and Margaret Avery is Shug Avery, in Steven Spielberg's 1985 adaptation of *The Color Purple*.

ing creative mother and aloof if not brutal father— would replay themselves throughout Walker's later fiction.

Poet and Activist in the Making

Walker spent more than two years at Spelman, during which time she became an activist in the fledgling civil rights movement. In 1963 she attended a World Youth Peace Festival in Helsinki, Finland. Not long afterward, she won a scholarship to attend Sarah Lawrence College in Bronxville, New York. At that time still an all-women's school, Sarah Lawrence provided Walker with the atmosphere to grow in the literary form that had increasingly become her passion: poetry. The summer before her senior year, Walker traveled to Africa, a watershed experience for the young woman, and later that same year she became pregnant. This traumatic pregnancy and a subse-

quent abortion pushed her to the verge of suicide, dreams of which she had experienced since she was a child. However, instead of death, she chose life. An outpouring of poetic activity filled the weeks following her abortion, poems she would slip under the door of Sarah Lawrence's writer-in-residence, Muriel Rukeyser, Walker's teacher at the time. Rukeyser not only read the poems and critiqued them, she passed them on to her editor at Harcourt. Some five years later, these poems from Walker's senior year became her first published book, *Once*. A short story from the time was published during her college years, however. "To Hell with Dying" later became a children's book; inspired by the death of a local Georgia guitar player, Mr. Sweet, it immortalized not only Walker's feelings for the musician, but for her life in the South in general.

Graduating from Sarah Lawrence in 1965, Walker was determined to become a writer. Moving to

New York City, she took a job in the city welfare department, writing at night. However, by 1966 she was in Mississippi, working on the voter registration campaign. There she met a young law student, Melvyn Leventhal. Returning to New York, the couple lived together, and Walker became an editor at *Ms* Magazine. It was during that year that she wrote the essay, "The Civil Rights Movement: What Good Was It?" which won a $300 first prize in the annual *American Scholar* essay contest. In 1967 the couple married and moved back to Mississippi, where Leventhal prosecuted high-profile civil rights cases. They were the only interracial, home-owning married couple in a state where such marriages were still illegal. For the next seven years, she and Leventhal would call Mississippi home; Walker continued writing, as well as working with Head Start programs and serving as writer-in-residence at Tougaloo College and Jackson State University.

The Early Stories and a Novel

Walker's collection of poems, *Once,* was published in 1968, and her daughter Rebecca was born in 1969. Living in the South again, she now looked from a new and more mature perspective at the survival tactics blacks employed. Another strong influence of these years was the discovery of the literary work of Zora Neale Hurston, which enhanced her appreciation of her underprivileged background as well as the difficulties which face the black female writer. In Hurston, Walked found a model: a woman who had left the South but not her heritage. Hurston preserved the oral culture of her people in her writing, and also dealt with her characters not as stereotypes of racial inequality, but as real, whole people.

Walker's readings of Hurston first influenced a short story she was at work on, "The Revenge of Hannah Kemhuff," later included in the collection *In Love and Trouble,* whose stories largely deal with black women victimized by men. Remarking on these stories, Thadious M. Davis wrote in *Dictionary of Literary Biography,* "Walker writes best of the social and personal drama in the lives of familiar people who struggle for survival of self in hostile environments." The triumph of black women over adversity is one of the major themes of the stories written largely in the late 1960s. In stories such as "The Child Who Favored Daughter," "Roselily," and "Really Doesn't Crime Pay?"

Walker introduces a wide gallery of protagonists, focusing primarily on strong women who are either thwarted in their dreams or punished for having them. As Davis noted, "Without shame or apology, Walker presents her characters and celebrates their efforts to be themselves. Her approach to characterization reflects a preoccupation with what she terms, 'spiritual survival, the survival *whole* of my people.' "

Collected in the 1973 publication, *In Love and Trouble,* these stories won critical praise as well as the Rosenthal Award of the National Institute of Arts and Letters. ("Everyday Use" and "The Revenge of Hannah Kemhuff" were included in the annual volume called *Best American Short Stories.)* Nikki Giovanni, reviewing *In Love and Trouble* in *Washington Post Book World,* noted that Walker's stories "are not pretty . . . nor happy—as one traditionally thinks of stories about black women and their men, black mothers and their children, old black ladies and their gods." However, Giovanni connected with Walker's message: "I applaud *In Love and Trouble.* I welcome the examination without polemics. I certainly welcome the love Alice so painfully shares." Reviewer Mel Watkins noted in *New York Times Book Review* that "these stories are perceptive miniatures, snapshots, that capture their subjects at crucial and revealing moments." Watkins concluded, "Some of these tales are small gems."

Likewise, Walker used the inspiration of Hurston to plough forward on her first novel, *The Third Life of Grange Copeland.* Walker's theme in this novel and in her collected short stories—of the sexism which existed in the black community—led to criticism by black leaders who were at this time focusing on racism. But Walker forged ahead with her exploration of the dynamics at work in black families, much inspired by what she had observed in her own family and in those of the people with whom she worked in Mississippi. In *The Third Life of Grange Copeland,* she wrote of three generations of the Copeland family, beginning with Grange, the family patriarch, who becomes a sharecropper in the 1920s. Unable to take out his frustrations on the white owners who employ him, who own his soul, Grange takes them out on his wife and son, Brownfield. This was what Walker herself had seen while growing up. But when Margaret, the wife, begins to live a dissolute life as well, and gives birth to another man's child, Grange leaves for the North. The wife kills herself and the new child, leaving Brownfield on his own. Brownfield grows up to be even more tyrannical than his father, beating his wife, Mem, who is an archetypal Walker female: wise and caring and courageous. Brownfield ultimately shoots her when she attempts to raise the family out of their miserable condition. Grange, returned from his long sojourn in the North a changed man, rescues his granddaughter, Ruth, by killing his own son.

Here in this first novel, are many of Walker's themes: the dehumanizing conditions of life in the South that turn black men into brutes, raging against their own families; the presence of strong women who try to snatch the best out of life; and the redemptive value of change. Writing in *Saturday Review,* Josephine Hendin noted, "This novel has heroines and villains. The villains are those who have a genius for hate, but no capacity for love. The heroes acquire the ability to care deeply for another human being." Hendin went on to remark, "Miss Walker skillfully depicts Brownfield turning into a murderous, whining beast. Her sympathy, however, is plainly with his wife, with all black women, whom she sees as the victims of both whites and their own husband's rage." Robert Coles, reviewing the novel in *The New Yorker,* felt that the tragic story was told "with particular grace; it is as if one were reading a long and touching poem." However, Coles noted, "Walker is a fighter as well as a meditative poet and lyrical novelist. She has taken part in the struggles her people have waged, and she knows the struggles they must yet face in this greatest of the world's democracies." And of Grange's redemption, his third life of the title, Coles wrote: "Grange Copeland can at last stop being hard on himself and look with kindness upon himself—and one wonders whether any achievement can be more revolutionary."

Toward the end of their seven years in Mississippi, Walker and her daughter took a hiatus to Wellesley College in Massachusetts, where Walker taught a class on black female writers, one of the first of its kind in the United States. She was also at work on a series of poems that was published in 1973 as *Revolutionary Petunias and Other Poems,* a collection nominated for the National Book Award and which won the Lillian Smith Award of the Southern Regional Council. As Donna Haisty Winchell commented in *Dictionary of Literary Biography,* "Petunias are, for Walker, an image

of survival," a recollection of her own mother's garden magic that could transform their meager cabins into homes. "In Walker's works the nurturing of flowers is synonymous with art," Winchell further noted. "In *Revolutionary Petunias* Walker specifically explores the role that art plays in time of revolution."

Walker's first collection of short stories, *In Love and Trouble,* was also published at this time. Her literary career was on sound footing, yet still she suffered from rage at the oppression she felt; a violent rage that she attempted to channel into her writing. In 1974, Walker, Leventhal, and their daughter moved back to New York.

On Her Own

In New York, Walker continued to work as a contributing editor for *Ms* and also started a new novel, published in 1976, *Meridian.* Marge Piercy writing in the *New York Times Book Review* called the book a "fine, taut novel that accomplishes a remarkable amount." Encompassing twenty-five years, the novel focuses on the height of the civil rights movement through the voices and actions of four main characters: Meridian, a black civil rights campaigner, her mother, Mrs. Hill; Lynne, a Jewish civil rights worker; and Truman, a black painter, once married to Lynne. A love triangle is at the heart of the novel: Truman has left Meridian for Lynne, whom he in turn leaves along with their daughter. When he wants to return to Meridian, she no longer wants him. Her commitment to working in the rural South and his commercial success in the art world are deeply at odds. And ironically Lynne can neither return to suburbia nor fit into the black community. As Piercy commented, "Meridian, the protagonist, is the most interesting, an attempt to make real in contemporary terms the notion of holiness and commitment." Writing in the *Dictionary of Literary Biography* Donna Haisty Winchell has pointed out that the theme annunciated in *Revolutionary Petunias* is further developed: "*Meridian . . .* explores at length the role of the artist in time of revolution."

Like Walker, Meridian wins a scholarship to a black woman's college in Atlanta, and there is thrust into the heart of the civil rights movement. But Meridian is a disappointment to her revolutionary friends because of her commitment to nonviolence; she travels around the South, much like Walker, helping to register voters. Having given up her baby to attend college, Meridian goes a long way to debunking some of the myths of black motherhood. She chooses a life of commitment over ease or personal happiness. Considered a classic of the civil rights movement, the novel is taught in both literature and history classes. *Newsweek* reviewer Margo Jefferson called *Meridian* "a novel as ambitious and complicated as the era it examines and elegizes." Jefferson further noted, "Walker is both ruthless and tender," and that her "eye for hypocrisy is painfully sharp." The *New York Times Book Review* added that this portrait of a young female black activist was "unsentimental yet tender . . . fascinating for its revelations, admirable for its deft telling."

Walker was also criticized, however, for heavy-handed polemics—a recurrent criticism—and for symbolism that is "one dimensional and fixed," as Greil Marcus remarked in a review of the novel in the *New Yorker*. No critics, though, could fault Walker's commitment, honesty, and ambition of purpose. Davis, writing in *Dictionary of Literary Biography*, commented, "Walker's treatment of the civil rights movement in Meridian's personal transformation is perhaps her greatest achievement in this novel. She astutely conveys its dynamic effect upon the lives of participants, and she does so without simplistic reductions." Davis concluded, "Meridian represents the possibility for new life, for catharsis, redemption, and hope. . . . *Meridian* is both [Walker's] elegy for the 1960s and her proclamation of her work ahead."

Walker's personal life also took on new dimensions around this time. Divorcing her husband, she remained in New York, sharing custody of their daughter. Then, in 1977-78, she won a Guggenheim Fellowship and began work on her big novel. Moving to the West Coast, she established herself in San Francisco and at a little cabin on the north coast in Mendocino. In the next few years, Walker published another book of poems, *Goodnight, Willie Lee, I'll See You in the Morning*, whose title was inspired by her mother's words of farewell to her dead husband, and a second book of short stories, *You Can't Keep a Good Woman Down*. In this collection Walker experiments in narrative forms with stories which deal with violence, rape, pornography, and abortion, all viewed "from a blatantly womanist perspective," according to Donna Haisty Winchell in *Dictionary of Lit-erary Biography*. "Walker's politics have shaped her art from the beginning, yet here some critics felt she goes too far, blurring completely the line between short story and political tract; feminist critics applauded her use of fiction, or pseudofiction, to advance their cause." Two controversial stories in the collection. "Porn" and "Coming Apart," treat the threat of pornography to relations between black men and women. Of the latter story Winchell remarked: "Here is early evidence that Walker's work is least successful as fiction when it is most polemical."

The Color Purple

However, with all of this, it was as if Walker were merely warming up for her longer fiction, for the novel that would make her a household name. In 1982 Walker published her third novel, *The Color Purple*. Nominated for the National Book Critics Circle Award, it won both the American Book Award and the prestigious Pulitzer Prize, making Walker the first African American woman to ever win that latter honor. This tale of "violence, incest, and redemption," as Dinitia Smith characterized the novel in the *Nation,* focuses on the life of young Celie, fourteen at the opening of the story, and her struggles for survival under the most difficult of circumstances. Told in epistolary form in black vernacular, the novel uses letters to bring the reader into the mind and heart of the main character, to identify with Celie absolutely. Once again, as in much of her early work, Walker casts a harsh eye at the cruel domination of black women not so much directly by the white establishment, but by black men.

The Color Purple spans some thirty years in Celie's life, beginning at the time she is a teenager and her father (actually her stepfather as she later learns) continually beats and rapes her. She bears him two children and is then forced into a loveless marriage with an older man she simply calls Mr. _____, a widower with the first name of Albert who beats her. This husband eventually moves his mistress, Shug Avery, into their home. Shug, a beautiful blues singer, soon becomes Celie's lover as well. Celie's letters are often addressed to God, but also to her older sister, Nettie, whom she saved from the lechery of her husband and who is now a missionary in Africa. However, there have been years of silence from Nettie; Celie fears that she is dead.

Award-winning Author of *The Color Purple*

ALICE WALKER

"Remarkable....superb fiction."
—*New York Daily News*

POSSESSING THE SECRET OF JOY

Including some of the characters who appeared in *The Color Purple*, Walker's 1992 follow-up story focuses on Tashi, the wife of Celie's son, Adam, who has been a victim of genital mutilation at the hands of African tribesmen.

Celie later discovers a cache of letters from Nettie that her husband has hidden from her. Nettie's letters provide a subplot of life in traditional African society among the Olinkas of West Africa. Women, it seems, are as oppressed in traditional African society as they are in America. Nettie's letters also let Celie know that her real father was lynched and that it was therefore her stepfather who had sired her children. Also, the reader learns that she, Nettie, is raising Celie's children, Olivia and Adam. All this—the letters, and her love for Shug—help to build a sense of worth in Celie. She ultimately throws her miserable husband out; female bonding and the redemptive power of love make Celie, in the end, a survivor. Leaving for

Memphis with Shug, she ultimately opens her own business, blending her love of color—especially purple—with sewing. Her Folkpants Unlimited becomes a successful business. In the end, her daughter and son, who have been raised by sister Nettie, are reunited with Celie, returning from Africa.

One of the central symbols of the novel, the color purple, represents royalty, creativity, even a sense of surprise and wonder at God. It is also, as has been pointed out, the symbolic color of lesbianism, and this along with sexism and racism, are vital thematic elements in the novel. Reviewers were heavy with praise for this novel. Peter S. Prescott, writing in *Newsweek*, pronounced it "an American novel of permanent importance," while Robert Towers, in the *New York Review of Books*, praised its lyricism and use of black idiom. "No other novelist . . . has so successfully tapped the poetic resources of the idiom," Towers noted. Other critics remarked on Walker's tendency to preach through characters, but Dinitia Smith, writing in the *Nation*, felt that despite its "occasional preachiness, *The Color Purple* marks a major advance for Walker's art. At its best, and at least half the book is superb, it places her in the company of Faulkner. . . . By infusing the black experience into the Southern novel, she enriches both it and us." Other critics pointed out the dangling plot threads left with Nettie's sojourn in Africa. Mel Watkins also remarked in the *New York Times Book Review* that Nettie's letters, by comparison to Celie's, "seem lackluster and intrusive." However, Watkins went on, "These are only quibbles . . . about a striking and consummately well-written novel."

In addition to such high praise, Walker also earned scorn from some members of the black community for her negative portrayal of black men. As the screenwriter Richard Wesley noted in *Ms*, "What angers black men as they read Alice Walker's novel, or watch the film version, is that *all* the black men are portrayed as fools; the women are portrayed as noble and long-suffering. If they have any weaknesses, they are weaknesses seemingly brought about by their long association with these foolish men." And as *The Color Purple* fell into the school canon, some districts also received complaints from parents who objected to the harsh language, the lesbianism, and the seeming incest. But Walker has weathered such criticism, insisting on her unflinching look at the role of black women. And such criticism often ignores the fact that the men do change in *The Color Purple:* Albert and Celie actually become near friends at the end with something of a gender shift in the two, and Albert's son Harpo straightens out and stops beating his wife. Redemption, for Walker, can be found in love as well as in turning your back on the dominant societal norms.

Maturation of Themes

Publication of *The Color Purple* and the release of its 1985 critically acclaimed movie adaptation by Steven Spielberg (eleven Oscar nominations), brought Walker fame and fortune. She felt, as she approached forty years of age, that her work was done, even confiding to her journal at one point that perhaps she had written down everything she had to say. However, she found new reservoirs of creativity, and in the next few years she published two volumes of essays: the 1983 *In Search of Our Mother's Gardens* and the 1988 collection, *Living by the Word,* as well as another volume of poetry, *Horses Make a Landscape Look More Beautiful.* The last two, especially, show a more reflective Walker, coming to terms with her own heritage—not only her African American blood, but also her white and Indian blood. Environmental concerns are voiced here; Walker advocated a more global approach to personal wholeness and well-being.

In 1989, Alice Walker published her fourth—and most agree—her least successful novel, *The Temple of My Familiar.* Indeed, some, such as J. M. Coetzee, writing in the *New York Times Book Review,* have observed that it "is a novel only in a loose sense. Rather, it is a mixture of mythic fantasy, revisionary history, exemplary biography and sermon. It is short on narrative tension, long on inspirational message." Miss Lissie, an old black woman, tells stories of reincarnation and tries to guide Fanny, Celie's granddaughter from *The Color Purple,* to a new understanding of the world. Lissie retells the last five hundred thousand years of human history in a myriad of voices and personas. The writer Ursula K. Le Guin remarked in the *San Francisco Review of Books* that the "richness of Alice Walker's new novel is amazing, overwhelming. A hundred themes and subjects spin through it, dozens of characters, a whirl of times and places."

But many critics felt that Walker had overreached with this novel. "Cover to cover, Alice Walker's *The Temple of My Familiar* is the nuttiest novel I've ever read," declared James Wolcott in the *New Republic.* David Nicholson, writing in *Washington Post Book World,* noted that "Walker seems to have been striving to write a *big* book, the kind writers used to feel they had to write at a certain part of their careers." Nicholson went on, "It would be nice to report that Walker has succeeded, but reading this new novel is much like watching a little girl on parade, all dressed up in her mother's clothes and high heels." At the same time, Luci Tapahonso, reviewing the novel in *Los Angeles Times Book Review,* pointed out that Walker "asks us to suspend literary expectations and be-

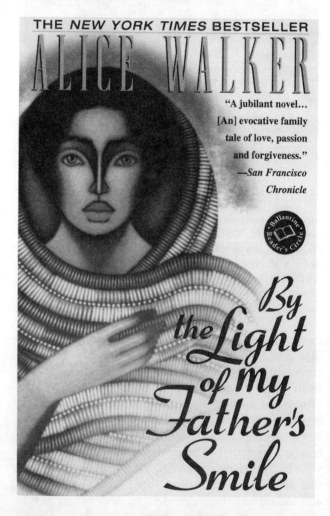

THE *NEW YORK TIMES* BESTSELLER

ALICE WALKER

"A jubilant novel... [An] evocative family tale of love, passion and forgiveness." —*San Francisco Chronicle*

By the Light of my Father's Smile

An anthropologist's anger for his daughter's love of a Mundo boy creates a sense of unforgiving bitterness in her in Walker's 1998 novel about sexuality and hypocrisy.

come part of the evolution of a people." For Tapahonso, Walker was indulging in the oldest of arts, storytelling, and if the narrative line zigged and zagged over millennia and in and out of hundreds of lives, that is part of such an oral tradition. The reviewer noted themes of racism, environmentalism, and love, among others, and concluded, "Alice Walker has written beautifully about dreams, the power of stories—and about the remarkable strength of our own histories."

Walker next published collected poems from 1965 to 1990 in *Her Blue Body Everything We Know*, and then in 1992 came out with the novel, *Possessing the Secret of Joy*, something of a continuation of the storyline of *The Color Purple* in that characters are carried over from that earlier novel. Tashi, the best friend in Africa of Celie's daughter Olivia, and the wife of Celie's son, Adam, arrives with the children in America at the end of *The Color Purple*. In this new novel, Tashi takes stage center, the victim of genital mutilation in the name of tribal tradition. As in *The Color Purple*, Walker again focuses on one major character with her theme of the oppression of women, and most critics felt that the novel was a success. As Winchell noted in *Dictionary of Literary Biography*, "The novel records Tashi's attempts throughout the rest of her life to come to terms with what has been done to her body and the bodies of generations of African women." Convicted of murdering M'Lissa who was responsible for the death of her sister in one such female initiation rite, Tashi breaks the silence about female circumcision and rallies the women of Africa to her cause. Winchell remarked that this novel, focused as it is, "is much more concise, more controlled, and more successful as art than its predecessor."

Other critics agreed. Writing in *Washington Post Book World*, Charles R. Larson commented, "It's the suffering of children, the wholesale mutilation of little girls, that finally haunts us in Walker's daring novel." Larson concluded, "I hope that *Possessing the Secret of Joy*, already on the bestseller lists, will be the most talked about book of the season." Laura Shapiro noted in *Newsweek* that Walker "has pulled off an amazing feat here: she's written a powerful novel about brutal misogyny, and she's made it both horrifying and readable, angry and warm-hearted, political and human."

Working with Pratibha Parmar, Walker expanded on this theme with a documentary and nonfiction

---

If you enjoy the works of Alice Walker, you may also want to check out the following books and films:

J. California Cooper, *Family*, 1991.
Lucille Clifton, *My Brother Fine with Me*, 1975.
Faith Ringgold, *Aunt Harriet's Underground Railroad in the Sky*, 1992.
Beloved, a film starring Oprah Winfrey and Danny Glover, 1998.

---

book on female circumcision, *Warrior Marks*, a "remarkable cross-cultural collaboration" which "should help break the deafening silence surrounding a taboo subject," according to *Publishers Weekly*. Another nonfiction title, *The Same River Twice: Honoring the Difficult*, published in 1996, records the events surrounding the filming of *The Color Purple*, and includes much autobiographical information about the author, including the illness of her mother and her reaction to the criticism leveled against her by black males. A further collection of essays, *Anything We Love Can Be Saved: A Writer's Activism*, appeared in 1997. Of that book *Publishers Weekly* remarked, "Walker's commitment to activism—in its myriad cultural, political and spiritual form—shines forth convincingly in this wide-ranging collection of personal essays, remarks, letters, speeches and statements. . . . Constantly testing and stretching her readers' imaginations and boundaries, Walker expresses her warmth, her anger, her optimism in this provocative, lively collection."

In 1998 Walker's sixth novel, *By the Light of My Father's Smile*, was published. Like Walker's earlier books, this one focused on female sexuality. The main characters are the Robinsons, a husband-wife team of black anthropologists, and the novel is told in flashback sequences. Unable to secure funding for research in Mexico in the 1950s, the husband poses as a minister to study the Mundo, a black and Indian tribe. The couple brings along their young daughters to this new life in the Sierra Madre. Sexuality is at the heart of the story, though the father reacts violently upon discovering his young daughter involved with a Mundo boy. This reaction has repercussions throughout the novel. Again, Walker experiments with points of view, even recounting the action through the eyes of the recently deceased patriarch of the Robinson clan.

Booklist's Donna Seaman remarked on the "boldly explicit" nature of the sex scenes in *By the Light of My Father's Smile,* also pointing out that "the message Walker conveys is that sex brings us closer to God." For Seaman this "is a seductive but flimsy foundation on which to base a novel." *Time* magazine's R. Z. Sheppard noted that Walker "flits gnomically through space and time" to tell the story of an American family which is transformed from "a repressed patriarchal unit to a spiritual sorority of free radicals." Sheppard felt that fans of "the well-focused *The Color Purple* may not appreciate Walker's looser style."

Walker continues to write penetrating critiques of the modern world, and of the position of black women in such a world. Whether in poetry, essays, short stories, or novels, she asks hard questions and takes chances. If she is in turn criticized for being polemical in her writings, that can only be expected. Donna Haisty Winchell called Alice Walker "a major voice for contemporary black women" in *Dictionary of Literary Biography.* In works such as *The Color Purple* and *Possessing the Secret of Joy,* the author's art is focused and critics responded favorably as a result. Yet at heart, those works are every bit as politically informed as her essays and speeches.

Alice Walker believes in the transformative power of words and of a life by example. For her *everything* we do is political. "Books are by-products of our lives," she told Gloria Steinem in a 1982 *Ms.* interview. "Deliver me from writers who say the way they live doesn't matter. I'm not sure a bad person can write a good book. If art doesn't make us better, then what on earth is it for?"

■ **Works Cited**

Review of *Anything We Love Can Be Saved,* *Publishers Weekly,* February 24, 1997, p. 77.

Christian, Barbara T., "Alice Walker," *Dictionary of Literary Biography,* Volume 33: *Afro-American Fiction Writers after 1955,* Gale, 1984, pp. 258-70.

Coetzee, J. M., "The Beginnings of (Wo)man in Africa," *New York Times Book Review,* April 30, 1989, p. 7.

Coles, Robert, review of *The Third Life of Grange Copeland, New Yorker,* February 27, 1971.

Davis, Thadious M., *Dictionary of Literary Biography,* Volume 6: *American Novelists Since World War II, Second Series,* Gale, 1980, pp. 350-58.

Giovanni, Nikki, "So Black and Blue," *Washington Post Book World,* November 18, 1973, p. 1.

Hendin, Josephine, review of *The Third Life of Grange Copeland, Saturday Review,* August 22, 1970.

Jefferson, Margo, "Across the Barricades," *Newsweek,* May 31, 1976, pp. 71-72.

Larson, Charles R., "Against the Tyranny of Tradition," *Washington Post Book World,* July 5, 1992, pp. 1, 14.

Le Guin, Ursula K., review of *The Temple of My Familiar, San Francisco Review of Books,* Summer, 1989.

Lystad, Mary, *Twentieth-Century Young Adult Writers,* St. James Press, 1994, pp. 676-77.

Marcus, Greil, review of *Meridian, New Yorker,* June 7, 1976.

Review of *Meridian, New York Times Book Review,* May 29, 1977, p. 23.

Nicholson, David, "Alice Walker Trips," *Washington Post Book World,* May 7, 1989, pp. 3, 5.

Piercy, Marge, review of *Meridian, New York Times Book Review,* May 23, 1976, pp. 5, 12.

Prescott, Peter S., review of *The Color Purple, Newsweek,* June 21, 1982, pp. 67-68.

Seaman, Donna, review of *By the Light of My Father's Smile, Booklist,* June 1, 1998, p. 1671.

Shapiro, Laura, review of *Possessing the Secret of Joy, Newsweek,* June 8, 1992, pp. 56-57.

Sheppard, R. Z., review of *By the Light of My Father's Smile, Time,* October 5, 1998, p. 96.

Smith, Dinitia, "Celie, You a Tree," *Nation,* September 4, 1982.

Steinem, Gloria, "Do You Know This Woman? She Knows You: A Profile of Alice Walker," *Ms.,* June, 1982.

Tapahonso, Luci, "Learning to Love Through Storytelling," *Los Angeles Times Book Review,* May 21, 1989, pp. 6, 13.

Towers, Robert, review of *The Color Purple, New York Review of Books,* August 12, 1982.

Walker, Alice, *In Search of Our Mothers' Gardens: Womanist Prose,* Harcourt Brace, 1983, p. 21.

Review of *Warrior Marks, Publishers Weekly,* October 25, 1993, p. 49.

Watkins, Mel, review of *In Love and Trouble, New York Times Book Review,* March 17, 1974, pp. 40-41.

Watkins, Mel, review of *The Color Purple, New York Times Book Review,* July 25, 1982.

Wesley, Richard, "*The Color Purple* Debate," *Ms,* September, 1986, pp. 90-92.

Winchell, Donna Haisty, "Alice Walker," *Dictionary of Literary Biography*, Volume 143: *American Novelists Since World War II, Third Series*, Gale, 1995.

Wolcott, James, "Party of Animals," *The New Republic*, May 29, 1989, pp. 28-30.

■ For More Information See

BOOKS

Allan, Tuzyline Jita, *Womanist and Feminist Aesthetics: A Comparative Review*, Ohio University Press, 1995.

Bestsellers '89, Issue 4, Gale, 1989.

Black Literature Criticism, Volume 1, Gale, 1992, pp. 1808-1829.

Christian, Barbara, editor, *Everyday Use*, Rutgers University Press, 1994.

Contemporary Literary Criticism, Gale, Volume 5, 1976, Volume 6, 1976, Volume 9, 1978, Volume 19, 1981, Volume 27, 1984, Volume 46, 1988, Volume 58, 1990, Volume 103, 1998.

Evans, Mari, editor, *Black Women Writers (1950-1980): A Critical Evaluation*, Anchor, 1984.

Gates, Henry Louis, Jr., and K. A. Appiah, editors, *Alice Walker: Critical Perspectives Past and Present*, Amistad Press, 1993.

Johnson, Yvonne, *The Voices of African American Women: The Use of Narrative and Authorial Voice in the Works of Harriet Jacobs, Zora Neale Hurston, and Alice Walker*, P. Lang, 1995.

Kaplan, Carla, *The Erotics of Talk: Women's Writing and Feminist Paradigms*, Oxford University Press, 1996.

Kramer, Barbara, *Alice Walker: Author of* The Color Purple, Enslow, 1995.

O'Brien, John, *Interviews with Black Writers*, Liveright, 1973.

Peden, William, *The American Short Story: Continuity and Change, 1940-1975*, 2nd revised and enlarged edition, Houghton, 1975.

Prenshaw, Peggy W., editor, *Women Writers of the Contemporary South*, University Press of Mississippi, 1984.

Short Story Criticism, Volume 5, Gale, 1990, pp. 400-24.

Winchell, Donna Haisty, *Alice Walker*, Twayne, 1992.

PERIODICALS

African American Review, spring, 1995, p. 67.

American Scholar, winter, 1970-71; summer, 1973.

Ann Arbor News, October 3, 1982.

Atlantic, June, 1976.

Black Scholar, April, 1976.

Black World, September, 1973; October, 1974.

Booklist, November 15, 1995, p. 514; August, 1996, p. 1875; March 1, 1997, p. 1067.

Chicago Tribune, December 20, 1985; April 23, 1989; June 21, 1992, p. 3.

Chicago Tribune Book World, August 1, 1982; September 15, 1985.

Commonweal, April 29, 1977.

Critique, summer, 1994.

Detroit Free Press, August 8, 1982; July 10, 1988; January 4, 1989.

Detroit News, September 15, 1982; October 23, 1983; March 31, 1985.

Entertainment Weekly, December 30, 1994, p. 64.

Essence, February, 1996, p. 84.

Freedomways, winter, 1973.

Globe and Mail (Toronto), December 21, 1985.

Jet, February 10, 1986.

Library Journal, November 15, 1994, p. 103; December, 1995, p. 110; May 1, 1997, p. 104; August, 1998, p. 136.

Los Angeles Times, April 29, 1981; June 8, 1983.

Los Angeles Times Book Review, August 8, 1982; May 29, 1988; July 5, 1992, p. 4; August 8, 1992, p. 3.

Ms., February, 1974; July, 1977; July, 1978; September-October, 1998, p. 42.

Nation, November 12, 1973.

Negro Digest, September/October, 1968.

New Leader, January 25, 1971.

New Republic, September 14, 1974; December 21, 1974.

Newsweek, April 24, 1989, p. 74.

New York Review of Books, January 29, 1987.

New York Times, December 18, 1985; January 5, 1986.

New York Times Book Review, December 30, 1979; May 24, 1981; April 7, 1985; June 5, 1988; June 28, 1992, p. 11; January 14, 1996, p. 18; May 12, 1996, p. 28; May 25, 1997, p. 17; October 4, 1998, p. 18.

New York Times Magazine, January 8, 1984.

Observer (London), October 11, 1992, p. 61.

Parnassus: Poetry in Review, spring/summer, 1976.

People Weekly, April 29, 1996, p. 36.

Poetry, February, 1971; March, 1980.

Publishers Weekly, August 31, 1970; February 26, 1988; March 1, 1991, p. 64; October 25, 1991, p. 66; July 6, 1998, p. 47.

Southern Review, spring, 1973.

Time, May 1, 1989, p. 69.

Times Literary Supplement, August 19, 1977; June 18, 1982; July 20, 1984; September 27, 1985; April 15, 1988; September 22, 1989, p. 1023; October 9, 1992, p. 22; August 15, 1997, p. 24.

Tribune Books (Chicago), July 17, 1988; April 23, 1989, p. 5; June 21, 1992,p. 3; January 21, 1996, p. 5.

Tulsa World, March 29, 1998.

Washington Post, October 15, 1982; April 15, 1983; October 17, 1983.

Washington Post Book World, October 30, 1979; December 30, 1979; May 31, 1981; July 25, 1982; December 30, 1984; May 29, 1988; January 16, 1994, pp. 4-5; January 21, 1996, p. 5.*

—Sketch by J. Sydney Jones

Margaret Weis

■ Personal

Born March 16, 1948, in Independence, MO; daughter of George Edward (an engineer) and Frances Irene (Reed) Weis; married Robert William Baldwin, August 22, 1970 (divorced, 1982); married Donald Bayne Stewart Perrin (an author), May 5, 1996; children: (first marriage) David William, Elizabeth Lynn. *Education*: University of Missouri, B.A., 1970. *Politics*: Independent. *Religion*: "No formal."

■ Addresses

Office—P.O. Box 1106, Williams Bay, WI 53191. *Agent*—Jonathon Lazear, Lazear Agency, 800 Washington Ave. N., Suite 600, Minneapolis, MN 55401. *E-mail*—mweis@mag7.com.

■ Career

Writer and editor. Herald Publishing House, Independence, MO, advertising director, 1972-81, director of Independence Press trade division, 1981-83; TSR Hobbies, Inc., Lake Geneva, WI, editor of juvenile romances and other special product lines, 1983-86; freelance writer, 1987—. Co-owner, The Game Guild, 431 N. Broad St., Lake Geneva, WI 53147. *Member*: Great Alkali Plainsmen (Kansas City, MO).

■ Writings

The Endless Catacombs (fantasy), illustrated by Jeff Easley, TSR (Lake Geneva, WI), 1984.

(Editor) *The Art of the Dungeons and Dragons Fantasy Game*, TSR, 1985.

(With Janet Pack) *Lost Childhood: Children of World War II* (nonfiction), Messner, 1986.

(Editor with Tracy Hickman) *Leaves from the Inn of the Last Home: The Complete Krynn Source Book*, TSR, 1987.

(Editor with Tracy Hickman) *Love and War*, TSR, 1987.

(With Tracy Hickman) *Dragonlance Adventures* (game source book), TSR, 1987.

(Editor) *A Dragon Lovers Treasury of the Fantastic*, Warner, 1994.

(With Tracy Hickman) *The Second Generation*, poetry by Michael Williams, illustrated by Ned Dameron, TSR, 1994.

(Editor and author of introduction) *Fantastic Alice* (short stories loosely based on Lewis Carroll's *Alice's Adventures in Wonderland*), Ace Books, 1995.

(Editor with Tracy Hickman) *The History of Dragonlance: Being the Notes, Journals, and Memorabilia of Krynn*, compiled by Maryls Heeszel, TSR, 1995.

(With husband, Don Perrin) *The Doom Brigade* (a "Dragonlance" novel), TSR, 1996.

(With Tracy Hickman) *Star Shield*, Del Rey, 1996.

(With son, David Baldwin) *Dark Heart*, Harper Prism, 1998.

(Editor and author of introduction) *New Amazons*, DAW, 2000.

"DRAGONLANCE CHRONICLES"; WITH TRACY HICKMAN; POETRY BY MICHAEL WILLIAMS

Dragons of Autumn Twilight, illustrated by Denis Beauvais, TSR, 1984.

Dragons of Winter Night, TSR, 1984.

Dragons of Spring Dawning, illustrated by Jeffrey Butler, TSR, 1984.

Dragons of Summer Flame, illustrated by Larry Elmore, TSR, 1995.

"DRAGONLANCE LEGENDS" FANTASY NOVELS; WITH TRACY HICKMAN; POETRY BY MICHAEL WILLIAMS

Time of the Twins, TSR, 1985.

War of the Twins, TSR, 1985.

Test of the Twins, TSR, 1985.

"DRAGONLANCE TALES II"; SHORT STORIES AND POEMS

The Reign of Istar, TSR, 1992.

The Cataclysm, TSR, 1992.

The War of the Lance, TSR, 1992.

Dragons of Krynn, TSR, 1994.

"DARKSWORD" TRILOGY; WITH TRACY HICKMAN

Forging the Darksword, Bantam, 1988.

Doom of the Darksword, Bantam, 1988.

Triumph of the Darksword, Bantam, 1988.

"THE ROSE OF THE PROPHET" TRILOGY; WITH TRACY HICKMAN

The Will of the Wanderer, Bantam, 1989.

The Paladin of the Night, Bantam, 1989.

The Prophet of Akran, Bantam, 1989.

"STAR OF THE GUARDIAN" SCIENCE FICTION SERIES

The Lost King, Bantam, 1990.

King's Test, Bantam, 1990.

King's Sacrifice, Bantam, 1991.

Ghost Legion, Bantam, 1993.

"DEATH'S GATE CYCLE" FANTASY SERIES; WITH TRACY HICKMAN

Dragon Wing, Bantam, 1990.

Elven Star, Bantam, 1990.

Fire Sea, Bantam, 1990.

Serpent Mage, Bantam, 1990.

The Hand of Chaos, Bantam, 1990.

Into the Labyrinth, Bantam, 1993.

The Seventh Gate, Bantam, 1994.

"MAG FORCE 7" SCIENCE FICTION SERIES; WITH DON PERRIN

Knights of the Black Earth, ROC, 1995.

Robot Blues, ROC, 1996.

Hung Out, ROC, 1997.

"STARSHIELD" FANTASY SERIES; WITH TRACY HICKMAN

Starshield Sentinels, Del Rey, 1996.

The Mantle of Kendis-Dai, Del Rey, 1997.

Nightsword, Del Rey, 1998.

"THE RAISTLIN CHRONICLES"; WITH DON PERRIN

Brothers in Arms, Random House, 1999.

"WAR OF SOULS" TRILOGY; WITH TRACY HICKMAN

Dragons of a Fallen Sun, TSR, 2000.

"SOVEREIGN STONE" SERIES; WITH TRACY HICKMAN

Water from the Well of Darkness, Harper Prism, in press.

NONFICTION; AS MARGARET BALDWIN

The Boy Who Saved the Children (remedial reader for young adults; based on autobiography *Growing up in the Holocaust* by Ben Edelbaum), Messner, 1981.

(With Pat O'Brien) *Wanted! Frank and Jesse James: The Real Story* (young adult biography), Messner, 1981.

Kisses of Death: A Great Escape Story of World War II (remedial reader for young adults), illustrated by Norma Welliver, Messner, 1983.

My First Book: Thanksgiving (juvenile), F. Watts, 1983.

Fortune-Telling (nonfiction), Messner, 1984.
My First Book of Robots (nonfiction), F. Watts, 1984.
My First Book of Computer Graphics (nonfiction), F. Watts, 1984.

OTHER

(With Don Perrin and Lester Smith) *Sovereign Stone Game System,* Sovereign Press, 1999.

Contributor to *The Dragonlance Saga* by Roy Thomas (includes adaptations of *Dragons of Autumn Twilight* and *Dragons of Winter Night*), illustrated by Thomas Yeates with Mark Johnson, TSR, 1987. Also author of *Lasers,* F. Watts; author, with Gary Pack, of *Computer Graphics* and *Robots and Robotics,* both F. Watts. Author of graphic novels *A Fable of the Serra Angel,* Acclaim Comics, and (with son, David Baldwin) *Testament of the Dragon,* Teckno Books.

Creator of trading card games, including *Star of the Guardians* and *Wing Commander.* Weis's books have been translated into many languages, including French, Spanish, Japanese, German, Portuguese, Italian, Russian, Czech, Rumanian, Hebrew, Danish, and Finnish.

■ Adaptations

An audio recording was made of *Elven Star,* Bantam Audio, 1991.

■ Work in Progress

Collaborating with Tracy Hickman on the second book in the "Sovereign Stone" series, and "The War of the Souls" trilogy for TSR, expected in 2000.

■ Sidelights

Wisconsin resident Margaret Weis is one of today's most prolific and popular authors and editors of fantasy literature; her books, which appeal to a wide audience and have been translated into at least a dozen languages, have sold more than twelve million copies worldwide. Weis is best known as the co-creator, along with role-playing games designer Tracy Hickman, of the "Dragonlance" adventures, set in the imaginary world of

Krynn. She has also collaborated with other authors—including her second husband, author Don Perrin, and her son, David Baldwin—on dozens of other titles. Weis was not always involved in fantasy fiction, however. She began her literary career writing juvenile books, remedial readers, and nonfiction.

Weis was born, raised, and spent all of her early life in Independence, Missouri, a city with a keen sense of history. Independence is famous as the birthplace of Harry Truman, the thirty-third president of the United States (1945-1953), and as the final resting place of the infamous outlaw Frank James. As a girl, Weis attended school just across the street from the cemetery where James is buried, and she was fascinated by tales of the Old West and the Civil War. "I was a lonely, introverted child, spending more time in my imagination and in books than playing with other children. I was the class story-teller. Before I could write, I told stories to the other children during rest periods," Weis said in a 1999 interview with *Artists and Authors for Young Adults* (*AAYA*).

Since the entire family loved to read, the Weis house was filled with books. Saturday trips to the library were a part of the routine for as long as Weis lived at home, and books were the usual gifts on special occasions. In those days, Weis had little interest in young adult literature; she devoured classic tales by Alexandre Dumas (*The Three Musketeers*), Sir Arthur Conan Doyle (*The Adventures of Sherlock Holmes*), and Louisa May Alcott (*Little Women*). "I was [also] fascinated by war stories. I read the *Guns of Navronne, Bridges of Toko Ri,* [and] Winston Churchill's account of WWII," Weis told *AAYA*.

She began writing her own stories as a girl, but had no plans to become a writer. In fact, Weis dreamed of becoming an artist. As she once recalled, "Several incidents caused me to change my mind, and they point out, I believe, how strong an effect good teachers can have on our lives." Weis's English teacher in her junior year was a free-spirited man named Mr. Smith who often ignored the official classroom curriculum, much to the dismay of school administrators. Weis has said that she learned from Smith about the importance of standing up for things one believes in, even if doing so is sometimes difficult. Even more important, Weis gained an understanding of the basics of good writing. "Our class spent the first semes-

MARGARET WEIS & TRACY HICKMAN

THE DARKSWORD TRILOGY

by the
bestselling authors of
THE DEATH GATE CYCLE

VOLUME II
DOOM OF THE DARKSWORD

This second book in the "Darksword" trilogy finds Joram returning to his home to reclaim his birthright by fighting Bishop Vanya and the fierce Duuk-tsarith.

ter writing sentences. That's all. Just one sentence every day. We started out with simple sentences— a subject and verb. Then we were allowed to add an adjective. . . . After sixteen weeks, Mr. Smith decided we were ready to move on. We wrote paragraphs—five sentences each," Weis recalled.

"I came to respect words in [Mr. Smith's] class. I came to realize how critical every word—no matter how insignificant—is in writing. I saw how sentences joined together to form paragraphs. When we read books in his class, we studied not only the literary content but how the writer created the effect he wanted by use of words and sentence structure. Mr. Smith showed me the door, but it still remained closed," Weis added.

Changing Directions

Upon graduating from high school in the spring of 1966, Weis enrolled at the University of Missouri. At this point in her young life, she was still intent on becoming an artist. That all began to change when a student English teacher asked Weis to stay after class and asked her if she had ever thought of studying writing. As Weis recalled, "She told me about the University of Missouri's English program. (The university was one of the few in the 1960s to offer a creative writing program separate from journalism.) I have often thought this young woman should have been an army recruiter. If she had, I would no doubt have joined on the spot. I investigated the writing program, liked it, and switched my major. [The student teacher] gave me the key to the door."

Having switched her major, Weis began studying with a poet and professor named Donald Drummond, another gifted and perceptive teacher, albeit an unorthodox one. It was her experiences in Drummond's classes that finally convinced Weis to become a writer. As she once explained, "We wrote poetry in Dr. Drummond's class. . . . The poet was required to read his [or her] work aloud, while his [or her] fellow poets sat, knives out, waiting to draw blood. . . . We came out battle-scarred, but we could write. . . .[Drummond] began by giving us a long list of subjects we were under no circumstances to write about. These included: Love (with a capital 'L'), truth, beauty, death, and the Vietnam War. 'And,' he growled, 'if I get one poem about a daffodil you will flunk the semester!' Needless to say, I never have, and I never will, write about a daffodil."

Weis married in 1970, the same year that she graduated from college with her bachelor's degree in creative writing and English/American literature. In 1972, she found work with the Herald Publishing House in Independence, Missouri. She worked there for the next thirteen years, until 1983, a year after she divorced her first husband. Seeking a change, Weis moved to Lake Geneva, Wisconsin, where she took a position with a company called TSR Hobbies Incorporated becoming an editor of juvenile romances and what she refers to as "special products."

Teams With Tracy Hickman

Weis had started writing young adult nonfiction books in 1981 under her married name of Margaret Baldwin; in 1984 she began using her maiden name (Weis). She also moved in a completely new direction. As part of her work with TSR Hobbies, Weis began writing and editing fantasy books, many of which were tied to the role-playing games which TSR Hobbies produced and sold. "We were churning out those game books very fast. It was quite a challenge. First, you had to write in the second person, which is very difficult, and you had to devise multiple endings for every situation," Weis told *AAYA*. Their success in the game book field led TSR to expand into adult fiction with the popular "Dragonlance" series, which Weis wrote in collaboration with TSR games designer Tracy Hickman. The Dragonlance books have enjoyed added success in the form of a variety of spin-off products that have included art books, trading cards, and new role-playing games.

The reality behind the series (and all the related merchandise) is that the fantasy world serving as the backdrop for all the action was meticulously plotted and chronicled before Weis and Hickman ever began work on the first book in the series, *Dragons of Autumn Twilight*. In this introductory tale, published in 1984, the main characters—who appeared first in Dungeons and Dragons—meet at an inn in a tree-top township called Solace. The cast includes a cross-section of the population of the complex fantasy world that Hickman created. The protagonist is a half-elf, half-human named Tanis; his companions include a kender (a hobbit-like kleptomaniac), a knight, a dwarf, a warrior, and a wizard. This motley group is joined by a barmaid and a couple of plains people when they go forth to do battle with an army of evil draconian hordes that is on the march. The heroes ultimately defeat these marauding invaders, of course, but not without an epic struggle that is played out in this book and in three subsequent adventures written in 1984 by Weis and Hickman: *Dragons of Winter Night*, *Dragons of Spring Dawning*, and in a fourth and final volume in the series, *Dragons of Summer Flame*, which appeared in 1995. Reviewing the first three books in the series in 1989, when the novels were anthologized in a 1,032-page edition, Eleanor Klopp of the *Voice of Youth Advocates* commented, "Taken as a whole, this is an amazingly sustained effort comprising

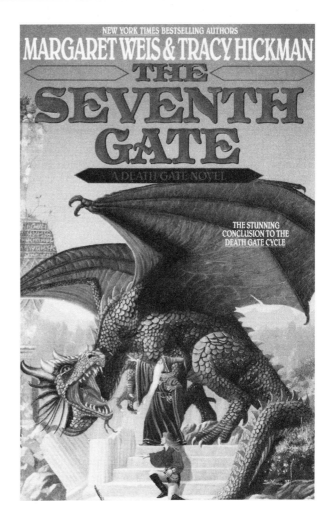

In this final chapter of the "Death's Gate Cycle," the Sartan and Patryns learn they must set aside their differences in order to defeat the evil serpents that threaten them all.

many characters, places, and events and, to its credit, the reader is quite able to keep them all straight."

Weis and Hickman subsequently have collaborated on at least a half-dozen more fantasy series, all of which have been hugely successful. Often, elements from one book or series spin-off into others; this includes characters as well as plot lines. "Tracy and I work on the plot outlines together," Weis told *AAYA*. "I do the majority of the writing, although Tracy will write chapters he feels strongly about. Then he goes over what I've written and comments. I do the final rewrite, so that the book has a single voice." This arrangement has evidently worked well, for Weis and Hickman have enjoyed enormous success with their books. With each new series they have created, the two have expanded and broadened their readership.

If you enjoy the works of Margaret Weis, you may also want to check out the following books:

Barbara Hambly, *The Silent Tower*, 1986.
Guy Gavriel Kay, *The Summer Tree*, 1985.
Melanie Rawn, *The Star Scroll*, 1989.
Jane Yolen, *Here There Be Dragons*, 1993.
Michael Swanwick, *Stations of the Tide*, 1991.

One of their most popular series is the "Dragonlance Legends," a trilogy that picks up the further adventures of the surviving characters from the original "Dragonlance" books; *Time of the Twins*, *War of the Twins*, and *Test of the Twins* all appeared in 1985. This time around, the authors send some of the characters back in time to the period just before the Cataclysm, the divinely-ordained catastrophe that has reshaped the world. Reviewing this new series, Pauline Morgan of the reference publication *St. James Guide to Fantasy Writers* commented, "The set . . . begins awkwardly, with information being repeated—a problem that can afflict any collaborative work—but also with a lot unsaid. . . . In general, there are too many characters, and as a result there is little depth to them. . . . There is, however, plenty of action, even if the writing is uneven."

In 1988, Weis and Hickman collaborated on the "Darksword" trilogy. This series recounts the adventures of a character named Joram who is born without magic, and as is the custom when this happens in the world of Thimhallen, he is abandoned for dead. But Joram is raised in secret and taught tricks that disguise his deficiencies. When he is eventually found out, he flees into a frontier zone known as the Outlands. There he falls in with the Technologists, a group of outcasts who live by technology, a mystery which the high priests have banned in Thimhallen. With the help of technology, Joram forges the Darksword—the instrument from which the series takes its title.

The Darksword enables him to overcome his lack of magic, and eventually to reclaim his rightful place as a lost member of Thimhallen's ruling Royal House. The three books in the Darksword odyssey of adventure—*Forging the Darksword*, *Doom of the Darksword*, and *Triumph of the Darksword*—were popular with readers, but received mixed reviews. Commenting on *Forging the Darksword*, the opening title in the series, a *Library Journal* reviewer wrote, "The authors of the `Dragonlance' series again demonstrate their talent for vivid characterization in a novel that will appeal to fans of epic fantasy." However, reviewer Ruth Cline of *Voice of Youth Advocates* was less enthusiastic about what she read. She wrote of *Doom of theDarksword*, the second volume in the trilogy, "There is humor, but most of the book is too violent and weird to enjoy it."

A Prolific Pair

Other Weis-Hickman collaborations include "The Rose of the Prophet" trilogy, written in 1989, and the four-book "Star of The Guardian" series (1990-1993), which Pauline Morgan writing in *Fantasy Writers* describes as "space-opera science fiction." Similarly, Morgan summarized the imaginative seven-book epic known as the "Death's Gate Cycle" (1990-1994), as an attempt to get away from the more usual kind of fantasy novel." The premise of the "Deathgate" series is that two god-like races, the Sartan and the Patryns, have, through mutual enmity, caused the world to divide into four distinctive parts separated by a magical labyrinth. Each of the first four books in the series, *Dragon Wing*, *Elven Star*, *Fire Sea*, and *Serpent Mage*, describes a different part of the world. Evil serpents threaten the existence of all four realms in two subsequent books, *The Hand of Chaos* and *Into the Labyrinth*, and by the last installment, *The Seventh Gate*, it has become clear that only by setting aside their differences, cooperating, and combining their magic can the Sartan and Patryns defeat their common enemy. A review in *Library Journal* stated that the "Deathgate Cycle" "bears the now-familiar complex villain/heroes, and an emphasis on moral responsibility."

To some critics, Weis and Hickman did a remarkable job of sustaining narrative energy and maintaining plot continuity throughout the thousands of pages required by such an ambitious series. It was inevitable that some critics would praise their efforts and others find fault with them. Reviewing *Dragon Wing*, the first book of the series, Eleanor Klopp of *Voice of Youth Advocates* commented, "Freed from the constrictions of *Dungeons and Dragons* whose characters are more often personifications than personalities, the authors have been able to use their remarkable talents to even greater advantage." Reviewing the same book, Scott Winnett of *Locus* wrote, "This is the most interesting and distinctive work from Weis and Hickman to date. . . . The plot gallops along, the narrative and dialog are unobtrusive and clichés are kept to a minimum."

Five books later, Weis and Hickman were maintaining their pace. Reviewing *Into the Labyrinth*, the sixth volume in the "Death Gate Cycle," Hugh M. Flick of *Kliatt* commented, "The complex world of this fantasy series is still intriguing, despite some of the narrative weaknesses . . . ." Assessing *The Seventh Gate*, the final book of the series, Roland Green of *Booklist* praised the authors' efforts, noting that "[Weis and Hickman] continue to demonstrate the qualities they displayed in [the "Dragonlance" series]—complete mastery of the art of turning classic fantasy elements into equally classic well-told tales." In another review of *The Seventh Gate*, a *Voice of Youth Advocates* critic pointed out that in the first six books in the series the authors had been "creating unique worlds, characters to believe in, and giving them dire circumstances to work through." In this final installment, the reviewer continued, "the message is what the reader wanted the characters to embrace all along. They all but say, 'there is that of God in all of us.' " Pauline Morgan did not share in the enthusiasm other reviewers felt for the series. Writing in the *St. James Guide to Fantasy Writers*, she commented, "In all these novels, good ideas have been swamped by poor, predictable plots and weak characterizations."

Such comments have done nothing to slow sales or dull interest in Weis and Hickman's novels, which continue to enjoy a wide and very devoted readership. "The reviews I care about are those the fans write," Weis told *AAYA*. For that reason, she continues to forge ahead with new initiatives. One of the most recent fantasy series from Weis and Hickman, the "Starshield" adventures, was launched in 1996 with the pilot novel called *Starshield Sentinels*. Initial reviews were not encouraging. A *Publishers Weekly* reviewer chided Weis and Hickman for "lackluster dialogue" and noted

that "the mythical, far-future and contemporary Earthling plot lines lack convincing linkages, boding ill for future volumes in this series." A reviewer from *Kirkus Reviews* expressed similar sentiments in dismissing *Starshield Sentinels* as "ambitious hogwash," but went on to note that the series was still "guaranteed to become a huge success."

In the next two books in the series, *The Mantle of Kendis-Dai* and *Nightsword*, Weis and Hickman relate the adventures of a group of what a *Publishers Weekly* reviewer described as "a motley collection of Earth astronauts, multiracial space pirates, and assorted Inquisitors led by Targ, an Oedipal misfit" as they struggle to recover a stolen sword from an arch-villain named Lokan. That same unnamed *Publishers Weekly* reviewer dismissed *Nightsword*, the third novel in the series, as an "exponentially inflated comic book." However, other reviewers had much more favorable opinions. A *Library Journal* review of *Nightsword* commented that "Weis and Hickman have reached the top of their storytelling form with this latest series, a fast-paced, panoramic blend of space opera and high fantasy." Roland Green of *Booklist* also offered praise for *Nightsword*, writing that "the lived-in space-opera universe; the engaging characters, both good and bad; and the streak of wit and zaniness that crops out unexpectedly in it are all signs that with 'Starshield,' Weis and Hickman are creating something most agreeable for all fans of swashbuckling space adventure."

No Time To Rest

It seems likely that Weis and her writing partners will continue their efforts. Weis shows no signs of slowing down. If anything, she is busier and more productive than ever. Weis attends fantasy literature conventions; she maintains her own Web site, and answers all of her own e-mail. Of course she also continues to write. "I write for the joy of words and for the fun of sharing the imaginary worlds I inhabit with the readers," Weis told *AAYA*.

Increasingly of late, Weis has also shared the joys of creating her unique fantasies with members of her own family. She teamed-up with her son, David Baldwin, on a 1998 fantasy novel entitled *Dark Heart*, and Weis and her husband, Don Perrin, have recently begun an ambitious new series called "The Raistlin Chronicles." In addition, Weis and Hickman continue their collaboration. They have finished *Dragons of a Fallen Sun*, a soon-to-be-published first book in a new "War of Souls" trilogy, and they have launched another new series, "Sovereign Stone," based on a role-playing game created by Weis, Don Perrin, and Lester Smith. The first "Sovereign Stone" book, *Water from the Well of Darkness* is written, and a second is in progress.

The prolific Weis told *AAYA* that she no longer has any idea how many books she has written, nor does she have a favorite. "Each book is a favorite in some way," she said. "I love the `Star of Guardians' series because I worked on it for ten years before it was finally published. I loved 'Dragonlance' because working with Tracy was, and is, such a joy. I love the 'Mag Force 7' books because those brought my husband [Don Perrin] and me together, and we had a great time writing them."

■ Works Cited

Cline, Ruth, review of *Doom of the Darksword*, *Voice of Youth Advocates*, October, 1988, p. 197.

Flick, Hugh M., Review of *Into the Labyrinth*, *Kliatt*, November, 1994, p. 25.

Review of *Forging the Darksword*, *Library Journal*, December, 1987, pp. 130-131.

Green, Roland, review of *The Seventh Gate*, *Booklist*, August, 1994, p. 2030.

Green, Roland, review of *Nightsword*, *Booklist*, May 15, 1998, p. 608.

Review of *The Hand of Chaos*, *Library Journal*, February 15, 1993, p. 196.

Klopp, Eleanor, review of "Dragonlance Chronicles," *Voice of Youth Advocates*, April, 1989, pp. 48-49.

Klopp, Eleanor, review of *Dragon Wing*, *Voice of Youth Advocates*, June, 1990.

Morgan, Pauline, *St. James Guide to Fantasy Writers*, St. James Press, 1996, pp. 594-596.

Review of *Nightsword*, *Library Journal*, May 15, 1998, p. 118.

Review of *Nightsword*, *Publishers Weekly*, April 27, 1998, p. 51.

Review of *The Seventh Gate*, *Voice of Youth Advocates*, February, 1995, p. 352.

Review of *Starshield Sentinels*, *Kirkus Reviews*, October 1, 1996.

Review of *Starshield Sentinels*, *Publishers Weekly*, October 21, 1996, p. 75.

Weis, Margaret, interview with *Authors and Artists for Young Adults*, September, 1999.

■ For More Information See

PERIODICALS

Booklist, September 1, 1990, p. 32; November 1, 1993, p. 505; April 15, 1995, p. 1484.

Kirkus Reviews, January 1, 1993, p. 30; October 1, 1993, p. 1234; June 15, 1994, p. 812; March 15, 1995, p. 530.

Library Journal, February 15, 1993, p. 196; April 15, 1995, p. 119.

Publishers Weekly, October 18, 1993, p. 67; January 17, 1994, p. 420; July 25, 1994, p. 38; April 24, 1995, p. 64; November 6, 1995, p. 88.

ON-LINE

Margaret Weis's Web site is located at http://www.mag7.com.home.html.

Frank Lloyd Wright

■ Personal

Born June 8, 1867, in Richland Center, WI; died April 9, 1959, in Phoenix, AZ; married Catherine Lee Tobin, 1889 (divorced); partner of Mrs. Mamah Bortwick Cheney, beginning 1909 (died in Taliesin fire, 1914); married Miriam Noel, 1915 (separated 1924, died, 1927); married Olgivanna Lazovich, 1925; children: (with Tobin) Lloyd, Catherine, Frances, David, Llewellyn; (with Lazovich) Iovanna, Svetlana (stepdaughter). *Education:* Attended University of Wisconsin, School of Engineering, 1885-87.

■ Career

Allen D. Conover, Madison, WI, junior draftsman, 1885-87; Lyman Silsbee, Chicago, IL, junior draftsman, 1887; Adler and Sullivan, Chicago, assistant architect, 1888-89, head of the Planning and Design Department, 1889-93; in partnership with Cecil Corwin, Chicago, 1893-96; in private practice in Oak Park, IL, 1896-97, and Chicago, 1897-1909; travelled in Europe and stayed in Fiesole,

Italy, 1909-11; built first Taliesin house and studio, and resumed practice, Spring Green, WI, 1911; re-opened Chicago office, 1912; Taliesin partially destroyed by fire and rebuilt as Taliesin II, 1914; established office in Tokyo, Japan, in conjunction with work on Imperial Hotel, 1915-20; worked on first concrete "texture block" houses, California, 1921-24; Taliesin II partially destroyed by fire and rebuilt as Taliesin III, 1925; worked in La Jolla, CA, 1928; established southwestern headquarters, Ocatillo, at Chandler, AZ, 1928-29; established Wright Foundation Fellowship at Taliesin, 1932; worked on major theoretical studies for Broadacre City from 1933; built Taliesin West, Paradise Valley, AZ, 1938; continued to practice in Wisconsin and Arizona until his death; students formed Taliesin Associated Architects on his death to complete various works. *Member:* National Institute of Arts and Letters; honorary member of Academie Royale des Beaux Arts (Brussels, Belgium), Akademie Royal der Kunste (Berlin, Germany), National Academy of Brazil, Royal Institute ofBritish Architects, National Academy of Architects (Uruguay), National Academy of Architects (Mexico), National Academy of Finland, Royal Academy of Fine Arts (Stockholm, Sweden).

■ Awards, Honors

Kenchiko Ho Citation, Royal Household of Japan, 1919; Royal Gold Medal, Royal Institute of British

Architects, 1941; Gold Medal, American Institute of Architects, 1949; Gold Medal, American Institute of Architects (Philadelphia chapter), 1949; Peter Cooper Award, 1949; Star of Solidarity, City of Venice, Italy, 1951; Medici Medal, City of Florence, Italy, 1951; Gold Medal, National Institute of Arts and Letters, 1953; Brown Medal, Franklin Institute, Philadelphia, PA, 1954; Freedom of the City, Chicago, IL, 1956. Honorary doctorates from Princeton University, 1947, Yale University, 1954, University of Wisconsin, 1955, Florida Southern College, 1950, and University of Wales, 1956.

■ Sidelights

The name Frank Lloyd Wright has become virtually synonymous with architecture in the American mind. Wright was a flamboyant, outspoken figure who was both praised and criticized for his controversial ideas about space and design. His restlessness and unbridled creativity gave rise to what he called his "organic" style. He was a master of technological concepts that would not become prominent until well after his heyday, and his productivity was legendary—Wright designed thousands of buildings, almost eight hundred of which were constructed. Each of his projects was unique. The body of work they represent continues to influence architects almost forty years after Wright's death.

Wright was born in Richland Center, Wisconsin, on June 8, 1867. His mother was sure her son would be an architect. Anna Lloyd-Jones Wright was a strong-willed, intelligent, and shy woman who taught school for many years. She claimed that before her son was born, she decorated the nursery with pictures of cathedrals from England so he would grow up to build beautiful buildings.

Anna Wright was the second wife of William Cary Wright, a minister. William Wright had three children from his first marriage, and he and Anna had three more. This large family moved often as William Wright served as minister for a variety of congregations in Wisconsin and Massachusetts. When Frank Lloyd Wright was about twelve, they settled in Madison, Wisconsin. Some of his mother's relatives lived on a farm in the nearby town of Spring Green. As a teenager, Wright spent several summers working on his uncle's farm. He

The "Robie House," built in Chicago in 1906, is a fully realized example of Wright's "Prairie Style" houses.

came to love the countryside of the area and eventually built a house there.

Became Draftsman to Help Support Family

As a boy Wright loved to read and "invent" things. But he did not enjoy school, disdaining the many rules he encountered there and deeming most of the curriculum useless; he quit high school just before graduation. At the time, his parents were in the midst of a divorce. Ultimately, Wright's father left, and the two never saw each other again. To help support the family, Wright took a job as a draftsman in the office of the city's civil engineer, making exact scale drawings of city buildings, roads, sewers, and the like. Wright displayed great talent for this work. Soon he began to share his mother's dream of him becoming an architect.

Wright's boss was also the dean of the engineering school at the University of Wisconsin in Madison. He was able to bend the rules and allow Wright to enroll without a high school diploma. There were few architecture schools in the United States in the 1880s; most would-be architects studied engineering, rarely developing new styles of design and mostly copying traditional structures while changing details and adding decoration. Popular designs included the neoclassicism of Greek temples, as well as the conventions of Egyptian and French architecture. Wright remained in engineering school for roughly eighteen months before frustration with these creative constraints drove him to leave at the age of twenty.

Despite his mother's objections, Wright left Madison and arrived in Chicago in 1887 with seven dollars in his pocket. With an uncle's help he landed a job in an architect's office where he helped design houses. These residences adhered to the traditional style of the period, characterized by large porches, turrets, and overhanging roofs. Wright soon became unsatisfied with this work. Eventually he won a position at the most important architecture firm in Chicago, Adler & Sullivan. The heads of this firm, Dankmar Adler and Louis Sullivan, had built several of the most important and progressively designed buildings in Chicago.

Wright was intrigued by Sullivan's conviction that "form follows function," that the design of a struc-

If you enjoy the works of Frank Lloyd Wright, you may also want to check out the following:

The sleek, modern structures of Walter Gropius, founder of the Bauhaus school of design and architecture in Weimar, Germany.

The elegant yet controversial architectural designs of I. M. Pei, including the East Building of the National Gallery of Art, Washington, D.C., and the glass pyramid in the courtyard of the Louvre, Paris, France.

ture should be determined by the structure's purpose. This became a key element of Wright's philosophy of architecture. He rose quickly in the firm, becoming chief draftsman and working his way toward an impressive salary within a year. He married Catherine Tobin in 1889 and settled in Oak Park, a prosperous town near Chicago. His mother and two sisters joined him and lived in a house next door. Wright and his wife had six children.

The Prairie Style

In 1894 Wright opened his own architecture firm and became busy designing homes for his prosperous Oak Park neighbors. By 1900 he had developed a new mode, the Prairie Style, based on the idea that a residence should blend into its surroundings. Wright believed that in the flat and wide midwestern landscape, houses should be similarly flat and wide. Prairie-style houses were comprised of one or two stories, with broad roofs and long rows of windows emphasizing their horizontal orientation. Wright also remade the interior space of the house; while traditional residences were divided into box-like rooms, Wright was convinced that the space should be more free-flowing and echo in design the exterior of the structure. The primary space of the house was frequently centered around a stone fireplace. This unity of environment was called the organic style. Wright even designed the furniture, rugs, tableware, and more to maintain consistency. The Robie House and the Willits House, both in the Chicago

Wright was acclaimed for his design of the Johnson Wax Building, completed in 1936, that featured unusual columns that some have compared to golf tees or mushrooms.

area, are fully realized examples of Wright's Prairie Style.

During the early 1900s Wright also designed two innovative public buildings. The Larkin Building in Buffalo, New York, was the first office building in the country to feature metal furniture, plate-glass windows, and air conditioning. Wright also included a recreation area and restaurant on the premises. His Unity Temple church in Oak Park was a pioneering structure because it was the first public building to be made of poured concrete.

By 1910 Wright's reputation was spreading. A book illustrating his work was published in Germany and began to influence European architects. He visited there to great acclaim that year. The trip was tainted by scandal, however, because Wright had left his wife and children behind and traveled with a married woman, Mamah Borth-

wick Cheney. When they returned from Europe, Wright built a new house for himself and Cheney near his old home of Spring Green, Wisconsin. He called the residence Taliesin, Welsh for "shining brow." It was a secluded retreat, constructed of materials from the area, that boasted a farm and studio.

Wright and Cheney lived there only about three years before tragedy struck: a mentally unstable household worker went on a murderous rampage, killing Cheney, her two children, and four others and burning the house to the ground. Wright was devastated. But rather than abandon the site, he rebuilt the house, naming it Taliesin II and dedicating it to Cheney.

From 1915 to 1922 Wright was consumed by the design and construction of the Imperial Hotel in Tokyo, Japan. This project was challenging in that its setting is prone to earthquakes. Wright's solution to this potential problem was criticized by many. The hotel was built on a deep bed of mud, with the foundation sunk only a short way into the ground. Wright reasoned that the hotel would be able to "sway" in the event of a quake, but would not "break" from stress. His theory was tested just a year after the hotel was finished when a major trembler struck Tokyo. Almost one hundred thousand people were killed in collapsing buildings and fires; the Imperial Hotel was the only large building left standing.

This vindication served to increase Wright's already strong sense of self-assurance and independence. In fact, he was renowned as difficult—inflexible, opinionated, and stubborn. These qualities were apparently only matched by his sense of superiority. He once asserted, "Not only do I intend to be the greatest architect who has ever lived, but the greatest who will ever live." His radical design principles and rampant egotism combined to create an eccentric persona. Wright was certain that his way was the way of the future. By and large, he was right.

Decade Marred by Misfortune

The 1920s represented a low point in Wright's career. He met and married sculptor Miriam Noel (his first wife divorced him in 1922), but they were divorced within a short time. Taliesin II burned in 1925, and Wright exhausted his fortune rebuilding it. He was often short on funds but could not seem to stop spending. When the bank threatened to foreclose on Taliesin III, a group of Wright's friends and relatives came to his aid.

The "Fallingwater House" is Wright's most famous and best recognized residential building, integrating stone and water in a natural, peaceful setting.

During this period he received few commissions, focusing instead on lecturing and writing.

In 1928 Wright married his third wife, Olgivanna Hinzenberg. Their relationship lasted thirty years, until Wright's death. Olgivanna provided him with much support and stability over the course of some of his most creative years. She was also responsible for maintaining the Taliesin Fellowship Wright had established long after the architect's death. Wright began the fellowship as an apprentice and teaching program at Taliesin III in the 1930s. Student apprentices assisted Wright with his commissions, benefiting immeasurably from the hands-on training, and contributed to the Taliesin community by working in the gardens, farm, kitchen, or wherever they were needed. In 1938 Wright built a "winter home" for the Fellowship called Taliesin West near Phoenix, Arizona. Many

of the fellows became close to Wright and considered themselves disciples of a great master.

Fallingwater

Wright's other major achievement of the 1930s was an amazing residence in the hills of Pennsylvania. He was commissioned by Pittsburgh businessman Edgar Kaufmann to build a country house for his family. The wooded property he owned was graced by a waterfall, and this is where Wright chose to build the house—over the waterfall. The stunning result, called Fallingwater, meshes perfectly with its setting. It displays all of Wright's concepts of organic design, among them the use of materials native to the area; interior and exterior spaces flowing into each other; and a central fireplace as the focus of the house-

Wright's last--and one of his most controversial--buildings was the Guggenheim Museum, completed in 1959.

hold. One historian called it "the most famous modern house in the world." Now open to the public, people flock from all over the world to visit Fallingwater and marvel at its beauty.

In 1936 Wright began work on the acclaimed headquarters of the Johnson Wax Company in Racine, Wisconsin. Particularly noteworthy are the structure's support columns, described alternately as tall, thin mushrooms or giant golf tees topped by massive discs. Wright also designed eighteen buildings for the campus of Florida State College during this period. Moreover, he developed a plan for construction of inexpensive, middle-class housing that was remarkable for its many work-saving innovations. Some of these "Usonian" homes– named for the first letters in United States—were built throughout the country in the late 1930s and early 1940s. Wright also designed many homes for wealthy patrons in these years, as well as during the 1950s.

Wright's final, most famous, and arguably most controversial project was the Solomon R. Guggenheim Museum in New York City. Nothing like it had ever been built. It was made of concrete and took the form of a gigantic spiral ramp; there are no rooms, just continuous gallery space. New Yorkers claimed it resembled a giant snail or spiral cinnamon bun. Needless to say, the Guggenheim contrasted markedly with the traditional buildings surrounding it. Artists feared that their works would not hang properly on the upward-sloping walls. In typical fashion, Wright proved everyone wrong. Though he died a few months before the museum was completed and was thus deprived the last laugh, today the Guggenheim is universally recognized as one of the world's great landmarks. Wright died on April 9, 1959, in Phoenix.

Wright is remembered as a genius whose uniquely "modern" ideas were far ahead of their time. He worked until he was ninety-two years old with vitality and conviction. Though his irritable nature may not have made him the most-loved architect in history, he is certainly among the greatest, as the numerous laurels bestowed upon him attest. One of the plans he left behind at his death was for a mile-high skyscraper. As one writer put it, "The sky was the only limit for Frank Lloyd Wright."

■ For More Information See

BOOKS

Boulton, Alexander O., *Frank Lloyd Wright, Architect: An Illustrated Biography,* Rizzoli, 1993.

Davis, Frances A., *Frank Lloyd Wright: Maverick Architect,* Lerner, 1996.

Levine, Neil, *The Architecture of Frank Lloyd Wright,* Princeton University Press, 1996.

Maddex, Diane, *50 Favorite Rooms by Frank Lloyd Wright,* Smithmark, 1998.

Murphy, Wendy B., *Frank Lloyd Wright,* Silver Burdett Press, 1990.

Wright, Frank Lloyd, *An Autobiography,* Horizon Press, 1977.

Wright, John Lloyd, *My Father Who Is on Earth,* Southern Illinois University Press, 1994.

Acknowledgments

Acknowledgments

Grateful acknowledgment is made to the following publishers, authors, and artists for their kind permission to reproduce copyrighted material.

DOUGLAS ADAMS. From a cover of *Last Chance to See* by Douglas Adams and Mark Carwardine. Ballantine Books, 1990. Cover photographs: Hippos (c) Douglas Adams; Komodo dragon, White rhinoceros, Tropic bird (c) Mark Carwardine/Biotica. All rights reserved. Reproduced by permission of Random House, Inc. / Cover of *The Hitchhiker's Guide to the Galaxy* by Douglas Adams. Ballantine Books, 1995. Reproduced by permission of Random House, Inc. / Adams, Douglas, 1993, photograph by Frank Capri. Archive Photos, Inc. (c) Frank Capri/SAGA. Reproduced by permission.

ALLEN APPEL. McGlynn, Katherine, photographer. From a cover of *From Father to Son: Wisdom for the Next Generation* by Allen Appel. St. Martin's Press, 1993. Reproduced by permission of St. Martin's Press, Incorporated. / From a cover of *Time After Time* by Allen Appel. Doubleday. Reproduced by permission by Bantam Books, a division of Random House, Inc. / From a cover of *Twice Upon a Time* by Allen Appel. Doubleday. Reproduced by permission by Bantam Books, a division of Random House, Inc. / From a cover of *Till the End of Time* by Allen Appel. Doubleday. Reproduced by permission by Bantam Books, a division of Random House, Inc. / Appel, Allen, photograph. Reproduced by permission.

ROBERT L. ASPRIN. Ruddell, Gary, illustrator. From a cover of *Time Scout* by Robert Asprin and Linda Evans. Baen, 1995. Copyright (c) 1995 by Bill Fawcett & Associates. Reproduced by permission.

NEVADA BARR. Greenberg, Jill/Photonica, photographer. From a cover of *Bittersweet* by Nevada Barr. Avon Books, 1984. Reproduced by permission of HarperCollins Publishers. In the UK by permission of the Dominick Abel Literary Agency, Inc. / From a cover of *Ill Wind* by Nevada Barr. Avon Books, 1996. Reproduced by permission of HarperCollins Publishers. In the UK by permission of Penguin Putnam, Inc. / From a cover of *Endangered Species* by Nevada Barr. Avon Books, 1998. Reproduced by permission of HarperCollins Publishers. In the UK by permission of Penguin Putnam Inc.

JANE CAMPION. From a cover of *Holy Smoke* by Jane Campion and Anna Campion. Hyperion Books, 1999. Cover photograph (c) Miramax Films. Reproduced by permission of Disney Publishing, Inc. / Hunter, Holly, with Anna Paquin in a scene from *The Piano*, 1993, photograph. The Kobal Collection. Reproduced by permission. / Kidman, Nicole, in the film version of *The Portrait of a Lady*, 1996, photograph. The Kobal Collection. Reproduced by permission. / Campion, Jane, filming *The Portrait of a Lady*, photograph by Juergen Teller. The Kobal Collection. Reproduced by permission. / Campion, Jane, photograph. Reuters/Corbis-Bettmann. Reproduced by permission.

KATE CHOPIN. From a cover of *The Awakening* by Kate Chopin. Avon Books, 1972. Reproduced by permission of HarperCollins Publishers. / Chopin, Kate, photograph. Missouri Historical Society, St. Louis. Reproduced by permission.

ARTHUR C. CLARKE. Heffernan, Phil, and David Stevenson, illustrators. From a cover of *Childhood's End* by Arthur C. Clarke. Ballantine Books, 1990. Reproduced by permission of Random House, Inc. / From a cover of *2001: A Space Odyssey* by Arthur C. Clarke. Roc Books, 1993. Reproduced by permission of Roc, an imprint of Dutton Signet, a division of Penguin Putnam Inc. / From a cover of *3001: The Final Odyssey* by Arthur C. Clarke. Ballantine Books, 1997. Reproduced by permission of Random House, Inc. / Scene from the film *2001: A Space Odyssey*, movie still. The Kobal Collection. Used by permission. / Clarke, Arthur C., photograph. AP/Wide World Photos. Reproduced by permission.

A. C. CRISPIN. Doriau, illustrator. From a cover of *Songsmith: A Witch World Novel* by Andre Norton and A. C. Crispin. Tom Doherty Associates Book, 1992. Reproduced with permission of St. Martin's Press, Incorporated. / Struzan, Drew, illustrator. From a cover of *Star Wars: The Paradise Snare* by A. C. Crispin. Bantam Books, 1997. Cover art copyright (c) 1997 by Lucasfilm Ltd. Reproduced by permission of Bantam Books, a division of Random House, Inc.

LYLL BECERRA DE JENKINS. Pedersen, Judy, illustrator. From a jacket of *The Honorable Prison* by Lyll Becerra de Jenkins. Lodestar Books, 1987. Reproduced by permission of Lodestar Books, a division of Penguin Putnam Inc. / De Jenkins, Lyll Becerra, photograph by Natalie Stultz. Reproduced by permission.

CHARLES DE LINT. Bergen, David, illustrator. From a cover of *Moonheart* by Charles de Lint. Orb Books, Tom Doherty Associates, Inc., 1994. Reproduced by permission of St. Martin's Press, Incorporated. / Howe, John, illustrator. From a cover of *Yarrow: An Autumn Tale* by Charles de Lint. Orb Paperbacks, Tom Doherty Associates, Inc., 1997. Reproduced by permission of St. Martin's Press, Incorporated. / From a cover of *Jack of Kinrowan* by Charles de Lint. Orb Books, Tom Doherty Associates, LLC, 1999. Reproduced by permission of St. Martin's Press, Incorporated.

GABRIEL GARCÍA MÁRQUEZ. / From a cover of *Chronicle of a Death* Foretold by Gabriel García Márquez. Ballantine Books, 1984. Reproduced by permission of Ballantine Books, a division of Random House, Inc. / Toelke, Cathleen, illustrator. From a cover of *The Autumn of the Patriarch* by Gabriel García Márquez. HarperPerennial, 1991. Cover illustration (c) by Cathleen Toelke. Reproduced by permission of HarperCollins Publishers. / Toelke, Cathleen, illustrator. From a cover of *One Hundred Years of Solitude* by Gabriel García Márquez. HarperPerennial, 1998. Cover painting (c) Cathleen Toelke. Reproduced by permission of HarperCollins Publishers. / Márquez, Gabriel García, 1982, photograph. AP/Wide World Photos. Reproduced by permission.

ALLEN GINSBERG. From a cover of *Collected Poems 1947-1980* by Allen Ginsberg. Harper & Row, 1988. Reproduced by permission of HarperCollins Publishers. / Counts, Wyatt/Outline, photographer. From a jacket of *Death & Fame: Last Poems 1993-1997* by Allen Ginsberg. HarperFlamingo, 1999. Front jacket photograph (c) 1996 by Wyatt Counts/Outline. Reproduced by permission of HarperCollins Publishers. / Ginsberg, Allen (reading poetry to audience under trees), 1966, Washington Square Park, New York City, photograph. AP/Wide World Photos. Reproduced by permission. / Ginsberg, Allen (speaking into microphone, in flowered tie), 1969, photograph. AP/Wide World Photos. Reproduced by permission. / Ginsberg, Allen, reading his poem "Howl" demonstrating in favor of Free Speech, Washington D.C., 1994, photograph by Dennis Cook. AP/Wide World Photos. Reproduced by permission.

S. E. HINTON. From a cover of *Rumble Fish* by S. E. Hinton. Bantam Books, 1989. Reproduced by permission of Bantam Books, a division of Random House, Inc. / Estevez, Emilio, with Rob Lowe, C. Thomas Howell, Matt Dillon, Ralph Macchio, Patrick Swayze, and Tom Cruise, standing in group, in the film *The Outsiders*, photograph. The Kobal Collection. Reproduced by permission. / Dillon, Matt (seated under tree, hands clasped, wrecked car in background), in the film *Tex*, 1982, photograph. The Kobal Collection. Reproduced by permission. / Dillon, Matt (center of clock), Mickey Rourke (right) and William Smith, in the film *Rumble Fish,* 1983, photograph. The Kobal Collection. Reproduced by permission. / Hinton, S.E., photograph by Thomas Victor. Reproduced by permission of the Estate of Thomas Victor.

EDWARD HOPPER. / *Nighthawks* (people in cafe), 1942, painting by Edward Hopper. AP/Wide World Photos. Reproduced by permission. / *Ryder's House*, 1954, painting by Edward Hopper, photograph. Art Resource. Reproduced by permission. / *People in the Sun* (people sitting on folding chairs, facing mountains), painting by Edward Hopper, 1960, photograph. National Museum Of American Art, Washington DC/Art Resource. Reproduced by permission. / *Self-Portrait*, painting by Edward Hopper, photograph. AP/Wide World Photos. Reproduced by permission. / Hopper, Edward, 1967, photograph. AP/Wide World Photos. Reproduced by permission.

ROBIN MCKINLEY. Clapp, John, illustrator. From an illustration in *The Stone Fey* by Robin McKinley. Harcourt Brace & Co., 1998. Reproduced by permission of Harcourt, Inc. / McKinley, Robin, photograph by Helen Marcus. Reproduced by permission.

L. E. MODESITT, JR. Jainschigg, Nicholas. From a cover of *Of Tangible Ghosts* by L. E. Modesitt, Jr. Tom Doherty Associates Book, 1994. Reproduced with permission of St. Martin's Press, Incorporated. / Sweet, Darrell K., illustrator From a cover of *The Magic Engineer* by L. E. Modesitt, Jr. Tom Doherty Associates Book, 1994. Reproduced with permission of St. Martin's Press, Incorporated. / Sweet, Darrell, illustrator. From a cover of *The Death of Chaos* by L. E. Modesitt, Jr. Tom Doherty Associates Book, 1995. Reproduced by permission of St. Martin's Press, Incorporated. / Modesitt, Leland E., photograph. Reproduced by permission.

LOUISE MOERI. Marchesi, Stephen, illustrator. From a jacket of *Downwind* by Louise Moeri. Dutton, 1984. Used by permission of the publisher, E. P. Dutton, an imprint of New American Library, a division of Penguin Putnam Inc. / Hillenbrand, William, illustrator. From a jacket of *The Forty-Third War* by Louise Moeri. Houghton Mifflin Company, 1989. Jacket (c) 1989 by William Hillenbrand. Reproduced by permission of Houghton Mifflin Company. / Moeri, Louise, photograph by Rose M. Albano. (c) 1988 Rose M. Albano. Reproduced by permission.

HARRY TURTLEDOVE. Watts, Stan, illustrator. From a cover of *Worldwar: In the Balance* by Harry Turtledove. Ballantine Books, 1994. Reproduced by permission of Ballantine Books, a division of Random House, Inc. / From a cover of *How Few Remain* by Harry Turtledove. Ballantine Books, 1997. Reproduced by permission of Ballantine Books, a division of Random House, Inc. / Pratt, George, illustrator. From a cover of *The Great War: American Front* by Harry Turtledove. Ballantine Books, 1998. Reproduced by permission of Ballantine Books, a division of Random House, Inc.

JEAN URE. Ure, Jean, photograph. Reproduced by permission.

RACHEL VAIL. Raymond, Larry, illustrator. From a jacket of *Wonder* by Rachel Vail. Orchard Books, 1991. Jacket illustration (c) 1991 by Larry Raymond. Reproduced by permission of Orchard Books, New York. / Johnson, Doug, illustrator. From a jacket of *Do Over* by Rachel Vail. Orchard Books, 1992. Jacket illustration (c) 1992 by Doug Johnson. Reproduced by permission of Orchard Books, New York. / Conrad, Sarah, illustrator. From a jacket of

Daring to Be Abigail by Rachel Vail. Orchard Books, 1996. Jacket illustration (c) 1996 by Sarah Conrad. Reproduced by permission of Orchard Books, New York. / Vail, Rachel, photograph by Bill Harris. Reproduced by permission.

ALICE WALKER. From a cover of *The Color Purple* by Alice Walker. Pocket Books, 1985. Cover art courtesy Warner Bros. Reproduced by permission of Pocket Books, a division of Simon & Schuster, Inc. / Morrison, John/Photonica, photographer. From a cover of *Possessing the Secret of Joy* by Alice Walker. Washington Square Press, Pocket Books, 1997. Reproduced by permission of Pocket Books, a division of Simon & Schuster, Inc. / Gonzales, Nivia, illustrator. From a cover of *By the Light of My Father's Smile* by Alice Walker. Ballantine Books, 1999. Reproduced by permission of Ballantine Books, a division of Random House, Inc. / Goldberg, Whoopi, and Margaret Avery in film *The Color Purple*, 1985, photograph. Archive Photos, Inc. Reproduced by permission. / Walker, Alice, photograph. AP/Wide World Photos. Reproduced by permission.

MARGARET WEIS. Elmore, Larry, illustrator. From a cover of *Doom of the Darksword* by Margaret Weis and Tracy Hickman. Bantam Books, 1988. Cover art copyright (c) 1988 by Larry Elmore. Reproduced by permission of Bantam Books, a division of Random House, Inc. / Youll, Stephen, illustrator. From a jacket of *The Seventh Gate* by Margaret Weis and Tracy Hickman. Bantam Books, 1994. Jacket illustration (c) 1994 Stephen Youll. Reproduced by permission of Bantam Books, a division of Random House, Inc. / Weis, Margaret, photograph by Peggy A. Murphy. Austin Studio. Reproduced by permission.

FRANK LLOYD WRIGHT. Solomon R. Guggenheim Museum designed by Frank Lloyd Wright, photograph by Alan Clifton. Archive Photos, Inc. Reproduced by permission. / Falling Water House designed by Frank Lloyd Wright, photograph. Corbis-Bettmann. Reproduced by permission. / Robie House, Chicago, Illinois, 1906, designed by Frank Lloyd Wright. Corbis-Bettmann. Reproduced by permission. / Johnson Wax Company Office Building, designed by Frank Lloyd Wright, Racine, Wisconsin, 1939, photograph. UPI/Corbis-Bettmann. Reproduced by permission. / Wright, Frank Lloyd, photograph. The Library of Congress.

Cumulative Index

Author/Artist Index

The following index gives the number of the volume in which an author/artist's biographical sketch appears.